Heirloom Gardening
in the South

AGRILIFE RESEARCH AND EXTENSION SERVICE SERIES

Craig Nessler and Edward G. Smith, General Editors

Heirloom Gardening in the South

Yesterday's Plants for Today's Gardens

WILLIAM C. WELCH & GREG GRANT

with Cynthia W. Mueller & Jason Powell

Foreword by Felder Rushing

TEXAS A&M UNIVERSITY PRESS   COLLEGE STATION

LIBRARY OF CONGRESS CATALOGING-IN-PUBLICATION DATA

Welch, William C. (William Carlisle), 1939–
Heirloom gardening in the South : yesterday's plants for today's gardens / William C.
Welch and Greg Grant ; with Cynthia W. Mueller and Jason Powell. — 1st ed.
p. cm. — (AgriLife Research and Extension Service series)
Revised and expanded edition of: The southern heirloom garden.
Includes index.

ISBN 978–1-60344–213–8 (pb-flexibound : alk. paper)
1. Gardening — Southern States.   2. Heirloom varieties (Plants) — Southern States.
3. Gardens — Southern States — Styles — History.   4. Landscape plants — Heirloom
varieties — Southern States.   I. Grant, Greg, 1962–   II. Mueller, Cynthia W.
III. Powell, Jason (Jason C.)   IV. Welch, William C. (William Carlisle), 1939– .
Southern heirloom garden.   V. Title.   VI. Series: AgriLife Research and Extension
Service series.
SB453.2.S66W43   2011
712.0975 — dc22
2010029554

General editors for this series are Craig Nessler, director of Texas AgriLife Research,
and Edward G. Smith, director of the Texas AgriLife Extension Service.

In memory of
Diane Welch,
Flora Ann Bynum,
Pam Puryear,
& Florence Griffin,
four amazing women
who left lasting impressions
on the Southern landscape
and its history

Contents

Foreword by Felder Rushing   ix

Preface   xi

Acknowledgments   xiii

Exploring Our Gardening Heritage   1

The Three Sisters: Native American Influence   3

Orange Blossoms and Spanish-Daggers: Spanish Influence   9

Formality and Order: French Influence   17

Out of Africa: African Influence   22

Gardening with Nature: English Influence   31

A Garden in a Wilderness: German Influence   39

Classics in the Garden: Italian Influence   51

Plant Explorers and Timeless Treasures: Asian Influence   62

Rediscovering a Wealth of Southern Heirloom Plants   73

Natives, Invasives, Cemeteries, and Rustling   75

"Slips and Starts": How Heirloom Plants Were Increased   86

Naturalizing Daffodils and Other Southern Bulbs   95

The Fruitful Garden   106

Enjoying the Bounty   115

The Right Plant in the Right Place   123

Designing Your Own Garden: Basic Design Principles   127

Fine-Tuning the Garden   143

Heirloom Plants of the South   151

How Our Gardens Grew: Creating Your Own Garden Traditions   499

A Country Cottage Garden: Fragilee   501

A Sense of Place: Emanis House   511

Index   527

Foreword

How to savor a good, homemade salsa sauce: Don't just gingerly dip your tortilla chip in the juice—*dig in*, with a deft but sure wrist movement to get as much spicy goodness as you can with each bite. This is how Bill Welch taught me, and it will always remind me of how he and his close friend and coauthor Greg approach life—and gardening.

For decades now I have skidded to many a stop along dusty Southern roads—from Texas to Virginia and many points in between—with both these men, backing up pickup trucks to take a closer look at flashes of color in rural cottage gardens. We have climbed over lichen-encrusted tombstones together, looking for better angles to photograph graveyard roses. I once coincidentally bumped into Bill on an island off the coast of France as we both searched for the original source of a certain Southern heritage bulb, and Greg and I have laughed over inane historic plant details as he lovingly tended his grandmother's cottage wildflowers.

These gentle men—longtime friends and co-mentors, as well as hard-core do-it-yourselfers—have crisscrossed the South and beyond, spending as much time or more in the backyards of "garden variety" gardeners as in fine estates and botanical gardens, in their quest for perfectly apt plants for our climate, our soils, and our Southern psyches and sensibilities. The proud Texans, real hands-on gardeners with a solid sense of place, know the South, they know our plants, they know and understand our garden wants and needs. In short, they know who we are and who our "mama 'n' them" are.

Along with thorough, hands-on knowledge of cutting-edge cultivars and horticultural fashion, these delightful teachers, in order to bridge gaps between like-minded people of all cultures and heritage, also share both a passion for and a delight in rediscovering and promoting overlooked heirloom plants that have been passed along, over, and under fences for generations. They have literally changed the way many Southern garden designers and teachers approach our craft.

With "right plant, right place" being the most important line in the mantra of Green Gardening, this book hits the nail squarely on the head in highlighting plants that survive with little or no artificial life support and rise above the acid tests of climate and fashion. The selection of plants featured here by the horticultural duo, along with historic tidbits and observations based on firsthand experience, is simply superb.

This book is more than a primer for new gardeners; it's a crucial research reference for writers and academics looking to glean special insights. And it is a treasure trove for lovers of Southern gardens and culture.

Now *dig in*!

—FELDER RUSHING

Preface

It is the wealth of our Southern gardening heritage—a wealth both stimulating and challenging to today's garden designers and makers—that inspired this book. *Heirloom Gardening in the South* is a celebration of cultures and plants as we look at how these came together to create memorable gardens, whether they be small swept plots or large formal landscapes. We wrote this book in hope that by examining our gardening heritage, we will be better equipped to create distinctive and useful new gardens and landscapes that truly reflect our region and its people.

Immigrants and Native Americans both played their part in building our nation, and both have contributed greatly to the beauty of our Southern gardens. The immigrants contributed diversity, and with it the fruits and flowers of many different cultural, economic, and religious traditions. Each immigrant brought from a distant homeland a mental picture of what a garden ought to be. Of course, new gardens were often simpler due to frontier conditions and priorities for food and shelter. But gardens also served new arrivals as links to the life they left behind, for each group brought treasured seeds and cuttings—remembrances of homes and family that were sometimes oceans away.

Since we believe that our own gardening experiences are integral to communicating with you, we have written about them in our chapter "How Our Gardens Grew." We are committed to helping you create the garden of your dreams and along with it one that expresses a strong sense of place and commitment to sustainability. This implies presenting information about many of our native plants. Our ancestors gardened largely within natural rainfall, soil, and weather conditions. The plants included in our list are not meant to be the only ones considered but are among the best-adapted and "time-tested" species for the South.

As we become more and more a nation of gardeners, the successful traditions and plants of our ancestors offer a unique opportunity with which to reflect and build our future. The most meaningful gardens of our past are those that reflected the lifestyle of their owners. We hope that you will find as much pleasure in remembering your own gardening heritage as we have in collecting and presenting the material included in this book. Our most sincere wish is to enrich your personal gardening experience.

Acknowledgments

Cynthia W. Mueller, originally a Galveston county Master Gardener, has worked in the Extension Horticulture office and has been involved with my landscape horticultural work for thirteen years. She also wrote the chapter in this book entitled "Slips and Starts" and has provided invaluable support through the years. Cynthia propagated many of the plants in this book including the white Lady Banks rose from Elizabeth Lawrence's garden and other rare and hard-to-find-treasures.

Jason Powell, who wrote "The Fruitful Garden" chapter in this book, spent his first six years in College Station. His dad, Arlie Powell, is an Extension Fruit Specialist and is involved with the family's Petals from the Past Nursery located in Jemison, Alabama. Jason received his undergraduate horticulture degree from Auburn University and his master's degree from Texas A&M University. After working part time at the Antique Rose Emporium while a student, he and his wife Shelley, also a horticulture graduate from Texas A&M University, founded Petals from the Past Nursery which features heirloom plants and fruit for the South on site and by mail order.

Other valued support and contributions include Marge Hurt, Nell Zeigler, Hazel McCoy, William Seale, Gene Bussell, Linda Askey, Staci Catron, Francis Parker, Patti McGee, Peggy Cornett, Dean Norton, Peter Hatch, Susan Haltom, Sally Reeves, Mary Anne Pickens, Mike Shoup, Chris Wiesinger, Neil Odenwald, Mike Arnold, Doug Welsh, Paul Greer, Martin Anderson, Tom LeRoy, Bill Adams, Keith Hansen, William Johnson, Neil Sperry, Ben Page, Gail Griffin, Davyd Foard Hood, Robert Smith, Mary Palmer Kelly Dargan, Hugh Dargan, Jerry Parsons, Ralph Anderson, Derick Belden III, Steve Bender, Susan Hitchcock, Jeff Lewis, Carleton Wood, Jane B. White, Ken M. McFarland, Felder Rushing, Ethyl Shingo Manard, Genevieve Trimble, Peggy Martin, Beverly Welch,

Aubrey King, Andrew King, Dave Creech, and Charlie Thigpen. Special appreciation goes to my wife Lucille Pressley Welch for her patience, knowledge and support, to my son, Will, for many years of enduring horticulture, and for my granddaughters Kathlyn Alyse and Ella Diane Welch with hopes for continuing a horticultural legacy. — WCW

I wish to thank David Creech, Dawn Stover, Elyce Rodewald, Barbara Stump, Trey Anderson, Duke Pittman, Thera Lou Adams, the late Cleo Barnwell, Jo Ann Carter, Nina Ellis, Sandra Field, Jackie Grant, Jeff Abt, Mary Beth Hagood, Annie Hoya, Bill & Mary Louise Jobe, Celia Jones, Aubrey & Cheryl King (King's Nursery), Dan McBride, Jerry Parsons, Ann Phillips, the late Theresa Reeves, Sue Ripley, Larry Shelton, and my other colleagues at Stephen F. Austin State University. — GG

Part One

EXPLORING OUR GARDENING HERITAGE

The Three Sisters

Native American Influence

WILLIAM C. WELCH

ontributions to our Southern gardening traditions are not normally associated with Native Americans. While Euro-Americans generally thought humans were the masters of nature, Native Americans believed they were but a small part of all creation and the circle of life. Native American contributions to our garden heritage were based on a well-developed understanding of the land, native vegetation, and food production related to, among other things, the location of trails and communities and the many uses of plants.

Research supports that Native Americans first arrived in the

Purple coneflower *(Echinacea purpurea)* was used as a medicinal plant by Native Americans. (Photo by William C. Welch)

Corn was a major crop grown by Native Americans. (Photo by Greg Grant)

southeastern part of the United States at least ten thousand years ago and were descended from people who crossed the Bering Sea ice bridge from Asia. When Europeans encountered these people, they probably numbered as many as five million and their descendants today include the Alabama, Caddo, Creek, Choctaw, Chickasaw, Seminole, and Cherokee. They practiced agriculture and used earthen mounds for burial and raised buildings.

Agriculture

Most of us grew up with a movie- and television-influenced image of Native Americans as nomadic hunter-gatherers and warriors, but many hunted wild animals and gathered wild plants only as a supplement to the food that they grew, especially in the South. Although they grew more than 150 domestic plants, these three dominated: corn (*Zea mays*), beans (*Phaseolus* spp.), and squash (*Cucurbita* spp.). The Iroquois of upstate New York called this trio the "Three Sisters." We will never know if native farmers knew the significance of the nutritional importance of this threesome as a balanced diet—corn as a source of carbohydrates, and squash and beans as vegetable protein. We now know that when eaten together, corn and beans produce lysine, which increases the amount of protein available in beans.

Three kinds of beans were favorites of native peoples of the Southern United States: scarlet runner beans (*P. coccineus*), lima beans (*P. lunatus*), and kidney beans (*P. vulgaris*). The beans were typically grown up the stalks of corn, and pumpkins of various sorts grew beneath. Field pumpkin (*C. pepo*), crookneck squash (*C. moschata*), and winter squash (*C. maxima*) were very important food sources because they could be stored for long periods or the flesh dried for winter use. Blossoms, young shoots, and even young leaves were eaten for greens.

Schoolchildren are familiar with the legend of Squanto showing the first Pilgrims how to plant corn in hills with a fish underneath the soil for fertilizer. The Native American farming practices of planting on hills, training bean vines up the stalks of corn, and using pumpkin leaves as ground cover to control weeds would today be considered advanced concepts in garden management.

Gourds, especially bottle gourds (*Lagenaria siceraria*) and other relatives, were grown for medicinal uses but also for the edible quality of the young shoots and fruits. They were used for making dippers, water containers, musical instruments, birdhouses (for insect control), containers for sacred honey or pollen, spoons, masks, and eating vessels.

Native Americans grew gourds and used them as utensils and birdhouses.
(Photo by William C. Welch)

Native Americans planted, gathered, and ate pecans, which are native to river and creek bottoms in Texas and the South. (Photo by William C. Welch)

Crops were not grown in huge single-crop acreages but in small garden and field plots. Men usually had the job of locating the fields and clearing the land; women and children then tended the crops. Seed sown in raised mounds helped control moisture and temperature, and fences kept out marauding animals. Fields were moved periodically, so the land was generally not exhausted. Centuries of trial and error resulted in locating fields in areas of natural fertility, such as in lowlands where periodic flooding provided sufficient nutrients. Native Americans of the Southwest also planted in depressions to take advantage of sometimes scarce rainfall.

Site Planning

Altering a tract of land to serve human purposes is considered site planning. Native peoples of the Southeast made many changes for their own purposes by clearing land for farms, building villages and roads, and mining minerals and other resources from the land. Among the most important and lasting alterations they made in the landscape were the many trails, paths, and roads created to accommodate local traffic and link communities to waterways, which served as larger-scale transportation systems. Sometimes these routes were marked by stones, but most were well-worn footpaths. Segments of a trail from Florida to Natchitoches, Louisiana, and San Antonio, Texas, became part of the Spanish colonial road El Camino Real, and the Occaneechi Path in present-day North Carolina and Virginia remains part of the right-of-way for U.S. Highway 40.

In addition to using these trails, European settlers took over Native American villages and farmlands, especially after epidemics of European diseases decimated the native populations. The good land-selection skills of these indigenous people were reinforced when many early colonial towns were built adjacent to existing native villages. Nacogdoches, Texas; Savannah, Georgia; Santa Fe and Taos, New Mexico, are examples.

Native American Contributions at a Glance

- Native plants used for food, medicine, and ceremonies
- Farming of corn, beans, and squash
- Site-planning skills for locating paths connecting communities and promoting trade
- An intimate knowledge of nature

Use of Wild Plants

Gathering plants was an essential task of survival for Native Americans. It is not always clear whether certain crops were cultivated or gathered from the wild. Some management was likely undertaken to clear or discourage competing growth of unwanted woody plants. Native plants such as camassia (*Camassia esculenta*) and purple coneflower or echinacea (*Echinacea purpurea*) served as food, medicine, and dye sources and were used in ceremonies and for smoking. Sometimes the cutting of trees took place in a wide area around towns, especially of desirable species like the tulip tree (*Liriodendron tulipifera*), which was much in demand by native craftsmen who burned the centers and made them into canoes.

Native Americans possessed a broad understanding of the plants in their environment and how to use them. They favored certain plants for gathering: persimmons (*Diospyros virginiana*), wild grapes (*Vitis* spp.), maypop (*Passiflora incarnata*), rose hips (*Rosa* spp.), and a variety of berries (*Vaccinium, Rubus, Viburnum,* and *Sambucus* spp.).

Popular nuts included hickories (*Carya* spp.), pecans (*C. illinoiensis*), and acorns from palatable oaks (*Quercus* spp.). They ground greenbrier tubers (*Smilax* spp.) to make starch for breads and ate the tips as greens. Jerusalem artichokes (*Helianthus tuberosus*), which contained high levels of fructose, were cooked in a variety of ways. Leaves such as those of pokeberry (*Phytolacca americana*) were eaten as greens as they are today.

Medicinal plants played an important part in the lives of Native Americans. Some of these included toothache tree (*Zanthoxyllum clava-herculis*), Indian pink (*Spigelia marilandica*), Virginia snake root (*Aristolochia serpentaria*), wild onion (*Allium* spp.), beebalm (*Monarda fistulosa*), blue flag iris (*Iris versicolor*), and witchhazel (*Hamamelis* spp.). The application and uses of these plants varied regionally, but each was used for at least one important application.

Plants used for ceremonial purposes included tobacco (*Nicotiana* spp.) smoked in ceremonial pipes; eastern red cedar (*Juniperus virginiana*) used as incense in purification rituals; and American ginseng (*Panax quinquefolius*) used in religious ceremonies, because Native Americans, like Asians, found that the roots took on human forms.

Native Americans used plant patterns and themes in their textiles and pottery, but little is known about their use of ornamental plants around their homes. In the early spring of 2001, Russell Studebaker, a well-known horticulturist and garden writer in Tulsa, Oklahoma, with knowledge about ornamental bulbs in Oklahoma, offered to take me through Tahlequah and other eastern parts of the state where many heirloom daffodils have naturalized. Old narcissus are there in great abundance, which attests to their adaptability. They are found at Native American cemeteries and schools in impressive numbers, but as for many other sites in the South where these bulbs exist, one can speculate how they came to be there, but no exact documentation of their origin exists.

The authors wish to acknowledge as the source of this material Nancy Volkman and her essay "With the Three Sisters: Native American Contributions to the Southern Landscape," which appeared in *The Southern Heirloom Garden* (Taylor Trade Publishing, 1995).

Orange Blossoms and Spanish-Daggers

Spanish Influence

WILLIAM C. WELCH

Gardeners may feel fortunate that Spanish ships first found the way from Europe to the southern part of North America, for Spain is a country with an old and especially rich horticultural tradition. The Spanish were expert gardeners and had a history of adapting freely from other cultures. Moreover, because they traveled so widely, establishing colonies in all of our Gulf Coast states, their influence on American colonial gardening was unusually pervasive and remains strong in the South today.

Early Settlement in Florida, Louisiana, Alabama, and Texas

The oldest continuously populated community of European descent in the United States is St. Augustine, Florida, which was established by Spain in 1565 as an urban setting for a colony of more than twenty-five hundred people. The original plan for the town was military in character since St. Augustine was established to provide refuge and protection during siege. Military considerations actually limited planting in the immediate vicinity of the town, and the planners allowed few tall trees or other plant masses in St. Augustine.

Individual properties were typically sixty-seven hundred square feet in size. The defining element of these landscapes was the white-washed walls of tabby (a mixture of oyster shells, lime, and sea-water), which were five and one-half feet tall and raised around the perimeter to enclose the areas as expansive courtyards. Planting was utilitarian: prickly pear (*Opuntia*) often topped the tabby walls to

These large specimens of 'White Marseilles' figs were planted at the Bishop of Canterbury's Palace in London in the mid 1500s. They are still productive and healthy today. Thomas Jefferson grew the same fig at his Monticello home, and it is featured today in the gardens and orchards of Petals from the Past in Jemison, Alabama. (Photo by William C. Welch)

Grapes were often grown on arbors in early Spanish gardens for shade and fruit. (Photo by William C. Welch)

Confederate jasmine *(Trachelospermum jasminoides)* is among the fragrant vines used in Spanish gardens. (Photo by William C. Welch)

serve as a natural sort of razor wire. *Yucca aloifolia* earned the common name of Spanish-dagger and was also used for fencing. Within the walled compounds were houses with windows to the south and solid walls to the north. The concept of zero lot lines was utilized throughout.

Arbors covered with grapes provided cooling shade within the courts, and archaeologists' excavations have uncovered wells in many of the original yards. Some of these featured shafts fashioned from shipping barrels; in others, coquina (a native rock made mostly of shell fragments) was used as a lining and to make walls around the

Lucinda Hutson's Austin, Texas, garden reflects Spanish influence with its bold use of color and herbaceous plant materials. (Photo by William C. Welch)

wellhead. Figs, onions, melons, citrus, peaches, grapes, mulberries, lemons, sour orange, pomegranates, and sweet orange trees were commonly planted within the walled spaces.

Louisiana was under Spanish rule from 1769 to 1803, although little remains or is known of its direct influence on the gardens and plant materials of the area. It is thought that the extensive use of con-

Early Spanish colonists distributed citrus of various kinds to the warm climates around the world. The oranges in this image are on Bolivar Peninsula near Galveston, Texas. (Photo by William C. Welch)

Bold use of bright colors, container plants, and citrus indicates a strong interest in gardening for food and pleasure in this Sealy, Texas, garden. These concepts are currently popular in Southern gardens even in the most modest neighborhoods. (Photo by William C. Welch)

tainer plants in the French Quarter courtyards in New Orleans may have its origins with the Spanish. The use of citrus trees, although enthusiastically adopted by French settlers, seems likely to have been a Spanish contribution. Early records refer to the planting of orange trees on the levees of New Orleans. In addition to citrus as a food source, their blossoms were valued for fragrance along with jasmine and other plants.

In the records of the Spanish period in New Orleans are references to roof gardens. These were made possible by a safety measure adopted after the catastrophic fires of 1789 and 1792: to inhibit the spread of fires, the city authorities required thereafter that all walls be brick and the roofs be flat and tiled. Because flat roofs almost always leak in areas of high rainfall (such as New Orleans), however, the new building code proved unenforceable in the long run, and the roof gardens did not persist. Nor did the Spanish colonial

Plants grown in containers are part of the Spanish contribution to gardening. Plants like these require little watering or care while contributing color and texture to the garden. (Photo by William C. Welch)

Arches of Wisteria (*Wisteria sinensis*) with large containers of native Mexican succulents (*Graptopetalum paraguayense*) accent this Houston garden. (Photo by William C. Welch)

Spanish Contributions at a Glance

- Open plazas in towns and cities
- Four-part garden plans that focused on a central water feature
- Structures built for shade
- Grapes and other vines to soften structures, provide fruit and shade
- Symmetrical plans (formal) often contrasted with informal plantings
- Intensely developed and utilized small garden spaces
- Boldly contrasting colors for garden materials with earth-toned backgrounds
- Use of many fragrant and colorful plants
- Water as a garden feature (often functional)
- Walls that enclose garden spaces
- Ornamental tiles for wall and pool adornment
- Extensive use of container plants

administration, which ended in 1803. Because the French influence on local culture was overwhelming, evidence of Spanish gardening, though intriguing, is hard to trace.

New Orleans has always given due credit to its Spanish roots. Far less well known is the role that Spanish colonists played in opening up Alabama. In fact, this state was also under Spanish control for a considerable period. It had been claimed by the French from 1702 to 1763, and then the English from 1763 to 1782, but for thirty-one years immediately thereafter (1782–1813) Alabama was ruled by a Spanish administration seated in Mobile.

According to research by the late Ed Givhan, a physician and historian from Montgomery, Alabama, the interior courtyards that are a traditional feature of older houses in Mobile were a relic of this period. Mobile remained a small town through the Spanish period—Dr. Givhan calculated that when the Spanish left in 1813, its total population was less than one thousand. But the city's population still remains 45 percent Roman Catholic in a state that is approximately 96 percent Protestant.

Texas Mission Gardens

Spanish domination lasted longer in Texas than in any other Southern state, and it is here that the finest examples of Spanish colonial-era architecture survive. These survivals are chiefly mission buildings that Spanish priests erected as centers for the Christianization of the native people. These have been carefully restored in San Antonio and other sites in South Texas. At the time of Maximilian (1832–67) and Carlota there was a great emphasis on planting as many trees on the squares and streets as possible. This appreciation for trees is evident to this day in Texas.

Built of native stone, these South Texas missions represented a spectacular architectural achievement for the period, especially when one considers that they were built largely by Native American labor supervised only by priests. Unfortunately, the earlier missions in East Texas were built of wood, and none remain.

From the garden historian's point of view, the mission restorations remain distinctly incomplete. To date, there has been very little research or restoration of the gardens that tradition says must have accompanied these structures.

Some tantalizing glimpses come from a preliminary study of Mission San Juan conducted in February 1993 by Rosalind Z. Rock, park historian for the San Antonio Missions National Historical Park. She found that intensive farming methods and use of irrigation ditches characterized the Spanish colonial farming there, in strong contrast to the more typical dryland farming the later settlers in Texas practiced. Crops of Mission San Juan included corn (maize) and other grains, cotton, figs, grapes, watermelons, cantaloupes, beans (a pinto type and a chickpea type most common), sugarcane, and squashes (gourds, pumpkins).

Formality and Order

French Influence

GREG GRANT

Though the French did not invent "their" style of landscaping, they certainly made it famous enough that the world generally gives them credit for it. Growing from Egyptian, Roman, Islamic, Spanish, and finally Italian roots, the rigid formality of the French style of landscaping became the norm in the seventeenth century and began spreading throughout Europe. Influential garden-design families like Mollet and Le Nôtre led the charge with trendsetting examples of their work. André Le Nôtre's work at Vaux-le-Vicomte and later at Louis XIV's palace at Versailles became the standard by which all others would be judged.

The seventeenth-century French garden ideology proposed that the natural landscape should be an extension of the architecture. This classic French design was characterized by a complete dominance over nature and featured plant materials in rigid order or meticulously clipped into architectural features, including stately avenues (allées), walls (palisades), rooms (*cabinets de verdure*), topiary, espalier, and parterres (*broderies*).

Topiary is the art of clipping a tree or shrub into a fanciful shape. Sometimes the shapes are rather simple (pyramids, cones, globes, etc.), while at other times they can be quite elaborate (animals, spirals, etc.). In Europe, boxwood (*Buxus sempervirens*) and yew (*Taxus baccata*) are often the clipped shrubs of choice. In the Southern nursery trade one most often sees wax leaf ligustrum (*Ligustrum japonicum*) or various junipers (*Juniperus* spp.) being used. The highly invasive Chinese privet (*L. sinense*) would have been clipped and shaped in older gardens as well. Our native yaupon holly (*Ilex vomitoria*) is my all-time favorite shrub for creating topiary. Creating fine topiary is time consuming, but maintaining it is even more laborious. Unfortunately, Americans often cheat today by using a preformed frame and planting a clinging vine on it, which is a poor substitute for the real thing.

An espalier is formed by training a tree into a two-dimensional flat plane. It is most often used with fruit trees like pears, apples, and figs and with plants like roses, magnolias, and wisteria. Espaliers are designed to save space by growing plants either flat against a wall or trained onto or in place of a fence. Growing tender plants on a heat-

A formal courtyard at Bayou Bend in Houston adds elegance to the wooded setting. (Photo by William C. Welch)

An allée of crape myrtles at the Dallas Arboretum focuses on a pool and fountain. (Photo by William C. Welch)

Clipped hollies at the Dallas Arboretum contribute a sense of formality to the garden. (Photo by Greg Grant)

Longue Vue Gardens in New Orleans includes a good example of parterre (pattern) plantings. (Photo by Greg Grant)

The French Legation in Austin once served as a political center during the Republic of Texas period (1836–45). Plantings include a small parterre. (Photo by William C. Welch)

absorbing wall also allows a gardener to take advantage of a select microclimate to extend the hardiness range of an otherwise tender plant.

The parterre, or *parterre de broderie,* was named for its resemblance to embroidery. Fanciful patterns to be viewed from above were laid out next to the main building and edged in clipped boxwood or other fine-textured shrubs. Inside, the living scrollwork was filled with different materials, including colored gravel, turf, flowers, or topiary.

After a hundred years of French dominance of formal landscape design throughout Europe, the English, in a somewhat rebellious gesture, turned to a more naturalistic style of landscaping. It thumbed its nose at all aspects of what was considered overly rigid French formal design. The naturalistic English style became the norm throughout Europe and led to the complete destruction of many fine French-style gardens. It became so popular that many remaining French gardens even added *jardins anglais* (wild or unstructured informal plantings) as prominent features. Luckily, many French formal gardens, along with their style and influence, remained.

Eventually these two competing styles blended together to form the typical "hybrid" European garden seen today, with French formal bones and an English informal planting style. Classic examples of this beautiful blending of styles include the gardens at Hidcote Manor, Sissinghurst, and Great Dixter, all in England.

American gardeners, of course, inherited all of the European landscape influences but relied heavily on the French "dominance-over-nature" theme in taming the new wild America. This was especially embraced in dealing with the exuberant semitropical growth in the Deep South. The Creole gardens of New Orleans and southern Louisiana showcased the French style like no place else in America. Even today one can't help noticing the stately live oak allées, the rectilinear garden patterns, and the occasional parterre. Today, remnants of the French style are seen as well in many everyday suburban foundation plantings.

French Contributions at a Glance

- Formal and often symmetrical landscapes
- Extensive use of shrubs and trees clipped into topiary
- Grand allées and vistas of trees
- Trees and vines trained on walls, fences, and small spaces as espaliers
- Trees trained and clipped (pleached) in the form of structures
- Highly trained pruning and shaping of fruit trees
- Ornate parterres as individual features to be viewed from above
- Expressed dominance over nature

A French olive jar serves as an accessory in a Baton Rouge, Louisiana, garden. (Photo by William C. Welch)

Out of Africa

African Influence

GREG GRANT

Although often overlooked and rarely researched, African influence in our Southern culture is widespread. Because African Americans make up the most common minority in the South, it is only natural that their ancient culture contributed heavily to and helps define that of the region. Despite the hardships that introduced slaves had to endure, an oppressive and deliberate attempt to strip them of their heritage and culture for the most part failed. Whether in language, song, dance, craft, church, farm, or garden, many seeds of Africana continued to sprout and thrive. I doubt many Southerners realize that the words *goober* (peanut), *yam* (sweet potato), and *gumbo* (okra) came to us via Africa. In fact, the entire South became a stew pot, mixing African influences with those of Europe, Native Americans, and others.

Many Southern dishes based on different types of "stews" served on rice can be attributed to Africa through the influence of slaves who did most of the cooking and farming in the plantation world of the South. Rice, yams, okra, peas, watermelon, sorghum, coffee, and catfish were all an existing part of the African culture. Guinea hens, a staple in early Southern yards, were from Africa as well. Thus, we are blessed today with the delicious Southern dishes of gumbo, étouffée, seafood creoles, jambalaya, and fried fish.

Another African influence that slipped quietly into all facets of Southern life was the swept yard. It's hard to image in today's world of lawn mowers, string trimmers, blowers, herbicides, and irrigation that most yards in the early South were scraped clean of all vegetation and swept like a kitchen floor. Early Southerners used dog-

wood twig "brooms," sage grass, or other native plants to fashion yard brooms or rakes for this purpose. Of course, one reason yards were swept is that most were used as workspaces, such as outdoor kitchens. Swept yards also kept away snakes and cut down on the danger of house-destroying fires. You can imagine how important bare ground was near a wooden house with a thatched roof in hot, dry Africa. The Stephen F. Austin Pineywoods Native Plant Center in Nacogdoches, Texas, has a "Firewise" demonstration garden that advocates, even today, having no vegetation in close proximity to a house in fire-prone areas.

Shangrila, in Orange, Texas, sports a striking allée of blue bottles and birdhouse gourds. (Photo by Greg Grant)

There seems to be some debate about the true origin of swept yards in America, but Richard Westmacott, author of *African-American Gardens and Yards in the Rural South* (University of Tennessee Press, 1992) states, "Although the swept yard clearly has African rather than European roots, it was adopted in the yards of the plantation houses throughout the South. . . . It is a fact that the swept yard is one of many examples of African tradition that found its way into all levels of Southern society." This even includes most early Southern cemeteries. To this day, my dad isn't at all fond of helping my mom mow the yard, as he was raised with a bare swept one and thinks the whole yard-mowing exercise quite pointless.

Many African American yards in the twentieth century were known for their yard art. A unique form of yard art with purported African origins is the bottle tree. Apparently, bottles were originally hung on trees to trap evil spirits. Then the bottles were stuck on dead tree branches and later, attached to posts with nails. Discarded bottles were used, so they often varied in color, size, and arrangement. Bottle trees worked their way into all cultures in the South as pure ornament. They have even been referred to as "the poor man's stained-glass window." While working for the Works Progress Administration (WPA) in 1941, the Southern author Eudora Welty

Pots of blue bottles act as focal points in a Southern cottage garden. (Photo by William C. Welch)

A spectacular multicolored bottle tree guards the grounds at Festival Hill in Roundtop, Texas. (Photo by William C. Welch)

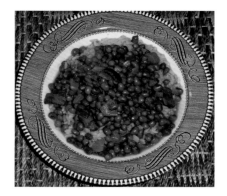

Peas with rice, a typical African dish, is also a Southern staple. (Photo by Greg Grant)

from Jackson, Mississippi, photographed haunting bottle trees in a Simpson County, Mississippi, yard. Popular garden writer, horticulturist, and good friend Felder Rushing, also from Jackson, is the father of the current popularity of bottle trees, advocating them in his lectures around the country.

Because African Americans were sold into slavery with literally nothing, no other culture in the South has been as adept at recycling and reusing discarded materials. Scientist and teacher George Washington Carver, who was way ahead of his time, even had his students construct an entire science lab at Tuskegee University out of materials found at dump sites. He also preached the use of organic waste as fertilizer and the preparation of edible plants from the wild. He is famous for discovering numerous ways to utilize by-products from the sweet potato, pecan, soybean, and especially that Southern staple, the peanut.

In an odd blending of cultures, many poor white Southerners

A native of Africa, castor beans (*Ricinus communis*) have graced many country gardens through the years. (Photo by Greg Grant)

unknowingly adopted these African recipes, raising of guinea fowl, swept yards, bottle trees, words, songs, and plants.

One of the still most common and important plants from Africa is the southern pea (*Vigna unguiculata*). Not actually a true pea (*Pisum*) and not really a true bean (*Phaseolus*), the high-protein, easy-to-grow "pea" became a staple on every plate in the South. Occurring in a myriad of types, the most common ones in Southern gardens were varieties of purple hull peas, black-eyed peas, cream peas, and crowder peas. Crowder peas were so named because the fat peas were so crowded in the large pods that they ended up being flat on the ends. Any good Southern pea sheller appreciates easy-to-shell crowder peas and cringes at having to shell that wonderful delicacy, the "lady finger" cream pea. Many a family in the South, both black and white, spent countless hours talking under a shade tree in the yard or on the porch as they shelled peas. To this day

Laura Plantation is a fine example of an accurately restored and interpreted Louisiana plantation home on the Mississippi River. (Photo by Greg Grant)

Long-abandoned slave quarters are nestled under majestic live oaks (*Quercus virginiana*) at Evergreen Plantation in Wallace, Louisiana. (Photo by Greg Grant)

I'm fond of shelling peas, as it takes me back in time, sitting with my grandparents and other relatives listening to the local "gossip." Although today most peas are stored in the freezer for later use, they would usually have been eaten fresh or stored dry in earlier times.

Okra (*Abelmoschus esculentus*) is another important contribution from Africa. Often served fried, boiled, or cooked with tomatoes and served over rice, it is truly a Southern dish, often looked upon with disdain by Northerners. When I was a child, Grandmother Emanis would boil okra in the same pot with the peas. We children wouldn't take a spoon of peas until Papaw scooped all the okra off the top. He produced a great spectacle by holding each pod over his head and slurping it down, like a bird eating a worm, as each of us looked on in horror. Of course, today I love boiled okra along with the fond memories. Okra's most important contribution to the Deep South is that wonderful, hearty soup known as gumbo. Although it can be prepared using any kind of seafood, chicken, or sausage, the ingredient that gave it its name is okra, a natural thickening agent.

The watermelon (*Citrullus lanatus*) is another Southern icon that originated in Africa. Though in ancient times watermelons would have been small fruited and mostly eaten for much-needed moisture, today watermelons occur in a myriad of types, including small "icebox" melons, large-fruited sorts, yellow fleshed as well as the popular red, and the fashionable seedless melons, which are pure "heart" and keep much longer. Many of the older cultivars, like the yellow-spotted 'Moon and Stars' my grandmother's parents used to grow, the big round 'Black Diamond,' and the striped 'Georgia Rattlesnake,' can be found in several specialty mail-order seed companies offering a range of heirloom seed. Many towns throughout the South celebrate watermelons with festivals, largest-watermelon competitions, and seed-spitting contests.

The bottle gourd (*Lagenaria siceraria*) is also from Africa. Grown for containers for thousands of years, they are now popular as pure ornament. They come in many shapes and sizes, including birdhouse gourds, dipper gourds, basket gourds, snake gourds, and the small, multicolored ornamental types. I was always fascinated as a child by the dipper gourds that Grandmother Emanis grew. The gourd even has its own society of growers now.

Another popular Southern plant from Africa is the castor bean (*Ricinus communis*). Once known as "Palma Christi," the palm of Christ, this large-leaved lover of heat was a prominent feature in Victorian gardens. My grandfather, Rebel Eloy Emanis, used to plant them in the chicken yard for summer shade. Today there are burgundy-leaved as well as red-flowered forms. It is also the source of castor oil.

Perhaps my favorite African plant is the crinum lily (*Crinum* sp.). A standard in many cemeteries and older yards, the crinum is "the lily" for the South. Whether white, pink, or striped, crinums have provided ornament and cut flowers to generations of Southerners. Though not all crinums are fragrant, or even pleasant smelling, most are known for their intoxicating fragrance, especially at night. They are so tough and hardy that many a surviving crinum marks a homesite long departed by its owners and remains the lone reminder that humans ever graced the site. Like the bottle tree, some species of

Aunt Chloe Preparing Dinner, original oil on board painting commissioned by the Landreth family in 1909. The painting was inspired by a photograph taken by Rudolph Eikemeyer between 1894 and 1900 (and included in a book of Eikemeyer's works, *Down South*). Eikemeyer traveled through the South in the 1890s documenting the life of African Americans who elected not to leave the plantation after they were freed. Photograph courtesy of D. Landreth Seed Company, New Freedom, Pennsylvania.

African Contributions at a Glance

- Swept yards
- The yard used as a working extension of the house
- Guinea fowl
- Bottle trees
- Many famous "Southern" plants like watermelons, okra, peas, castor beans, and crinums

crinum were even grown around yards in Africa to keep out evil spirits. They have the opposite effect on me!

It is essential that we not forget that many of the fine gardens in the South were installed and maintained by slaves. The swept yards were swept by slaves. The crops were tended by slaves. The produce was harvested by slaves. The sorghum and sugarcane was made into syrup by slaves. The homegrown meals were prepared by slaves. Though acquired under deplorable circumstances, African Americans today have a deep legacy of expert gardening and farming.

It's amazing, considering the often tumultuous race relations in the South, that the African culture so permeates our landscape and culture. Whether drinking coffee, listening to rock and roll, eating gumbo, picking crinum lilies for a church celebration, or watching cattle egrets from Africa following a rancher cutting his African bermudagrass hay, our society owes a great debt to that continent for helping shape our cultural history.

Gardening with Nature

English Influence

WILLIAM C. WELCH

The English tradition has been responsible more than any other in determining how we design and garden in the South. The earliest of our gardens in America were borrowed from the "old-style" English garden and laid out in a grid pattern. This influence grew from the Egyptian, Roman, Islamic, Spanish, and Italian roots of French gardens and later came to be widely known as the "French" landscape style. The gardens were designed in a formal manner with a walk system defining the grid. The open spaces were the garden plots. The main walk was directly in front of the main entrance and echoed the central hall of the dwelling. This central walk was usually broader than the central hall while physically and visually extending the house out into the garden.

Examples of this type of early English garden may be seen at Bacon's Castle near Surrey, Virginia, and in Rachel Jackson's garden at the Hermitage near Nashville, Tennessee. The Paca Garden represents the classic colonial view of a well laid-out estate garden in the style of Capability Brown combined with American sensibilities. In contrast, the area closer to the house is a series of garden rooms. Dumbarton Oaks, near Washington, D.C., combines wilderness aspects as well as highly structured formality of English and French design. These are, however, examples of gardens of people with means. Ordinary citizens had simpler gardens usually in a square or rectangular space with walks and raised beds between. These gardens were not as likely to be integrated with the house. A good example is the Tully Smith House at the Atlanta History Center.

Montisford Abbey in England combines roses, perennials, and evergreen shrubs into a year-round garden display. (Photo by William C. Welch)

This type of garden changed radically in the early eighteenth century in England when the "natural style" of gardens became popular. These gardens were created with the natural topography in mind, with walks tending to follow the curves and contours of the land. Streams were dammed to form lakes that appeared "natural," and the straight lines of the old-style gardens were replaced.

Lancelot "Capability" Brown (1716–83) created and made popular this naturalistic style in England and strongly influenced Thomas Jefferson's layout of Monticello. Brown was responsible for more than 170 landscapes surrounding the finest English country homes, such as Blenheim Palace, Stourhead, and Warwick Castle. His style included grassy slopes, artificial lakes, and vistas that ran straight to the house. Brown utilized clumps, belts, and scatterings of trees as well as serpentine lakes created by invisibly damming small rivers within the English landscapes. It was basically a gardenless form of landscaping that swept away almost all remnants of the previous formal garden styles. Sheep and cattle kept the grass low by grazing on the grounds. They were kept away from the buildings by a "ha ha," a retaining wall and/or ditch that kept animals at bay while allowing an unbroken view of the landscape from the manor house.

George Washington's Mount Vernon eventually reflected this style, although it still retained a walled garden. The William Paca Garden (1760s) in Annapolis, Maryland, is a good example of having both the old style and the naturalistic movement apparent in the garden. The Paca Garden was designed by the owner and has been meticulously restored after extensive archaeology and research.

Bernard M'Mahon's *American Gardener's Calendar* (1811) was the first book to espouse this type of garden and covers just about

Susan Lee's garden on the Isle of Jersey includes an outstanding example of a mixed shrub border set off by a broad expanse of turf. (Photo by William C. Welch)

A memorial garden at Susan Lee's Isle of Jersey home includes silver-colored foliage plants and a beautiful metal obelisk. (Photo by William C. Welch)

The William Paca Garden in Annapolis, Maryland, created in 1764, combines formal and informal concepts. (Photo by William C. Welch)

every aspect of gardening. M'Mahon (1775–1816) borrowed extensively from earlier English gardening authors. Thomas Jefferson considered the book his "Bible" for horticulture and consulted it extensively for guidance at Monticello. M'Mahon was also the curator for the Lewis and Clark plant collection.

Later, Andrew Jackson Downing (1815–52) published *Treatise on the Theory and Practice of Landscape Gardening* (1848), which was devoted entirely to the natural style. Downing included extensive plant lists to support this picturesque style of gardening. Many garden authorities credit Jackson with our modern garden designs that include a largely public front space, more private rear garden, and utility spaces. This same concept of naturalistic tree and shrub groupings, roads and paths that followed the contours of a hilly site, and lakes being made in low, boggy areas was used to design and develop cemeteries. These were often used like parks for Sunday outings where families enjoyed visiting the gravesites of loved ones.

William Robinson (1838–1935) was instrumental in changing the high-Victorian pattern of planted-out bedding schemes (carpet bedding) to more naturalistic "cottage-garden" style plantings as emphasized in his book *The English Flower Garden* (1883). Through his book *The Wild Garden* (1870) he greatly influenced the concept of naturalistic plantings of wildflowers, shrubs, and trees, both native and exotic. Robinson's garden at Gravetye Manor is still recognized as an inspiration for diversified plantings of bulbs, woodland plants, rambling roses, and herbaceous mixtures. He rejected Victorian ideas about filling the garden with statuary, fountains, topiaries, and formal bedding schemes. The *Leucojum* 'Gravetye Giant' is still commercially available and as well adapted to the South as the species form *L. aestivum*, which is found in hundreds of historic gardens throughout the South.

Frederick Law Olmsted (1822–1903) is known as the originator of landscape architecture in America. His inspiration came from the naturalistic movement and developed areas such as Central Park in New York City. After his travels to the South, Olmsted wrote his

The perennial border at Dumbarton Oaks in Georgetown, Washington, D.C., creates a separate room enclosed by evergreen hedges. (Photo by Gail Griffin)

A cottage garden at the Antique Rose Emporium in San Antonio includes self-seeding annuals and heirloom roses. (Photo by William C. Welch)

impressions of the region in books such as *A Journey through Texas: Or a Saddle-Trip on the Southwestern Frontier* (1857). He was a keen observer of the landscape and wrote extensively about it.

Gertrude Jekyll further popularized the naturalistic style of gardening. Through her books and garden designs, as well as more than one thousand magazine articles, she inspired an entire generation of gardeners with her manipulation and use of color in the garden. She designed more than four hundred gardens in the United Kingdom, Europe, and the United States. Her use of pastel colors and plants arranged in elongated masses she called "drifts" strongly influenced estate gardens from 1900 to 1940. Her combination of plant heights, textures, color, and repetition communicated a strong design message. Some of her long herbaceous borders were famous for beginning with cool blue, blue-violet, and purple to yellows, hot oranges, and reds, interspersed occasionally with white and the many greens of foliage.

The gardens at Reynolda House, Winston-Salem, North Carolina,

The perennial border at the Antique Rose Emporium in San Antonio utilizes water-efficient perennials and roses for year-round seasonal color. (Photo by William C. Welch)

English Contributions at a Glance

- A natural style rather than rigid geometry
- Parklike landscapes
- Perennial borders, popularized by Gertrude Jekyll around 1900
- Cottage gardens as individualized, traditional eclectic plant mixtures surrounding small homes
- New ways of using color, introduced by Gertrude Jekyll in the early 1900s

are an excellent example of Gertrude Jekyll's style. Jekyll's association with English architect Sir Edwin Lutyens brought her into prominence in the arts and crafts movement. She also collected plants solely for their preservation. Jekyll is known today for going against the grain of conventional gardening ideas of her day.

The "cottage garden" most typically refers to a highly individualized garden surrounding a modest cottage. The "cottager" would often have small fruit trees, herbs, perennials, roses, berries and vines, vegetables, and annual flowers all coexisting beautifully. Historically, gardeners would bring home starts of plants from a nearby castle, dig them from the surrounding woods and meadows, or barter for them with friends and family.

This type of garden was usually enclosed by a fence or hedge to keep out unwanted animals and did not include lawns or mass plantings of the same plants. Anne Hathaway's garden at Stratford-upon-Avon is an authentic example. Hollyhocks, roses, foxgloves, and delphiniums are often shown in romantic-style paintings and illustrations. The phrase "rose-covered cottage" signifies this style. There is a new renaissance of interest in cottage gardens because lots are becoming smaller, the desire for large lawns is decreasing, and gardeners enjoy having a wide variety of plants. The informality and "anything-goes" idea appeals to modern sensibilities. Some of us just enjoy giving a dignified name to our personalized collections!

The gardening ideas we are expressing in this book are inspired by the English naturalistic movement. This includes the utilization of native plants, low-water-use landscapes, and creation of a sense of place.

A Garden in a Wilderness

German Influence

GREG GRANT

With the exception of Missouri, no Southern state received such a massive influx of German immigrants as did Texas. Ship after ship filled with Germans seeking their "new Germany" arrived into the ports of Galveston, Indianola, and New Orleans. In 1846, about eight thousand arrived in Galveston alone. Because the immigrants tended to settle together, the German influence was often far more pronounced, or even overwhelming, locally. According to *German Seed in Texas Soil* (Terry G. Jordan, University of Texas Press, 1975), the populations of Galveston, Houston, and San Antonio during the 1850s were roughly one-third German.

A rustic cedar grape arbor re-creates an inviting German-style outdoor space for a New Braunfels, Texas, garden. (Photo by William C. Welch)

Antique roses, perennials, and reseeding annuals were typical of early German homes. (Photo by William C. Welch)

German settlement in Texas centered most heavily around two regions. The town of Industry, in east-central Texas, was the initial focus of immigration, with the first German settlers arriving in 1838. Immigrants soon began spreading to other towns in that area. By 1845, German settlement had begun in the Hill Country of west-central Texas, with settlers arriving that year in New Braunfels and in Fredericksburg the following year.

As new arrivals, the Germans gardened to feed themselves. In addition to what they could grow, the immigrants harvested a great many foods from the wild, including wild grapes, plums, blackberries, and anything else deemed edible. As one German settler put it, "We ate what we liked and we ate what we didn't like."

Like most early settlers, the Germans grew such edible crops as sweet potatoes, Irish potatoes, corn, and cabbage. It doesn't appear that the Germans were responsible for introducing any new types of vegetables to Texas, but they can be credited with new uses for existing crops. It was the German influence that led to an increased consumption of white, or "German" potatoes, and the use of cabbage for kraut, tobacco for cigars, and wheat for "light bread" and flour tortillas.

At least in their own estimation, the German immigrants were generally better gardeners than their Anglo neighbors. In 1845, Prince Carl of Solms-Braunfels, the first commissioner-general of the Society for the Protection of German Immigrants in Texas, pointed out, "All of the garden vegetables grow abundantly if one takes the pains to plant them. The American is usually too lazy to prepare a garden. Rather than go to such trouble, he prefers to live on salted meat, bacon, corn, and coffee and to deny himself any greenery either for nourishment or for beautifying the home. However, the German settlements are distinguished by their beautiful gardens, vegetables, and flowers."

The Adolphus Sterne home in Nacogdoches, Texas, is open to the public. (Photo by Greg Grant)

The popular perennial *Gaura lindheimeri* is named for the "father of Texas botany." (Photo by Greg Grant)

Apparently, Germans were among the first settlers in Texas to adorn their surroundings with flowers and ornamental plantings. Traveling across Texas in 1854, Frederick Law Olmsted described his accommodations for a night he spent in the German community of New Braunfels: "A little room it proved, with blue walls again, and oak furniture . . . two large windows with curtains, and evergreen roses trained over them on the outside—not a pane of glass missing or broken—the first sleeping-room we have had in Texas where this was the case."

The love of flowers and an ornamental garden setting were part of the three gardens of Adolphus Sterne (1801–52), one of the first German immigrants to Texas. Born in Cologne on the Rhine, he came to New Orleans at sixteen and in 1826 moved to Nacogdoches, where he remained the rest of his life. (Today, the Sterne home is open to the public.) In 1923, his son, C. A. Sterne, described the lush gardens:

> My father's house stood in Nacogdoches on the Lanana Creek, near where the Bonita and Lanana meet, with about 30 acres surrounding it. . . . My father took great pride and interest in his gardens and orchard. There were three gardens on the place.

A simply constructed grape arbor provides shade and fruit. Much leisure time was spent under arbors during the hot summer months. (Photo by William C. Welch)

The one on the north was devoted to flowers, with a great variety of roses and rare shrubs and plants, which he had brought from Louisiana, and which had been imported from France.

In the center of the garden was a summer house, which was covered with morning glories and multiflora roses. The fence was covered with woodbine and yellow jessamine. The south garden had vegetables of every variety. The west garden was the orchard with a variety of fruit trees and a butter bean arbor running the entire width of the garden. My father often resorted to this butter bean arbor to read and study.

Perhaps even more telling were the recollections that Louise Romberg Fuchs recorded in 1927 about her first home in Texas: "I had some work to do all my life, in the house, in the field, and in the garden. The garden always interested me and I always had flowers in the house, too. . . . My dear grandmother in Germany always sent me all kinds of flower seeds: wonderful stocks, pinks, mignonette, hyacinth bulbs, all of which were my standing favorites."

In the *History of the Romberg Family*, Helene R. Mackensen, a Romberg granddaughter, recalled her grandparents' farmhouse where "the path leads up past a rosebush with dark red, velvety roses, up to the old log house. Just in front of the walk is a trellis overgrown with Madeira vine, fragrant with waxy, white blossoms, and with roses that grow in clusters in shades from the faintest pink into dark red, some even into blue." And in a letter she sent home to Germany in 1850, Elise Willrich asked for "all the bulbs you can get together (but no seeds) without causing you too much trouble, like Queenscrown, Lilies, Tulips, Hyacinths, Narcissus, etc., etc., packed in buckwheat chaff, also cuttings from Gardenias of good quality."

Because many German immigrants were college educated (some were even university professors), they quickly made their mark in the educated professions. For example, gardeners owe much of primary research on Texas' native flora and fauna to several German naturalists.

Oxblood lilies (*Rhodophiala bifida*) have naturalized in many areas of Texas. (Photo by Greg Grant)

Among the most important of these pioneering naturalists was Ferdinand Jakob Lindheimer from Frankfort-on-the-Main. He spent fifteen years collecting and classifying previously undescribed plants around Houston, Galveston, San Felipe, Columbus, Cat Springs, New Braunfels, Fredericksburg, and San Antonio. Most of his collecting was done for Asa Gray, a professor at Harvard, and fellow German George Engelmann of the Missouri Botanical

'Veilchenblau,' "the blue rose," was bred in Germany in 1909. (Photo by Greg Grant)

Garden. Considered "the father of Texas botany," Lindheimer has been honored in the names of one genus of Texas wildflowers and twenty native Texas plant species, including *Gaura lindheimeri* (commonly known as gaura or Lindheimer's gaura), now a popular garden perennial.

Lindheimer's dream (which he carried with him through all his moves around the frontier) was to establish Texas' first botanical garden. In an 1842 letter he stated: "I have kept back one specimen of every plant known to me. I must decide upon a more secure location somewhere here in Texas when I can establish an herbarium of indigenous plants. I must also have a botanical garden somewhere hereabouts where I can protect rare perennials" (quoted in Minetta Altgelt Goyne, *A Life among the Texas Flora,* Texas A&M University Press, 1991).

After finally settling in New Braunfels, Lindheimer served from 1852 to 1872 as the editor for the *Neu-Braunfelser Zeitung,* the local German-language newspaper. Today Lindheimer's home in New Braunfels stands as a small museum with a garden such as he might have cultivated.

Also making a name for himself was Friedrich Ernst, who before coming to Texas had served as head gardener and bookkeeper for the Duke of Oldenburg. Ernst, considered "the father of German immigration" in Texas, founded and helped settle the town of Industry in 1838. He is perhaps most famous for the overly enthusiastic letter he sent in 1832 to a friend in Oldenburg, Germany, extolling the virtues of his newly beloved home:

> The ground is hilly and alternates with forest and natural grass plains. Various kinds of trees. Climate like that of Sicily. The soil needs no fertilizer. Almost constant east wind. No winter, almost like March in Germany. Bees, birds and butterflies the whole winter through. . . . Principal products: tobacco, rice, indigo grow wild; sweet potatoes, melons of an especial goodness, watermelons, wheat, rye, vegetables of all kinds; peaches in great quantity grow wild in the woods, mulberries, many kinds of walnuts, wild plums, persimmons sweet as honey, wine in great quantity. . . . Meadows with the most charming flowers.

Texas is still home to the most charming meadows of wildflowers, in this case the wild blue hyacinth (*Camassia scilloides*). (Photo by Greg Grant)

Old-fashioned German practicality is at work by reusing large tin cans to protect young tomatoes and peppers in early spring. (Photo by William C. Welch)

Ernst's influence on Texas horticulture extended beyond his role as a cheerleader, however. He was known as a skilled gardener and shared much useful information on fruit and garden culture.

Another skilled gardener and an accomplished student of the natural sciences was the former baron Otfried Hans Freiherr von Meusebach. Serving as second commissioner of the Society for the Protection of German Immigrants in Texas, the baron dropped his

An early German homestead with an 1840s house still in excellent condition includes an orderly German-style vegetable garden. (Photo by William C. Welch)

title upon arriving in Texas and became simply John O. Meusebach. Meusebach is remembered for having founded the town of Fredericksburg. While he lived there, he was one of that community's leading citizens, forging a lasting peace treaty with the Comanches of the Texas Hill Country and serving as a state senator. He later moved to Loyal Valley, where his farm and garden became a showplace.

Visiting the Meusebach farm in 1877, N. A. Taylor wrote in *The Coming Empire:* "Loyal Valley is indeed a garden in a wilderness; a garden in which one can linger and be happy. Here is a nursery in which sixty varieties of roses grow, and hundreds of the finest flora of three continents; sixty varieties of pear, forty of peach, and an array of apples, plums, and grapes—all cultivated and arranged with taste and skill that cannot be excelled."

In a letter dated March 14, 1884, Meusebach himself stated, "We have planted onions, [German] potatoes, beans, and sugar corn in the garden. We had plenty of turnips, and sold about $30.00 worth. As I bought no new trees this year, I trimmed all the old trees severely, and made 2000 cuttings of grape-vines, as well as 1000 of crepemyrtle and other shrubs" (*Wurzbach's Memoirs and Meusebach Papers*). His crapemyrtles evidently presented quite a spectacle when in bloom.

The naturalized offspring of Meusebach's flowering willows (*Chilopsis linearis,* related to catalpas, not willows) and jujubes (*Zizyphus jujuba,* also called Chinese date) remain on his old property today. These help the visitor form some idea of what the garden looked like in its heyday. But it is challenging to imagine the effect of another of the former baron's fancies—the open-air Roman bath constructed of whitewashed native stone set beneath a bathhouse covered with purple and white wisteria.

To supply the needs of their horticulturally minded neighbors, a number of German immigrants established nurseries. Several of these were to play important roles in the development of gardening within Texas. Particularly notable in this regard were Johann Joseph Locke's Nursery, founded in 1856 at New Braunfels; Johann Friederich Leyendecker's Pearfield Nursery, established in 1876 at Frelsburg; and Gustav A. Shattenberg's Waldheim Nursery, established at Boerne before 1895. I had the fortunate experience of getting to know Johann Locke's ninety-plus-year-old grandson, Otto Locke Jr., while I was the county horticulturist in nearby San Antonio. Unfortunately, the historic family nursery died shortly after he did. Shattenberg is credited for transplanting a number of baldcypress (*Taxodium distichum*) from the headwaters of the Blanco River to the site of today's San Antonio River Walk. He also had a large commercial pear orchard in Boerne. Surviving pear trees can still be seen along Interstate 10 west of San Antonio. Today, San Antonio sports a multi-million-dollar wholesale nursery industry and a host of farmers and gardeners descended from German immigrants. Despite marginal soils and an erratic climate, the Texas Hill Country

Remains of a tenant house reflect the modest beginnings of settlers in America. (Photo by William C. Welch)

German Contributions at a Glance

- Good gardeners and keen horticulturists
- Scientific interest in plants, production, botany, and new plant material
- Heavy emphasis on fruit and vegetable culture; many early market farmers
- Houses frequently adorned with ornamentals
- High value on trees for shade, ornament, and lining streets
- Summerhouses in gardens
- Yards and cemeteries often neatly swept
- High degree of craftsmanship in stone, wood, and iron

claims the state's largest peach and grape production area and the state's only apple industry.

At least one of these old-time German Texan plantsmen succeeded in establishing a truly international business. Peter Heinrich Oberwetter was an excellent botanist and a pioneer in the study and cultivation of bulbs, particularly amaryllids. He is often credited with the introduction into the United States of the oxblood lily (*Rhodophiala bifida*), a fall-blooming "miniature amaryllis" from Argentina that has appropriately naturalized throughout the German areas of Texas.

In addition to the oxblood lily, several other ornamental plants popular in modern Texas gardens can be linked to the influence of German pioneers. Such plants include the German, or bearded, iris (*Iris × germanica*) and a number of rose cultivars, including 'Crimson Glory,' 'Eutin,' 'Grüss an Aachen,' 'George Arends,' 'Skyrocket', 'Leverkusen,' 'Dortmund,' 'Kordes Perfecta,' 'Trier,' 'Frau Karl Druschki,' 'Tausendschon,' and 'Veilchenblau.'

The German immigrants brought plants as well as such customs tied to nature as the Christmas tree. In her *Memoirs of a Texas Pioneer Grandmother, 1805–1915,* Ottilie Goeth remembers: "Somehow our first Christmas seemed a little meager in comparison to our German Christmas celebration with its fragrant fir tree, always decorated with so much loving care by our good parents for us children. At Cat Springs, Texas, where we first settled, Father had nailed a large cedar limb to a stump. They were the only cedar trees in the vicinity. Homemade yellow wax candles and small molasses cookie figures, baked by my two older sisters—that was the entire decoration."

The gardeners who introduced so many beloved plants are long gone. Yet while traveling the Germanic areas of Texas today, one cannot help noticing the skillfully constructed limestone buildings, the traces of European *fachwerk* (half-timbered) construction techniques, and the intricate patterns of the "gingerbread" that adorns the houses. Within the fine ironwork of the fences lie yards lush and neat—living legacies to the German immigrant's ingenuity, perseverance, and spirit of self-help.

Classics in the Garden

Italian Influence

WILLIAM C. WELCH

I taly is home to much of our gardening heritage because of the impact the Romans (who themselves were influenced by the Greeks) had on the whole of Western civilization. The classic garden of today includes Roman and Greek statuary, garden styles, and furniture.

When the Romans conquered Middle Eastern, Asian, and African territories, they brought back plants and gardening ideas, although in general Italian gardens were basically green, with varying textures, shades, and sizes of plants enhanced with statuary and assorted flowers. Gardens were formally designed with a strong

A rural home in Tuscany illustrates bold use of color and the importance of the garden. (Photo by William C. Welch)

An ancient olive tree adds character to an Italian landscape. (Photo by William C. Welch)

axial development (meaning that they were created rectilinearly and retained equal visual balance) and included ponds and walkways.

During the first century BC, Roman general Lucius Lucullus acquired firsthand experience of Persian gardening styles as he seized and burned many of the royal palaces of central Asia. When he returned to Rome, he put to use the gardening ideas and plants he brought back from his triumphs. Lucullus's rural villas in the hills of Tuscany were set in lavish garden settings. Pliny writes of

An ancient pomegranate (*Punica granatum*) adds interest to an Italian churchyard garden. (Photo by William C. Welch)

A series of garden rooms unfolds as the visitor strolls through the garden at Villa d'Este. (Photo by William C. Welch)

Lucullus cutting a channel through a mountain on his Naples estate to allow seawater to circulate in his fishpond. It is widely thought that he brought back apricots and cherries to Italy.

The basic agricultural crops grown in what is now Italy were olives (the historian Pliny described at least fifteen varieties), grape vines for wine production, and a form of wheat. As time passed, more and more of the small farms tended by individual families were combined into larger estates owned by wealthy Romans. A shift from growing grain domestically to purchasing it from a source such as Egypt encouraged the luxury of ornamental gardening. Wealthier citizens built small villas near the city for relaxation and enjoyment,

Formally arranged fountains and a wall of maidenhair fern are major features at Villa d'Este. (Photo by William C. Welch)

and larger farms were converted to villas with pavilions, shady groves, and formal gardens. Details show that many villas had a portico, which opened onto a garden terrace featuring turf, violets, lilies, or crocuses surrounded by box hedges or other suitable shrubs. There was often a lower garden as well, with ramps and steps connecting the two with terraces. The *gestatio*—an area suitable for horseback riding—often included examples of the Syrian art of topiary, featuring the pruning and shaping of box hedges and dwarf plane trees (similar to our sycamore, but with very handsome mottled bark). Ponds were popular for ornamentation and for keeping fish and eels. The historian Cato suggested that gardens include ceremonial plants such as laurel (*Laurus nobilis*) and myrtle (*Myrtus communis*).

Fruit became an important part of the landscape as well as for farm production. Peaches and jujubes (*Zizyphus jujuba*) were introduced from Persia. Figs, dates, pomegranates, and grapes became important staple fruits of Italian gardens.

In the second century AD, Columella described the garden of a typical large estate as containing roses, daffodils, pomegranate flowers, marigolds, acanthus, poppies, and fragrant flowers from foreign lands. It would include irrigation channels, sunken paths, and raised flower beds, all laid out in a formal pattern and enclosed by a wall or hedge to keep out intruders. Romans seem to have loved their gardens, whether the grand gardens of imperial country estates or the small private spaces tucked behind city houses. Gardens provided places for relaxation as well as plots to grow ornamental plants, fruits, and vegetables. The soothing sound of fountains often added further to the pleasures of life in the garden. Romans constructed gardens in every corner of their empire from Britain to North Africa and from Portugal to Asia Minor. As the population grew to over one million people, apartments took the place of many small houses and gardens. The Romans planted rooftop gardens with arbors of

Potted white hydrangeas line the entrance walk at an Italian churchyard. (Photo by William C. Welch)

A cloister garden in Italy serves as an outdoor living space with a central water well. (Photo by William C. Welch)

vines and fruit trees as well as ornamental plants in containers. This theme can be seen today in the cities and villages of Italy.

Long after the empire collapsed, the gardens Romans had planted continued to exert influence in the far-flung corners of their former world. There were many kinds of Roman gardens, from small vegetable and fruit plots to vast, carefully landscaped spaces filled with marble furniture, bronze and marble sculptures, mosaics, pools, and fountains—grand spaces suitable for lavish entertainment of guests. Whether large or small, gardens were an extension of the interior living space of Roman houses, which were surrounded by covered walkways and served as cooling refuges in hot climates.

The Roman House

The *peristyle* (a court enclosed by columns) contained the garden of the house and was incorporated into the house structure itself. In it were grown herbs and flowers, particularly roses, violets, and lilies. Small statues and statuettes and other ornamental artwork or out-

door furniture would adorn the space that, on sunny days, would be used as an outside dining area. In homes of wealthy Romans, the gardens served as meeting points and were designed to be shady and comfortable.

The *atrium* (a skylighted rectangular court) was open to the sky to allow rainwater to fill the *impluvium* (shallow pool) and to provide natural illumination to the interior of the house. Because the entire house was secluded behind walls as protection from outsiders, the public could not see the garden areas. Hadrian's villa in Tivoli and the gardens of Pompeii and Herculaneum were among the most impressive of their era.

After the fall of Rome (about AD 400) the populations of the Italian city-states declined along with pleasure gardening for a

The ruins at Hadrian's villa near Rome emphasize the formal use of sculpture and water in Italian gardens. (Photo by William C. Welch)

Italian cypress (*Cupressus sempervirens*), terra-cotta tile roofs, and Italian stone pines (*Pinus pinea*) help define "sense of place" in the Italian countryside. (Photo by William C. Welch)

number of centuries. During this time, through the efforts of the Roman Catholic Church, knowledge of gardening and landscape design were kept alive, and, as the Renaissance began, some ancient grounds and buildings were restored to their former glory. As the Renaissance unfolded, sculpture and painting began to feature Christian themes and motifs rather than the earlier pagan emphasis. The Medici and d'Este families created splendid examples of grand villas. Along with Frascatti and Villa Lante, which were also built by prominent families interested in the arts, these are some of the most acclaimed garden sites in the world, and today's architects and landscape architects still pay homage to them as standards.

Italian Sense of Place

"Sense of place," or *genius loci* (essential character and spirit of an area), the Latin phrase used by Romans, was created by lavish use of towering Italian cypress (*Cupressus sempervirens*), Italian stone pines (*Pinus pinea*), cedars of Lebanon (*Cedrus libani*), chestnuts, ancient olive trees (*Olea europa*), and gnarled grape vines. These gardens are defined by classic statues, grid patterns, decorative pebble and tile works, and grottoes (artificial caves usually with pools, springs, hanging ferns, and mosses along with bas relief mythological figures such as nymphs and satyrs or shell motifs). Wealthy owners scoured the world for classic statuary and furniture for their gardens.

Romans applied great skills in distributing, collecting, and managing water in their gardens as well as their communities. Waterworks displays such as the Fountain of Giants at Villa Lante or the Water Organ at Villa d'Este are impressive feats of engineering and aesthetics by any standards.

The ruins of the old house at Afton Villa (St. Francisville, Louisiana) reflect its distinctive classical Italian influence. (Photo by William C. Welch)

The parterre at Afton Villa (St. Francisville, Louisiana) was re-created from the old garden and influenced by classical Italian style. (Photo by William C. Welch)

Larger gardens included promenades where visitors could sit or stroll and contemplate the scenery. Entertaining features like pools, grottoes, and arbors for shade were often enhanced with large specimen trees such as Italian stone pines, Italian cypress, cedars of Lebanon, and olives. Plane trees (*Platanus orientalis*) lent themselves to a pruning technique known as "pollarding" where the limbs are annually pruned back into a ball-shaped top, which produces a very architectural but unnatural effect.

Topiary (clipping or trimming live shrubs, trees, or vines into ornamental shapes such as animals or geometric shapes) is a time-honored element of Italian gardens. Some are small enough to be contained in a pot, while others can be major features in the garden.

Creating and maintaining topiaries are high-maintenance activities that usually begin with a wire or other structured frame stuffed with peat, sphagnum, and other mosses. Providing the regular pruning and watering to maintain topiaries can be a challenge.

Other plants that help define Italy's sense of place include capers (*Capparis spinosus*), wall flowers (*Cheiranthus* varieties), and figs (*Ficus carica*), all of which grow in the joints of stone walls and other structures. Capers are small, underdeveloped buds pickled in a salt solution and eaten as a relish. Thomas Jefferson knew and appreciated capers but could not grow the real thing in Virginia. Instead, he pickled green nasturtium buds. Figs can be trained against walls having a southern exposure and have been grown in Italy for many centuries. Acanthus plants were so well known and loved that their stylized leaves and flowers were incorporated into bas reliefs on columns and statues. Lemons, limes, and other citrus are grown in the ground in warmer parts of Italy or as container specimens in cooler areas.

Madonna lilies (*Lilium candidum*) have been associated with depictions of the Madonna for hundreds of years. Their bulbs thrive in limy, stony soils and make splendid displays in the early summer garden. Geraniums, bougainvillea, and poppies of various sorts are typical. Olives are remarkable in their adaptability to transplanting and ability to endure the tests of time, with some being a thousand or more years old. Silver-leaved plants such as olives, lavender, lamb's ears, bearded irises, artemisias, and sages do particularly well in drier soils such as those of Italy.

Italian Influence at a Glance

- Signature plants like Italian cypress, olives, and grapes
- Extensive use of statuary, columns, and containers
- Extensive and innovative use of water
- Structural elements more important than the plants
- Strong axial development (formal balance)

Plant Explorers and Timeless Treasures

Asian Influence

WILLIAM C. WELCH

Asian ideas about design and plant materials have had a large impact on Southern gardens, which are dominated by plants from China, Japan, and Korea. Try to imagine the South without the shrubby flowering quince, forsythias, crapemyrtles, bridal wreath (spirea), banana shrub, mondo (monkey) grass, flowering almonds, azaleas, gardenias, wisteria, Confederate jasmine, and camellias. They have all made their mark because people like them and they are sufficiently well adapted, as well as beautiful.

Nandinas (*Nandina domestica*) are another example. Even though some people may consider them invasive, for many they have become a dominant and loved landscape plant. A new homeowner in the mid-nineteenth century depended on friends or family to "divide" their nandinas. Established clumps were dug and separated into individual plants or smaller "starts" and reset as the dominant evergreen. Sometimes called "heavenly bamboo," its compound, reddish foliage is crowned with clusters of bright red berries for several months each year.

The shrub althea (*Hibiscus syriacus*) was the most often mentioned woody ornamental offered in Southern nursery catalogues at the turn of the last century (1900). It is not from Syria, as the scientific name implies, but came from China and India. Japanese and Chinese wisterias have leapt from the urban landscape to our forests and are more common than the native wisteria. Indica and kurume azaleas are major features in gardens across the South.

Nandina (*Nandina domestica*) has become a staple in Southern gardens. The bright red fruit ripens in winter and lasts for several months. (Photo by William C. Welch)

Why are so many Asian plants used in Southern gardens? While fashion trends for plants played a part, I believe the major reason for the popularity was their beauty and usefulness. Another reason could be that Asian plants were new and different, and local plants were taken for granted. We can see now how popular U.S. natives are in Europe and Asia. Also, while some Asian species may have been temperamental, others adapted so well that they became pests. Japanese honeysuckle (*Lonicera japonica*) and Chinese privet (*Ligustrum sinense*) are two prime examples. Although there was some dissent, notably from Andrew Jackson Downing, a well-known landscape designer and author in the 1850s who advocated using native plants in American gardens, most gardeners considered the showy blooms, shrubby forms, and ease of propagation sufficient reason for popularity of these new "exotics" from Asia.

Where did these plants come from? An era of plant exploring began when Great Britain and China signed the Nanking Treaty in 1842, and Robert Fortune was selected as a plant collector for China

A "drift" of kurume azaleas provides a multicolor display. (Photo by William C. Welch)

and Japan in an exciting career that lasted from 1843 to 1862. Fortune was a Scotsman who had been trained as a hothouse gardener in Chiswick, west of London. He was initially charged by the Royal Horticulture Society to collect "seeds and plants of an ornamental or useful kind, not already cultivated in Britain" and to record information about Chinese agricultural practices and how climate affects vegetation.

Other collectors had been sent to Asia, but most had returned with only dried herbarium specimens. Fortune used for the first time closed, terrarium-like cases named for their creator, Nathaniel Bagshaw Ward of London. These Wardian cases allowed the plants to grow without adding water. At the end of his first China trip, he transported eighteen Wardian cases filled with 250 plants.

Fortune collected from private gardens and nurseries but also from cemeteries, and he observed that at tombs in China the plants were generally not the "expensive camellias or peonies" but were simpler plants, such as anemones, roses, or tall, waving grasses. Near Shanghai he noted a species of *Lycoris* covering a grave with its "mass of brilliant color."

Of considerable importance during his visit to China was his account of tea districts that produced some of China's famous tea from the foliage of *Camellia sinensis*. Fortune learned how the Chinese flavored green and black teas with flowers, and tea plants were among the species he brought back from China, although the Chinese were very protective of their tea plants and the processes used to produce tea. Fortune was later hired to collect and send tea plants

Chinese wisteria (*Wisteria sinensis*) is an aggressive vine and can be spectacular when trained properly. (Photo by William C. Welch)

Chinese fringe trees (*Chionanthus retusus*) thrive in the South, providing spectacular white flowers and beautiful bark on a fifteen- to twenty-foot tree. Robert Fortune, a Scottish plant explorer, brought the first ones to England from China in 1845. (Photo by William C. Welch)

to the United States, where it was being considered as a crop in the Southern states; however, the Civil War was looming and caused the government to cancel Fortune's trip. Fortune expressed his disappointment at never having an opportunity to visit the United States and work with the tea project.

The list of plants utilized in the South originally introduced by Fortune is long and impressive. It includes many of my personal favorites, like the kumquat (*Fortunella japonica* and *F. margarita*). In the Mandarin dialect, *kumquat* means "gold-orange," a perfect description of the color of this beautiful and tasty fruit. To quote Fortune, "I think if the Kumquat was better known at home it would be highly prized for decorative purposes during the winter months." He also introduced *Poncirus trifoliata,* the hardy or wild orange that is now found naturalized across the South and is used as a rootstock for citrus production.

Another personal favorite is the Chinese fringe tree (*Chionanthus retusus*). I have grown and loved this tree since Lynn Lowrey gave me a one-gallon container specimen in the late 1970s. Pearl-bush (*Exochorda racemosa*) has never been hugely popular but is often found in old Southern gardens and has a peculiar beauty, with its pearl-like buds and delicate spring flowers. 'Fortune's Double Yellow' rose was among the earliest old roses I acquired, but I am even more fond of *Rosa* × 'Fortuniana,' which is often confused with the white form of Lady Banks rose (*R. banksiae* 'Alba Plena'). Although well worth planting as an ornamental itself, 'Fortuniana' is probably the best understock for warm climates with sandy soils. Grape holly (*Mahonia bealei*) and Fortune's mahonia (*M. fortunei*) are still major landscape plants; popcorn spirea (*Spiraea prunifolia* 'Plena'), Chinese snowball (*Viburnum plicatum*), and forsythia (*Forsythia viridissima*) provide spectacular displays in zone 8 and north. The windmill palm (*Trachycarpus fortunei*) has long been popular on the Gulf Coast. Gold dust plant, the variegated form of *Aucuba japonica,* has been popular as a useful foliage plant for shade gardens. In addition to the wisterias, Fortune found what has become yet

Banana shrub (*Michelia figo*) fills the late spring air with the fragrance of bananas borne on a large, evergreen shrub. (Photo by William C. Welch)

Crapemyrtles are a favorite small flowering tree or shrub across the South. The trunks provide year-round beauty; the flowers appear for at least three months each summer. (Photo by William C. Welch)

another Southern favorite, Confederate jasmine (*Trachelospermum jasminoides;* often now called "star jasmine").*

Much of the information concerning Robert Fortune is from "Spoils of Fortune" by Mary Anne Pickens and published in the Proceedings of the 6th Annual Fall Gardening Symposium, Oktober Gartenfest, October 22–25, 1999, hosted by the University of Texas Winedale Division and Texas Agricultural Extension Service, the Texas A&M University System.

Future Acquisitions

Continuing the tradition of plant exploration in China, David Creech, director of S.F.A. Gardens at Stephen F. Austin State University in Nacogdoches, Texas, has made numerous trips to China and continues to interact with nurseries and collectors of note. The "reopening" of China in recent years continues to stimulate exciting finds. According to Creech, "Plant hunting in Asia and the transfusion of plants into the Western world has a relatively recent history, three centuries for the bulk of the introductions. While the great plant introductions have left us with an undeniable Asian influence, there remains much to be done. The long-term nature of woody plant evaluation makes the point that arboreta, botanical gardens, and private gardens can drive the landscape picture of the future by acquiring, testing and promoting the superior performers."

Asian Influence on Floral Design

For more than thirteen hundred years the Japanese have had a keen awareness of the beauty of nature and a philosophy that required that they demonstrate that appreciation. "Ikebana" brings the simple beauty of flowers, branches, and fruit to the performance of the tea ceremony, and flowers also enhance worship in shrines. Samurai, the ancient warriors of Japan, meditated about the beauty of flowers in their gardens to cleanse their minds of evil thoughts.

James L. Johnson, director of the Benz School of Floral Design at Texas A&M University, has great respect for the Asian influence on floral design:

This dwarf form of monkey grass (*Ophiopogon japonicus*) has become a popular ground cover in Southern gardens. (Photo by Greg Grant)

Asian Contributions at a Glance

- The Southern plant palette (bamboo, cherries, Japanese maples, kudzu, azaleas, camellias)
- Deep-seated appreciation for nature and simplicity
- Bonsai, bridges, lanterns, moon gates, koi
- Quiet water features
- Stonework

From the Orient we get philosophy, meditation and contemplation connected with the appreciation of flowers and their arrangement. It is a history in opposition to that which we discover in the Occident. All great cultures in the West have used flowers to adorn their ceremonies, their great buildings and their people. Color and mass are the hallmarks of Western floral design. Line and space are the distinguishing characteristics of Eastern floral art. Lavish and unexpected uses of materials are appreciated in the West while prescribed order and detail are taught in the classical schools of Ikebana.

Asian Influence on Garden Design

Chinese and Japanese gardens are inspired by nature. It is said that nothing in these gardens can be something that nature itself cannot be. For example, in nature you would never find a square pond. Rocks can represent mountains, and pools become lakes. A small area of raked sand can become an ocean. Another emphasis in these gardens is that they be visited and appreciated in every season, not just when most colorful. Summer is the time for contrasts of lush foliage against cool shadows and the splash of koi in the pond. Spring is enjoyed for the awakening and swelling of the bright green buds. Fall features the brilliant colors of the dying leaves before the snows and grayness of the winter season.

Enclosing the garden is essential, since a method to enter and leave various rooms within it is a necessary part of the Asian garden experience. Fences and gates have great importance. Sometimes a small window is cut in a solid wall to present the passerby with a small, tantalizing glimpse of what lies inside. The round moon gates of Chinese gardens are an exciting way to enter. The garden is meant to be an experience unto itself.

Japanese and Chinese gardens are created and enjoyed all over the world. Two notable ones are in Texas. A major feature of

Texas' oldest botanical garden, the Fort Worth Botanical Garden, is the Japanese Garden. Another garden of interest is located at the Nimitz Museum in Fredericksburg, Texas. The Japanese Garden of Peace was a gift from the military leaders of Japan to the people of the United States in honor of Fleet Admiral Chester W. Nimitz, who reached out to the Japanese people after World War II. Here, the three base elements of water, stone, and plants are beautifully articulated. The San Antonio Botanic Garden in Texas has an important garden that was constructed by Japanese workers; and the Birmingham Botanic Garden in Alabama also has a lovely Japanese garden.

Asian influence on our plant palette and floral and garden design, as well as in our kitchen gardens, continues in Southern gardens, with interesting and beautiful results.

Part Two

REDISCOVERING A WEALTH OF SOUTHERN HEIRLOOM PLANTS

Natives, Invasives, Cemeteries, and Rustling

GREG GRANT

inding wonderful Southern heirloom plants for your garden is often easier than you would think. Although many of the plants our ancestors grew are no longer common in these days of the "big-box" garden center, a number of them survive in specialty nurseries, old gardens, cemeteries, and even in the wild.

Rounding Up the Natives

Of course, many of the original plants our ancestors acquired and grew were plants native to the regions in which they settled. Nature offered up many wonderful plants to the Southern palette, including edibles like the pecan, black walnut, persimmon, pawpaw, mayhaw, mulberry, muscadine, blackberry, and blueberry. Others were adopted solely for their beauty. These include many fabulous shade trees like oaks, elms, baldcypress, and maples, along with the showy dogwood, Carolina jessamine, coral honeysuckle, oakleaf hydrangea, redbud, assorted hollies, coneflowers, black-eyed Susan, liatris, beebalm, Turk's cap, rose mallow hibiscus, and many more.

Although many early settlers dug native plants from the wild, obtaining nursery-propagated specimens or producing them from seed or cuttings is recommended in most cases today. If circumstances are such that one has an opportunity to dig a native plant to save it from destruction, doing so while it is dormant and leafless ensures the greatest chance of success.

Flowering dogwood *(Cornus florida)* (Photo
by Greg Grant)

Unfortunately, many plants found in the "wild" now are not
actually native but introduced exotics from other continents. These
plants found growing feral in their new home are now naturalized,
reproducing on their own. Regrettably, some grow so vigorously
that they are extremely invasive, taking over large areas of the country, while squeezing out less vigorous indigenous species. Many of
these invasive exotics were originally brought in and used as ornamental landscape plants and then spread by birds and other means.
Such examples in the South include mimosa *(Albizzia julibrisson)*,
Chinese tallow *(Sapium sabiferum)*, chinaberry *(Melia azedarach)*,
Chinese privet *(Ligustrum sinense)*, glossy privet *(L. lucidum)*, Jap-

anese climbing fern (*Lygodium japonicum*), McCartney rose (*Rosa bracteata*), Japanese honeysuckle (*Lonicera japonicum*), and kudzu (*Pueraria montana* var. *lobata*). The invasive exotics that were included for historical purposes in *The Southern Heirloom Garden* have now been removed. Their planting, cultivation, and tolerance are no longer accepted, as much of the American landscape is being degraded before our very eyes. Forests from Texas to the East Coast are now inundated with Chinese privet instead of delicate native spring ephemerals, fence rows are choked with Japanese honeysuckle instead of the showy trumpets of our native coral honeysuckle, and beautiful coastal prairies full of wildflowers and native grasses have been replaced with endless thickets of Chinese tallow. It's very important to know how all plants behave before introducing them to your landscape. The beauty of heirloom plants is that we know their entire history and how they will perform.

Other plants persist at abandoned homesites but do not spread across the country. Many are old sterile hybrids and generally lack the ability to form seed. This gives them added toughness as well as prevents them from spreading. Good examples are 'Grand Primo'

Flowering dogwood (Cornus florida) (Photo by Greg Grant)

Fruit of flowering dogwood (*Cornus florida*)
(Photo by Greg Grant)

narcissus, campernelle and Texas star jonquils, Byzantine gladiolus, St. Joseph's lily, milk and wine lilies, double orange daylily, tiger lily, snowflakes, spider lily, cemetery iris, bouncing bet, rosemary, Confederate rose, flowering pomegranate, flowering quince, figs, and many tea and China roses. Though they set seed, other tough introduced heirloom plants have shown over the past few centuries that they pretty much stay on the property where you plant them. These include crapemyrtles, common myrtle, rose of Sharon, mock orange, blackberry lily, prickly pear, old-fashioned petunia, and fruiting pomegranate.

Collecting Etiquette

Carolina jessamine (*Gelsemium sempervirens*) (Photo by Greg Grant)

Collecting starts of these existing plants at abandoned sites is known as "rustling." The world-famous Texas Rose Rustlers, founded by Bill Welch along with our late friends Pam Puryear and Margaret Sharpe, made this practice famous. Because many precious heirloom plants fell out of favor and were no longer planted or available in the nursery trade, they became rare or extinct. Rustling doesn't mean indiscriminate harvesting or stealing. I have had bulbs and

Eastern redbud (*Cercis canadensis*) (Photo by Greg Grant)

other plants stolen from my properties, leaving gaping holes in their places. There are unwritten mannerly codes to rustling. This is the South after all. One should always request permission before collecting cuttings or starts of a plant. Stealing and trespassing are crimes. Many folks in the rural South own guns and often aren't afraid to use them! I always offer money, plants, or seed in exchange for time-tested precious heirlooms. They are certainly worth more than much of the ill-adapted species for sale in many of today's garden centers. Property owners are often proud their plants have been admired and are pleased to share them.

Unless the plant is in imminent danger of being destroyed by development, one should never dig the plant but always use vegetative propagation. It's important to carry hand pruners, plastic bags to put cuttings in, and some water to slightly moisten them. Cuttings are very perishable. Bulbs are not. In the case of bulbs, the whole clump can be lifted and divided. Many individual bulbs can be taken from an old clump while returning the largest ones to the hole. This allows the old clump to keep blooming, and the following year's floral production will be similar to the last. It is also easy to obtain a start from certain spreading perennials and clump-

Oakleaf hydrangea *(Hydrangea quercifolia)*
(Photo by Greg Grant)

ing shrubs by merely cutting a piece with attached roots from the base of the plant. In my opinion, these surviving specimens deserve to remain in their homes, no matter how rundown the setting. They often mark property lines, former flower beds, and pathways. And of course, somebody may inherit or purchase the property and wish to carry on the horticultural legacy that is rooted there. In other cases an interested family member may wish to propagate a plant or move it to their home. But most often, they were planted in their terrestrial homes with love. They are obviously happy enough or they would not still be alive. And for heaven's sake, leave things as you found them. If it's pretty enough that you take a picture, leave it that way!

Cover up any holes you dig, and pick up your trash. I often deadhead the plants, trim them up, and fertilize them to make them even stronger and better looking. You at least owe that to the parent plant.

Grave Situations

Old graveyards used to be a great place to see Southern heirloom plants. Sadly, "perpetual" care, with its monocultured turfgrass and associated string trimmers and herbicides, have almost eliminated this historic association. And even worse, these fabulous pieces of living history have been replaced by mass-produced fake plants made of petrochemical by-products. What a sad waste of resources and even sadder commentary about our values. Many cemeteries are named for plants, including cedars, roses, oaks, and myrtles. These same plants, along with lilies, were often favorites of individuals who were buried there and planted on their graves out of respect and honor by their loved ones. These same ancestors and loved ones used to clean the cemeteries on at least an annual basis,

Plants make up an integral part of this East Texas cemetery. (Photo by Greg Grant)

often followed by "dinner on the grounds." The original parks in America were cemeteries, designed to be inviting and user-friendly for visitors. Today's prevailing mentality of them being places to be avoided is heartbreaking. I love visiting cemeteries to this day because my grandmother used to take me to them to introduce me to my many relatives. It's very sad when that running bond is broken. With today's world of global travel, cell phones, e-mail, and urban life, our traditional rural lifestyles, ethics, and values drift into the past unseen, searching for some flower-laden cemetery to die in. What a loss.

Of course, wimpy plants do not grow well in cemeteries. It is critical that tough survivors be used and that they be planted in raised, curbed graves to keep them away from the mowers, trim-

Camellia 'Rose Dawn' surviving in a Fredericksburg, Virginia, cemetery under low-maintenance conditions. (Photo by William C. Welch)

mers, and herbicides. In our rural family cemetery I have marked each direct ancestor's grave with oxblood lilies that bloom in the fall and a collection of crinums for summer bloom. In one particular plot where my Emanis great-grandparents are buried, I've planted one of my great-grandmother's crapemyrtles propagated from the old homeplace, Byzantine gladiolus next to the headstones, crinum lilies in the corners, and Texas star jonquils along the inside of the curbs. I have also introduced reseeding old-fashioned petunias and periwinkles there. If I feel like weeding around them, I do; if not, I mulch the whole thing with pine straw.

The mere fact that these Southern heirloom plants survived untended in hidden cemeteries and old homesites is what makes them so appealing in today's "green world." After all, they've managed to make it for decades and sometimes even centuries without added water, pesticides, and labor. These survivors, like crinums, China roses, cemetery iris, lycoris, oxblood lilies, and crapemyrtles, are ideal for low-maintenance plantings at schools, businesses, and streetscapes. In my opinion such survivors, along with equally adapted locally native plants, should form the backbone of all landscapes. Why intentionally choose plants that need water, pesticides, and labor to survive? The time for a change is upon us.

Easy-to-grow plants for Southern cemeteries

Early-blooming narcissus (*N. tazetta, N. jonquilla,* and hybrids), especially 'Grand Primo,' campernelle (*N. × odorus*), and Texas star (*N. × intermedius*)

Snowflake (*Leucojum aestivum*)

Old-fashioned iris (*Iris × albicans* [white], and *I. × germanica* [purple])

Byzantine gladiolus (*Gladiolus byzantinus*)

St. Joseph's lily (*Hippeastrum × johnsonii*)

Canna (*Canna* spp. and hybrids, especially older, taller types)

Orange daylily (*Hemerocallis fulva,* especially double 'Kwanso')

Tiger lily (*Lilium × lancifolium*)

Society garlic (*Tulbaghia violacea*)

Old orange montbretia (*Crocosmia* × *crocosmiaflora*)

White spider lily (*Hymenocallis caribaea* 'Tropical Giant')

Crinum lily (*Crinum* spp. and hybrids)

Oxblood lily (*Rhodophiala bifida*)

Red spider lily (*Lycoris radiata radiata*)

Esperanza (*Tecoma stans* 'Gold Star')

Bush morning glory (*Ipomoea fistulosa*)

Firebush (*Hamelia patens*)

Oxalis (*Oxalis crassipes*), pink and white

Bouncing bet (*Saponaria officinalis* 'Flore Plena')

Mexican petunia (*Ruellia malacoperma* and *R. brittoniana*)

Turk's cap (*Malvaviscus drummondii*)

Jewels of Opar (*Talinum paniculatum*)

Lantana (especially old bush types of *Lantana camara*)

Garden phlox (*Phlox paniculata*), old garden cultivars are
    superior

Variegated Georgia cane/giant reed (*Arundo donax* 'Variegata')

Four-o'clock (*Mirabilis jalapa*)

Purple Jew (*Setcreasea pallida* 'Purple Heart')

Obedient plant (*Physostegia virginiana*)

Cigar plant (*Cuphea micropetala*)

Mealy cup sage (*Salvia farinacea*), especially taller, native forms

Mexican bush sage (*Salvia leucantha*)

Michaelmas daisy (*Aster oblongifolius*)

Confederate rose (*Hibiscus mutabilis* 'Plena')

Kashmir bouquet (*Clerodendrum bungei*)

Red yucca (*Hesperaloe parviflora*)

Prickly pear (*Opuntia* spp.), especially spineless forms

China rose (*Rosa chinensis*)

Tea rose (*Rosa* × *odorata*)

Polyantha rose (*Rosa* × *polyantha*)

Coral vine (*Antigonon leptopus*)

Lindley's butterfly bush (*Buddleia lindleyana*)

Finding these Southern treasures for cemeteries and home land-scapes used to be problematic, but thanks to a number of specialty nurseries dealing in heirloom plants, it has become easier. Two of the most celebrated in the South are the Antique Rose Emporium in Texas and Petals from the Past in Alabama. Bill Welch and Mike Shoup started the Antique Rose Emporium in 1982 near Brenham. It grew out of the Texas Rose Rustler movement, which developed in the same area. Today it is owned by Mike and Jean Shoup. With another location in San Antonio and one formerly in Dahlonega, Georgia, plus a mail-order business, its impact on the garden world has been far reaching. Many heirloom roses and other plants grace landscapes throughout the country thanks to the Antique Rose Emporium's objective of sharing these once-lost treasures with the public. In addition, the fabulous cottage garden landscapes at their locations have inspired numerous such designs throughout Texas and the South.

Jason and Shelley Powell opened Petals from the Past nursery in Jemison in 1994. The beautiful nursery flanked by fruit orchards has been a popular destination for many gardeners in the South. While a student at Texas A&M, Jason worked developing Bill Welch's for-mer Cricket Court garden and took the cottage garden idea, the Antique Rose Emporium experience, and his wife, Shelley, back to his Alabama home. The rest is history. Their fruitful endeavor also includes a mail-order business and has further spread the heirloom plant and cottage garden movement across the South. It's so nice in this world of mass global marketing to have specialty niche nurser-ies catering to local Southern gardeners and trendy new horticul-tural movements. We're all better off with these heirloom treasures unearthed.

"Slips and Starts": How Heirloom Plants Were Increased

CYNTHIA W. MUELLER

In America's early years there were very few nurseries and precious little money to spend on the purchase of plants. Gardeners had to find, or increase, their own plants by trading with friends and neighbors, saving seed, or rooting cuttings of plants. Ferns and medicinal herbs as well as ornamentals such as dogwood, magnolia, and holly were sometimes dug in the woods and brought home.

"Starts"

Some plants, such as chrysanthemums, iris, old fashioned day lilies, monarda (beebalm), and violets, and herbs, such as mints, oregano, thyme, and horseradish, could be pulled apart and the pieces replanted to multiply the gardener's stock. These were often known as "starts." With bulbs such as paperwhites or amaryllis (hippeastrum) that become too crowded in their containers, the new offsets may be carefully cut away from the parent bulb, dusted with sulfur or other disinfectant, and potted up independently to produce new plants.

"Slips"

"Slips" were usually cuttings of anything from dianthus (carnation), grapes, geraniums (pelargonium), roses, and hydrangeas to boxwood, citrus, tops from pineapples, and many other plants capable of rooting easily.

Rescuing an antique rose from a Central Texas cemetery helps preserve these hardy and unique plants. (Photo by Cynthia W. Mueller)

Today, many perennials, shrubs, and trees can be rooted from cuttings. It's best to use semihardwood for these (this year's wood that is still flexible when bent). Most will root in early to midsummer, although some (such as grapes and pomegranates) need to root more slowly while dormant during fall and winter. Sometimes rooting cuttings is the only way to have your own plant of such hard-to-find beauties as the 'White Empress' or 'Alba Plena' camellia, or keepsake plants such as the white Lady Banks rose given to Bill Welch from the former garden of Elizabeth Lawrence in Charlotte, North Carolina. He brought the precious cutting home to Texas, and it was nurtured into a fine climbing specimen at his country home, Fragilee.

A favorite image of old-fashioned plant propagation is Grand-

By dividing clumps of *Narcissus*, it is possible to have true copies of the original plant. (Photo by Greg Grant)

This geranium (*Pelargonium hortortum* cross) is growing from a cutting. (Photo by Cynthia W. Mueller)

mother's habit of putting out a row of cuttings of such things as roses, lemons, vitex (chaste tree), or carnations in the soil along the drip line of the roof on the east side and covering them with an inverted mayonnaise jar for protection from drying out or insect attacks. Of course, in Texas sometimes the plants were better off without a jar, because the heat of the sun could raise the interior of the jar to ovenlike temperatures!

Before the use of rooting powders or even willow water—created by steeping freshly cut willow twigs in hot water for a few hours, which leaches out chemicals that encourage rooting—care and attention were required to succeed with rooting slips. It's much easier now that four- to six-inch cuttings can be severed at a slant, scraped a bit down the lower half inch with a sharp knife on one side

Many plants such as this geranium (*Pelargonium*) have complex heritage, but most are easily grown from cuttings. (Photo by Cynthia W. Mueller)

Using canning jars to cover rooting cuttings is still a favorite practice. (Photo by Cynthia W. Mueller)

of the stem, lightly dipped in rooting powder, and set into a plastic container of quality potting media mixed with coarse sand. Adding a label identifying your cuttings is helpful, even though gardeners usually think they can easily remember the variety! Add the date so you will learn how long it takes to root various plants. Make a note of where your cuttings came from. Press down the medium around the cuttings. Insert a cut wire coat hanger or stick to rise a few inches above the remaining leaves (take off all but a tuft on top). After watering, rest the container in a clear, breathable plastic bag such as a grocery produce bag, and tie the top shut above the stick. This will preserve the moist atmosphere in the "rooting chamber." The best place for the cuttings is beneath a shrub where sunlight will be relatively indirect.

Enclosing the cuttings in a plastic bag helps retain moisture during the rooting process. (Photo by Cynthia W. Mueller)

A typical rose slip (cutting) is five to seven inches long. (Photo by Cynthia W. Mueller)

Successful rose cuttings are usually well rooted within six to eight weeks. (Photo by William C. Welch)

Following is a list of woody plants to root from cuttings:

- Roses
- Citrus
- Winter honeysuckle
- Camellia
- Gardenia
- Flowering almond
- Pomegranate
- Special magnolia varieties
- Hollies
- Grapes
- Salvias
- Vitex
- Bridal wreath (*Spiraea*)
- Crapemyrtle—especially the old-fashioned Indica varieties

Fruit trees are difficult to root from cuttings, though ornamental flowering almond (*Prunus glandulosa*) is easy to root and was sometimes used for low hedges surrounding early cottage gardens. In Texas, hedges might be made of closely trimmed, small-leaved myrtle or dwarf Barbados cherry (*Malphigia glabra*). These were quite drought tolerant and had the extra benefit of a few small fruits for the birds. (In warmer Southern areas where boxwood grew poorly, dwarf yaupons made a good substitute.)

Planting Large Seeds and Pits

To create more peach, plum, or apple trees, gardeners resorted to planting seeds and pits of extra tasty fruit, even though the quality of the resulting trees was uneven, depending on whether they were allowed to bear fruit or used for grafting. If the young seedling tree was used for grafting, a bud or portion of a limb of another peach or plum with known, superior fruit quality was inserted into its main stem and allowed to grow and dominate, and all the limbs

The electric blue-purple seeds of this large form of monkey grass (*Ophiopogon clarkei*) germinate easily. (Photo by Cynthia W. Mueller)

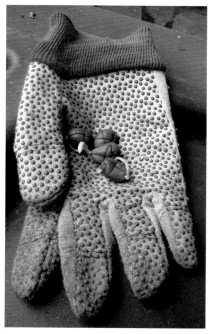

When you start plants from seed, there is always the excitement of a new and beautiful discovery. (Photo by Cynthia W. Mueller)

of the seedling tree were pruned away. As a result, the seedling tree provided the roots and a portion of the trunk but never bore its own fruit. This is the way choice fruit varieties were propagated. But often people carefully saved the pits of fruit they enjoyed and planted the seeds to increase their stocks. The resulting trees could be a mixed lot: some produced good fruit, and others produced fruit of poorer quality. Occasionally an excellent new variety would reward the gardener. It is said that the Native Americans enjoyed peaches so much that they were instrumental in spreading the peach pits far and wide throughout the United States.

At Monticello, Thomas Jefferson planted fruit pits (or "stones") one to two inches deep in a large heap of good earth, as soon as possible. As the young trees emerged, they were picked out and replanted in nursery rows for the first year or so of life, then set into orchard rows.

The modern gardener can plant heirloom seeds of fruit trees, hip gardenia, magnolia, holly, and others—such as cherry laurel for hedges—approximately three times as deep as the size of the seeds, in a good mixture of potting media and coarse sand. It's not recommended to use 100 percent actual garden soil in containers, as it is too apt to harden up. Tamp the media down firmly, water, and put away in a bright but shady place. Remember to water occasionally. Many seeds require a period of dormancy and/or cold chilling before the seeds will sprout. Often at least one winter is needed before sprouting, and sometimes as many as three years for vines such as clematis. Keep sprouting weeds and annual grasses picked away. As the young plants appear, they may be dug out and set into individual pots for their first year or two of life. It's amazing to see a small oak seedling that is only four or five inches in height that has already established roots as much as a foot long—thus ensuring its survival during any upcoming dry periods.

Layering

For shrubs and trees a bit more difficult to root, the old-fashioned gardener sometimes "layered" low-hanging limbs. To do this, bring a branch down to ground level, scrape it to the green cambium layer (which is just below the bark) on the bottom side with a sharp knife, and partially bury it. It might be necessary to put a stone or brick on top of the leafless part of the branch to keep it down. Water occasionally. After several months, test to see if roots have formed. The branch may then be cut free from the parent plant and allowed to grow on its own for a while before transplanting. This is an excellent way to start more difficult shrubs such as cassias, in case there are no seeds produced.

Saving Your Own Heirloom Seeds

There is nothing mysterious about saving seeds from one's own garden. It is useful to know the difference between "open pollinated,"

Select unusual plants as gifts, such as this Vitex 'LeCompte,' for your gardening friends. (Photo by Cynthia W. Mueller)

which describes most old-fashioned strains, and more modern hybrid seeds, which may not grow true to the parent plants. Gather seeds before they scatter, preferably in the afternoon. Allow them to dry well, and seal in paper envelopes with name and other details. Keep out of the sun and away from excessive heat and dampness.

Crinum and hymenocallis seeds, which are usually large and easily grown, may be started in a container of potting media and coarse sand. In order to discourage rotting, many gardeners let crinum seeds rest in a clear plastic container with whole, slightly damp sphagnum moss until the first signs of the shoot, or radicle, appear. This may emerge from any part of the seed—there is no distinct "spot" that needs to be planted downward. Keep this container on a windowsill out of direct sunlight or on a shelf in the greenhouse until germination occurs. Even though it may take two or three years, it's always thrilling to see the first bloom from bulbs you have grown yourself from seed.

Learning More about How Heirloom Plants Were Grown

Many gardeners who become interested in antique and heirloom plants will enjoy further readings in early books on horticulture. Some of these can be found in local libraries; others need to be located in the libraries of larger cities or ordered through bookstores, eBay, or Web catalogues. Listed below are several classics:

Liberty Hyde Bailey, *The Standard Cyclopedia of Horticulture* (Macmillan, 1900), several editions. This large volume covers most of the plants known in American horticulture "sold in the trade in the U.S. and Canada" at the time. There are countless descriptions of plant varieties and much good information on how to grow them.

Joan P. Dutton, *Plants of Colonial Williamsburg* (Colonial Williamsburg Foundation), many printings.

R. Favretti and J. Favretti, *For Every House a Garden: A Guide for Reproducing Period Gardens* (University Press of New England, 1990).

Bernard M'Mahon, *M'Mahon's American Gardener (American Gardener's Calendar)* (Colonial Williamsburg Foundation, 1806), many editions. This very comprehensive book covers every aspect of gardening, from plant descriptions to techniques used to create hotbeds and insect fumigators, from storing and preserving fruits and vegetables to making paper from the paper mulberry plant (*Morus papyrifera*). A large portion of the book is devoted to a monthly calendar of activities.

Sally K. Reeves, *New Louisiana Gardener* (Louisiana State University Press, 2001). This is a translation of the 1838 original by Jacques-Felix Lelievre and possibly the first book written in the United States for American gardeners.

Naturalizing Daffodils and Other Southern Bulbs

WILLIAM C. WELCH

Fantasies can become reality in my garden, especially as I travel about. In late winter and early spring I start looking for fields, old homesites, cemeteries, and similar places where bulbs are still thriving from earlier times. I become inspired by the natural way bulbs distribute themselves on these sites. Occasionally they may be in rows where they have outlined a walk or flower bed, but most often they are in large masses or drifts.

Naturalizing daffodils are as cheerful, dependable, deer resistant, and aesthetically pleasing as they were to our ancestors two hundred years ago. Their presence in woodland and shrub borders as well as open meadows, where they blend with native grasses and wildflowers, can provide memorable landscape settings, although meadows require careful management to ensure that desirable bulbs and grasses coexist and thrive. It is essential, for example, to allow time for the bulb foliage to ripen in spring before mowing.

To create these memorable settings, keep in mind that scale is important. Large masses or drifts of narcissus are much more visually effective than individual plantings or clumps.

We are fortunate in the South to have a number of old narcissus that are appropriate for naturalizing. Some, like *Narcissus* 'Grand Primo,' *N. italicus,* and Chinese sacred lily (*N. orientalis*) will adapt as far south as the Gulf Coast. They begin flowering as early as December. The early, all-white cluster flowering narcissus are called "paperwhites." Some of these bloom as early as Thanksgiving. *Narcissus* 'Grand Primo' is probably the most universally successful

A gate made of vintage wagon wheels is painted to match the nearby daffodils. (Photo by William C. Welch)

narcissus across the South. In coastal areas it begins flowering in late January and is a continuous show for a month or more. *Narcissus italicus* fills a nice void after the Chinese sacred lilies bloom in December or January and just prior to the 'Grand Primo.' *Italicus* is distinctive for its pointy petals, creamy color, and delightful fragrance. The slightly northern areas (mainly zone 8 and northward) have even more choices with campernelles (*N.* × *odorus*), jonquils (*N. jonquilla*), Lent lilies (*N. pseudonarcissus*), and others. All these are "time tested" and require little, if any, watering, fertilizer, or pest management to thrive. Jonquils and campernelles are among the most prolific and fragrant of all the narcissus and thrive best in acidic to neutral soils. During the later season *N.* 'Golden Dawn' is a favorite with its clusters of medium-sized, fragrant yellow flowers.

Perhaps almost as useful as narcissus are snowflakes (*Leucojum aestivum*). In both the old species form and 'Gravetye Giant' (which does equally well but has larger flowers), snowflakes thrive from the Gulf Coast to much more northern locations.

In addition to meadow plantings of these bulbs they are useful planted under deciduous trees. Here they bloom under such Southern favorites as pecans and oaks and seem to enjoy the summer of natural dryness when planted in the root flares (large, exposed roots near the trunks) of these trees. The color show does not end with the last narcissus. Bulbs such as *Lycoris* species, surprise lilies (*L. squamigera*), spider lilies (*L. radiata*), and Philippine lilies (*Lilium formosanum philippense*) carry the display through summer till midfall.

Establishing Naturalized Plantings

Whether you are dealing with a subdivision-sized lot or a multi-acre country property, the opportunity for success is greater when you properly prepare the site. Begin by selecting an area that has good drainage and at least some direct sunlight during the fall and winter months. Examine the existing vegetation. If coastal or common bermudagrass is present, it is best to apply an herbicide such as

Campernelle jonquil (*Narcissus × odorus*) surrounds a restored log corncrib at Arcadia, Texas. (Photo by Greg Grant)

Masses of campernelle jonquils (*Narcissus x odorus*) thrive alongside native grasses in a northeastern Texas pasture. (Photo by William C. Welch)

glyphosate (Roundup) according to label instructions. This needs to be done while the grass is growing actively and may require more than one application. Next, it is helpful to disk or till the area to be planted and add about five pounds of alfalfa or cottonseed meal per hundred square feet of planting area. Greg Grant's preference is to add no fertilizer and not kill the grass. He uses a sharpshooter spade to open the soil and plugs the bulbs right into the existing soil. This works best in naturally good, sandy loam soils.

For spring-blooming narcissus and snowflakes the ideal time for this preparation is late summer or early fall. Since visual impact is closely associated with the number of bulbs planted and the scale of the spaces, place the bulbs about six inches apart or even a bit closer for best effect. For a long season of color in hardiness zones 8–10, start with *N. orientalis* in either the single- or double-flowering forms, followed by *N. italicus, N.* 'Grand Primo,' and then *N.* 'Golden Dawn.' If more variety is desired, include jonquils, campernelles, or some of the suitable early-flowering paperwhites. I prefer keeping these together in masses or drifts, but they can also be mixed. For most soils, set the bulbs about twice the depth of the height of the bulb. Planting should be easy if the soil has been disked or tilled. Natural fall rains are usually sufficient to get the bulbs to start sending out roots and shoots. To conserve moisture and help control weeds, apply several inches of coastal bermudagrass hay (it should not contain seeds since it is vegetatively propagated), alfalfa, or other hay.

You may wish to broadcast wildflower seeds in the same area, in which case the hay mulch should be applied much more sparsely to allow the seed to germinate and emerge. As the bulbs complete their blooming, allow their foliage to mature before mowing them down. This stage causes some gardeners concern since the area will be a bit shaggy or "scruffy." If bluebonnets, Indian paintbrushes, coreopsis, Mexican hat, ratibida, or other wildflowers have been interplanted, they can help conceal the bulb foliage. Usually by late May or early June the spring wildflower seeds and bulb foliage are sufficiently mature that you can mow.

'Grand Primo' narcissus (*Narcissus tazetta* × *'Grand Primo'*) is probably the best adapted and most vigorous for the entire South. (Photo by William C. Welch)

Edges of the Developed Landscape

Perimeters of naturally wooded areas and shrub borders offer possibilities for naturalized daffodils and other bulbs. Root competition from shrubs and trees may be a limiting factor, but it can be overcome with soil preparation. Incorporating several inches of compost and organic fertilizers similar to the recommendation for meadow plantings can help. I have been pleasantly surprised at how well narcissus, leucojum, Philippine lilies, oxblood lilies (*Rhodophiala bifida*), and lycoris can perform even in fairly shaded areas close to trunks of deciduous trees. The tallest of these naturalizing bulbs are the Philippine lilies at four to six feet tall. Plant these at the back of borders where dark masses of shrubs and trees provide a suitable background for the clusters of striking white trumpet-shaped flow-

Chinese sacred lily (*Narcissus tazetta orientalis*) is among the best naturalizing narcissus for hardiness zones 8–10. (Photo by William C. Welch)

ers that appear in mid- to late summer. Bulbs and lilies need to be allowed to ripen their foliage so they can develop next year's flowers. This implies that companion plants should be selected to grow with lilies that will "mask" the fading foliage. Although they grow well in full sun, their flowers last longer where they receive at least some afternoon shade. The areas close to the trunks of trees where aboveground roots flare out is very dry in the summer but a good habitat for narcissus and the other naturalizing bulbs mentioned.

Schoolhouse (oxblood) lilies bloom following the first fall rains and closely resemble miniature amaryllis. They were once included in the amaryllis family. Originally from Argentina, schoolhouse lilies were distributed and popularized by Peter Oberwetter, a German immigrant to the Texas Hill Country who imported them from Argentina. Gardeners have spread them prolifically from Central Texas throughout the South, and they require no care or attention after planting. Plant and treat them like the narcissus and leucojum, but remember that these fall bloomers have foliage that appears after their bloom.

Spider lilies (coral red *Lycoris radiata* and its relatives, golden yellow *L. aurea*, and white *L. × albiflora*) mark many old Southern

Snowflakes (*Leucojum aestivum*) naturalize all over the South. (Photo by William C. Welch)

gardens. These spring- and fall-flowering bulbs are native to parts of the world where the summers are very dry. They remain dormant and prefer little or no watering in the summer, which makes them particularly useful in water-efficient gardens. By far the most common and best adapted is the coral red form. The strap-shaped foliage is somewhat similar to that of liriope but has a silver stripe down the center. Leaves remain lush and green all fall and winter when few garden plants are in good foliage. For gardens in the central South another option is *L. squamigera* with its large clusters of funnel-shaped, pink flowers following a good summer shower in July and August. These have the common name "naked ladies" and appear suddenly "overnight."

Close-up of the bell-shaped flowers of snowflake (*Leucojum aestivum*). (Photo by William C. Welch)

Rain lilies—*Zephyranthes candida* (white), *Z. grandiflora* (pink), and relatives *Habranthus robustus* (pink) and *Z.* × 'Grandjax' (apricot-pink)—are repeat-flowering, summer-blooming perennials that have great potential for our gardens. They are useful in the landscape for borders or mass plantings and require little attention once planted. Seeds of rain lilies, like those of other amaryllids, should be planted as soon as they are gathered. The bulbs increase somewhat like narcissus, but some reseed prolifically. Although some are native to the South, the most useful and well-adapted forms are from Argentina. Like the oxblood lilies, they have naturalized in Texas and parts of the South and do well on our natural rainfall, even in relatively dry regions like South and Central Texas.

Narcissus tazetta italicus naturalizes well from hardiness zones 8–10 and blooms before *N. tazetta* × 'Grand Primo.' (Photo by William C. Welch)

I have observed areas of *Z. candida* naturalized along roadsides, such as Interstate 20 in northeast Texas and Louisiana. They were probably part of old gardens that were bulldozed during highway construction and redistributed by accident. The flowers are pure white and appear from late summer well into fall, usually beginning with late summer or early autumn showers. The foliage is dark green and at first glance looks somewhat like monkey grass (*Ophiopogon japonicus*). Flowers are six petaled, starlike, and about two inches in diameter. Although they will grow just about anywhere, white rain lilies prefer a sunny location and moist soils. In fact, they will grow partially submerged.

Oxblood lilies (*Rhodophiala bifida*) naturalize all over the South and continue to increase even under stressful soil and climate conditions. (Photo by William C. Welch)

Oxblood lilies (*Rhodophiala bifida*) closeup of. (Photo by Greg Grant)

This naturalized meadow includes wildflowers, bulbs, and grasses. The curving mowed path invites visitors to explore what is beyond. (Photo by William C. Welch)

Habranthus robustus does not have a common name but truly lives up to the species name. Another native of Argentina, *H. robustus* is the most useful rain lily I have grown. Their foliage is evergreen, and the plants are tough enough to endure stressful growing conditions while providing an abundance of seasonal color. I first obtained some bulbs from Cynthia Mueller about ten years ago, and they have reseeded and multiplied profusely in my College Station garden. Following summer showers, blooms occur in great profusion with large, pink, funnel-shaped flowers with tones of apricot. They thrive in sun or partial shade and bloom five or six times during the growing season from late spring till early fall. Equally as gardenworthy is *Z.* × 'Grandjax,' which is a cross between *Z. candida* and *Z.* × 'Ajax.' It is a vigorous grower, multiplier, and bloomer and will flower many times through the warm seasons.

Philippine lilies (*Lilium formosanum philippense*) thrive in partially shaded areas at the edges of woodlands. (Photo by William C. Welch)

Spider lilies (*Lycoris radiata*) are thriving in the root flare of an old pecan tree. They are interplanted with old-fashioned single orange daylilies. (Photo by William C. Welch)

Currently, quite a bit of breeding is under way with rain lilies. They are not only wonderful as heirlooms but also a good source of new and useful garden plants. Because they are repeat flowering, insect and disease resistant, and water efficient, they make great choices for almost any garden.

Managing rain lilies in naturalized settings can be compatible with management of *Narcissus, Leucojum, Lycoris,* and oxblood lily (*Rhodophiala*). There is no really ideal time to mow them, but a late spring or early summer mowing when the spring bulbs and wildflowers have mature foliage should not be harmful. One of my favorite uses of rain lilies is as a border for rose plantings. Drifts and masses of them fit beautifully into perennial borders.

Rain lilies like *Zephyranthes* 'Grandjax' can naturalize in meadows and provide repeat color during summer and early fall. (Photo by William C. Welch)

Dividing the Bounty

Dividing established clumps of bulbs is a way to share with friends and extend the plantings while alleviating overcrowding. In reality, dividing these bulbs may be done at any season. Perhaps the ideal time is in late spring when the foliage is dying back and you can still find the clumps. Begin by using a spading fork to loosen the clump. Carefully separate each bulb, and be sure to dig deeply enough to not damage the basal plate (where the roots come out). Reset the bulbs immediately in prepared soil where organic material and slow-release fertilizer (such as five pounds of alfalfa or cottonseed meal per 100 sq. ft. of bed area) have been incorporated, or store them in paper bags in a shaded, well-ventilated area.

The Fruitful Garden

JASON POWELL

The oldest garden written about was one that featured a great many fruiting plants. And the first gardeners, Adam and Eve, were given the responsibility of caring for the plants in this Garden of Eden. This plot of land likely featured perfect soil, ideal weather, and just the right amount of rain. But we all know how this story ends: the fruit from the tree of knowledge was a little too tempting, and Adam and Eve later adopted a wardrobe that relied heavily upon the fig leaf.

Every generation since that time has cultivated plants that produce fruit for both enjoyment and consumption. As Southern gardeners, we inherited a great many types of both native and introduced small fruits and tree fruits that enjoy our long growing season. For some gardeners the idea of having an edible landscape may seem a little implausible. Many consider fruit gardening to be appropriate only if segregated into an orchard setting. However, incorporating fruit directly into the landscape was the norm in ancient Egypt where flowers, grape arbors, vines, and fruit trees were blended together to great effect. During the Renaissance, fruit trees, vegetables, and herbs were separated into their own areas as gardens became more formal. For an extended period of time, gardens were considered either ornamental or edible.

In the 1970s, edible landscaping experienced renewed interest. People became interested in doing more with their land. New publications were started, and nurseries specializing in fruit-bearing plants began to experience sales boosts. That trend continues today as gardeners have learned the lesson my granddad taught me: "It never tastes better than when you grow it yourself." It does not

'Changsha' tangerines are among the most cold-hardy citrus and are adapted from hardiness zone 8 and south. (Photo by William C. Welch)

matter if you have fifty acres or a quarter acre; you can produce fruit in a setting that is both functional and aesthetically pleasing.

Living in the South means we have a wide variety of fruit from which to choose. Maybe apples are hard to grow in South Texas, but loquats (*Eriobotrya japonica*) are good shade trees with dark evergreen foliage and a nice texture, plus these "Japanese plums" are delicious. Add to that pomegranates, figs, blackberries, blueberries, pomegranates, tangerines, kumquats, strawberries, persimmons, muscadines, pineapple guavas, satsumas, grapefruit, lemons, kumquats, olives, plums, jujubes, grapes, and pears, and you discover that plants that grow in the South can provide a veritable banquet.

Among small fruits, the blackberry seems to reign supreme in most people's memories. Many of us grew up making those ventures to the woods to fight thorns, red bugs, and the potential snakebite for a gallon of small, sweet blackberries. The danger we faced was rewarded when the blackberry cobbler was removed from the oven and a scoop of ice cream was placed on top. The blackberry, depending

Kumquats (*Fortunella japonica*) are an attractive addition to the garden. Fruit ripens in the fall and winter following fragrant spring and summer flowers. They are reliably cold hardy in zone 9 and often used as container specimens in colder areas. (Photo by William C. Welch)

on variety, can be either thorny or thornless, and it is self-fruitful, so the gardener can have one plant or many and still produce fruit. Semi-erect varieties can be trellised for easy harvest and provide a lovely backdrop for a perennial border or vegetable garden. Early summer would be a bit less tasty without them. Strawberries may be reserved for beds or borders.

Rabbiteye blueberries, in my opinion, are a plant with twelve months of interest. Beautiful white bell-shaped flowers appear in spring followed by delicious, sweet blue fruit in the summer. Blueberries prefer acidic soil and partial shade, much like their azalea relatives. Autumn rewards us with orange and red foliage, and after it falls, an exfoliating bark that is cinnamon in color is visible through the winter. Maintaining a height and width of five to seven feet, these plants are as valuable a shrub in the landscape as a burning bush or a hydrangea. Blueberry plants can provide an excellent hedge to define property lines or can be incorporated into a mixed border. Nutritionists continue to find healthy attributes to blueberry fruit as well.

As late summer melts into fall, I look forward to the arrival of muscadine grapes. Scuppernongs, as the bronze form of this fruit is

Blueberries (*Vaccinium* spp.), an attractive deciduous shrub with fruit ripening in midsummer, are combined here with beebalm (*Monarda* spp.) and salvia. (Photo by Greg Grant)

Blueberries prosper in acidic soils with growing requirements similar to those of azaleas and camellias. (Photo by Jason Powell)

called, provide a sweet-flavored grape uniquely Southern. As a vigorous vine this grape makes the perfect cover for a pergola, yielding both shade and scrumptious fruit. Blend it with a purple muscadine and you have all the makings for jams, jellies, and wine you need. My only problem is that once I begin eating, I cannot seem to stop. Not all parts of the South can grow wine grapes, but most areas can grow bunch grapes (other than muscadines). Muscadines thrive on natural rainfall and are rarely attacked by insects or disease.

Tree fruits provide another opportunity to address landscape challenges as well as a harvest of fresh fruit. It would not be summer for me unless I can sit beneath the shade of a fig tree and eat until my tongue is numb. As a young boy I learned to appreciate the flavor of fig preserves from a kind neighbor. Our unwritten agreement was that if I climbed to the top of her 'Celeste' fig tree and beat the birds to the harvest and picked a bucketful, she would have warm biscuits for me topped with butter and preserves. Those birds never had a chance. If space is limited, my preference is to espalier a fig against a wall. The vigorous growth of a single plant and its self-fruitfulness make it an ideal way to soften a harsh blank wall.

'Celeste' fig, also known as sugar fig throughtout the south. (Photo by Willam C. Welch)

Apples are not exclusive to Northern gardens. Heat-tolerant heirloom varieties such as 'Carter's Blue,' 'Yates,' and the 'Horse' apple can be grafted onto dwarf, midsize, or large rootstocks to fit any landscape. Selection of appropriate varieties offers harvest from July through October. Trellising or espaliering apples is a technique perfected by our European ancestors and my preferred way to grow them. They can be trellised to allow harvest from both sides or grown flat against a wall. There is also a beautiful crabapple native to the South (*Malus angustifolia*) that has fragrant, pink flowers and tart little apples that make a wonderful jelly.

At one time, most everyone had an old 'Kieffer' hard pear in

Figs are popular in Southern gardens because they are relatively trouble-free and productive. They may be allowed to branch naturally or trained as a single trunk standard or as espaliers against a wall or trellis. (Photo by William C. Welch)

Strawberries may be grown in containers as shown here or in rows in the garden. (Photo by William C. Welch)

the yard. Most were left unpruned and allowed to grow to fifteen or more feet in height. In August these pears would be picked into five-gallon buckets and turned into preserves. In addition to 'Kieffer,' other hard pears such as 'Orient,' and common pears such as 'Warren,' 'Ayers,' and 'Moonglow,' have passed the test of time. With a little early pruning these pears can offer an attractively shaped tree that will add showy white flowers to the spring garden and enough shade to picnic underneath in the summer. The flexibility of the limbs provides excellent espalier opportunities as well.

One of the oldest fruits that is acclimated virtually everywhere in the Deep South is the pomegranate. The majority of the varieties we see today have orange-red flowers that occur from spring to early summer. They yield sweet, multicelled fruit in the late summer and fall. The best landscape use for pomegranate is as a multitrunked shrub in a hedge. Without a common insect or disease problem, it is hard to resist. Mrs. Sellers, an elderly neighbor helped me to appreciate this fruit and taught me a lesson in patience at the same time.

Persimmons (*Diospyros virginiana*) that are native to the South are astringent forms that will turn your mouth inside out and make

Japanese or Asian persimmon (*Diospyros kaki*) is a beautiful small to medium-sized tree with delicious fall ripening fruit. (Photo by William C. Welch)

Japanese persimmons are highly ornamental, productive, and trouble-free. (Photo by Jason Powell)

Japanese persimmons are a popular crop at Petals from the Past Nursery in Jemison, Alabama. (Photo by Jason Powell)

Chinese dates (*Zizyphus jujube*) are drought- and pest-resistant small trees adapted throughout the South and Southwest. (Photo by Mike Arnold)

a great snack for the opossums. However, if we graft their Asian cousin (*D. kaki*) onto them, we have the opportunity to produce a delightful, nonastringent fruit. As a specimen tree an Asian persimmon should reach a height of around fifteen feet. October and November yield a beautiful orange seedless fruit shaped like a squashed tomato. The fall color of the foliage is the same color as the fruit.

Unusual fruits such as jujube (*Zizyphus jujuba*), feijoa, and pawpaw (*Asimina triloba*) probably are not available at your local grocery store. Their interesting, edible fruits grow on cold-hardy plants in the South. Even if they taste a bit strange to us, the birds will certainly appreciate them. The silver foliage and unusual flowers of the feijoa, or pineapple guava (*Feijoa sellowiana*) are certainly eye-catching. The unusual rick-rack growth habit and upright form of the jujube are great for height and lines in a garden. Sometimes known as "Chinese dates," jujubes are among the most heat-, drought-, and pest-resistant plants I know. The fruit is delicious dried or candied like dates and is very popular among Asian populations. The pawpaw has beautiful large leaves and soft yellow fall color, making it an excellent small tree for a shady area. It is also the host plant for the beautiful zebra swallowtail butterfly.

Gardeners in the South have enjoyed a rich heritage of growing fruit, whether in a perennial border or an orchard. The variety of choices is outstanding. Don't forget that a tractor shed really isn't finished until a fig tree is planted next to it.

Enjoying the Bounty

GREG GRANT

Eats and Treats

To me, having a garden without using and enjoying its "fruits" is like having a cookie jar with a lock on it. Why have one at all?

As far as I'm concerned, all gardens should contain edible plants. Whether these plants are confined to their own vegetable, orchard, or herb garden, or interspersed throughout, they are essential elements in a truly functional garden. Today's world is so spoiled, with produce available from all corners of the globe, that most homeowners do not even consider growing their own. But think about the cost of this culinary cornucopia. Many fruits and vegetables have been bred for mass production and thick skins, not taste. Many are sprayed with all kinds of pesticides, a number of which may be banned in this country and injurious to your health. And of course, most are trucked or flown in from all corners of the planet, using great quantities of fuel and labor. There used to be a season for each product, when it was plentiful, fresh, flavorful, and locally grown. But we traded all that for often tasteless produce available year-round. We lost out on the deal.

With help from university extension programs in each state, local Master Gardeners, or regional botanical gardens, anybody can learn to grow his or her own food. It mainly involves basic horticulture and adapted plant selection. The same flowers, fruits, vegetables, and herbs that grow in the North do not grow during the same season in the South, or even at all. Therefore, plant selection and time of planting are extremely important.

It's very satisfying to grow what your family likes to eat. My family's favorites have always been cucumbers for dill pickles, yellow summer squash for my mom, onions for my dad, sweet potatoes for pies, spinach, lettuce, sweet corn, purple hull and cream peas, okra

Greg's farm is home to a nice pea patch every year. (Photo by Greg Grant)

for frying, tomatoes, and sweet peppers. My mom and I have also grown fond of sweet basil for pesto. It's fun to try new things as well. I have grown yard-long beans; Indian popcorn; red, white, and blue potatoes; purple bell peppers; maroon carrots; raspberries; boysenberries; and anything else my plethora of seed catalogues offers up. I, like many gardeners across the country, look forward to appraising the catalogues each winter while dreaming of the next season's harvest. If for some reason you cannot grow your own produce, purchase locally grown eats from your community farmers' market or grower. The produce is fresher, supports your local economy, and helps conserve precious natural resources.

Greg's daily basket of produce contains a variety of colorful, healthy, homegrown veggies. (Photo by Greg Grant)

Cutting Up

Most people love cut flowers, but we Americans seldom take the time to enjoy them. For some the reason is time, and for others, money. Both problems can be alleviated by producing your own. Many of us think the only acceptable cut flowers are those we see at the florist. However, most commercial cut materials are grown in other parts of the world. They are standard varieties that hold up to mass production and shipping. They have the same negatives that produce from far-flung regions has. Many fabulous cut flowers can be produced right in your home landscape, including narcissus, jonquils, daffodils, spider lilies, crinums, hydrangeas, camellias, coneflowers, sweet peas, cockscomb, bachelor's buttons, buckeyes, black-eyed Susans, goldenrod, zinnias, and most tall grasses. Good cut greenery includes southern magnolia, red cedar, palms, ferns, hollies, Jackson vine, and pittosporum. If in doubt, cut something and give it a try. Flowers are best cut in the early morning when they are the most turgid. The water in the vase holding them should be

Homegrown sweet potatoes make the best Thanksgiving and Christmas pies in the Grant house. (Photo by Greg Grant)

replaced every day. If not, a good homemade floral preservative can be made with one teaspoon of bleach and one tablespoon of sugar in one gallon of water. We all appreciate flowers in the garden, so why not bring some in with you?

Flapping About

Two of the best lagniappe pleasures in the garden just happen to fly in for free. Many, including myself, consider birds and butterflies to be "flying flowers." Some birds, like bluebirds, cardinals, buntings, grosbeaks, and goldfinches, are just plain beautiful to gaze upon. But all, whether feeding, bathing, or nesting, are fascinating to watch. I have always found watching a bird feeder mesmerizing and downright therapeutic. While I study specialized bills cracking sunflower seeds with speed and ease, or inspect tiny feet clinging to a suet feeder, all cares in the world amazingly disappear. As many bird feeders are plastic and unsightly, I used to be an advocate for feeding the birds only with appropriate native plants in the landscape. But for the healing and educational powers alone, I think everyone should have a close view of a functioning bird feeder of any kind. While watching my active bird feeder or listening to the mesmerizing call of a pileated woodpecker, a bluebird, or a white-throated sparrow, I forget my problems and pains. Free and effective medicine is very hard to come by, so take advantage of it.

Of course, birds need more than just food. They also need shelter, the proper habitat, and water. Water for drinking and bathing can be provided through a birdbath, an ornamental water garden, or if you are lucky enough to have one, your own stream, pond, or lake. Be sure to check your birdbath daily to make sure it is not dry or frozen over.

Different birds prefer different habitats. Some, like woodpeckers, prefer mature forests. Others, like bluebirds and buntings, would rather be in wide-open spaces. And some, like the common yellow throat warbler, need wetlands. If you own larger tracts of land, try to preserve the natural landscape in order to maintain and perpetuate the indigenous bird population. If you own a typical urban landscape,

Native goldenrod makes a wonderful, long-lasting cut flower arrangement. (Photo by Greg Grant)

All the heirloom spring bulbs make outstanding cut flowers. (Photo by Greg Grant)

Native goldenrod makes a wonderful, long-lasting cut flower. (Photo by Greg Grant)

try to provide a multilayered landscape consisting of open ground space, shrubs and small trees, and a taller tree canopy. This will help invite the greatest variety of birds for your enjoyment.

A Wing and a Prayer

Butterflies are more fleeting and shorter lived than birds, but they are no less impressive. Though most gardeners are attracted to the larger, showier sorts, like the swallowtails, all are special. The natural world is an amazing interconnected web of host plants, dependent butterflies, and opportunistic predators. The more I study and pay attention, the more I realize that every plant, from the largest and showiest down to the homeliest little weed, supports some butterfly or moth. My favorite, the zebra swallowtail, is one of the showiest ones. It is restricted to eastern Texas and the forested eastern United States. The delicate but striking wings of this beauty are striped black and white with small blue and red highlights. The reason

Possumhaw holly (*Ilex decidua*) and evergreens from the garden create a wonderful holiday wreath. (Photo by Greg Grant)

Adorable baby eastern bluebirds nesting in a cedar box of native loblolly pine straw. (Photo by Greg Grant)

Dallas, Forth Worth, Austin, Houston, and El Paso do not have zebra swallowtails is that, like a picky child, this butterfly eats nothing but pawpaws (*Asimina triloba*), which do not grow in these cities.

To preserve our outstanding bird and butterfly population, limit the amount of pesticides used in your landscape. First of all, they are dangerous to your health. As a horticulturist with neurological troubles, I implore you to heed this warning. Pesticide exposure has been linked to many ailments, including Parkinson's disease. The

Our spectacular native zebra swallowtail nectaring appropriately on butterfly weed (*Asclepias tuberosa*). (Photo by Greg Grant)

same insecticides that are toxic to ants, beetles, and worms are also toxic to butterflies and their larva. And the dead insects that you kill are food to wonderful little songbirds like the bluebird and the Carolina wren. Most Southern heirloom plants are tough enough to survive diseases and insects, which is what first interested me about them. They would not still be around if they were not tough. Learn to tolerate some damage, and think about how those insect populations support other wildlife like lady bugs, praying mantis, toads, anoles, and birds. Your life will be richer for it.

Part Three

THE RIGHT PLANT
IN THE
RIGHT PLACE

WILLIAM C. WELCH

It's all right to have your favorite plans and/or themes in your own garden! Here are some guidelines and suggestions on how to achieve the best effect.

Perhaps the cardinal canon of design is simplicity or clarity. This implies the elimination of confusion and the portrayal of the entire composition as a clear and orderly relationship among all the components. Whatever the style, an overall vision should prevail. If the designer has done the job well, the layout should be perceived as a work of art. To quote Greg, "Tossing a bunch of plants into a yard and expecting a nice landscape is like throwing a bunch of ingredients into an oven and hoping a pie jumps out!"

A wildflower meadow contrasts with the "built" environment around a pool. (Photo by William C. Welch)

A border of *Sedum acre* provides a unifying element to this azalea planting. (Photo by William C. Welch)

These 'White Queen' crinums are very drought-tolerant perennials once established. (Photo by William C. Welch)

A well-designed garden should not only be pleasing to the eye but must function as a living space. It must address needs such as privacy, outdoor living, vehicle and pedestrian circulation, drainage, and a relationship to the community as well as the specific site. Successful landscapes should reflect a "sense or spirit of place." This involves a critical look at the site and its surroundings to understand what you have. Take a look at the native plants on or near the site, the topography, and the architecture, and be sensitive to these factors in trying to enhance what is already there rather than overwhelm it.

One important issue facing gardeners is the use of water resources. Extensive turf areas and introduced plant material can use large quantities of irrigation water. It is interesting to note that our ancestors created beautiful and meaningful gardens without modern irrigation or use of chemicals. Many of the plants they grew have become "heirlooms" and have proven to be "time tested."

Professional landscape architects are trained to address all these issues. But if you choose to create your own design, an ideal way to

A combination of living and nonliving materials (gray-foliaged plants, gray gravel, and a gray metal obelisk) provides a handsome setting. (Photo by William C. Welch)

begin is to draw an existing map of your property. This should be done to scale (such as one eighth inch equals one foot). Although making a map is a bit of a chore, it can serve as a valuable reference for the future. Whether you are working with a professional or designing your own landscape, it is critical to decide what you want your garden to be.

Garden landscapes are a combination of living and nonliving materials. Nonliving elements include paving, walls, trellises, arbors, plant containers, and other art objects. Plants are the most obvious living material, but it is helpful to view them also as building materials to be used as masses, screens, and ground covers, as well as individual specimen plants.

Designing Your Own Garden

Basic Design Principles

WILLIAM C. WELCH

Greg and I agree that it is impossible to create good landscape designs without using the following design principles.

Design Principles

The design principles of balance, repetition, scale (proportion), dominance, and contrast are essential to good landscape design.

BALANCE
Balance is the equalization of visual weight from one area of the composition to another. Every landscape view should normally

A perennial garden at Dumbarton Oaks in Georgetown, Washington, D.C., reflects symmetrical balance. (Photo by William C. Welch)

This Spanish-influenced garden is an example of asymmetrical balance. (Photo by William C. Welch)

be balanced. There are two general types of balance. *Symmetrical* (formal) balance is achieved by repeating the arrangement of elements on one side of the composition on the opposite side (mirror image). *Asymmetrical* (informal) balance is created by implying equal weights, although the same plant materials are not repeated in the same quantity or the same relative position on either side of the axis, so it is not a "mirror" image.

Steepled arches of 'Cl. American Beauty' roses provide a lasting impression at the Antique Rose Emporium, Independence, Texas (Photo by William C. Welch)

A repetition of the color purple and daisy petal shape enhances this intimate garden. (Photo by William C. Welch)

Another view emphasizing the repetition of the color purple throughout the design. (Photo by William C. Welch)

REPETITION

Repetition is the technique of using one element, form, size, tone, or texture throughout a composition. We consider repetition to be a very important design principle. Repetition of an element at different locations in the design provides a common tie or visual link among the various parts. Repetition helps establish unity. It is achieved by *minimizing* the number of different elements and materials used in a design composition or *repeating* the limited elements and materials used throughout the entire design.

SCALE (PROPORTION)

Scale is the relationship of one part to the other and the relationship of each part to the whole. In establishing scale within the landscape, the human being is the measure of all things. All aspects of the design must be in scale with its users, its site, and its structure.

This garden conversation area is a nicely scaled resting place. (Photo by William C. Welch)

A nicely scaled area provides a restful space in the garden. (Photo by William C. Welch)

DOMINANCE

Dominance is the authority of one element of a design composition over all other parts. Due to the dominant element's size, shape, texture, or location, all other elements of the composition are subordinate to it. This principle should be used sparingly. As a rule, use only one dominant element in each view.

The vertical lines of the birches and iron railings are dominant in this famous design by Fletcher Steele at Naumkeag, in Massachusetts. (Photo by William C. Welch)

Purple foliage and the effects of sun and shade (shadows) dominate this outdoor living area. (Photo by William C. Welch)

CONTRAST

Contrast is the introduction of an unlike element. It serves to emphasize the similarity of the remaining features. Contrast can add richness to a composition. Too much contrast results in chaos.

Art Elements

The building blocks of landscape design are known as art elements. These are common to all forms of art and design and are helpful to keep in mind as one designs or evaluates a garden. They include color, line, form, texture, and pattern. We will take a brief look at each as they relate to garden design.

COLOR

The most obvious of the elements is color. Similar to how its elements compose an impressionist painting, clumps or "drifts" of bloom and foliage colors help compose garden design. The classical English borders from the turn of the century utilized either

Drifts of azaleas provide unifying colors during the spring season. (Photo by William C. Welch)

Bright colors in herbs, flowers, and pottery work together to create a warm and inviting atmosphere in Lucinda Hutson's Austin, Texas, garden. (Photo by William C. Welch)

"single-theme" colors or subtle gradations of pastels. In the plans with which Gertrude Jekyll illustrated her book of 1908, *Color Schemes for the Flower Garden,* she often began at the far end of her borders with blue-grays and grays, passing on to blues, whites, pale yellows, pale pinks, and from there shading into stronger yellows, then to oranges and reds, and then gradually paling again into the light pastels with the addition of lilacs and purples. Almost always, springtime in these herbaceous gardens featured light yellows and pale lilacs amid whites.

Special "color-theme" gardens were also popular in classically designed English shrub and perennial borders. Perhaps the most common of these was the white garden, a display of white flowers accented with gray-foliaged plants. The archetype of all English white gardens is Vita Sackville West's creation at Sissinghurst Castle in Kent. About the same time, Christopher Lloyd (1921–2006), in his book *Color for Adventurous Gardeners,* showed that creativity in the cottage garden included the use of unorthodox color combinations, like mixing colors that are opposite rather than adjacent on the color wheel, such as blue-green and red-orange.

Color comes to the landscape from several sources. In addition to perennial and annual flowers, structural materials such as walls, fences, pavings, and buildings can contribute a colorful note. Trees, shrubs, turf, and ground covers also play their part. Seasonal changes of plant materials provide a challenge in subtle uses of color. Even the brightest flower colors are subdued by the neutral values of green, which are usually present in abundance. In outdoor light, and with patterns of shade and shadow, color is an all-important tool in the hands of the clever designer. For this reason it is important in choosing plant material to see the plant at its maturity to form an accurate judgment of its color and other artistic considerations.

Late winter, early spring color is predominantly from heirloom bulbs followed by prairie phlox (Phlox pilosa), daylilies, and garden mums. (Photo by William C. Welch)

Chris Wiesinger, an authority on heirloom bulbs and garden history, has a philosophy about color preferences. "Color combination is definitely a personal preference, but designer beware that bold, unconventional mixtures must be balanced by proper texture, hardscape, and green spaces. Avant-garde mixtures can make a bold statement but usually require a matching personality of the gardener to be successful."

LINE

In design disciplines, line is usually a mark made by pencil, ink, brush, or other device to firm the basis of the design pattern as distinguished from shading, shadows, or colors. In garden design, all

The curving line of a stone path invites guests to the next area of the Hairston Garden at the Antique Rose Emporium in Independence, Texas. (Photo by William C. Welch)

Diagonal lines of boxwood hedges at the Dallas Arboretum and Botanical Garden provide visual contrast. (Photo by William C. Welch)

types of lines are employed to create interesting space relationships. Because lines serve for definition of space, they must be considered one of the most valuable tools in the hands of a designer.

Lines may be either straight or curved. Since herbaceous and shrub borders use line to define their shape, the overall design is greatly enhanced and strengthened when backed with a wall, fence, or tall, dark green hedge.

Walls, fences, hedges, and the edges of planting areas themselves should make strong design statements. When a design relies on curved lines, they should be definite and sweeping. Edges of the border should be neat and easily maintained, of materials such as well-constructed brick, concrete, wood, or metal edging. Edging is especially important when herbaceous borders join turf or ground-cover areas and the line itself becomes an important element of the overall design.

By its crispness, the well-defined edge creates very definite effects. It dramatizes the plants that spill or cascade across it, and it furnishes a strong contrast to the pleasantly muddled look of the plant combinations within the bed or border. Well-designed and constructed edges also make maintaining the garden less of a chore.

FORM

Architectural forms are an obvious concern of the landscape designer, but so are plant forms, since every plant has a distinctive form in its natural condition. Pruning can modify this, and under its influence a plant may lose its natural identity. Even without this artificial modification, plant forms are usually less prominent than the architectural forms of buildings, walls, and walks.

Individual plant forms vary from mounds and pyramids to cones and the cascades of weeping specimens, and it behooves the designer to study these carefully before making selections. Combining individual plants into larger compositions involves other decisions as well. As previously noted, Gertrude Jekyll favored planting in drifts rather than in clumsy, block-shaped patches. In shrub and herbaceous borders, the plants arrange themselves most naturally into three categories by height: the tallest plants fall to the back of the border; the midsize ones to the center; and the shortest up front. Some irregularity in this order is desirable, however, to prevent an appearance of boring predictability.

Individual flower forms are extremely important in compositions. Spike and ray flowers are the two most basic flower forms, although there are numerous variations. Familiar examples of spike flowers are the salvias, lythrum, and gladiolus. These provide dramatic statements in the border but are best when contrasted liberally with ray flowers, such as daisies, coreopsis, and asters. Some flowers, like alyssum and verbenas, contribute large masses of color from numerous tiny flowers. The flower form in these plants is less important or distinctive than the larger and more individual ray and species flowers. Instead, these mass-flowering plants serve an important role in providing unity and linkage among the many species that may constitute a well-designed border.

TEXTURE

As a product of the plants' surface qualities, texture appeals to the senses of sight and touch. More specifically, the texture of a plant is a result of the relationship of various parts of a plant, the size and

The bold texture of a mullein plant contrasts with the fine texture of the surrounding plantings at the Fort Worth Arboretum and Botanical Gardens. (Photo by William C. Welch)

The fine texture of grasses like this native Gulf Coast muhlygrass (*Muhlenbergia capillaris*) provides contrast in the garden. (Photo by William C. Welch)

arrangement of the leaves, the composition of the twigs into limbs, and the overall structure of the plant. Texture is relative, and placing two dissimilar textures in close proximity heightens the effect of each. The garden canna appears even coarser planted next to the fine-textured herb rosemary. The ferny yarrow gives an even softer effect next to the broad, smooth-leaved aspidistra. And a carpet of

Sedum acre seems neater in contrast to the spikes of Mexican bush sage (*Salvia leucantha*).

Blending these combinations of textures offers a fascinating method of developing the principle of contrast in the landscape. Using plants exclusively of similar texture creates monotony in a composition, whereas a variety of textures will add interest and distinction. Form is very closely related to interpretation of texture; the difference is often only one of scale as it is viewed in a composition. The majority of plants used in landscapes are of intermediate texture. As in any art composition, too much variety can result in visual confusion.

PATTERN

Pattern implies repetition or reappearance of combinations of plants, structures, colors, textures, lines, or forms. When used with restraint and forethought, pattern helps to create unity and richness in a composition. When overused, it becomes monotonous. Pattern may also be defined as an arrangement of forms repeated within a design. "Parterre" is a term that describes ornamental garden areas

The geometric pattern of clipped boxwood at Bayou Bend Gardens in Houston provides contrast to the woodsy setting. (Photo by William C. Welch)

in which the flower beds and paths form a pattern. Other examples are repeating arrangements of several varieties of climbing roses on a wall or the reappearance of certain bulb groupings. Pattern may also serve in paving designs, fences, and walls to add interest and detail to the garden.

The Collector's Garden

Many gardeners become extremely fond of particular species or groups of plants and want to have large collections. There is nothing inherently wrong with this, and gardens need to be individual expressions of their owners. Sometimes, however, there is a lost opportunity in these gardens. Although challenging to design a garden with a major emphasis on one or a few types of plants, it can be very rewarding. When an overall plan incorporates this idea, a really meaningful and beautiful landscape can result.

One way to design such a garden is to have a strong infrastructure of walks, walls, and other structures. Providing some unity

Frances Parker's garden in Beaufort, South Carolina, illustrates a wide variety of plants such as these topiaries of star jasmine and pots of amaryllis. (Photo by William C. Welch)

A grouping of plant collectibles in Frances Parker's garden in Beaufort, South Carolina. (Photo by William C. Welch)

with hedges and masses of similar materials can provide a good setting for plant collections. Another possibility is to use plants that combine well with the favored choice, such as using perennials in a garden where roses are the favored plant. Another possibility is to integrate the design by using a single color for annual and perennial color. Using containers of a similar design is another way to achieve unity.

Fine-Tuning the Garden

WILLIAM C. WELCH

Antiques

As a lifelong plant collector, I realize that many of the specimens we grow and love are true living antiques. A cutting from George Washington's favorite rose or Elizabeth Lawrence's cherished 'White Empress' camellia is an actual part of the original plant. Enjoying these heirlooms is like having a personal visit with the family and friends who grew them before you.

Sculpture, urns, finials, furniture, and other accessories add richness and personality to the garden, and a few well-chosen antique pieces can set the tone for a garden. Recent years have seen a huge increase in prices and declining availability of objects that were once common and inexpensive. Today, recycling architectural and other objects as garden art can be economical while also having a positive impact on our environment. But how do we ensure that acquiring them is right for our landscape?

SCALE IS IMPORTANT

If the urn, sculpture, finial, or other object is too small or too large, it is not going to look right. Generally, outdoor objects need to be somewhat larger than those used inside. Most garden accessories can be tried in various areas of the garden before permanent placement.

IS THE LOOK COMPATIBLE?

Compatibility can be a bit more complicated. The patina of weathered lead or copper, or peeling paint, generally looks best surrounded by period architecture. Sometimes, however, the contrast of some-

This terra-cotta reproduction is at home in a restored Texas garden. (Photo by William C. Welch)

An antique container like this European olive jar can provide an opportunity for display or stand alone as a garden accessory. (Photo by William C. Welch)

A cast-iron French gutter purchased from a New Orleans garden shop provides a wall planter for succulents. (Photo by William C. Welch)

thing old in a very new setting can also work. Let the architecture provide clues to the selection of your accessories.

WHAT ABOUT SECURITY AND MAINTAINING THE VALUE?

When even cemeteries are not safe from looting, security is an issue. Firmly anchoring pieces and having them inside locked gates are two possibilities. Maintaining quality and value is another issue. Wood, terra-cotta, cast iron, and even concrete need maintenance and protection. To prevent accelerated weather damage, many gardeners move fine garden antiques inside. I realized the sense of this after paying rather handsomely for several hand-crafted whirligigs (wind-driven folk art sculptures). I move them outside for special occasions but enjoy them indoors most of the time.

Heirloom sweet peas like these 'Painted Lady' and 'Cupani' are the essence of fragrance and self-sowing hardiness in the garden. (Photo by William C. Welch)

WHERE TO BUY?

If your eye is good and you have the time, you can sometimes find great values in flea markets and at garage sales. Antiques shows, estate sales, and Internet purchases can also be productive. Trying to find a particular piece for a specific place in the garden can require time and patience. It can also be highly rewarding!

Even if you don't "need" a particular item but really like it and think it is fairly priced, my advice is to go for it! Having a small inventory of good pieces is a joy and allows flexibility in garden displays.

A WORD ABOUT REPRODUCTIONS

In reality, few of us can afford original, antique garden art. Poorly crafted reproductions are abundant. So are high-quality items. Look for detailing and crispness in workmanship. Today's reproduction could well be tomorrow's valuable antique. A little weathering usually helps the piece to look older and treatments are available that can facilitate this process.

These heirloom sweet peas (*Lathyrus* × 'Painted Lady') are hardy garden plants. (Photo by William C. Welch)

Garden Furniture

Comfort, style, durability, and cost are major considerations when choosing garden furniture. Benches, which can add a decorative touch while providing additional seating, may be built in or movable. I particularly like the built-in bench in the parking area of Martha's Bloomers Garden Shop in Navasota, Texas. It is constructed of native stone and nestled into a natural rise in the elevation.

Many years ago I purchased a set of Brown-Jordan garden furniture. Although the paint has chipped and faded over the years, the aluminum alloy frames and vinyl straps are still strong and attractive thirty years later. The same is true of a pair of wrought-iron spring chairs. I have repainted them for the third time, and they are as comfortable and handsome as ever. Wooden furniture has a nice look but does not hold up as well when exposed to the elements. I have enjoyed some rustic cedar furniture, but the life expectancy is usually about ten years, even when wood preservatives and stains are applied. Keep in mind that continuing maintenance is essential for most outdoor furniture and accessories.

An antique table and rockers in a sea of fragrant old-fashioned petunias. (Photo by William C. Welch)

A recycled kitchen chair adjacent to an antique cast-iron urn fits well in this heirloom garden. (Photo by William C. Welch)

Accessories

Among my favorite garden accessories is a *faux bois* (or "fake wood") concrete birdbath made in San Antonio and purchased about ten years ago from an antiques dealer in Fredericksburg, Texas. *Faux bois* became an art form in Europe during the late 1800s and continues to receive international interest. The work of artist Dionicio Rodriguez in San Antonio and elsewhere has been the subject of a recent book. Although being constructed of concrete makes these pieces very heavy and sometimes immovable, good examples command very high prices. Quality is often associated with the amount of detail in the work.

An antique garden bench adds color and interest to a shady setting. (Photo by William C. Welch)

A reproduction faux bois (false wood made of concrete) birdbath in the Welch College Station garden. (Photo by William C. Welch)

Birdbaths are another way to add color and interest to the garden and provide for the birds as well. There has also been an explosion of interest in both practical and decorative birdhouses in recent years. Many gardeners have become especially interested in attracting eastern bluebirds and purple martins, whose houses require particular specifications.

Containers

Plant containers have been a part of gardening for hundreds of years. Orangeries were included in gardens for the wealthy and centered around large container plants such as citrus trees, which were moved into glass houses during the winter months. Clay, stone, iron, and concrete are the most popular and practical materials for containers. Clay pots remain a frequent choice, although they are subject to breaking and disintegrating over time. (Grubb Pottery white clay pots from Marshall, Texas, are known for their durability and longevity, however.) Recently, it has become difficult to distinguish clay from some of the new plastic and other lightweight materials. Their lack of weight is usually an advantage, but blowing over can be a problem. Large containers are often in better scale in the garden, and the plants in them require less watering. Antique iron, marble, and concrete containers sometimes offer more detailing as well as the patina that comes with age. Topiary—the training of plants into various architectural animal or geometric forms—is often but not always grown in containers and has been popular for centuries.

Art

Sculpture, tile mosaics, and paintings can all be a part of the landscape. A rich heritage of tile mosaics that began with early Roman and Spanish gardens can contribute color and richness of detail in both modern and restored gardens. Paintings, such as murals, can be created with products that withstand the elements.

Every garden should reflect the owner's tastes and lifestyle. Having a collection of living plant antiques as well as garden accessories can add significantly to everyone's enjoyment.

Part Four

HEIRLOOM PLANTS OF THE SOUTH

Show me your garden and I shall tell you what you are.
—Alfred Austin, 1835–1913

Gardening is one of those primordial forces in our lives that we can't hide from. Even the most brown thumbed is compelled to torture a houseplant or wonder why the grass won't grow. Like love itself, horticulture speaks a universal language, recognizes no race or culture, and is free to all. Since the beginning of modern civilization, all peoples have gardened, first for food and then for flowers. This section of the book takes a look at a number of the most commonly cultivated plants in early Southern gardens.

Southern heirloom plants belong in Southern gardens. They have earned the right. These plants are still with us for two reasons. First of all, they are tough and adapted. The testing has already

been done. They want to grow here. Also, they are pretty and useful. People don't save ugly, useless plants. What more could we possibly ask for? And we can't forget the nostalgia evoked by the sight or smell of plants that Grandmother grew or for those that we grew up with as children.

Another important aspect of these living antiques is that they are necessary components of accurate historic restoration projects. The days when we would surround a carefully restored Victorian house with a twentieth-century landscape are gone. If we believe that restoration involves the exact nails and original paint pigments, then we should have an appropriate landscape design and authentic plant materials as well.

Most of the plants included here, such as roses and jonquils, were grown for their beauty and fragrance. Others, such as figs and persimmons, were cherished for their culinary uses. Bill and I have included as many historically grown Southern heirloom plants in this section as we were able. Of course, our selection certainly is not exhaustive. We relied on personal observation, historic garden documentation, early garden literature, the advice of others (if we liked it!), and nursery catalogues to come up with our entries. If your mama's favorite was left out, please forgive us and cherish it none the less.

We borrowed from the wonderful book *Passalong Plants* by Steve Bender and Felder Rushing, and our initials are included with each plant description to indicate its author.

If you take away nothing else from this book, we hope that you will at least gain a respect for those plants that have kept us gardening for over a hundred (sometimes a thousand) years.

May you stay young and your plants grow old. Enjoy.—*GG*

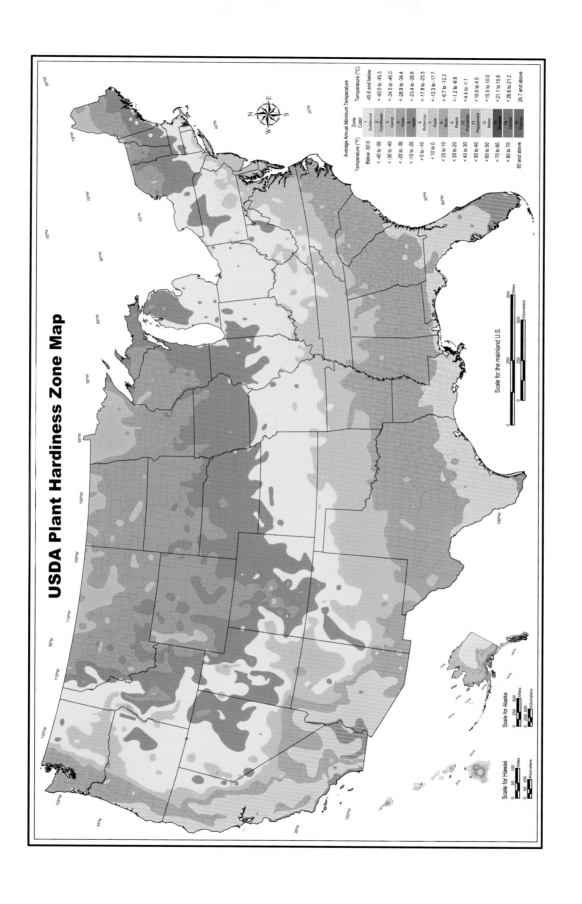

USDA Plant Hardiness Zone Map

Average Annual Minimum Temperature

Temperature (°F)	Zone Color	Temperature (°C)
Below -50.0	1 Goldenrod	-45.6 and below
< -40 to -50	2 Cornflower	< -40.0 to -45.5
< -30 to -40	3 Carrot	< -34.5 to -40.0
< -20 to -30	4 Violet	< -28.9 to -34.4
< -10 to -20	5 Apple	< -23.4 to -28.8
< 0 to -10	6 Buttercup	< -17.8 to -23.3
< 10 to 0	7 Rose	< -12.3 to -17.7
< 20 to 10	8 Moss	< -6.7 to -12.2
< 30 to 20	9 Peach	< -1.2 to -6.6
< 40 to 30	10 Periwinkle	< 4.4 to -1.1
< 50 to 40	11 Peppermint	< 10.0 to 4.5
< 60 to 50	12 Melon	< 15.5 to 10.0
< 70 to 60	13 Bluebell	< 21.1 to 15.6
< 80 to 70	14 Orchid	< 26.6 to 21.2
80 and above	15 Plasma	26.7 and above

Scale for the mainland U.S.

Scale for Alaska

Scale for Hawaii

Acer spp.

Maples
Family: Aceraceae (Maple)
Size: 6–50 ft
Zones: 5–8
Deciduous trees
Colorful foliage and samaras (winged "seed holders"); sweet sap

I will be the first to admit that maples are not exactly Southern heirloom plants or even that commonplace in much of the South. But our ancestors certainly lived and worked among them, and as plants that don't seem "Southern," maples certainly deserve more recognition.

The few maples that were available from early commercial nurseries were usually the least desirable from a horticultural standpoint. These included several forms of silver maple (*Acer saccharinum*) and boxelder (*A. negundo*). Red maple (*A. rubrum*) was occasionally available, as well as the sugar maple (*A. saccharum*).

The sugar maple, familiar to most Americans, is ill adapted for all but the northern fringes of the South. Luckily, ancient climate changes left us with our own Southern sugar maples. In the days when advanced glaciers turned the country into an icebox, our plant palette was much more like that of Canada and the North. Everyone is familiar with the sugar maple represented on the Canadian flag and as Vermont maple syrup. Thanks to the chilling events, the very same sugar maple grew throughout the South, including Texas and even Mexico. When the glaciers receded, creating the warmer Southern climate we know today, most of the sugar maples died out. Those near moist streams, ravines, and cooler canyons slowly adapted and survived. This created the surprising "sugar maple" diversity we have today in the southern United States.

One of our most common native maples in the South is the southern sugar maple (*A. barbatum*). It grows in woodlands

Southern sugar maple *(Acer barbatum)*
(Photo by Greg Grant)

'Crimson Queen' Japanese maple *(Acer palmatum* 'Crimson Queen') (Photo by Greg Grant)

across the South and sports beautiful golden fall color highlighted by peach, orange, and occasionally red tones, depending on the weather. In deep East Texas, where I live, our best fall color is most often in late November and even December. During the growing season, the undersides of the leaves are whitish, adding interest when the wind blows. It is available from specialty nurseries dealing in native plants as well as by mail order. It makes a beautiful shade tree and is most landscape worthy. Supposedly syrup and sugar can be made from its sap, as from its northern cousin. With some experience under my belt producing ribbon cane syrup, I plan to give our southern sugar maples a try one day. It is a sweet tree regardless.

A less common "sugar maple" found in special woodlands across the South is the chalk maple (*A. leucoderme*), named for its whitish bark, although I don't find it that chalky. It is pretty much a smaller-growing, green-backed version of the southern sugar maple. When fall comes, however, it's much different, as the foliage turns orange and red, more like that of a red maple. This is one of my favorite maples and belongs in all Southern landscapes.

Japanese maple *(Acer palmatum)* (Photo by Greg Grant)

The Hill Country region of Texas, as well as parts of the Southwest, is home to another sugar maple variant adapted to the South. The big tooth maple (*A. grandidentatum*) looks similar to the southern sugar maple but is more heat and alkaline tolerant. Lost Maples State Park in Texas celebrates this special maple among the hills and beautiful streams there.

The hills of southern Oklahoma claim a special sugar maple as well. Just as the big tooth maple did, the Caddo maple (*A. saccharum* 'Caddo') evolved to be more adapted to heat, drought, and alkaline soils. Studies at Kansas State University showed it to be the most tatter-resistant sugar maple. These traits make the big tooth maple and the Caddo maple the most logical sugar maple choices for the drier alkaline gardens of Dallas, Austin, San Antonio, and other western regions of the South. It, too, is rare in the trade but well worth seeking out.

Even farther south occurs what I call the Mexican sugar maple (*A. skutchii*), often called the Guatemalan sugar maple. It resides in the forested hills of Mexico and Guatemala and looks very much like a northern sugar maple. It's very rare but makes an outstanding shade tree with typical sugar maple fall color as well.

Perhaps the most outstanding maple for fall color in the South is the red maple (*A. rubrum*). It is represented by three different varieties, *A. rubrum rubrum* in the northeastern areas, *A. rubrum trilobum* in the forested middle South, and *A. rubrum drummondii* in the swamps of the Deep South. The first is most common in the trade, known for brilliant red and orange fall color but less heat and drought tolerance. The smaller-leaved trilobed variety is common throughout much of the South, native where I live, and more heat and drought tolerant. It, too, is known for its brilliant hues of red, orange, and yellow. The undersides of its leaves are often dramatically whitish. The leaves of variety *drummondii* also have white undersides but are very fuzzy beneath. It grows in Southern swamps and has showy spring blooms in colors of yellow, brown, orange, red, or maroon. Some are as showy as redbuds in the spring. Unfortunately, this variety often sports the least showy fall color.

Red maple (*Acer rubrum rubrum*) (Photo by Greg Grant)

Sugar maple *(Acer saccharum)* (Photo by Greg Grant)

Red maple *(Acer rubrum trilobum)* (Photo by Greg Grant)

There are a number of beautiful Asian maples that shine in Southern landscapes. The most popular landscape maple is the delicate Japanese maple (*A. palmatum*). There are hundreds of cultivars of this fashionable small tree, ranging from green-leaved types to burgundy ones, cut leaved to full leaved, and weeping or upright habits. There are even special selections that grow no higher than dwarf shrubs and some with variegated foliage. The easiest by far to grow are the inexpensive green-leaved seedlings. All are spectacular in the fall, however, with colors usually ranging from glowing oranges to eye-popping reds.

The trilobed maple (*A. buergerianum*) is becoming more popular as a landscape tree across the South. It has three-lobed leaves and is quite adaptable to a range of sites. Like other Asian maples, it shines with a variety of brilliant fall colors. It also has an interesting flaking bark.

The Shantung maple (*A. truncatum*) has risen in popularity as well because of its shiny tatter-resistant foliage and showy fall colors. It has also proven to be heat and alkaline tolerant in the western fringes of the South.

I love maples so much that I have created a small "aceretum" around what will one day be my retirement home. It's a Creole cottage–style house with a tall hipped roof and a central double fireplace. In the early 1900s it belonged to the Arcadia general store owner and community matriarch. I have planted all the maples native to Texas in the yard along with thousands of daffodils, jonquils, and narcissus. I have also planted pink and white rain lilies, pink and white lycoris, and pink oxblood lilies for the fall. There are no flower beds, just a broad low-maintenance lawn that can be mowed with the tractor when the bulbs finish. When I'm old and can't get around anymore, I'll sit on the porch and admire the view. — *GG*

Asimina triloba

Pawpaw
Family: Annonaceae (Custard Apple)
Size: 15–20 ft
Zones: 5–11
Small deciduous tree
Maroon flowers, edible fruit, and butterfly host

Pawpaw *(Asimina triloba)* (Photo by Greg Grant)

> *Where, oh where is pretty little Susie?*
> *Where, oh where is pretty little Susie?*
> *Where, oh where is pretty little Susie?*
> *Way down yonder in the paw-paw patch.*
>
> *Come on, boys, let's go find her,*
> *Come on, boys, let's go find her,*
> *Come on, boys, let's go find her,*
> *Way down yonder in the paw-paw patch.*
>
> *Pickin' up paw-paws, puttin' 'em in her pockets,*
> *Pickin' up paw-paws, puttin' 'em in her pockets,*
> *Pickin' up paw-paws, puttin' 'em in her pockets,*
> *Way down yonder in the paw-paw patch.*
> *—Traditional folk song*

I have seen different variations on the lyrics of this song with different lost names and searchers, but they all end up picking up pawpaws and putting them in their pockets. The pawpaw is a very interesting member of a tropical fruit family. It is native throughout the eastern United States along creeks and streams. Although I have not located any examples of early nurseries that carried it or specific gardens that grew it, I'm sure early settlers were aware of it. The genus name *Asimina* comes from a French variation of its Native American name. In the spring, small maroon bell-like flowers emerge before the large drooping leaves appear. The crushed

Pawpaw *(Asimina triloba)* (Photo by Greg Grant)

leaves smell like bell peppers to some. The small banana-like fruit ripens in the late summer and is relished by opossums and raccoons. Some folks relish the fruit as well (including my uncle Noel), while others find its soft, fragrant, highly flavored pulp more than they can bear. In addition to being eaten fresh, it probably has been used to make pies, custards, and even ice cream. One year my mom and I substituted pawpaws for bananas while making banana bread, and it was delicious. The only drawback is the number of large seeds in the fruit. Breeders, however, have made progress in selecting fruit with fewer and smaller seeds.

This tropical fruit relative also lures a tropical butterfly relative northward. It is the lone host for the beautiful zebra swallowtail butterfly, my favorite since I was a child. This prized beauty has black and white stripes, like a zebra, highlighted with touches of blue and red and a long "swallow's" tail. The butterflies start out in the spring in the deep woods, and by summer populations are nectaring on lantanas and vitex in the sunny garden. As they only reproduce in pawpaw patches, it's important to preserve bottom-land hardwood forests and riparian zones in their range. If you don't have that luxury, at least plant one (or more) in your garden and please don't spray the odd-shaped, brown-striped caterpillars if you are lucky enough to have them. Natural predators seem to dispose of most of them.

Pawpaws are difficult to transplant but can occasionally be found in specialty nurseries or mail-order catalogues. They perform best in well-drained soil with regular moisture and prefer a bit of shade. Trees can be produced from seed by planting them in the fall or giving them a cold, moist (stratification) treatment for three months. Pick up a pawpaw seed and put it in your pocket, and your garden. —GG

Belamcanda chinensis

Blackberry Lily
Family: Iridaceae (Iris)
Size: 2 ft
Zones: 6–9
Perennial
Speckled orange flower and showy black fruit

The foliage of the blackberry lily so closely resembles that of its relatives the bearded irises as to fool the gardener—if the plant isn't in flower. For blackberry lily blossoms are quite distinctive: as much as two inches across, deep orange with red freckles. Individual blossoms last only a day, but dozens of buds gracefully adorn each of the airy flower stalks, and these continue to emerge from late spring into fall, ensuring a long succession of flowers. The source of the blackberry lily's common name becomes apparent when the flowers fade in late summer and the fruit and seed

Blackberry lily *(Belamcanda chinensis)*
(Photo by William C. Welch)

form, producing a cluster that looks very much like a shiny, ripe blackberry. These seed structures are attractive as well as intriguing and may be used fresh or dried in floral arrangements.

Originally from China and Japan, where the plant was used for medicinal purposes, the blackberry lily has made itself very much at home in most areas of the South and provides gardeners of that region with an attractive and easily grown perennial. Blackberry lilies are effective when massed in borders or in containers. I was pleased to have the opportunity to collect a few specimens at Ingleside, former home of Thomas Affleck, the well-known writer and nurseryman of the 1840s and 1850s, in Washington, Mississippi. Earl Rawlings, the current owner of the property and a distant relative of Affleck's wife, Anna Dunbar Affleck, showed me the plants, which were still growing near the ruins of the head gardener's cottage.

One reason for this plant's popularity is the ease with which it is propagated from divisions or seeds. To divide, lift and separate the rhizomes of mature plants in fall or early spring. Both divisions and seedlings usually bloom the first year after planting and continue to thrive for years.

Blackberry lilies prefer well-drained soils and a sunny location, but partial shade and less than ideal soils will do. —*WCW*

Buxus sempervirens

Common Boxwood
Family: Buxaceae (Box)
Size: 2–15 ft
Zones: 6–10
Evergreen shrub, small tree
Flowers insignificant except to hairstreak butterflies and bees

> And so with the Tree Boxes—the neatest and prettiest of evergreen trees; always fresh and pleasant to look on. They grow better here than even in their native climate; as does, also, the Dwarf Box, for edgings.
> —Thomas Affleck in a letter to the editor of the *Natchez Daily Courier,* October 28, 1854

This shrub has been in cultivation in America for over two hundred years. It is the hedging and topiary box of many historic European and American gardens, including those of Colonial Williamsburg. In the heyday of the parterres in the Southeast and the upper South, this was *the* plant. Supposedly, it is a native of both Europe and Asia, though some authorities speculate that actually it may have been introduced to Europe in ancient times. Some say that box foliage smells somewhat like the smell of a wet dog. To me, it just smells like classic boxwood.

Historically, two forms were cultivated: tree box or American box (*Buxus sempervirens* 'Arborescens') and dwarf box, edging box, Dutch box, or slow box (*B. sempervirens* 'Suffruticosa'). Tree box grows to be a good-sized shrub or even an attractive small tree, but the shorter, more compact dwarf box normally stops growing at a height of less than three feet. The dwarf is the one primarily used for edging and parterres.

According to Raymond Taylor's book, *Plants of Colonial Days,* Abigail Davidson advertised imported box "for edging of walks" in the Boston *Gazette and Country Journal* of March 12, 1770.

Common boxwood *(Buxus sempervirens)*
(Photo by Greg Grant)

Dwarf box *(Buxus sempervirens*
'Suffruticosa') (Photo by William C. Welch)

Taylor also points out that Captain Ridgeley, of Hampton, Mary-land, left a will in 1787 directing that his box gardens be main-tained. I can't get anybody to look after my plants when I'm gone for a week, much less eternity.

Martha Turnbull made numerous references in her garden diary (1836–95) to her boxwood and parterres at Rosedown Plantation in St. Francisville, Louisiana. On October 5, 1837, for example, she wrote that she "set out box in yard," while on November 15, 1841, she mentions trimming the box. She made a note of sticking box cuttings in January and November 1849; on October 20, 1855, she recorded a day spent "putting down box around my *parterre.*"

Many early nurseries in the South, especially those of the upper South and the east, carried boxwood. In an 1851–52 catalogue, Thomas Affleck's Southern Nurseries of Washington, Mississippi, listed "Tree and Minorca" box. Montgomery Nurseries (Wilson's Nursery) of Montgomery, Alabama, listed dwarf box in an 1860 catalogue; in an 1881–82 catalogue, Langdon Nurseries, near Mobile, Alabama, offered *B. communis*, *B. argentea*, *B. myrtifolia*, *B. latifolia*, *B. japonicum*, and *B. variegata*. However, common box does not seem to have been very common in Texas.

The Japanese or little-leaf boxwood (*B. microphylla;* formerly known as *B. japonica*) was not introduced to Europe until 1860 but may have arrived in the American South somewhat earlier. An 1857 landscape plan by Henry Watson in Greensboro, North Carolina, listed a Chinese box, which could possibly be a very early use of Japanese boxwood. Today the little-leaf box is more common in modern Southern gardens than the common box, probably because the Japanese species is slightly better adapted to our region's constant heat and humidity.

All forms of boxwood require good drainage. They are susceptible to nematodes, and the newest leaves are prone to frost damage during severe winters or sudden cold snaps. Propagation is by cuttings.—*GG*

Calycanthus floridus

Sweet Shrub, Carolina Allspice, Strawberry Shrub, Sweet
Bubby
Family: Calycanthaceae (Calycanthus)
Size: 6–9 ft
Zones: 6–9
Deciduous shrub
Fragrant maroon (sometimes yellow) flowers

Sweet shrub is also known as strawberry shrub and is native to
the South. It is legendary for the fragrance of its flowers, which
occur as the foliage emerges in spring. Sweet shrub is associated with old gardens of the colonial period. The scent is said to
resemble ripe fruit and is strongest in warm, humid situations.
The bark is sometimes used as a filler in the production of cinnamon spice. Propagation is from seeds or offsets. The foliage
is aromatic when bruised, and the shrub itself combines nicely
with other native or introduced plants. It typically matures to a

Sweet shrub *(Calycanthus floridus)*
(Photo by Greg Grant)

Sweet shrub *(Calycanthus floridus)* (Photo by William C. Welch)

four- to six-foot rounded shrub in the sun or partial shade in sandy, acidic soils.

Flowers are reddish brown and one to two inches in diameter. I received my start from the late Catherine Sims, a friend and noted plant collector from Birmingham, Alabama. Catherine shared a division from her six- to eight-foot specimen, saying that "it had the largest and most fragrant flowers of any sweet shrub I have seen." I set out my plant in the back fence row at Mangham in Louisiana in the early 1990s, and it has thrived. I recently shared divisions with Greg so that he can include them in the collection at the Mast Arboretum of Stephen F. Austin University in Nacogdoches. Now he can share the responsibility of passing along this rather unique selection!

Although known as an easy plant to grow, sweet shrub does not like the alkaline soils and water in my area of Central Texas. It is native across the Southeast, but is never found in large colonies. — *WCW*

Camellia spp. Camellia,

Sasanqua, Tea
Family: Theaceae (Tea)
Size: 4–15 ft
Zones: 7–10
Medium to large shrub or small tree
White, pink, or red flowers in fall, winter, or spring

Although camellias may be found in many modest gardens today, historically this group of shrubs has served as a status symbol in the South. The difficulty with which camellias are propagated has put this task beyond the skills of most amateur gardeners; in the past, even professional nurserymen found the propagation of camellias challenging, and for generations this was reflected in a relatively expensive price of nursery-grown stock. Cost and the difficulty of cultivation have prevented camellias from following the classic path of exotic plants introduced into the South— camellias never filtered down from the gardens of wealthy collectors to the cottage gardeners' plots. Until recently, to have camellias blooming in your garden was proud evidence not only of horticultural skill but also of prosperity.

"Red Survivor" camellia *(Camellia japonica* 'Red Survivor') (Photo by William C. Welch)

'Delores Edwards' camellia *(Camellia japonica* 'Delores Edwards') (Photo by William C. Welch)

Like so many of the South's cherished ornamental plants, camellias originated in China and came to North America via Europe, but in this case, the steps in that progression are not easy to trace. Two volumes have helped to guide me through the long and fascinating history of these beautiful and important plants. One is H. Harold Hume's *Camellias in America,* which was a gift many years ago from Lynn Lowrey, a well-known horticulturist in Houston. My other resource has been *The Camellia: Its History, Culture, Genetics and a Look into Its Future Development,* a handbook edited by David L. Feathers and published by the American Camellia Society in 1978, which is available from the society headquarters in Ft. Valley, Georgia.

The genus *Camellia* includes many species, but of these, three are of special importance and interest as heirloom Southern plants: *C. sinensis, C. japonica,* and *C. sasanqua.* Of these three, the one that evoked the most intense interest in the early days of the Southern colonies was *C. sinensis,* a shrub that, truth be told, is of no special ornamental value.

Camellia sinensis is a reasonably attractive evergreen shrub that bears single, cream-colored flowers. The blossoms were of no concern to colonial planters, though; what they were interested in was the plant's foliage, which when dried and processed may be brewed into tea. This was an ancient taste in China and Japan, and cultivation of the tea plant had been carried on in those lands since ancient times. Tea drinking became the fashion in England in the late sixteenth or early seventeenth century, but because the leaves had to be shipped in from China, for a long time tea remained an expensive luxury. In fact, tea was brewed only at the "best homes," and the leaves were stored in locked boxes. Still, the growing passion for tea led to a serious trade imbalance with China, whose merchants accepted payment only in silver and who showed little enthusiasm for British goods. The British, in turn, resolved to establish a domestic tea industry, and it was hoped that the new colonies in southern North America would prove a suitable site.

The famous Trust Garden in Savannah was the first to receive seeds of tea. This shipment arrived from the East Indies in 1744; unfortunately, according to contemporary observer Francis Moore, these first seeds, "though great Care was taken, did not grow." Plants were sent to Georgia in 1772 and are recorded as growing on Skidaway Island, near Savannah, before 1805. This attempt to grow tea near Savannah also failed, apparently because of a combination of undercapitalization and a climate that proved to be very unhealthy for the gardeners.

By 1813, a serious effort to grow tea was under way at Charleston, South Carolina, in the nursery of Philippe Noisette. The planting did not flourish there nor in Texas—there is a record by the Cat Springs Agricultural Society of unsuccessful attempts at tea culture by early German settlers there. Tea growing never did become a viable industry in the Southern colonies, though curiously, an English company finally succeeded in establishing a successful plantation near Charleston long after independence. The Lipton Tea Company planted the tea bushes, whose foliage is harvested every year now and marketed under a private label. This success, however, has not been duplicated, for tea is not

'Duchess de Caze' camellia (Camellia japonica 'Duchess de Caze') (Photo by William C. Welch)

easily cultivated in North America and has never been widely grown in the South. Greg considers *C. sinensis* quite easily cultivated in East Texas and the Southeast. There are some large specimens thriving at the Stephen F. Austin Mast Arboretum in Nacogdoches, and Greg is brewing his own green tea at his home in nearby Arcadia.

The tea bush has a more beautiful relative, *C. japonica,* one that did take root in the American South. This species is best known to Southern gardeners for its handsome foliage and elegant winter and early-spring flowers. A native of Korea, China, and Japan, this camellia has flower colors that range from white to turkey red, with many variegated forms. Although well adapted to much of the South, *C. japonica* has a reputation for being difficult to grow when exposed to less than its ideal growing conditions. It is, however, by far the most important species of the three in relation to our Southern gardening heritage, and specimens of *C. japonica* mark the site of many important plantations and old homesteads throughout the South. Its less popular rival in the Southern garden is *C. sasanqua,* a shrub of Japanese origin.

Individual blossoms of the sasanqua camellias, though beautiful, are much less spectacular than those of *C. japonica.* Nevertheless, *C. sasanqua* fills an important garden niche because it is fall blooming—*C. japonica* cultivars (known as "japonicas" in the South) bloom in late winter or early spring.

Of the two ornamental species of camellias, *C. japonica* was the first to arrive in North American gardens. Though frost sensitive, this plant actually made its first entry into the United States as a single red form imported by John Stevens of Hoboken, New Jersey, in 1797 or 1798. Presumably, Stevens succeeded in the cultivation of this plant, for in 1800 Michael Floy, a nurseryman across the river in the Bowery of New York City, wrote to a friend that he had brought back from England that July another japonica camellia, "a plant of the Double White [later named 'Alba Plena'] for John Stevens, Esq. of Hoboken, New Jersey, who had two or three years previously imported the Single Red."

For a Northerner such as Stevens, camellias could only succeed as a greenhouse crop, and that was how they were viewed by nearly all the early importers, who were located in the coastal areas of the northeastern United States. Boston, actually, was the first American center for camellia cultivation, for the wealthy gardeners of that city competed in obtaining new varieties as they moved from China into Europe. In addition, Boston's amateur growers succeeded in raising some new varieties of their own from seed, and these, too, were introduced into the florist and nursery trade. The Massachusetts Horticultural Society took the lead in popularizing new camellias, but a New York nursery, William Prince's Linnaean Botanic Garden in Flushing, in 1822 became the first American firm to list camellias in its catalogue. It advertised a stock of seventeen varieties, including one sasanqua camellia, "Lady Banks' tea leaved sasanqua."

Philadelphia soon overtook both Boston and New York as a center for camellia cultivation. That city's leading nurserymen, Robert Buist and David Landreth, both gave liberal space to camellias in their catalogues and were active in promoting these shrubs. In 1829 three camellia varieties were displayed at the Philadelphia Horticultural Society Show, and by April 1830 the number of entries had grown to twelve.

It was from Philadelphia that ornamental camellias finally entered the South. David Landreth's nursery kept a representative in Charleston, South Carolina, and in 1819 opened a branch store in that city. Clearly, the Landreths took this venture seriously, for David Landreth Jr., the son of the nursery's founder, took over the management of the store and continued to work there until April 22, 1862, when the real estate and stock were confiscated by an order of the Confederate States District Court.

Most importations of camellias into the South came from growers along the Atlantic seaboard from Washington, D.C., and north, though some were also imported from Europe. Plants from both sources were eagerly sought, and private camellia collections grew rapidly as planters realized how well adapted the

'White Empress' camellia *(Camellia japonica* 'White Empress') (Photo by William C. Welch)

plants were to the warmer and moister parts of the South. Plants often grew to a great size and age, and camellia blossoms became a part of plantation life in Charleston, Savannah, Wilmington, Mobile, New Orleans, and ports of the Mississippi River. Of particular note among the early collections were those at Magnolia Gardens and Middleton Place near Charleston.

The birth of Magnolia Gardens came in 1848, when the Reverend J. G. Drayton planted the first camellias and azaleas of what were to become remarkable collections. He eventually assembled more than three hundred camellia varieties, many of them seedlings he had raised. When Hume wrote his 1955 book, many of the Magnolia Garden plants had reached a height of twenty-five or more feet tall and had trunks measuring thirty inches or more in circumference—such a specimen might carry thousands of flowers at its peak of bloom.

Magnolia Gardens' chief local rival was Middleton Place, another Charleston-area garden that boasts many fine old camellias, although here they were not among the garden's original plantings. This was inevitable, for when the landscape at Middleton Place was first laid out in the years 1764–74, camellias were not available anywhere in America. But Middleton Place has proven well adapted to camellia cultivation, for these shrubs have actually naturalized there, and in the past thickets of "volunteers" formed around seed-bearing specimens.

The most important name in the history of Southern camellias is Prosper Julius Alphonse Berckmanns, who was born on October 13, 1830, in Aschot, Belgium, and acquired a good background in horticulture and botany before immigrating to America. His first stop on this side of the Atlantic was Plainfield, New Jersey, but after a short stay there he resettled in Augusta, Georgia, in 1857, purchasing a half interest in a nursery that had been started by D. Redmond. The following year he bought up the other half of the business and went on to build Berckmanns Fruitland Nurseries into one of the most important and influential nurseries in the South.

Fruitland introduced many fruit and ornamental trees and shrubs such as oriental persimmons, peaches, grapes, roses, and azaleas into the South and was a pioneer in the popularization of southeastern natives. This nursery was also a leading camellia producer; indeed, following the Civil War, Fruitland was for many years the sole source for camellia plants in the South. Berckmans and his sons, Louis, J., Robert, and P. J. A. Jr. (who followed him into the business), kept in touch with Hovey, Wilder, Landreth, and other camellia experts in the North and regularly ordered their new introductions. But most of Fruitland's camellias were imported from the founder's native Belgium, which throughout much of the nineteenth century was the center for camellia propagation and breeding in Europe.

Throughout its half century of operation, Fruitland served as a source for prized camellia specimens all over the South. After the nursery went out of business, its site became part of the Augusta Country Club, and as late as 1955, when Hume was publishing his camellia guide, venerable plants of 'Prof. C. S. Sargent,' 'Lady Hume's Blush,' and 'Alba Plena' still flourished there.

Excellent growing conditions for camellias are found all through the coastal regions of North and South Carolina and Georgia and along the Gulf Coast through Mobile, Alabama. They have been important garden plants in the Mobile area since early times. Actually, the southeastern Gulf Coast as a whole is excellent territory for camellias—its well-drained acidic soils, high humidity, and abundant rainfall provide ideal growing conditions. Even in areas where camellias do not thrive in the ground, they may be grown in large containers under an overhang providing afternoon sun protection. My plant of 'Delores Edwards' grown on my College Station porch has provided hundreds of blooms along with 'White Empress,' which we have enjoyed for many years. 'Duchesse de Caze' was a favorite of Ima Hogg at her Bayou Bend garden in Houston. It is still viewed by thousands of visitors annually.

As early as 1839, Gilbert R. Rotton reported finding in Mobile

'Rose Dawn' camellia *(Camellia japonica* 'Rose Dawn') (Photo by William C. Welch)

"about fifty varieties of camellias," many of which, he said, had been imported from England. In 1853, C. C. and D. W. Langdon established Langdon Nurseries about twenty-eight miles north of Mobile, and camellias were among the wide variety of plant materials they grew. The Langdon's catalogue for 1890–91 listed thirty-nine varieties by name and assured customers that it could get for them many more. C. Ravier & Sons established a florist business in Mobile shortly after the Civil War and imported and distributed large numbers of camellias from France. Today, Mobile's Bellingrath Gardens is known for a collection of large old specimens.

Louisiana also has its share of heirloom camellias. The finest of these are found around St. Francisville in West Feliciana Parish, a small Mississippi River village where in antebellum days many fine plantation homes and gardens prospered. Early plant introductions were brought upriver from New Orleans by boat. Of all the gardens in St. Francisville, the very finest, in its heyday, was Rosedown, the beautiful plantation home and garden that Daniel Turnbull built for his bride, Martha, in 1835.

In her garden diary in November 1855, Martha Turnbull mentioned having one hundred japonicas (camellias). On September 22, she had mentioned having purchased commercially propagated camellias but also referred to camellias she had budded and rooted herself. In addition, she grew large numbers of camellias from seeds. In her April 1858 diary entry she wrote, "April we had 29 pretty japonicas, 59 from seed in ground, 45 seedlings in jars, 196 all together. Six of them are of Augustus' propagation, 5 also cockade and besides thousands are coming up from seed, two layers of the pretty white by the summerhouse." The original garden covered twenty acres, and the remnants of those plantings, which are open to the public now, contain many heirloom plants, in particular many fine old camellia specimens. Aged plants of 'Alba Plena' and 'Fimbriata' are also reported to exist in the cemetery of the Grace Episcopal Church in St. Francisville.

South of St. Francisville along the Louisiana coast is Avery Island and the former estate of E. L. McIlhenny of pepper sauce fame. This enterprising businessman was a noted authority on camellias and a collector who was also active in the propagation and dissemination of the plants. There are many old specimens surviving at his Jungle Gardens today.

The camellia's historical progress across the South eventually culminated in Houston, Texas, the point that marks the far western edge of suitable climate and soils. In tracing the history of camellia cultivation in that city, I have had the help of Sadie Gwin Blackburn, whose research in the River Oaks Garden Club archives has yielded intriguing insights. What she has found is that although there are mentions of camellia plantings in Houston before the turn of this century, the real japonica craze did not start until the birth of the River Oaks Garden Club Azalea Trail in 1936. One of the favorite stops in the early days of the tour was the four-acre estate garden of the John E. Green Jr. family. The interesting feature of the Green garden was its collection of 150-plus camellias, plants that had been transplanted from old gardens across the South or imported from Belgium and France. In addition to such historic favorites as 'Lady Hume's Blush,' 'Purple Dawn,' 'Alba Plena,' 'Chandleri Elegans,' and 'Magnoliaflora,' the Greens cultivated a specimen of 'Leucantha,' which had been planted in 1898, according to a 1936 *Houston Chronicle* article.

Another Houston garden of note was that of the H. R. Cullen. According to a March 1937 article from the River Oaks Garden Club archives, the six-acre Cullen garden contained over eight thousand plants of azaleas and camellias, which made it the largest known collection of these plants outside of Bellingrath Gardens.

Elizabeth Lawrence (1904–85) is revered as one of the greatest garden writers of the South and is immortalized by her books. Her garden in Charlotte, North Carolina, is of modest size but contains a remarkable collection of plant materials. Among her plants are two beautiful specimens of *C. japonica* 'White Empress' located on either side of an axis in the back yard. I obtained cuttings from Lindie Wilson (then-owner of Lawrence's home) in 2006 and successfully rooted them. I placed each of them in a twelve-inch clay pot and placed them on either side of the doors leading from my living area to the back porch (east facing). They have thrived and bloom beautifully from January through March each year. I am convinced that Elizabeth Lawrence's 'White Empress' is the best-performing camellia I have grown. I have at least a half-dozen various plants from the Lawrence garden that have proven to be favorites.

Camellia Culture

Camellias require a soil that is both well drained and yet sufficiently moisture retentive to maintain the plants through dry spells. If an existing soil is too heavy or sandy, it should be modified by the addition of organic materials. For healthy camellias, the soil must also be acidic, and any water used for irrigation should also be acidic or at least neutral in pH. Mulches are beneficial, since they help insulate the soil from temperature and moisture extremes. Camellias are happiest in a spot protected from the hot afternoon sun, especially during the summer months. Large pine trees are excellent for providing such protection, as long as they are not planted too closely together.

Propagation is by seed, cutting, or grafting. When propagating superior clones by grafting, seedling plants of *C. japonica* or *C. sasanqua* are commonly used as understocks. Grafts are usually made just before growth begins in spring or when plants go dormant in August.

Although they are quite specific in their cultural requirements, camellias are not otherwise demanding. Southern gardeners who can meet camellias' basic needs should certainly try these handsome and historic shrubs. For generations, camellias remained the preserve of the wealthy. But advances in nursery techniques and in our understanding of the camellias' needs have brought these shrubs within the reach of the average gardener. Why not let them add some elegance to your period plantings?—*WCW*

Crossvine *(Bignonia capreolata)* (Photo by Greg Grant)

'Helen Fredel' crossvine *(Bignonia capreolata* 'Helen Fredel') (Photo by Greg Grant)

Campsis radicans

Trumpet Creeper, Trumpet Vine, Trumpet Flower, Cow-itch (*Campsis radicans*), Crossvine (*Bignonia capreolata*)
Family: Bignoniaceae (Trumpet Creeper)
Size: 15–30 ft
Zones: 5–11
Deciduous vine
Orange or red (occasionally yellow) flowers and hummingbird nectar

Our native trumpet creeper is a common sight on fence rows over the entire South. This tenacious, deciduous vine will not be denied—it grows where it wants. Fortunately, it is showier and not as rampant as kudzu, and the hummingbirds like it. If trumpet creeper grew like kudzu, we would have to fog the hummingbirds like we do mosquitoes.

According to Raymond Taylor's *Plants of Colonial Days,* this species was sent to England as early as 1640 as *Tecoma radicans.* A century later, early American plant collectors Mark Catesby,

'Flava' trumpet creeper (Campsis radicans 'Flava') (Photo by Greg Grant)

'Flava' trumpet creeper (*Campsis radicans* 'Flava') (Photo by Greg Grant)

Trumpet creeper (*Campsis radicans*) (Photo by Greg Grant)

William Bartram, and Thomas Walter were collecting it as *Bignonia radicans*. It has always been cultivated in the South and was offered by a number of early Southern nurseries. Today several forms of *Campsis radicans* are available, including the yellow variety, 'Flava,' and one with variegated foliage.

Campsis × *tagliabuana* 'Madame Galen'
(Photo by Greg Grant)

The Chinese species, *C. grandiflora,* was found by Engelbert Kaempfer, chief surgeon to the Dutch East India Company, in Japan as early as 1691 but not introduced to England until 1800. It has very large, showy flowers and is only hardy to zone 7. It is extremely showy but is often short-lived in the South. Hybrids between the Chinese and American species, *C.* × *tagliabuana,* were developed in France. The most common and popular of these, a cultivar introduced in 1889, is 'Madame Galen.' This plant bears huge, showy red-orange flowers and is fairly common in the nursery trade.

In its 1881–82 catalogue, Langdon Nurseries near Mobile, Alabama, listed "*Bignonia radicans*-orange scarlet trumpet flower" and "*Bignonia grandiflora*-Japan trumpet flower." The 1906–7 catalogue of Fruitland Nurseries in Augusta, Georgia, listed "*Bignonia grandiflora*" and "*Bignonia hybrida.*"

Our native crossvine (*B. capreolata*) was also cultivated in old-time Southern gardens. A member of the same family, it was often offered by Southern nurseries along with the trumpet creeper. A spectacular bright orange-and-yellow-flowered cultivar named

'Tangerine Beauty' Crossvine *(Bignonia capreolata)* (Photo by William C. Welch)

'Tangerine Beauty' is now available in the nursery trade. It came from a yard in San Antonio just down the street from the botanic garden. The brick red 'Atrosanguinea' is also available. Bill and I introduced an orange-flowered cultivar named 'Helen Fredel,' which he found in Helen Fredel's yard in Bryan, Texas. She originally obtained it from a large old home in her neighborhood. It has the largest flowers of any known cultivar. We sell it each year at our arboretum plant sales. These new selections of this tough evergreen vine are sure to make this native heirloom even more popular in the future.—*GG*

'Tangerine Beauty' Crossvine *(Bignonia capreolata)* (Photo by William C. Welch)

Canna spp. and hybrids

Cannas, Canna Lilies
Family: Cannaceae (Canna)
Size: 3–6 ft
Zones: 7–11
Perennial
Cream, pink, yellow, orange, or red flowers; host for Brazilian skipper butterfly

Cannas have two givens in this world: they are typically Southern, and they are much maligned. There's a reason for both. There are twenty or more *Canna* species in the world, all from tropical regions. Therefore, they cannot tolerate much cold and are adapted as showy annuals only in the North. This actually makes them more desirable in the North. Folks always like plants that don't grow in their area. If you have to work much harder for something, the value always goes up. Northerners groom the foliage and deadhead the flowers throughout the season, followed by digging and storing them for the winter. In the South, they thrive with no care in ditches and in the wrong parts of town, which of course makes their "value" decrease.

This is just part of the reason for their being maligned. They are often plagued by canna leaf rollers. It's only a plague, however, if you are not a nature lover and a butterfly enthusiast. For the canna leaf roller is the larva of the little Brazilian skipper butterfly, also from the tropics. Skippers are named for their quick, jumpy flight pattern. They reproduce and follow annual canna plantings up through the United States during the summer and return each year as "snowbirds" to spend the winter in South Texas, southern Florida, and the tropics. If you hate butterflies, the larvae are easily controlled with the organic, biological insecticide *Bacillus thuringiensis*.

Wild cannas tend to be tall plants with small flowers. Cannas occur in a wide range of colors from yellow, orange and reds, to

'Tropicana' canna lily *(Canna × generalis)* (Photo by Greg Grant)

'Cleopatra' canna lily *(Canna × generalis* 'Cleopatra') (Photo by Greg Grant)

'Ehemanii' canna lily (Canna × iridiflora
'Ehemanii') (Photo by Greg Grant)

'Ehemanii' canna lily (Canna × iridiflora
'Ehemanii') (Photo by Greg Grant)

pinks and creams. Many have bicolor or spotted flowers. They can also be green leaved, red leaved, or variegated. Those with variegated foliage have been all the rage over the last decade. Many use the showy foliage in floral design. Over the years, cannas were bred to be dwarf plants with larger and larger showy flowers. They were very popular as bedding plants during the Victorian period.

Though they are not in vogue with upscale gardeners, I have to admit that I have always been a bit fond of them. My favorite is the old French hybrid *Canna × iridiflora* 'Ehemanii.' It is tall and voluptuous with hot pink "iris" flowers that droop down from stalks that each produce repeated crops of flowers. It literally looks like a cross between a banana and a fuchsia. 'Ehemanii' is sterile, producing no seed. This is one reason it blooms so prolifically. The banana-like foliage is an added plus. It really is a piece of living sculpture.

Cannas perform best with rich, moist soil and plenty of sunlight. Unfortunately, many cannas are plagued by somewhat unsightly virus-contaminated foliage these days, which has no cure. —*GG*

Catalpa bignonioides

Southern Catalpa, Common or Eastern Catalpa, Indian Bean, Cigar, Fishbait or Worm Tree
Family: Bignoniaceae (Trumpet Creeper)
Size: 20–50 ft
Zones: 6–9
Deciduous tree
Fragrant white flowers in early summer; long beans follow; prized worms for fishing

Our native southern catalpa was once highly regarded as an ornamental tree in the landscape; a long and handsome double row on the Palace Green at Colonial Williamsburg attests to the tree's former glory. Unfortunately, the southern catalpa is seldom planted these days and is sometimes considered a weed tree. Like many American natives, it is more revered in Europe than it is at home.

"Catalpa" is a Latinized version of a Cherokee name, and it was in Cherokee country that the naturalist Mark Catesby discovered this species in 1726. He introduced the plant to gardens in America and England and included an illustration of it in volume 1 of the work he published in 1731, *The Natural History of Carolina, Florida, and the Bahama Islands.* In this book he wrote:

> This tree was unknown to the inhabited parts of Carolina until I brought the seeds from the remote parts of the country. And though the inhabitants are little curious in gardening, yet the uncommon beauty of this tree had induced them to propagate it and 'tis become an ornament to many of their gardens and probably will be the same to ours in England.

There is some evidence that catalpas were planted at the Governor's Palace in Williamsburg as early as 1737, and a journal entry from 1782 makes reference to the catalpas at the palace. Those growing there today were planted after 1930 as part of the restoration.

Eliza Lucas (later Eliza Pinckney) mentions in a 1743 account of William Middleton's gardens at Crowfield near Charleston, South Carolina, "a large square boleing [*sic*] green . . . with a walk quite round composed of a double row of fine large flowering Laurel and Catulpas [*sic*] which form both shade and beauty."

We have a copy of a page from a 1789 Baltimore, Maryland, newspaper with a nursery advertisement listing "Catalpa Flower-tree" for sale. And George Washington is known to have planted two catalpas at Mount Vernon in 1785.

The Moravians in Salem, North Carolina (the area of Winston-Salem known today as "Old Salem"), obviously prized the catalpas, as their records mention this tree a number of times: for example, the planting of catalpas on the square in 1782, the planting of a double row running from the Girls School to the parish graveyard in 1809 and 1815, and in the graveyard itself in 1820; and a catalpa struck by lightning in front of the Pottery in 1809. In the front yard of the Stauber farm in Bethania, another Moravian settlement near Winston-Salem, are two tremendous old catalpa trees that, judging from their size and alignment with the house, must have been planted when the house was built in 1852. The larger tree stands sixty-four feet tall, with a trunk

180 inches around at a height of four and one-half feet from the ground. The spread of the crown is fifty-two feet.

The southern catalpa has a limited natural range and is thought to be native only to western Georgia, western Florida, Alabama, and eastern Mississippi. It has large, broad, heart-shaped, light green leaves that end in a tapering point. In late spring the showy flowers appear in large pyramidal clusters. Orchidlike and ruffled on the edges, the blossoms seem to be all white at first glance, but closer scrutiny reveals yellow striping and purple-brown spotting inside the flowers. A few weeks after the flowers are gone, long, thin, green, beanlike pods hang in clusters all over the trees. It is occasionally available in a dwarf form, a golden-leaved form, and one with variegated foliage.

The other American species of catalpa is the northern or western catalpa (*C. speciosa*), which is native to the Mississippi Valley from Indiana to the Gulf and is more cold hardy. It is more common in the wild in East Texas, while southern catalpa is more common in landscapes. When settlers began moving into that area and found catalpas, they thought they belonged to the same species as the southern catalpa. However, John Ashton Warder of Cincinnati, Ohio, the publisher of the *Western Horticultural Review,* recognized the new trees as a distinct species and published the first description of the northern catalpa in his magazine in 1853.

Distinguishing the two species is difficult, especially when the trees are young and not in flower. Even foresters sometimes confuse the two. The northern catalpa is a much taller tree, growing straight up like a hickory, and may reach a height of one hundred feet. The southern species has a much broader crown and at maturity may measure sixty feet tall. In addition, the southern catalpa starts branching very low on its central trunk, so that its heavy, stout branches form a loosely rounded crown. Its bark is dark grayish, thin, and scaly, while that of the northern catalpa is thick and ridged. But for the amateur the easiest distinguishing mark of the northern catalpa is that it blooms two weeks earlier

Southern catalpa *(Catalpa bignonioides)*
(Photo by Greg Grant)

than the southern catalpa. Though they are both beautiful, I'm partial to the northern catalpa (despite the name) because of its stately size and habit. Both are native and widely naturalized in the South.

Catalpas are easy to move, even from the wild, and can be transplanted almost bare root. They grow rapidly, and a large catalpa in full bloom is a magnificent sight.

If catalpas have today lost their fame as an ornamental tree for Southern gardens, they are still beloved by fishermen as a source of catalpa worms, which are prized as freshwater fish bait. Harvesting catalpa worms with my Papaw, Eloy Emanis, was a particular treat for me growing up. He would even freeze them in milk jugs of cornmeal for later use. The worm is a three-inch-long, greenish yellow caterpillar similar to the tobacco worm; when mature, it exhibits distinctive, horizontal green and black stripes. It is the larva of the catalpa sphinx moth and feeds only on catalpas. Its appetite matches its size, and an infestation of catalpa worms may defoliate a tree entirely—fortunately, the tree soon recovers, rapidly producing a new crop of leaves.—*GG*

The authors would like to thank their late dear friend Flora Ann Bynum for her research and contribution to the catalpa information.

Celosia cristata

Cockscomb
Family: Amaranthaceae (Amaranth)
Size: 1–5 ft
Zones: NA
Warm-season annual
Velvety red or pink (occasionally orange or yellow)

The name *Celosia* comes from the Greek word *kelos,* meaning "burned"; this, apparently, refers to the look of the flowers in some species. In China, where it is extensively cultivated, this

Cockscomb *(Celosia cristata)* (Photo by Greg Grant)

flower is called *chi kuan* (cockscomb). Most believe *C. cristata* developed from *C. argentea,* which is listed as native to India but is common in the wild in China. Cited by the English herbalist John Gerard in 1633 as "Velvet Floures Gentle (*Amaranthus pannicula incura holifera*)," it was also known in early times as purple amaranth, floramor, and flower gentle. Under any and all of these names, cockscomb has been grown in American gardens since the eighteenth century.

Three forms were introduced into England from Asia in 1570. In 1709, John Lawson, author of *A New Voyage to Carolina,* noted, "Prince's Feather very large and beautiful" in the gardens of Carolina. According to Raymond Taylor, the plant was in Virginia in 1739. In 1760, "Indian Branching cockscombs" were listed for sale in Boston, and Thomas Jefferson sowed seeds of cockscomb on April 2, 1767, at Monticello.

There are three main types of celosia: crested, plumed, and spiked. My favorite has always been the crested or fasciated type, maybe because my family has always raised chickens. Flowers may be red, pink, orange, yellow, or variegated, and there are attractive red-leaved varieties as well. Although many dwarf cultivars are available today, the original types were fairly tall plants. My late dear friend Flora Ann Bynum found one over seven feet tall one summer in North Carolina. And I thought everything in Texas was bigger!

In addition to Flora Ann's type, my mom grows a smaller branching type. Both make excellent fresh or dried cut flowers and are highly variable in size, shape, and branching habit. It's very important to grow only one type per garden and to save seed from only the most desirable forms, however, as they will cross and revert to inferior "prince's feather" types with tassels instead of combs.

Apparently the branching type has been in and out of favor. Joseph Breck, in his book *The Flower Garden* (1851), writes, "There are the tall and the dwarf varieties, and some that are somewhat branching; but these last should be rejected." But this opinion is directly contradicted by Thomas More in an article in *Floral Magazine* that I found quoted in a book of 1906—*Hortus Veitchii* by English nurseryman James Veitch. More wrote, "It is not improbable the more branched . . . forms, if carefully selected might in time yield a plumy crimson variety analogous to the golden one we already possess; and this is the result at which growers should aim, rather than to obtain large expanded combs which take away from the elegant aspect of the plant."

I have been fond of these gaudy crested cockscombs since I first saw a row of them planted in a vegetable garden on the way to town with my grandparents. The hot pink velvet heads on stalks taller than I was got burned into my brain for life. I still think of them as "Elvis flowers on sticks."

Whether your cockscombs are branched or unbranched, old or new, they require full sun and adequate moisture. Cockscomb is easily propagated from seed collected in the fall and sown in late spring when the soil warms up. This plant self-sows and may become something of a weed, though it is very easy to pull. Unfortunately, unlike the heirloom strains of taller cockscomb, the dwarf bedding types available from many garden centers today are short-lived and nonreseeding. If you see one you like, you are better off begging some seed from a friendly gardener. Or just place a cut flower in a vase, and the shiny little black seed will fall to the table and appear to crawl about, causing quite a stir among your visitors. There's nothing like seed ticks as dinner guests!—*GG*

Chaenomeles speciosa, Cydonia oblonga, and
Pseudocydonia sinensis

Quince, Japonica, Flowering Quince
Family: Rosaceae (Rose)
Size: 3–20 ft
Zones: 5–9
Deciduous shrub or small tree
Showy white, pink, or red flowers in late winter; edible hard fruit

The chief attraction of the flowering quinces is their early bloom — the flowers appear on bare twigs, before the leaves emerge in spring. These blossoms may be red, white, pink, or salmon. The flowers are followed in late summer by oblong to rounded, yellowish green fruits that somewhat resemble pears. These fruits have a pleasant aroma and, though very hard, have been used for making conserves and marmalades. Fruiting on the flowering quinces is erratic, however, in quality and quantity.

Flowering quince *(Chaenomeles speciosa)*
(Photo by William C. Welch)

Flowering quince (*Chaenomeles speciosa*)
(Photo by William C. Welch)

Flowering quinces form a thorny, multistemmed clump and vary from three to six feet or more tall and wide, depending upon the cultivar and the growing conditions. There is an orangish red cultivar sometimes sold as 'Texas Scarlet' that is compact in form and grows well even under poor conditions. My experience with other cultivars is that they prefer well-drained, acidic soils and sunny or partially shaded exposures. Propagation is from cuttings or division of mature clumps.

These plants are of Chinese and Japanese origin. Joseph Banks of the Royal Botanic Garden at Kew introduced them to Western gardening in 1796 under the name *Pyrus japonica*. This was only the first of several names, however; for a time the ornamental flowering quinces were classified as *Cydonia* but now seem to have settled under *Chaenomeles*. Many gardeners still refer to the flowering quinces as "japonicas," and the situation is confusing for anyone trying to trace these plants back through historical documents and descriptions.

Complicating this problem is the existence of a second group of garden plants, the tree quinces, which grow much taller than the flowering quinces, forming (as the name suggests) a small tree. These, which have played a bigger role in the history of Southern gardens, are currently listed under two separate genera. I have invested considerable effort in determining "the correct" name for the heirloom tree quinces and believe that common quince of European origin is properly identified as *Cydonia oblonga,* while the Chinese quince, which is similar in appearance and habit, is named *Pseudocydonia sinensis.*

Taxonomists point to several differences between the two species. Most apparent are that *C. oblonga* has no serrations on the leaf margins and keeps its sepals in the fruit. *Pseudocydonia sinensis* has deeply serrated leaf margins and deciduous sepals. Both of these tree species differ in several ways from the flowering shrub, *Chaenomeles speciosa.* One difference is that the tree types have no thorns.

Chinese quince is an attractive small tree. Pink flowers, peeling reddish bark, and outstanding fall leaf color add to the landscape value of the tree, which usually reaches fifteen to twenty feet. Fire blight has been reported as an occasional problem with quinces. Lynn Lowrey, well-known horticulturist and nurseryman from Houston, extolled the virtues of Chinese quince for many years and successfully planted them as far south and west as New Braunfels, Texas.

The pedigree of this species as a Southern garden plant reaches

Flowering quince *(Chaenomeles speciosa)* (Photo by Greg Grant)

Flowering quince *(Chaenomeles speciosa)*
(Photo by Greg Grant)

back well into the last century. This I learned from a reference I found in the Cherokee Garden Library in Atlanta, W. W. Meech's book of 1888, *Quince Culture*. In the section titled "Varieties of the Quince," Meech states:

> Chinese Quince (*Cydonia sinensis*) is a variety cultivated for ornament. [The name for Chinese quince was changed to *Pseudocydonia sinensis* around 1990.] In the Southern States it is in favor for its fruit, which sometimes attains a weight of two and a half pounds. I have found the quality good for a preserve, though the grain is a little course [*sic*]. The tree grows to the height of thirty feet or more. The foliage assumes a beautiful

red tint in autumn. The flowers are rosy red, with a violet odor.
It blooms in May. The fruit is a very large, smooth, oblong-
oval, and of a greenish yellow. The flesh is firm; and when
preserved turns a beautiful pink. It ripens late, and keeps a
long time in sound condition. . . . It succeeds . . . in the United
States south of Maryland.

An even earlier reference to the Chinese quince comes from
P. Barry's *The Fruit Garden* (1851). In a section titled "Quinces
for Ornament," Barry remarks:

Chinese . . . quite different in appearance from other quinces.
The leaves are glossy, sharply and beautifully toothed; the fruit
is large, oblong, bright yellow, and keeps until spring; little
used. The flowers are large and showy, with the fragrance of
the violet; worked on the other sorts, rather tender, requiring
a sheltered situation. Usually cultivated for ornament. A very
tardy bearer.

Bill and Florence Griffin of Atlanta procured a handsome specimen of quince for the Tullie Smith garden at the Atlanta History
Center. Serrations on the leaf margins indicate that this specimen
is *P. sinensis*. The fruit of this tree is ovoid in shape and, when
ripe, is golden yellow in color and from four to six inches long. I
also remember nice specimens of this species planted by Emory
Smith at his garden on Highland Road in Baton Rouge (now
Hilltop Arboretum). The fruit is highly aromatic and was traditionally displayed in bowls in the home. Its pink flowers and
handsome fruit make it an attractive small tree. *Cydonia oblonga*,
the second species of tree quince prominent in Southern gardens, is the common fruiting quince naturalized in the hills and
woodlands of Italy, the south of France, Spain, Sicily, Sardinia,
and North Africa. According to the ancient Roman encyclopedist
Pliny, "There are many kinds of this fruit in Italy; some growing wild in the hedgerows, others so large that they weigh the

boughs down to the ground." The Romans boiled the fruit of this plant with honey, much as modern cooks make marmalade. Today, *C. oblonga* is important as an understock for pears as well as for its own fruit.

The late Flora Ann Bynum, former secretary-treasurer of the Southern Garden History Society, lived in Old Salem, North Carolina. After visiting the quince at the Tullie Smith garden in Atlanta, Flora Ann wrote in a letter to me dated October 17, 1990, about a quince that appears to be *C. oblonga:*

> There is an old quince tree here in a yard in Salem, which I trotted up to see as soon as I got home Tuesday; it is in leaf much like the Tullie quince, but the edges of the Tullie quince leaves are very serrated, while the leaves of the Salem quince have a smooth edge. Also, the Salem quince has one glorious fruit on it, a beautiful golden yellow, shaped just like a very, very large Golden Delicious apple, but flatter. The fruit was obviously mature because of the color, but nowhere near the size or shape Florence Griffin tells me the Tullie quince gets.

The selection of quinces available to gardeners of the last century seems to have been rich, at least in Georgia. In the collection of antique nursery catalogues at the Cherokee Garden Library in the Atlanta History Center, I found references to the following: Fruitland Nurseries (1858) had 'Portugal' and 'Angers' varieties; Pomona Hall Nursery (Clarksville, Georgia, 1856) listed pear-shaped quince, apple-shaped quince, and 'Angers'; and Down-ing-Hill Nursery in 1855–56 noted 'Apple,' 'Orange,' 'Portugal,' and 'Cocksackie,' while in 1870–71 it listed 'Apple,' 'Orange,' and 'Angers.'

In my own files, I also turned up some indications of the availability of quinces in other areas of the South. For example, Affleck's Southern Nurseries, near Natchez, Mississippi, in its 1851–52 catalogue lists both Chinese quince and *C. oblonga:* "Quince-Apple shaped, Lemon, Portugals, Pear shaped and Chinese; a handsome and hardy plant; fruit very large and excel-

Flowering quince (*Chaenomeles lagernaria*), providing late winter color when little else is blooming (Photo by William C. Welch)

lent. 75 cents." Another listing came from nearer my home, in the catalogue of Fairview Fruit Farm in Brenham, Texas, which in its 1875 catalogue advertised "Quinces—'Angers,' 'Apple' or 'Orange,' and 'Chinese'—of immense size, rather coarse, but desirable for its magnificent appearance."

Martha Turnbull provided forty-eight years (1837–95) of illuminating details of her gardening activities at Rosedown Plantation near St. Francisville, Louisiana. She refers several times to "eating quinces" and described growing plants from seed. She also refers to specific quinces as "Aunt Sarah Quince" and "Aunt Isabelle's" quince (1864).

A. J. Downing, in his classic *Fruits and Fruit Trees of America* published in 1857, provides considerable insight into the culture of quinces:

> The Quince grows naturally in rather moist soil, by the side of rivulets and streams of water. Hence it is a common idea that it should always be planted in some damp neglected part of the garden, where it usually receives little care, and the fruit is often knotty and inferior. This practice is a very erroneous one. No tree is more benefited by manuring than the quince. In a rich, mellow, deep soil, even if quite dry, it grows with thrice its usual vigour and bears abundant crops of large and fair fruit. It should, therefore, be planted in deep and good soil, kept in

constant cultivation, and it should have top-dressing of manure every season, when fair and abundant crops are desired. As to pruning, or other care, it requires very little indeed—an occasional thinning out of crowding or decayed branches, being quite sufficient. Thinning the fruit, when there is an overcrop, improves the size of the remainder. Ten feet apart is a suitable distance at which to plant this tree.

Gilbert Onderdonk, a well-educated and successful nurseryman in Victoria County, Texas, was influential in all areas of the nursery business but specialized in fruit. In his Mission Valley Nurseries descriptive catalogue for 1888 he wrote concerning quinces, "When properly treated the quince does well here. Nothing turns up its nose quicker at a poor soil than the quince. Plant in rich soil, apply a little salt on the surface of the ground each year. The Apple or Orange quince is well tested here. Priced 50 cents." Judging from his description, the quinces Onderdonk was describing were probably *Cydonia oblonga*.

For a tree that once was listed in almost every nursery catalogue in the South, quinces are surprisingly rare today. This is especially true in the case of *C. oblonga;* the *P. sinensis* is certainly not common but is found more often than *C. oblonga*. Fire blight, quince rust, and other diseases seem to be responsible for this near disappearance of a once-classic plant. My own experience with them in Richland Parish, Louisiana, has shown considerable difficulty with fire blight. Some trees have been completely killed, and others severely damaged. My plants were seedlings and were somewhat variable. They have produced some fruit. It will be interesting to continue to observe them.

Yet there are faint promises of a return. Lynn Lowrey in Houston reported little or no fire blight on the Chinese quinces he had planted, and Flora Ann Bynum reported of the specimen in Old Salem that as of the summer of 1994 it was thriving and loaded with fruit. The quinces were once an important part of the Southern landscape and cuisine—perhaps they will be again.—*WCW*

Chilopsis linearis

Desert Willow
Family: Bignoniaceae (Trumpet Creeper)
Size: 10–25 ft
Zones: 8–11 (particularly in the Southwest)
Small deciduous tree
Purple, pink, or white flowers in late spring and summer

I first encountered this native Texas tree as a xeriscape plant for the Southwest and assumed it was a modern introduction—so imagine how surprised I was to learn that almost every early Texas nursery carried desert willow.

As is so often the case, the common name for this plant is deceptive. The desert willow is not a willow at all, though it looks like one, with its narrow foliage and somewhat weeping habit. Native to dryland habitats in West Texas, the southwestern United States, and Mexico, desert willow is a drought-tolerant,

Desert willow *(Chilopsis linearis)* (Photo by Greg Grant)

Desert willow *(Chilopsis linearis)* (Photo by
Greg Grant)

deciduous small tree that blooms on and off from summer till
frost, bearing lavender and white, snapdragon-like blossoms.

A purple form and a white one were listed in Gilbert Onderdonk's 1888 Mission Valley Nurseries catalogue from Nursery,
Texas. About the white form the catalogue says, "A new variety,
now for the first time introduced to the public. It was found by
Dr. Atlee of Laredo, Texas in the sand of the Rio Grande near the
seminary at Laredo. We obtained it from him, and now have a
few plants for sale. It will be considered very beautiful by all who
see it. The foliage is of a paler green than the purple which we
began to disseminate when we first started our nursery in 1870."

By 1898, this same nursery was also offering the cultivar 'Major,' "the largest flowering variety."

In 1895, G. A. Shattenberg's Waldheim Nursery at Boerne, Texas, listed "Purple Flowering Willow. Leaves resemble very much those of the willow. Covered with beautiful clusters of tubular flowers, somewhat like those of Snap Dragon, throughout the season. Drought has no effect on it."

Other early Texas nurseries that carried the desert willow were D. G. Gregory and Son's Val Verde Nurseries at Alleytown, J. F. Leyendecker's Pearfield Nursery at Frelsburg, W. A. Yates's Nursery at Brenham, F. T. Ramsey's Austin Nursery at Austin, and Anna B. Nickels's Arcadia Garden at Laredo. I also found it listed by P. J. Berckmans Fruitland Nurseries of Augusta, Georgia.

Desert willow was grown and admired by early German Texan John Meusebach, a naturalist, nurseryman, politician, and founder of Fredericksburg, Texas. This tree even naturalized around his old homesite and nursery in Loyal Valley in the Hill Country.

Several decades ago Texas A&M University released a number of new cultivars of desert willow, but none seems to have caught on in the trade. A number of dark-flowered selections, including 'Burgundy' and 'Burgundy Lace,' are available in the wholesale nursery trade, however. In addition, Lone Star Growers of San Antonio, Texas, introduced a Paul Cox (San Antonio Botanical Garden) selection named 'Bubba,' which has dark early-blooming flowers, darker green foliage, and an uncharacteristic compact, upright habit. It's a favorite at the Stephen F. Austin Mast Arboretum in Nacogdoches. There is even a seedless one on the market now.

Desert willow is very easy to grow on any site with well-drained soil and full sunlight. It is an extremely drought-tolerant species. Use it in the landscape as you would a crapemyrtle. Propagation is by seed or cuttings of improved selections. —GG

Chionanthus spp.

Fringe Tree, Grancy Graybeard
Family: Oleaceae (Olive)
Size: 10–20 ft
Zones 7–10
Small deciduous tree
Fleecy white flowers in spring

Grancy graybeard (*Chionanthus virginicus*) is one of the best-known and loved native trees of the South. Also known as fringe tree, it is native from Pennsylvania to Florida and west to Texas. It most often occurs in upland pine forests. Mature size is in the range of twenty feet tall and ten feet wide. Flowers are loose and delicate in panicles with fringelike petals to eight inches long. Propagation is from seed or grafting or budding onto ash, a close relative. Grancy graybeard trees prefer acidic soils and tend to be relatively slow growing.

The Chinese fringe tree (*C. retusus*) was discovered by the great Scottish plant explorer Robert Fortune (1812–80) in China in 1845. He found it growing in a garden near Foo Chow and introduced it into commerce. I consider it one of the very best small flowering trees for the South. Dave Creech of Stephen F. Austin University, a connoisseur of trees, also thinks this is "one of the stellar large shrubs or small trees for the South." The SFA Mast Arboretum planted seventy-five Chinese fringe trees in February 1999 to celebrate the seventy-fifth anniversary of the university. It is considered by many to be superior to the native form (*C. virginicus*) with its showy carpet of pure white blooms in April and May. The shiny foliage is deciduous and oblong, three to five inches long and half as wide. Mature size is fifteen to twenty feet tall and almost as wide.

I first became acquainted with Chinese fringe tree in 1977 when I obtained one from native plant legend Lynn Lowrey of Houston. I was at Lynn's nursery when a truck arrived from Tom

Chinese fringe tree (Chionanthus retusus)
(Photo by William C. Welch)

Dodd's Nursery near Mobile, Alabama. Among the plants were a few one-gallon-size Chinese fringe trees that were in bloom. I couldn't resist having one but thought it would probably end up a casualty in my College Station garden. I set it out in an east-facing raised bed at our then-new home on Langford Street. We lived there until 1999, and the Chinese fringe tree became more beautiful each year.

When we built our new home in 1999, I couldn't leave the Chinese fringe tree behind and had it professionally moved to the new location in another raised planting area, but this time facing west. It has continued to prosper and creates a sensation each spring when it blooms. There is also a pleasant fragrance from the flowers.

Although easily grown, Chinese fringe trees are not readily propagated. Seeds require a complicated double-dormancy treatment; young juvenile hardened cuttings taken in June and treated with rooting hormone are a starting point for a several-month-long rooting process. For this reason, plants are more expensive and less available than we would like.

Grancy graybeard *(Chionanthus virginicus)*
(Photo by Greg Grant)

Robert Fortune was a colorful plant explorer who brought back many fine plants from the East. In addition to the Chinese fringe tree he brought and introduced to Europe and America *Rosa × fortuniana, Lonicera fragrantissima,* holly fern (*Cyrtomium falcata*), and Japanese anemone (*Anemone japonica*). According to research by Texas plant historian Mary Anne Pickens,* Fortune introduced 190 plants, 120 of which were completely new to science. —*WCW*

*Proceedings of the Sixth Annual Fall Gardening Symposium, October 1999, University of Texas Center for American History and Texas Cooperative Extension Service.

Citrus spp., *Fortunella* spp., and *Poncirus trifoliata*

Citrus
Family: Rutaceae (Rue)
Size: 6–20 ft
Zones: 9–10
Large shrub or small tree
Fragrant flowers in spring and edible fruit, generally in the fall

There are at least sixteen species and several genera that compose plants that we call citrus. All are native to South and Southeast Asia and the Malay Peninsula.

Most citrus species are tropical in origin and are killed outright or severely damaged when temperatures drop below freezing. They are highly prized for their fruit but, with their large, shiny, evergreen foliage and highly fragrant white to purplish flowers, are also valuable as ornamentals. Some are best cultivated as shrubs, while others are useful as small trees. Most are grown as grafted plants with the common understocks being sour and trifoliate orange.

Kumquat *(Fortunella margarita)* (Photo by William C. Welch)

Trifoliate orange *(Poncirus trifoliata)* (Photo by William C. Welch)

A mature specimen of sweet orange *(Citrus sinensis)* thriving in an old section of the Bolivar Peninsula (Photo by William C. Welch)

'Changsha' tangerine (Photo by William C. Welch)

The Spanish are usually credited with bringing citrus to North America. The sweet orange (*Citrus sinensis*) had been introduced into the lands of the western Mediterranean region by the Romans around the first century AD, following their conquest of the Near East. Columbus is known to have taken orange, lemon, and citron seeds from the Canary Islands with him to Hispaniola on his second voyage in 1493. Thirty years later Oviedo's testimony stated that sweet oranges were already abundant in Hispaniola. Spanish colonists subsequently introduced the trees into coastal areas near Charleston; Savannah; Mobile, Alabama; New Orleans; and St. Augustine, Florida; as well as into South Texas, California, and Mexico. Commercial production of oranges, grapefruit, lemons, limes, satsumas, mandarin oranges, and kumquats has been successful in the South at various times.

The appeal of their fruit and their ornamental qualities had also led to citrus trees' cultivation well to the north of their natural, warm-weather range. Once again, the Romans pioneered this practice, building houses glazed with sheets of mica to cultivate citrons as early as the first century AD. Special glasshouses, later known as "orangeries," designed for growing sweet oranges were common features of northern Italian estates by the fourteenth century, and by the seventeenth century, orangeries were appearing throughout northern Europe. The various kinds of citrus continue to be grown as container and greenhouse plants over much of the world.

A greenhouse is not necessary for growing citrus in much of the South, if the gardener is willing to experiment with the less familiar sorts. Some citrus species are considerably more cold hardy than others. Satsumas and tangerines (*C. reticulata*), kumquats (*Fortunella* sp.), and calamondins (*C. Citrofortunella mitis*) are probably the most cold-hardy edible citrus.

The trifoliate orange (*Poncirus trifoliata*) has inedible fruit, but the plant is prized for its hardiness as an ornamental into zone 7. Its green stems, large and fragrant white flowers, and ease of culture make it useful for very thorny hedges and specimen plantings all over the South. It is an aromatic small tree that can reach thirty feet tall. The fruit is like a small, pubescent, thick-skinned orange.

A native of China, the trifoliate orange was introduced into England in 1850 and by 1894 was listed in the catalogue of J. F. Leyendecker's Pearfield Nursery, Frelsburg, Texas. Leyendecker recommended this species as an ornamental shrub or hedge plant. The ease with which trifoliate oranges are cultivated may be deduced from the fact that they have escaped cultivation in some areas of the South to flourish in the wild. Flying dragon (*P. trifoliata* var. *monstruosa*) is a well-known variety of trifoliate orange that has a most interesting zigzag branching pattern. It is popular as an understock for other citrus or as a specimen landscape plant.

The late Pam Puryear, a garden historian from Navasota, Texas, remembered a handsome four-foot clipped hedge of *P. trifoliata* that used to grow at the Presbyterian manse (c. 1869) in Navasota. It was destroyed in the 1970s when the home was demolished to make way for a new building. Trifoliate oranges are also used for breeding with other citrus for their ability to withstand freezing temperatures.

Satsuma "Brown Select' growing in a sheltered spot in College Station, Texas (Photo by William C. Welch)

‘Changsha’ tangerine growing at Fragilee (Washington County, Texas) (Photo by William C. Welch)

The kumquat (*Fortunella* sp.) is named for Robert Fortune, the great Scottish plant explorer of the mid-1800s, who introduced it to Europe. It has never been found in the native state but is said to be indigenous to China, where it has been cultivated for many years, as it has been in Japan, Indochina, and Java. There are two common cultivars of kumquats: Nagami (*F. margarita*), which is oblong, and Meiwa (*F. margarita × japonica*), which is round. They form dense shrubs that can reach ten to twelve feet in height and spread to about eight feet but may also be kept smaller for many years by confining the roots in containers. Kumquats are among the most cold-hardy citrus and also highly ornamental. With warmer winters of recent years they are becoming more popular. Handsome evergreen foliage, fragrant flowers, and abundant fruit over a long ripening period add to their value.

Kumquat trees flower and fruit much of the year and are prized as container plants, shrubs, hedges, or specimens. The fruit of the kumquat is about one and a half inches in diameter and is sweet and edible when fresh—the entire fruit is eaten, skin and all. Kumquat fruits are also commonly preserved, either as whole fruits or in a high-quality marmalade.

Kumquats are usually budded onto trifoliate orange rootstocks. Although hardier than most citrus, they occasionally freeze or are damaged by cold. Kumquats are extensively used in the restored parterre garden of the Hermann-Grima House in the French Quarter of New Orleans.

Grapefruit is now considered to be a hybrid between the pomelo and the sweet orange. The production of grapefruit is a major enterprise in Florida, South Texas, and California. It is a fruit primarily of American origin with major varieties being developed in the last fifty years or so in the states where they are produced. Grapefruit are among the least cold hardy of citrus.

A cluster of 'Republic of Texas' oranges (Photo by William C. Welch)

As early as the 1960s I was introduced to an interesting citrus—'Changsha' tangerine—by Lynn Lowrey in Houston. Lynn considered it the most cold hardy of all the citrus he knew. It also was sweet and produced lots of fruit when mature. Most of the ones we were familiar with were grown from seed. Although they mostly came true from seed, they required four or five years to begin producing fruit. Several severe freezes in the 1980s and 1990s damaged the trees, but most survived. They reportedly were cold hardy as far north as Fort Worth at the O. S. Gray Nursery and in College Station. Although this tangerine is productive and handsome as a small tree, the sweet fruit is fairly seedy, making it less desirable than satsumas and other slip-skin tangerines. 'Changsha' tangerines are rarely available in the nursery trade but are an asset to the garden while extending the northern range of citrus.

Fruit of 'Republic of Texas' oranges. The tree produces good-quality fruit every year at Fragilee (Washington County, Texas). (Photo by William C. Welch)

Satsuma mandarins (*C. unshiu*) are particularly popular and successful in the South. They are Greg's (and many others') favorite citrus for fresh eating because of their delicate low-acid flavor, seedless fruit, and "kid-glove" skin that practically falls off with minimal peeling required. These are the same fruit most are familiar with from cans and used in ambrosia salads. Canned fruits do not hold a candle to fresh picked ones, which are occasionally available from roadside stands along the Gulf Coast. They are among the easiest citrus to grow in backyard gardens and more cold hardy than oranges, grapefruit, lemons, or limes. Jerry Parsons and Larry Stein with Texas AgriLife Extension, along with the late Joe Bradbury, have introduced three new Japanese cultivars to the nursery trade: 'Miho,' 'Okitsu,' and 'Seto.' Traditionally, 'Owari' was the only cultivar available. They are all delicious.

Sweet oranges were especially important to the early gardens of Charleston, South Carolina, where they were grown commercially as well as in many of the famous courtyards of the city. The devastating freezes of 1898–99 killed most of the trees in the area. New Orleans also has a tradition of orange trees that go back to the Spanish period, and remnants of a thriving area of commercial orange production still remain south of New Orleans in Plaquemines Parish.

Lemons (*C. limon*) and limes (*C. aurantifolia*) are even less cold hardy than oranges and can be grown outdoors only in tropical areas. 'Meyer Lemon' is slightly more cold hardy than other lemons and is productive when grown in containers as well as in the ground. Most limes are propagated as seedlings and named for their point of origin, such as Key, West Indian, or Mexican limes. Limes are also useful as container plants since they are compact in growth and have fruit or fragrant flowers many months of the year. Citrus trees grow best in well-drained soils and require vigilant pest and weed control to thrive and produce well. Scale insects, white flies, and numerous diseases attack the fruit and plant. Members of the citrus family are the host plant for the beautiful black and yellow giant swallowtail butterfly. — *WCW*

Cortaderia selloana

Pampas and other grasses
Family: Poaceae (Grass)
Size: 5–8 ft
Zones: 8–10
Perennial
Showy flower spikes in summer and fall

The ornamental use of grasses has always seemed modern to me. A native of South America, pampas grass was the only ornamental grass in common use in the South as I was growing up. It was so common that upper-crust gardeners considered it tired and coarse. Then in the 1980s the ornamental grass wave started. Beginning in Europe and then the northeastern United States, landscapes began to appear with great sweeps of ornamental grasses, including Japanese maiden grass (*Miscanthus* spp.), feather reed grass (*Calamagrostis* spp.), and fountain grass (*Pennisetum* spp.). Designers Wolfgang Oehme and James Van

Pampas grass *(Cortaderia selloana* 'Pumila') (Photo by Greg Grant)

Pampas grass (*Cortaderia selloana* 'Pumila') (Photo by Greg Grant)

Sweden started a lasting naturalistic trend, including ornamental grasses, known as "the new American garden." Naturally, I assumed these grasses were new and modern as well. Imagine the surprise when I thumbed through my collection of old nursery catalogues to see that many nineteenth-century Southern nurseries carried ornamental grasses. It does make sense that they would have worked well as architectural specimens in Victorian landscapes. In 1888, Gilbert Onderdonk's Mission Valley Nursery in Nursery, Texas (near present-day Victoria), listed both white and pink pampas grass along with ravenna grass (*Erianthus ravennae*), variegated Eulalia grass (*M. sinensis* 'Variegatus'), and lemon grass (*Cymbopogon citratus*). Other nurseries listed the nonvariegated Eulalia (Japanese maiden) grass as well.

Ornamental grasses are very easy to grow, requiring limited maintenance. As a rule they need little to no fertilizer and modest amounts of water, have few insect or disease problems, and only require cutting back once a year before their new growth emerges. They are outstanding as specimen plants either in the ground or in containers and as mass bedding plants. They are

Inland sea oats (*Chasmanthium latifolium*) (Photo by Greg Grant)

exceptional at softening harsh elements in the landscape such as building corners, benches, and sharp turns along paths. They also impart a pleasing sense of calm near sitting areas. And their long-lasting blooms (either fresh or dried), as well as foliage, are perfect for floral design.

If introduced grasses were kings of the twenty-first century, then native American grasses are set to rule in the twenty-second century. Less than 1 percent of the grass-covered Great Plains that lie in the heart of America remains today. Almost all of the grass- and wildflower-covered coastal plains of Texas have been either destroyed by development, farming, and grazing or taken over by the highly invasive Chinese tallow tree. Conservation of these ever-important natural resources is now a great concern. Let's hope it's not too late.

Some of our native American grasses are useful as ornamental plants in gardens. Among those currently in use in Southern gardens are Gulf Coast muhly (*Muhlenbergia capillaris*), Indian grass (*Sorghastrum nutans*), little bluestem (*Schizachyrium scoparium*), sugarcane plume grass (*Saccharum giganteum*), inland

Japanese maiden grass *(Miscanthus sinensis* 'Gracillimus') (Photo by Greg Grant)

Variegated Eulalia grass *(Miscanthus sinensis* 'Variegatus') (Photo by Greg Grant)

Zebra grass (*Miscanthus sinensis* 'Zebrinus') (Photo by Greg Grant)

sea oats (*Chasmanthium latifolium*), and switch grass (*Panicum virgatum*). In addition to being considered for biomass fuel production, ornamental cultivars of switch grass are available. My personal favorite is the compact, upright 'Northwind.'

As some are using native grasses in their beds and borders, others are taking on more substantial restoration projects such as small "pocket prairies" and even large-scale prairie re-creation and restoration. I have created a pocket prairie of my own next to my great-grandparents' old dogtrot house. Many of the plants in it have been rescued from the imperiled roadside running in front of the house. Improper mowing, careless herbicide use, and highway repair projects have all but eliminated the incredible and beautiful diversity that was there. I am especially aiming to re-create a scene from just down the road that includes masses of the pink drooping "purple" coneflower (*Echinacea sanguinea*) and the electric blue Carolina larkspur (*Delphinium caroliniana*). Other local favorites that I'm concentrating on include button blazing star (*Liatris aspera*), prairie phlox (*Phlox pilosa*), white spider lily (*Hymenocallis occidentalis eulae*), and white

Japanese maiden grass (*Miscanthus sinensis*) (Photo by Greg Grant)

Gulf Coast muhly *(Muhlenbergia capillaris)*
(Photo by William C. Welch)

Gulf Coast muhly *(Muhlenbergia capillaris)*
(Photo by William C. Welch)

false indigo (*Baptisia alba*). I'm encouraging little bluestem, split-beard bluestem (*Andropogon ternarius*), and sideoats grama (*Bouteloua curtipendula*) as my short-grass cover, while trying to discourage the invasive, introduced Bahiagrass, bermudagrass, and annual ryegrass, which all heavily compete with native wildflowers.

Nearby I'm also creating a ten-acre tallgrass prairie seeded with a number of southeastern native grasses, including big bluestem (*Andropogon gerardii*), bushy bluestem (*A. glomeratus*), little bluestem, broomsedge bluestem, Indian grass (*Sorghastrum nutans*), Eastern gamagrass (*Tripsacum dactyloides*), Canada wildrye (*Elymus canadensis*) and Virginia wildrye (*E. virginicus*), sideoats grama (the state grass of Texas), switchgrass, purpletop (*Tridens flavus*), sand dropseed (*Sporobolus cryptandrus*), and sand lovegrass (*Eragrostis trichodes*). Prairie creation requires much patience, something many avid gardeners are short on. It took thousands of years for these American treasures to develop, and they can't be duplicated in a single season. It will be my particular pleasure to help it succeed. I just hope the missing quail and turkey come back as well. —*GG*

Sugarcane plume grass *(Saccharum giganteum)* Greg Grant

Crataegus opaca

Family: Rosaceae (Rose)
Size: 10–20 ft
Zones: 4–9
Small deciduous tree
White flowers in late winter and edible fruit for jelly in late spring

This is an attractive and unusual small tree, an asset to almost any garden. Yet its interest for our ancestors lay in its fruits. In the mid-1800s and early 1900s, Southerners relied mainly on the native fruits that were growing close by and ate whatever was in season. Therein is the mayhaw's special value: it is the first native tree to flower in the late winter, so the first to ripen fruit, yielding its harvest in early spring (April and early May).

The mayhaw fruits are unfamiliar to most Southerners today, and for information on them we turned to Marty Baker, formerly extension horticulturist at the Texas A&M Research

Mayhaw (*Crataegus opaca*) (Photo by Greg Grant)

and Extension Center in Overton. He has a special interest and expertise in mayhaws and has provided the following information on them.

Ripe mayhaws signal the end of winter in the South. This event comes in April or May, when the small (five-eighths to one inch in diameter), applelike, fragrant fruits are gathered and processed into syrups, jellies, pies, wine, and vinegar. The fruit has ornamental value while still on the tree, and the showy white blossoms that precede them (opening in January and February) are especially welcome. L. H. Bailey in his *Sketch of the Evolution of Our Native Fruits* (1898) refers to mayhaws as thorn-apples and states: "Several of these thorn-apples produce fruit of great beauty, and some of the fruits are pulpy and edible, and are esteemed in various localities."

The mayhaw is native to wetland areas across much of the South. As a teenager in the 1930s, Marvin Baker (Marty Baker's father) rode twelve miles on horseback from Burke, Texas, to Taggert's Flat, located two miles east of the Neches River in Angelina County to gather mayhaw fruit in late April. The fruit was gathered from flooded, flat river bottoms filled with one to three feet of water for nine months of the year. After being swept from the water's surface, the mayhaws were put into cotton sacks. At home, Marvin's mother would boil the whole fruit in water to make syrup, which was the first fresh fruit product to appear on the table after the cold winter months.

Selections have been collected from various regions—from the Neches River bottom, in flooded flats north of Buna, and in groves close to Deweyville, Texas; in the Pearl River swamps of Mississippi; in lowlands around Logansport, Louisiana; and in groves near Thomasville, Georgia—and planted in upland orchards to produce numerous clones, some of which are available today. Although native to wetlands, mayhaws also thrive on drier sites and are sufficiently attractive to plant in shrub or herbaceous borders, where they will form fifteen- to thirty-foot trees. They grow best in acidic soils.

Cooking mayhaw fruit *(Crataegus opaca)* to make jelly (Photo by Greg Grant)

The following recipes are from J. S. Akin of Sibley, Louisiana, and Billie Jean Capps of Diboll, Texas.

Mayhaw Syrup
1 cup mayhaw juice (as for jelly)
½ cup sugar
½ cup white Karo (to prevent jelling)
Boil rapidly 18–20 minutes.

Mayhaw Jelly
To cook mayhaws:
1 gallon mayhaws and 1 gallon water
Cook until tender; strain through a cloth; squeeze out all juice. This should make 10 cups of juice. If not, add enough water to make 10 cups.

To make jelly:
5 cups mayhaw juice
7 cups sugar
1 box Sure-Jell
Cook as directed on Sure-Jell instructions.

Mayhaw (*Crataegus opaca*) (Photo by William C. Welch)

Mayhaw seed viability varies greatly from tree to tree. Pulped fruit from trees with viable seeds can be fermented from three to six days at warm room temperatures above seventy-five degrees Fahrenheit. The seeds are then removed from the pulp and washed with water through a screened colander. These seeds generally have excellent germination percentages. A more tested method is to clean the seed and store in damp sand at about thirty-five degrees Fahrenheit for eight months before planting. Also, many gardeners have had success by removing the pulp from fresh fruit and planting seed under intermittent mist systems.

Mayhaw cuttings can be rooted under intermittent mist or in a humidity chamber during the summer. Dipping in a root-promoting hormone may facilitate rooting. Plants grafted onto understocks or rooted from cuttings will produce fruit like the plant from which the cutting or graft was taken.

After World War II, a few hobbyists and farmers tinkered with mayhaws and marketed small amounts of jellies and syrups at roadside stands. The mayhaw's full potential has not been recognized yet, but it is receiving a degree of attention now. In at least four states, including Texas, agricultural scientists are learning how to manage the mayhaw as a crop, like apples, pears, and other fruit. Unfortunately, the plants are proving susceptible to fire blight, cedar apple rust, and other problems that challenge fruit crops.

Cultivation may be important to the mayhaw's survival, for many native stands have been destroyed or threatened by development and changes in natural drainage patterns. This tree is a distinctive part of our Southern heritage and is worth cultivating in our landscapes as an ornamental or edible fruiting plant. —*WCW*

Crinum spp.

Crinum, Crinum Lily, Milk and Wine Lily
Family: Amaryllidaceae (Amaryllis)
Size: 1–4 ft
Zones: 7–11
Perennial bulb
Showy white, pink, or striped flowers in spring, summer, or fall

> The various species of Crinum belong to the most important,
> the most beautiful and the most popular of Florida garden
> plants. No plants grow so easily, with so little attention, and no
> plants are so floriferous and so deliciously fragrant.
> —Henry Nehrling, *Bailey's Standard Encyclopedia of Horticul-*
> *ture,* volume 2, 1917

Although they do not rank among the oldest horticultural heirlooms of our region, in the past hundred years, crinums have
become synonymous with Southern gardens. In many ways, they
remind me of Texas and the South. They're huge, the biggest of
all bulbs. They're so showy and fragrant that they border on being
obnoxious, so tough that Bill claims none have ever died—and
he may be right.

As members of the amaryllis family (not the lily family),
crinums are often found listed as *Amaryllis* in old references.
According to *Hortus Third,* there are about 130 species of crinums, native mainly to the tropics and South Africa. Originally
grown as greenhouse specimens, these bulbs became common
Southern dooryard plants around the turn of the century.

Most early crinums made their trip to the United States by
way of the Caribbean, some as early as the mid-1800s. Many
were introduced through Florida nurseries. The first U.S. nursery to list crinums was likely Reasoner's Royal Palms Nursery
at Manatee, Florida, which began selling the bulbs as early as
1886. Some crinums also arrived by way of Dutch nurseries

Crinum jaegus ratrayii (Photo by William C.
Welch)

'Carroll Abbott' crinum (*Crinum* × 'Carroll Abbott') (Photo by Greg Grant)

'Cecil Houdyshel' crinum (*Crinum* × 'Cecil Houdyshel') (Photo by Greg Grant)

such as Krelage and Van Tubergen. Around 1837, Krelage listed seven crinums, including *Crinum americanum* and two forms of *C. bulbispermum*. The southern swamp lily (*C. americanum*) is our only native crinum and, as the name indicates, is native to local wetlands. It is often confused with our native white spider lily (*Hymenocallis* spp.). *Crinum bulbispermum* (formerly *C. capense, C. longifolium,* and *Amaryllis longifolia*) is our most commonly cultivated species and the most cold hardy as well. A native of South Africa, it is often found naturalized in ditches, in cemeteries, and around old homesites in the South. Its rather small, drooping, trumpet-shaped flowers may be white, pink, or striped. Usually the first crinum to bloom in spring, it may continue flowering until frost. Its wide, straplike, blue-gray foliage, which cascades and twists upon the ground, reminds me of a giant allium. This species is one of the parents of most of our common hybrid garden crinums, which inherit *C. bulbispermum*'s mounding foliage along with its cold hardiness and vigor. It seems that this may be a very old garden plant, for in 1629, John Parkinson made reference to a *Narcissus marinus exoticus,* "the strange sea daffodil," which may have been *C. bulbispermum*. In 1859, this crinum also won a mention in Charles Darwin's *Origin of Species* as part of the great naturalist's discussion of William Herbert's work with the pollenization of *C. bulbispermum*.

'Ellen Bosanquet' crinum *(Crinum* × 'Ellen Bosanquet') (Photo by Greg Grant)

This work deserved a mention, for Dean William Herbert (1778–1847), an English minister, botanist, naturalist, artist, and reform politician, has been called the "father of the Amaryllis family." His 1837 *Amaryllidaceae* is considered the greatest taxonomic treatment of this family ever undertaken, and until recently the record for breeding the greatest variety of crinum hybrids indisputably belonged to Herbert. Today, the record is probably held by two Texans, the late Thad Howard, formerly of San Antonio, and David Lehmiller of Kountz.

Certainly, the most commonly cultivated hybrid crinums in the South are *C.* × *herbertii,* a hybrid Herbert first produced around 1837 by crossing *C. scabrum* and *C. bulbispermum*.

Milk and wine lily *(Crinum × gowenii)* (Photo by Greg Grant)

A number of other breeders later produced different variations of this same hybrid. Plants of this group typically have cascading, slightly glaucous green foliage, large flower stalks, and drooping, candy-striped flowers—the source of the common name, "milk and wine lilies." These bloom heavily from summer to fall, shortly after any good rain or irrigation.

Like many crinums, *C. × herbertii* clones are very fragrant. As a child, I always thought they smelled like my mom's hand lotion. To this day when I smell them, they take me back to Grandmother Emanis's porch where the two large clumps on both sides of the steps bathed us with their perfume as we rocked in the swing. In addition to many unnamed forms I have collected, I cultivate one dubbed 'Carroll Abbott,' which has bold dark maroon stripes and is a heavy bloomer. The late Carroll Abbott was considered "Mr. Texas Wildflowers" by many and introduced this bulb to the geophyte world.

It is possible that some of Herbert's material filtered into Florida by way of Bermuda or other British possessions. Crosses between *C. zeylanicum* and *C. bulbispermum* are also considered milk and wine lilies, with the timeless *C. × gowenii* being our most historic example. According to Scott Ogden this Southern

Milk and wine lily *(Crinum × herbertii)* (Photo by Greg Grant)

'Mardi Gras' crinum (*Crinum* × 'Mardi Gras') (Photo by Greg Grant)

stalwart was bred by J. R. Gowen in England around 1820 and probably came into the South in the mid-1800s. It has pointed "fingernails" on the ends of the buds and petals and is another favorite of mine. My start came from an old home in historic Nacogdoches, Texas, that was demolished to make way for a new surgery center. The pale striped flowers appear almost white during the summer heat. Generally, all crinums with striped flowers are collectively known as milk and wine lilies.

The most common hybrid crinum in the upper South is the relatively cold-hardy *C.* × *powellii*. This cross between *C. moorei* and *C. bulbispermum* was described in 1887 and introduced in 1888. A number of variations of this hybrid exist, including the varieties *album* (white), *roseum* (pink), and *rubrum* (red). Van Tubergen listed three clones in 1895. *Crinum* × *powellii*, a summer bloomer, has neater foliage than *C.* × *herbertii* and tall slender flowers stalks with more erect flowers—not quite as gaudy. It is available from a number of commercial bulb sources. 'Cecil Houdyshel' is a small-flowered pink form that produces many blooms throughout the season.

'Mrs. James Hendry' crinum (*Crinum* × 'Mrs. James Hendry') (Photo by Greg Grant)

'Sangria' crinum (*Crinum* × 'Sangria')
(Photo by Greg Grant)

Another hybrid commonly encountered in the South is 'J. C. Harvey.' This plant is a cross between *C. kirkii* and *C. moorei* or *C. kirkii* and *C. yemense* that J. C. Harvey developed late in the last century in southern California and grew later on the Isthmus of Tehuantepec in Mexico. The Reasoner Brothers of the Royal Palms Nursery first marketed it in 1902. 'J. C. Harvey' has neat, cornlike foliage and blooms in summertime, bearing light

Pink crinum lilies (*Crinum* × 'Bradley')
(Photo by Greg Grant)

'Mrs. James Hendry' crinum (*Crinum* × 'Mrs. James Hendry') (Photo by William C. Welch)

pink flowers similar to those of *C.* × *powellii* on slender stems. Though it multiplies rapidly, it is a rather shy bloomer, which probably explains why most crinums given away turn out to be 'J. C. Harvey.' I once rescued a whole clump sitting cheerfully by the roadside in San Antonio among discarded trash. Another frequently found, fairly hardy hybrid is 'Ellen Bosanquet,' a Louis Bosanquet introduction. It is apparently a cross between *C. scabrum* and *C. moorei* and has semi-erect and wavy green foliage that may burn a little on hot, sunny sites. From summer to fall 'Ellen Bosanquet' bears attractive dark pink flowers. Some even call it a "red" crinum. It makes a very striking cut flower and has a nice scent. It was Grandmother Emanis's favorite, and I have hundreds of them. 'Mardi Gras' is a similar Thad Howard hybrid with even darker pink flowers, while 'Bradley' is a more delicate interpretation from Australia.

There are a number of rather common hybrids of *C. americanum,* including 'Elsie,' which Elizabeth Lawrence originally found in an Atlanta garden. This cultivar is reportedly common in old gardens of coastal North Carolina. Like most of our enduring hybrids, its other parent appears to be *C. bulbispermum.* These

Crinum jaegus ratrayii (Photo by William C. Welch)

hybrids are known as *Crinum × digweedii*. One that is common throughout Texas is 'Royal White,' a milk and wine type. It is also known as the Nassau lily. I got my start from Granny Ruth and planted it on her grave. These *C. americanum* hybrids have loose, somewhat spidery blossoms and a pleasing fragrance.

One of my favorite species of crinum is *C. macowanii,* which has fat balloonlike bulbs and reflexed petal tips. It, too, is from Africa. It has given rise to a number of beautiful hybrids, including one of my all-time favorites, 'White Queen,' which was bred by the late Luther Burbank of Santa Rosa, California. In my eyes, he is no doubt the most prolific and talented plant breeder that has ever lived. Friend, teacher, and author of *Bulbs for the South,* Scott Ogden first shared this crinum with me. I also grow what appears to be a huge *C. macowanii* hybrid that I obtained from Fanick's Nursery years ago in San Antonio that I call "Fanick's Giant White." It is a very prolific bloomer with faint pink stripes and the same striking reflexed petals. The late Eddie Fanick and his son John were my dear friends and mentors. Luckily the third generation of Fanicks continues the historic nursery today.

Scott also shared 'Sangria' with me, the only hardy maroon-leaved crinum available. It is a chance hybrid of the tender red-leaved *C. procerum* 'Splendens' and, of course, *C. bulbispermum.* It has delicate pink *Nerine*-like flowers and is very slow to multiply. Following Scott's recipe, I re-created the same cross while working at Mercer Arboretum in Humble by using *C. bulbispermum* 'Album' as a seed parent. All the seedlings were green except one. It bloomed for the first time last year with a pale pink flower. I was hoping for an Aggie crinum with white flowers and maroon leaves! It must be pretty good, however, as somebody tried to steal it but couldn't get it out of the ground. One of Bill's favorite crinums is 'Mrs. James Hendry,' a Henry Nehrling introduction, whose delicate pink blossoms are known for their delicious fragrance. To me, it smells like Fruit Loops and perfume. Many consider Henry Nehrling to be the father of amaryllid culture in the South. Bill also loves *C. jaegus ratrayii,* which has pristine white tulip-shaped flowers that smell like vanilla above attractive upright foliage. There are many other cultivars of crinums in a wide range of shapes, sizes, and colors. Thanks to tissue culture and specialty sources, they are becoming more and more available.

Crinums are very easy to grow throughout the South. They multiply best, however, in loose, sandy loam soils. Although quite drought tolerant, they bloom best with regular irrigation. Many of the everblooming types tend to bloom after each rainfall or heavy irrigation. A light application of high-nitrogen fertilizer can also stimulate repeat blooms, as well as promote healthy, lush foliage. When my crinum foliage grows ragged or becomes infested with thrips, as it periodically does, I cut it off. The plants quickly replace the loss with healthy, new leaves. Propagation is by division with a good strong back and a sturdy sharp shooter. I own only one of the two!

In addition to Dean Herbert, Henry Nehrling, Luther Burbank, and Cecil Houdyshel, Theodore Mead of Florida was another breeder of classic crinums who reportedly received a collection of nearly one hundred different crinums from India around 1900.

I don't know of any plant that has been so ignored by modern Southern gardeners as have been the crinums. There is probably no other flowering perennial that adapts well to either extreme drought or aquatic conditions, all the while providing stunning displays of fragrant, cut-flower-quality blossoms. Crinums belong in the South, so I say plant them whether you like them or not. Once while actually reading one of the books in my collection, *Bulbs and Tuberous Rooter Plants* (1893) by C. L. Allen, I found that the author saw the potential of crinums early on: "They are, however, in many respects especially interesting, and when the time comes that plants are grown for what there is in them, rather than for what can be made from them, in way of profit, we shall expect to see many of the Crinums pretty generally cultivated." I'm still waiting. —*GG*

Deutzia scabra

Deutzia
Family: Saxifragaceae (Saxifrage)
Size: 8–10 ft
Zones: 6–9
Deciduous shrub
Showy white flowers in spring

Deutzia was named for J. Deutz, a sheriff of the Dutch city of Amsterdam, and was introduced to Western gardens from Japan and China in 1822. The species name, *scabra,* refers to the roughness of the leaves, which in this plant's native country, Japan, are

Deutzia *(Deutzia gracilis)* (Photo by Mike Arnold)

used by cabinetmakers in polishing finer woods. The plant is a graceful, deciduous shrub with a height and spread of eight to ten feet that bears showy, upward-pointing, cylindrical panicles of beautiful white flowers in midspring. The arching branches have attractive, peeling brown bark. They seem better acclimated to the middle South than zone 9 and the coastal areas. Deutzias are easily propagated by cuttings, divisions, or layers. A related species, *D. gracilis,* grows only three to four feet tall and blooms earlier in spring, often with tulips and daffodils. In describing both these species of deutzias, nurseryman Peter Henderson wrote in *Practical Floriculture* in 1890 that they are "exceedingly showy when in blossom, and are two of the most desirable shrubs in cultivation." He further extolled the value of *D. gracilis* as a plant to force in winter and spring for the cut-flower trade.

As a landscape plant deutzia lends itself well to massing in shrub borders or, occasionally, to planting as a specimen or hedge. The plants provide a lovely background for bearded irises, which bloom about the same time as the deutzias. Deutzia flowers last about two weeks in spring, and after that, aside from their rather interesting flaking brown bark, these shrubs provide little visual benefit to the garden for the rest of the year. They prefer good, well-drained loamy soils but are tolerant of a fairly wide range of soil pH. Once established, deutzias are quite drought tolerant. —*WCW*

Diospyros kaki, D. virginiana, and *D. texana*

Persimmon
Family: Ebenaceae (Ebony)
Size: 12–30 ft
Zones: 7–9
Small to medium-sized deciduous tree
Edible and ornamental fruit in fall

With their bright orange fruits borne on naked stems, persimmons have few rivals for fall display. They are practical, too: persimmons are among the longest lived and least troublesome of the fruit trees that may be grown in the South. And the fruit, once thoroughly ripe, is delicious—the botanical name for this tree, *Diospyros,* which means "fruit of the gods," is no exaggeration.

The type of persimmon commonly seen in the produce section is the fruit of a Chinese species, *D. kaki,* which has a long history of cultivation in Japan. This species was brought to Europe in 1796 and traveled to North America in the nineteenth century,

Japanese or Asian persimmon (*Diospyros kaki*) (Photo by William C. Welch)

so it is an authentic planting for historic gardens. But the species that should be of special interest to the Southern gardener is our native *D. virginiana,* whose species name refers to the colony of Virginia. Don't be misled by this, however; this persimmon is indigenous and common all over the South.

The persimmon is dioecious, that is, the male and female flowers are borne on different trees and only female trees bear fruit. This fruit is oblong in shape and ranges in size from three-fourths to one inch in diameter. Fruit size and quality vary markedly from tree to tree, as does the season of maturity. Some trees start ripening their fruit as early as August, while others are not ready for harvest until February. In any case, the fruit should not be picked until soft and dead ripe, for underripe fruits are highly astringent and pucker the mouth like alum does. When fully ripe, though, the native persimmons can be sweet, tasty, and nutritious, as good as the fruit of the grocery store Japanese types, even though much smaller. There are nonastringent Japanese cultivars, like 'Fuyu,' that don't pucker the mouth even when firm, however. They can be eaten as soon as they have color and have a texture more similar to that of an apple than of a ripe persimmon.

Early settlers and explorers knew and appreciated native persimmons. They were mentioned in writings of De Soto in 1539, Jan de Laet in 1558, and John Smith in the seventeenth century. These pioneers probably learned of the persimmon from Native Americans, who mixed persimmon pulp with crushed corn to make a kind of bread. Nor is the fruit the persimmon's only valuable product—woodworkers prize the hard, tough wood, which has been used to make tool handles and golf clubs. In addition, many species of birds and animals find the fruit attractive as a food source. Some old-timers have even said you could predict the weather by cutting a persimmon seed open and observing whether there was a spoon or a fork inside!

Texas or Mexican persimmon (*D. texana*) is an interesting plant that is native to South Texas and Mexico. The fruit is somewhat

Japanese or Asian persimmon (*Diospyros kaki*) (Photo by William C. Welch)

smaller than that of the eastern persimmon and is black when ripe, at which time it is sweet and may be used in the same ways as *D. virginiana*. The foliage of the Texas persimmon is smaller, too, and unlike the rough, alligator-skin-like trunk of the eastern persimmon, that of the Texas persimmon is smooth and gray, with thin layers of bark flaking off the surface. Reaching a height of forty feet, the Texas persimmon is a handsome tree sometimes used for landscape purposes, especially in areas of alkaline soil, where this species thrives. It is also important as a source of food for wildlife.

Persimmons have a taproot system that makes them difficult to transplant. Early Southern gardeners sometimes grafted wood from superior fruiting types onto small seedlings or more mature trees. *Diospyros virginiana* varies in size but can reach forty to fifty feet under ideal conditions.

Excerpts from nursery catalogues give insight into the adaptability and interest in persimmons: Mission Valley Nurseries (Victoria County, Texas, 1888): "Japan Persimmon—We planted trees of this fruit in 1878. They are thrifty and productive. We believe this fruit will prove an acquisition to Southern Texas." Waldheim Nursery, Boerne, Texas, 1895–96:

> Japan Persimmons. A new and valuable fruit. Its perfect adaptability throughout the South coupled with the extreme oddity and delicious flavor of its fruit, the later somewhat resembling that of a date or fig when dried, makes it a very desirable fruit for this section. The tree is rather dwarfish in growth with large, glossy foliage and bears very young often at the age of 2–3 years and is enormously productive; the fruit will ship safely to the most distant market and will stay on the tree until frost. There are a number of varieties varying in shape and color. Price .50 cents.

The Pearfield Nursery (Frelsburg, Texas) 1888 catalogue states: "We have some other varieties which we are now testing. At the Dallas Fair and Exposition in 1886 we received a premium and diploma for the best display of Japan Persimmons. The secretary of the Exposition writes: They attracted marked attention being such a novelty. Hundreds and thousands of people stopped in wonder and admiration and asked me questions. Many could hardly believe their eyes, and a few even asked if they were 'wax.'"—*WCW*

Exochorda racemosa

Pearlbush
Family: Rosaceae (Rose)
Size: 10–15 ft
Zones: 7–9
Medium to large shrub or small tree
Showy white flowers in spring

When my late friend Cleo Barnwell from Shreveport provided me with a plant and suggested in her gracious way that it is an "overlooked gem" for our Southern gardens, I took notice. Such is the case with pearlbush. Although I am sure that my two plants of pearlbush would be happier in the moister, acidic soils of the Southeast, they have adapted well to both our country and city gardens in Central Texas.

This plant's common name evokes the five-petaled blossoms that this ten- to fifteen-foot-tall shrub bears on terminal branches in early spring. The expanding flower buds, which appear soon after this deciduous shrub's first flush of spring growth, do indeed look like pearls, and in this stage of their development they make fine cut material for floral arrangements. Pearlbush prefers a sunny or partially shaded location and loamy, well-drained soil. Adapting well to both acidic and alkaline soils, this shrub is also quite drought tolerant once established.

Pearlbush comes to us from eastern China and was introduced to England in 1849. Propagation is by seed (a cold treatment for thirty or sixty days improves germination) or by semihardwood cuttings taken and rooted under mist in summer. The genus name, *Exochorda,* describes the structure of the fruits, which are suspended by cords and consist of five small, compressed, bony carpels adhering around a central axis in a starlike manner.

In 1890, Peter Henderson described pearlbush as "a beautiful hardy shrub, from China, introduced a few years since, and as yet comparatively little known. . . . It is still a rare plant in the

Pearlbush (*Exochorda racemosa*) (Photo by William C. Welch)

United States, chiefly because it is difficult to propagate, and in consequence is not easy to get. It is propagated by seeds, layers, or suckers."

In older references you will find pearlbush classified as *Spiraea grandiflora,* and this is the alias under which it appears in historic garden plans. Best landscape use is probably in the shrub border or as a specimen; be sure to allow it ample space, for it can become a substantial plant. The largest plant I have seen is in Madison, Georgia, and that specimen had a multibranched, rounded form and stood about fifteen feet tall and nearly as wide. After the relatively short bloom period in spring, pearlbush offers little other landscape interest. Still, though short-lived, the blossoms are beautiful enough to earn this plant a place in the garden. Pearlbush has never been common, but once experienced, it is never forgotten. —*WCW*

Ficus carica

Fig
Family: Moreaceae (Mulberry)
Size: 5–15 ft
Zones: 7–11
Deciduous small tree
Edible fruit in summer

Figs are believed to have originated in Syria, but wild forms now occupy a much larger area than they did in the past. Today, they are commonly found growing wild from eastern Iran to the Canary Isles and through the Mediterranean. In cultivation, the fig's range is much wider—truly cosmopolitan, in fact. The ancient Phoenicians seem to have begun the process of exporting the plant, taking it to the east and the west, and figs soon passed along the early trade routes to China and India. Their arrival in the Americas was more recent, dating to the arrival of the Spanish colonists who introduced figs into Florida and Mexico. From there they quickly spread to other areas of the South.

When the cultivation of figs began is unknown, but drawings of the fruit found in the Giza pyramids date back to several centuries before the birth of Christ. Figs were known in Babylon, and the fruit is mentioned three times in the *Odyssey*. The Greek geographer Strabo, who attended school near the present town of Aidin, the center of the Smyrna fig district, reported that the figs of that region were already highly esteemed in his day and brought the highest price in the market. According to W. T. Swingle (1908), "This record goes to show that fig culture has been the principal industry in this region for two millennia, the oldest fruit industry of which we have any record, for the date orchards that were the admiration of Herodotus at Palmyra and Babylon perished ages ago" (quoted in Ira Condit's *The Fig*).

Today figs are cultivated extensively in Spain, Turkey, and Italy. They are also grown commercially in California and, until

'Celeste' fig (*Ficus carica* 'Celeste') (Photo by Greg Grant)

recently, in Louisiana and Texas. The fig's fruit is popular for eating fresh and dried figs stuffed with walnuts, almonds, or small pieces of orange or citron are a delicacy in many parts of the world. Figs were also put up as preserves in the American South, and early gardeners of this region sometimes made wine from figs.

Figs have been grown in the south of France at least since the time of Thomas Jefferson, who visited Marseilles and Toulon in 1787. In his memoranda he wrote that the most delicate figs known in Europe were those growing about this district, where they were known as "figues Marcellaises" to distinguish them from others of inferior quality. (quoted in Condit). Figs are mentioned frequently in the Bible. In the Old Testament we find in Numbers 19 that Moses was asked by his followers, "Why did you bring the Lord's community into this desert? That we and our livestock should die here? Why did you bring us up out of Egypt to this terrible place? It has no grain or figs, grapevines or pomegranates. And there is no water to drink!"

'White Marseilles' fig (Ficus 'White Marseilles') (Photo by William C. Welch)

In May 2007, I was fortunate to visit the gardens at the palace of the Archbishop of Canterbury in London. I had heard of a very old specimen of 'White Marseilles' fig growing there. Alistair Cook is the horticulturist at the palace and takes great pride in the tree. He says that it is documented to have been planted in the 1500s and is still thriving and fruiting. Frances Parker, well-known landscape designer from Beaufort, South Carolina, has propagated plants from this specimen and circulated them among some of her friends.

In the South, figs were once found in nearly every home garden. Both John Bartram (1765–66) and William Bartram (1791) ran across fig trees in their travels. Some forty miles north of Mobile, Alabama, William Bartram noted that "the fig trees were large as well as their fruit, which was then ripe (August), of the shape of pears and as large, and of dark purplish colour."

In 1821, James G. Forbes observed that Andrew Turnbull had established a colony of fifteen Greek and Minorcan immigrants at New Smyrna, Florida, in 1763, and that the colonists had grown grapes, figs, and pomegranates, all familiar fruits in their native lands.

Figs were, evidently, familiar to George Washington from earliest childhood. Charles A. Hoppin (1926), in his writings about the birthplace of Washington at Wakefield, Virginia, stated that in 1851, in the middle of a two hundred–acre cornfield stood a mammoth fig tree and a stone slab inscribed "Here the 22nd of February, 1732, Washington was born." Close by was a thicket of shrubby fig trees covering a circular space nearly fifty feet in diameter, thickly matted together, the largest being three inches in diameter at the base and eight to ten feet high." As an adult, General Washington planted fig trees at Mount Vernon, probably cuttings from the bushes at his boyhood home. In 1830, Edith Sale visited Mount Vernon and found some "upshoots" of the original fig tree. She stated that "a row of fig bushes stands

'Celeste' fig (*Ficus carica* 'Celeste') (Photo by William C. Welch)

'Celeste' fig (*Ficus carica* 'Celeste') growing in Central Texas (Photo by William C. Welch)

beside the box hedge and doubtless the children after lessons would delight in their abundance" (quoted in Condit).

Figs also make their appearance in the writings of early nurserymen. Thomas Affleck, when he visited Washington, Mississippi, in 1842 reported that he found "figs now in perfection, the last certainly the greatest luxury in the fruit line I ever partook of." A year or two later, when he settled at Washington, six miles from Natchez, Affleck planted an orchard of fifty fig trees. Still later, he published a series of almanacs and calendars titled *Affleck's Southern Rural Almanac and Plantation and Garden Calendar;* the one for 1852 lists fifteen varieties of figs.

According to a dubious story, the fig industry in Texas was based primarily upon one cultivar known locally as 'Magnolia.' This came into the state with a tree peddler who traveled throughout the coastal regions selling trees labeled "Magnolia" that he sold as specimens of that favorite Southern ornamental. Purchasers soon learned that what they had bought were in fact figs, but the name remained attached to the cultivar. J. C. Carpenter admired its fruit when he arrived in Houston in 1900. Upon settling at Aldine, Carpenter set out ten acres of the 'Magnolia' trees, eventually increasing the planting to twenty-three acres. In 1902, he started a preserving business that was the real beginning of the commercial fig industry in Texas.

Although occasionally damaged by cold, these trees are sufficiently hardy to be successfully grown several hundred miles inland from coastal areas. There are more than seven hundred varieties of figs in cultivation, but only a handful were common in gardens of the old South. Prominent among these are 'Brown Turkey,' 'Magnolia,' 'Celeste,' and 'Texas Everbearing.'

Figs grow fairly quickly to a maximum of fifteen to twenty feet, and they prefer fertile, well-drained soil, though they adapt to most soils and moisture conditions. Pruning is not necessary for good fruit production, but shaping and removal of crossing limbs make the trees neater and more acceptable as landscape plants. I remember visiting the Jamison commercial fig orchard about thirty years ago at Pearland, where the trees were pruned to a height of about seven feet with single trunks and scaffold branches much like those of peach trees. The result was very attractive.

Occasional hard freezes can kill the branches, but the trees recover quickly and are soon back in production, since most cultivars bear fruit on new growth ('Celeste' does not). As the trees mature, their cold tolerance increases. But in areas where their hardiness is questionable, figs are most safely grown against south-facing walls. Espaliering a fig tree against a sunny wall not only protects the plant against frost but also allows the gardener to cultivate the plant in much less space than it would occupy if allowed to grow free.

I remember figs trained as small trees when I was growing up in Houston. They were fun to climb, but the leaves were irritating to the skin. 'Magnolia,' with its very large reddish brown, pink-fleshed fruit, was the preserving fig of choice in my family. Recent years have seen less interest in 'Magnolia' because it is an open-eye fig, which has a small hole at the tip of the fruit. This makes it susceptible to attack by the dried-fruit beetle, which causes the fruit to sour. Closed-eye types like 'Celeste,' 'Texas Everbearing,' and 'Alma' form a drop of clear, sticky material in the eye that prevents entry of the damaging insect.

Figs are among the easiest fruiting plants to grow. They benefit from a mulch placed over the roots in summertime to help keep the soil moist, and to watering during prolonged dry spells. Figs often produce for long periods, bearing a first crop in June on the last year's growth and then a second, more prolific crop in August and September on the current season's growth.

Nematodes are sometimes a problem in sandy soils, and over-fertilization can cause fig trees to produce an abundance of foliage and little fruit. Stress from lack of moisture can cause fruit drop. In addition, cultivating the soil around the base of the tree may damage the figs' shallow roots. Figs are easily rooted from cuttings taken during the trees' dormant period and stuck deeply into good garden soil. Newly rooted plants often bear the third year.

Many Southern nurseries listed fig trees for sale in the late 1800s and early 1900s. Among them was Waldheim Nursery (Boerne, Texas) who listed in its 1895–96 catalogue 'Celestial,' 'Brown Turkey,' 'Adriatic,' and 'San Pedro.' The Alvin Fruit & Nursery Co. (Algoa, Texas) offered the following: "50,000 fig trees in Nursery, We have the largest commercial orchard of figs in the South and make a specialty of growing the trees. Varieties listed . . . Brunswick, Celeste, Lemon, Green Ischia, & Magnolia (Magnolia is the most profitable fig known). . . . Don't fail to plant a few Magnolia figs."—*WCW*

Gardenia jasminoides

Gardenia, Cape Jasmine, Cape Jessamine
Family: Rubiaceae (Madder)
Size: 2–8 ft
Zones: 7–11
Small, medium, or large evergreen shrub
Creamy white, heavenly scented flowers in summer

> In May, 1879, I had the first opportunity to enjoy its beauty in almost every garden at Houston, Texas. The effect was not only very delightful, but I was charmed with its dignified and noble appearance, its wealth of powerfully fragrant flowers and its dense masses of large thick glossy leaves. I saw that the gardens were replete with it, as single specimens, in groups, and as borders around the cemeteries. Everywhere, wherever planted, it added a peculiar charm to its surroundings.
> —Henry Nehrling, *My Garden in Florida,* 1944

Gardenia hips (*Gardenia jasminoides*)
(Photo by Greg Grant)

There are certain floral fragrances that slap you in the face; among them are gardenia, magnolia, sweet olive, banana shrub, butterfly ginger, and Japanese honeysuckle.

Though this shrub has been called cape jasmine, it is not from the Cape of Good Hope (or Cape Cod or Cape Fear, for that matter), nor is it a jasmine. This plant actually originated in China and belongs to the same family as coffee, pentas, firebush, and ixora. Its more popular name, "gardenia," commemorates Alexander Garden of Charleston, South Carolina, who studied medicine and botany in Scotland. More important, he was an enthusiastic pupil and friend of Linnaeus, who named the plant.

Gardenias were originally adopted by Western gardeners as greenhouse specimens cherished for their creamy white blossoms and heavenly fragrance. Originally known as *Gardenia florida,* the gardenia's exact date of introduction into North America is unknown. The Brooklyn Botanic Garden's 1968 handbook,

'Martha Turnbull' hip gardenia (*Gardenia jasminoides* 'Martha Turnbull') (Photo by Greg Grant)

America's Garden Heritage (volume 23, number 3), lists no date but says it was introduced during colonial days. Certainly there are plenty of references in our early garden literature. In 1806, the Philadelphia nurseryman Bernard M'Mahon mentioned in his book, *The American Gardener's Calendar,* planting seeds of gardenias. In her detailed garden diary on February 2, 1841, Martha Turnbull of Rosedown Plantation referred to trimming her cape jessamine hedge. In 1860, Robert Buist made note of *G. florida flore pleno* as the cape jasmine in his *American Flower-Garden Directory.* He also listed dwarf cape jasmine (*G. radicans*), and *G. longifolia, G. multiflora, G. latifolia, G. fortunii,* and *G. camelliaflora,* all as greenhouse plants and probable varieties of *G. florida.*

Almost all early nurseries of the South listed the cape jasmine. Thomas Affleck's 1851–52 Southern Nurseries catalogue listed "cape jessamine, the old double" and a "fine new variety, a Southern seedling." An 1860 catalogue from Montgomery Nurseries (Wilson's Nursery) of Montgomery, Alabama, also offered cape jessamine along with dwarf cape jessamine. Gilbert Onderdonk's

Cape jessamine (*Gardenia jasminoides*) (Photo by Greg Grant)

Mission Valley Nurseries catalogue of 1898–99 called gardenia "the most charming flower of the South."

Rosedown and Oakley Plantations of St. Francisville, Louisiana, both have what they call the "hip gardenia" naturalized on-site. Although they were originally identified by local horticulturists as *G. thunbergia,* I'm pretty sure they are just single "wild" seedlings of *G. jasminoides.* They bear single white blossoms, have narrow foliage, and in the fall produce attractive red-orange fruit that somewhat resembles rose hips. My experience has shown that they are self-sterile and require at least two selections (cross-pollination) to produce their showy fruit. There are a number of single-flowered gardenias available now. They tend to be easier to grow and are more forgiving than the double-flowered sorts. I even selected a particularly floriferous clone from a batch of seedlings and named it 'Martha Turnbull.'

Today there are many gardenia cultivars on the market, including the dwarf *G. jasminoides radicans,* 'August Beauty,' 'Mystery,' and 'Veitchii,' a less hardy, earlier-blooming type historically used for cut-flower production. My favorite is still the original big-leaved, large-growing, big-flowered *G. jasminoides,* the perfume of the South. According to Grandmother Emanis, it's the true "cape jasmine."

Gardenias are a little troublesome to grow, but their fragrance makes them well worth the effort. An acidic, well-drained, sandy loam soil amended with organic matter is essential. Some filtered shade during the hottest part of the day is also beneficial. In alkaline soils iron chlorosis is a severe problem. The most common pest encountered is the white fly. Propagation is from cuttings or by seed in the case of fruiting types.—*GG*

Gelsemium sempervirens

Carolina Jessamine, Yellow Jasmine
Family: Loganiaceae (Logania)
Size: 10–20 ft
Zones 7–11
Evergreen native vine
Sweet-scented yellow flowers in spring

This state flower of South Carolina is native to the southeastern United States from the Carolinas all the way to Texas. Though often called yellow "jasmine," this vine is not a true jasmine, nor is it even related to that genus. The average gardener doesn't care about such distinctions, though. All early gardeners knew was that this vine bore beautiful, yellow, and powerfully fragrant flowers—and that's why it has been cultivated in the South from the beginning of our ornamental gardening heritage.

On August 12, 1786, Thomas Jefferson wrote to Richard Cary, his kinsman and friend in Virginia, requesting a number of plants, including *Bignonia sempervirens* (this was the original botanical name for this species; it was also classified under the name *Gelsemium nitida* for a while). Bourne's 1833 *Florist's Manual* states, "The *Bignonia sempervirens,* or Yellow Jasmine, is a very beautiful shrub or tree. . . . That of the Southern States gives out a delicious fragrance in the night. In New-England it is reared with some difficulty. It is, however, generally found growing in our gardens, and is much admired."

There is a listing for yellow jessamine in an 1860 catalogue of Montgomery Nurseries (Wilson's Nursery) of Montgomery, Alabama. Langdon Nurseries, also of Alabama, lists *G. nitidum* and *G. nitidum, Fl. Pl.* in an 1881–82 catalogue in which he states about the latter: "This is the well known Carolina Yellow Jasmine, differing from the proceeding [*sic*] in that the golden yellow flowers are as double as a tube rose. Hardy, grows rapidly, flowers freely early in the spring, and though not new, has not

Carolina jessamine (*Gelsemium sempervirens*) (Photo by Greg Grant)

received that degree of attention to which its merits entitle it. We are not aware that it is offered by another Nursery in the country, but think it worthy of cultivation wherever a rapid evergreen vine is wanted." I assume that this is the same as the cultivar sold today as 'Pride of Augusta.' Although not as heavy blooming, it is certainly worth growing.

I often associate plants with the people from whom I obtained them. In the case of yellow "jasmine," I remember how excited I was when my first-grade teacher, Mozelle Johnston, an avid gardener, shared two plants of yellow jasmine with me. I planted one on the gas lamp in the front yard and one at the base of a double-trunked post oak.

The double-flowered jessamine growing in my garden now came from the late J. C. Raulston of the North Carolina State Arboretum. He also shared a pale yellow-flowered form with me that was introduced by Woodlanders Nursery of South Carolina.

Carolina jessamine (*Gelsemium sempervirens*) (Photo by Greg Grant)

Carolina jessamine is very easy to cultivate. Although native to acidic woodland soils, it grows quite well in alkaline types as well. It is quite shade tolerant, although it blooms best in full sun. Due to its vining habit, it shows to best advantage when trained up a supporting structure. Propagation by cuttings under high humidity is possible but fairly difficult. Any suckers springing from the soil at the base of a plant can be detached and transplanted with ease. —*GG*

Gladiolus byzantinus

Byzantine Gladiolus
Family: Iridaceae (Iris)
Size: 3–4 ft
Zones: 4–11
Perennial corm
Magenta flower spikes in spring

The heirloom gladiolus most common in Southern gardens is *Gladiolus byzantinus*. This species thrives in old cemeteries, near abandoned homesites, and along ditch banks, for unlike the fussy modern hybrids, *G. byzantinus* is a survivor and a true perennial. The color of its blossoms is typically a beautiful magenta-purple, though there is also a white form found here and there. Although I'm not exactly sure when this native of southern Spain, Sicily, and North Africa was introduced to American gardens, I do know that William Prince offered it in an 1820 catalogue from the Linnaean Botanic Garden in Long Island, New York. It seems to have arrived in Southern gardens around the same time.

If *G. byzantinus* is to thrive, it must be given a sunny location, and it prefers well-drained soil. The corms are much smaller than those of the hybrids commonly advertised in nursery catalogues today. It multiplies readily and may be divided as the foliage dies in early summer. The disappearance of the foliage at that season makes it risky to delay digging the corms until fall or winter, the season generally recommended by growers of modern gladiolus. Unless you are well enough organized to have marked the place where the plants were growing, you probably will not be able to find the corms.

Another species of gladiolus occasionally found in old Southern gardens is *G. dalenii* (sometimes listed as *G. natalensis* or *G. psittacinus*), an African native that is sometimes called parrot gladiolus. The source of this common name is the hooded, orange and yellow flowers. Today there are selections available

Byzantine gladiolus (*Gladiolus byzantinus*)
(Photo by Greg Grant)

Byzantine gladiolus (*Gladiolus byzantinus*)
(Photo by Greg Grant)

Byzantine gladiolus (*Gladiolus byzantinus*)
(Photo by Greg Grant)

in yellow, red, or peach as well. Borne on three-foot-tall stems in April, these blossoms make striking cut flowers. This species thrives in loamy or clay soils.

Evidence of use of the parrot gladiolus in mid-nineteenth-century American gardens may be found in Joseph Breck's book, *The Flower-Garden; or, Breck's Book of Flowers,* published in Boston in 1851. Breck remarked that "*Gladiolus natalensis,* called by some *psittacinus,* has not been known many years among us, and was considered, when first introduced, as being very superb: but it has such a propensity to increase, that it has become very common, and is now looked upon with indifference. The flowers are scarlet, on a greenish-yellow ground, produced in long, one-sided spikes: the stems sometimes four feet high, with fifteen or twenty buds and blooms." Elsewhere Breck also refers to *G. byzantinus,* noting that even in coastal New England it was winter hardy, so its corms could be left in the ground year-round.

Byzantine gladiolus (*Gladiolus byzantinus*)
(Photo by William C. Welch)

The name "gladiolus" derives from the Latin word *gladius,* which means "sword"—this refers to the bladelike foliage. Various names commonly used for this plant are "hardy glad," "corn flag," "sword-lily" and "Jacob's ladder." The old-time species types are more compact in growth than the hybrids and usually require no staking. Bloom time is usually April, at the same time as the bearded irises.

Traditionally, gladiolus were often planted in rows in the vegetable garden as well as flower borders. Both species described here were common in Southern cottage gardens of the nineteenth century. They deserve widespread use as perennials in period and modern gardens, though at present they are available only from specialty sources dealing in Southern heirloom bulbs and perennials.—*WCW*

Parrot gladiolus (*Gladiolus dalenii*) (Photo by William C. Welch)

Gomphrena globosa

Bachelor's Buttons, Globe Amaranth, Gomphrena
Family: Amaranthaceae (Amaranth)
Size: 2–3 ft
Zones: NA
Warm-season annual
White, pink, or purple cut flowers in summer and fall

Once again, common names are likely to lead us astray. Go shopping in the catalogues for bachelor's button and you are liable to end up with a northern European weed, *Centaurea cyanus* (also called corn flower), which has become popular in the "wildflower" meadows so fashionable in recent years. What you want to get is the real Southern bachelor's button *Gomphrena,* which has also been known as globe amaranth and immortelle. Gomphrena is from Central Asia, so it likes our climate, and it has roots here, too, having been grown in Southern gardens for a long time.

This flower is a warm-season annual easily grown from seed

Bachelor's button (*Gomphrena globosa*) with petunias (*Petunia* × *hybrida*) (Photo by Greg Grant)

planted in a sunny location after all danger of frost has passed. It is useful as a bedding plant and/or for cut flowers and is famous for its cloverlike clusters of brightly colored bracts that can be pink, white, or purple. There are early references to a violet and a striped variety—I would very much like to locate seed of those. In all gomphrena flowers, what appear to be the blossoms are really colored bracts that hide the true flowers, which are small and inconspicuous.

The normal height for this plant is approximately two and one-half feet, although dwarf cultivars are now available that grow approximately one foot tall. My experience has shown that the dwarf forms don't last through the summer in the South. Sometimes it pays to be big!

Bachelor's buttons are very popular as an "everlasting flower" because the "flowers" hold their color after drying. The plants are very easily dried by harvesting them at their peak of bloom and hanging them upside down in a warm, dry, dark area. Early Southern gardeners took advantage of the gomphrena's year-round beauty by growing the plants in their garden until fall and then using them for indoor dried bouquets throughout the winter. The following spring, the dried flower heads were crushed, releasing the seeds, which were then resown into the garden.

The gomphrena is reportedly used as a heart remedy in Central America. It always does my heart good to look at them! There are also references to the leaves being boiled and eaten as food.

I have found a number of references to the cultivation of gomphrena in eighteenth- and nineteenth-century American garden handbooks. In 1847, Thomas Bridgeman listed it in *The Young Gardener's Assistant,* while Joseph Breck mentions it in *The Flower-Garden; or Breck's Book of Flowers* (1859): "Globe Amaranth—white, purple, and striped are desirable. A popular immortelle." Thomas Jefferson grew the bachelor's button in his garden at Monticello. On April 2, 1767, he recorded in his garden book: "Sowed Carnations, Indian Pink, Marigold, Globe Amaranth, Auricula, Double Balsam, Tricolor, Dutch Violet,

Bachelor's button (*Gomphrena globosa*) (Photo by Greg Grant)

Bachelor's button (*Gomphrena globosa*), purple variety (Photo by Greg Grant)

Bachelor's button (*Gomphrena globosa*)
with cypress vine (*Ipomoea quamoclit*)
(Photo by Greg Grant)

Sensitive Plant, Cockscomb, a flower like the Prince's Feather, Lathyrus."

I'll never forget my great-grandmother Flossie Wallace's garden at "Thrill Hill" in Center, Texas. The entire front yard was a Monetlike maze of reseeded bachelor's buttons in their full array of colors. I was a small child when she lived there, so they were as tall as I was. I had to weave through them just to get to the door. —*GG*

Hemerocallis fulva

Tawny Daylily, Fulvous Daylily
Family: Liliaceae (Lily)
Size: 2–4 ft
Zones: 2–11
Perennial
Orange (plus yellow and many other colors in hybrids) flowers in late spring

Although many people may think of the daylily as a modern flower, in fact this perennial's roots run a long way back into the history of gardens. As early as the year AD 70, the Greek herbalist Dioscorides made reference in his writings to a form of the plant we now know as lemon or custard daylily. The plant he was describing had to have originated from cultivation, for this species is of Asian origin.

According to Chinese literature, various forms of daylilies have been cultivated by that nation's gardeners for thousands of years. The earliest references date to 2697 BC and the *Materia Medica* commissioned by Emperor Huang Ti, when the daylily was already in use as a food crop as well as a source of medicines. The consumption of daylily plants and flowers was thought to benefit the mind and strengthen willpower as well as to "quiet the five viscera." The flower buds, which may still be found on the shelves of Oriental markets, are palatable, digestible, and nutritious. The root and crown were widely employed as a medicine to relieve pain, and, later, juice extracted from the fresh roots by pounding was administered to patients suffering from cirrhosis and jaundice.

Carolus Linnaeus, the "Father of Botany," in his *Species Plantarum* of 1753 chose *Hemerocallis* as the scientific name for the daylily. This choice reflects a peculiarity of the flower; the name combines two Greek words meaning "beauty" and "day," and as this suggests, an individual daylily flower opens for only a day.

Double orange daylily (*Hemerocallis fulva* 'Kwanso') (Photo by Greg Grant)

However, since each scape (flower stalk) bears many buds, and these open in series, a single plant maintains a display over a number of days.

Daylilies resisted hybridization until the twentieth century, and old-time gardeners were limited in their choices to just a few kinds: the lemon daylily (*H. asphodelus*), the tawny or common orange daylily (*H. fulva*), and the double orange daylily (*H. fulva* 'Kwanso'). These were probably the only daylilies available to most Western gardeners until the 1920s.

Despite this lack of variety, daylilies have been popular garden plants in Europe for many centuries. The late sixteenth-century botanist Mathias de L'obel (who also styled himself as de Lobel or Lobelius) of France, noted that by 1575 both the lemon daylily and the tawny daylily had been introduced into European gardens. Writing from London in 1733, Philip Miller says in *The Gardener's Dictionary* of the lemon and tawny lilies:

The species are:
1. *lilio-asphodelus, luteus*
    The Yellow Day Lily.
2. *lilio-asphodelus, puniceus*
    The Red Day Lily.
    These plants are very common in most of the old English gardens. The first is called the Yellow Tuberose, from its being a very agreeable scent; but the other is called the Day Lily, or the Tuberose Orange lily in most places.

According to some sources, daylilies were extensively used in early American settlements. Alice Lockwood, in a caption for a picture of *H. asphodelus* in *Gardens of Colony and State* (volume 2), says, "Used in all gardens from the seventeenth to the twentieth century." Yet from the mid- to late nineteenth century, daylilies were conspicuously absent from American gardening literature, perhaps because American gardeners were distracted by the huge influx of new plants coming into the country at that time.

I have found two references to daylilies from that period. The first is in Jane Louden's *Gardening for Ladies: And Companion to the Flower Garden* (New York, 1845), where the author praises daylilies as "handsome perennial plants with yellow or copper-coloured flowers. They are quite hardy and only require a moist soil and a shady situation. They are propagated by dividing the roots."

In the same year, Robert Buist wrote glowingly of daylilies in his *American Flower Garden Directory* (Philadelphia, 1845): daylilies "flower well and are remarkable among the border flowers for their large yellow or copper-coloured corollas, some of them almost six inches in diameter; bloom from May to July and will grow in almost any soil." The lemon daylily has narrow, grasslike foliage and grows to three feet or less. Its lemon yellow, four-inch trumpets are known for their sweet scent. Joseph Breck in *The Flower-Garden; or, Breck's Book of Flowers* (Boston, 1851) described the species this way: "Yellow Day Lily,—has brilliant yellow

'Kindly Lights' daylily (*Hemerocallis* 'Kindly Lights') (Photo by William C. Welch)

lily-shaped flower in June: two feet high; leaves long keeled, linear." Although known as a very reliable and low-maintenance perennial, the lemon lily is difficult to find, and what is sold under this name in today's nursery trade often proves not true to type.

Hemerocallis fulva has naturalized so successfully throughout much of this country that it now functions as a wildflower in many areas. It is almost beyond belief that this plant could propagate so successfully and so far only by root spread. This particular species is a triploid "mule" and cannot produce viable seed. Several cultivated clones and various wild forms are included under the specific name *H. fulva*.

The oldest, most common, and best known of these is the clone 'Europa,' which Lobel described in 1576 as having cinnabar-red coloring in the flowers and as being distinctly different from the lemon daylily. By 1601, according to Clusius, 'Europa' was commonly found in the gardens of Austria and Germany. The Swedish botanist Linnaeus first considered 'Europa' a hybrid (1753) but later (1762) classified it a species with the name *H. fulva*.

The double forms of *H. fulva* are almost as durable and well adapted as the single-flowered type, and their blossoms mark many deserted homesites and cemeteries throughout the South. They, too, are sterile and do not spread by seed. According to herb and heirloom plant expert Art Tucker, two historic doubles are in cultivation. He says that *H. fulva* 'Flore Pleno' was displayed by Veitch and Son for the Royal Horticultural Society in 1860 and has fully double flowers (nine to fourteen petals, three stamens, and no pistil) and more bluish green foliage that appears earlier in the spring than that of 'Green Kwanso.' His research indicates that the original 'Kwanso' had variegated foliage and was introduced by Philipp von Siebold from Japan in 1864. It had less double flowers and fewer petals. It apparently is not stable and continually reverts to the green form, which Tucker says was first introduced in 1917.

I remember my excitement as an early teen when I learned that there was a double daylily. I rode the school bus each day, and the driver knew of my gardening interests. One day she left me a grocery sack full of double daylilies. Those plants bloomed that same year and thrived for as long as we lived in our Houston home.

For meadow gardens and naturalistic plantings, these species-type daylilies still make valuable additions to the designer's palette. In the eighteenth and nineteenth centuries, many gardeners relegated daylilies to out-of-the-way areas of the garden—they were sometimes known as "privy lilies" because they were commonly used to line the path to that outbuilding. Since the early 1930s, however, the activities of British and American hybridizers have revolutionized this ancient flower.

According to research conducted by Nell Crandall of Houston, George Yeld, an English schoolteacher and hobby gardener, carried out the first hybridization of the daylily in 1877. His cultivar 'Apricot' (*H. flava* × *H. middendorfii*) was first exhibited in 1892. A. Herrington of New Jersey registered the first known American clone, 'Florham,' in 1899 (*H. aurantiaca major* × *H. thunbergii* hybrid). Luther Burbank of California is credited with introducing four cultivars between 1914 and 1924.

A. B. Stout was the acknowledged pioneer of this new era of research on the genus *Hemerocallis.* His work began in 1921 as a result of his friendship with Albert Steward, who while teaching botany at the University of Nanking met and taught many of China's young botanists. Steward's home became the center of activity for people of many interests, and through them Stout was able to procure plants and information about daylilies that had been previously unavailable outside their native land. Stout received twenty-seven living plants and seeds from central China in 1924 and fifty more between 1920 and 1942. With this unprecedented wealth of material he was able to produce viable seed from a number of species, often for the first time. He propagated *H. fulva,* for example, by introducing its pollen into the flowers of fertile relatives.

Stout's work literally opened the door and laid the foundation for the modern breeding work with daylilies. Since his initial efforts, many scientists and amateurs have become involved in hybridizing daylilies, and tens of thousands of new cultivars have resulted. Whereas daylilies formerly offered the gardener only a yellow and an orange color, this flower is now available in countless shades of near white, yellow, orange, pink, vivid red, crimson, purple, pastel, and handsome blends. As of the end of 1993, there were 36,486 cultivar names registered in the Daylily Check List.

Most of the new introductions soon fall by the wayside and are displaced by the continuing supply of new cultivars. One of the early hybrids, however, has remained popular since its introduction in about 1925. 'Hyperion' was developed by Franklin B. Mead and is considered by many to be unexcelled in its class. 'Hyperion' stands about four feet tall, blooming midseason with fragrant, large, widely open, canary yellow flowers with a green-flushed throat and prominent stamens. It is often confused and sold as the old lemon daylily, but that has daintier flowers,

Double orange daylily (*Hemerocallis* 'Kwanso') (Photo by William C. Welch)

is smaller, and has more grasslike foliage. Another difference is time of bloom; Elizabeth Lawrence, in Charlotte, North Carolina, gives the earliest date of first bloom for 'Hyperion' as June 3, and the latest date of first bloom June 26, whereas first bloom for the lemon lily she sets as early as April 19 and as late as May 10. In addition, the lemon daylily sometimes repeats in fall.

Recent daylily breeding is focusing on tetraploids. From 1960 to 1965 only seventeen tetraploids were registered with the Daylily Society, but now the registered count exceeds five thousand. This explosion of popularity has to do with the tetraploids' greater potential. Since they have twice as many chromosomes as the normal plant, the tetraploids offer a correspondingly greater array of genetic material with which breeders can produce, for example, brighter flower colors, stronger and sturdier scapes, and more flower substance. Not all gardeners agree, however, that tetraploids are universally desirable. Plant historians and traditionalists point to the simple beauty and natural adaptability of the species forms of daylilies and wonder why it is necessary to "mess with a good thing." In reality, both interests are valid and worthy of support. The beauty of some of the new hybrids is truly impressive, but so are the long history and elegant simplicity of the species forms.

Daylilies are fibrous-rooted, hardy, herbaceous perennials. Their roots are fingerlike to large, round, and fleshy. There is a crown at the spot where the roots and leaves join. The foliage is narrow and long and assumes the shape of a fan. Basically, all daylilies fall into one of three types, according to their foliage: the dormant type, which loses its foliage completely during the winter; the evergreen type, which retains its green foliage all year unless there is an unusually severe winter; and the semi-evergreen type, which loses part or most of its leaves during the winter. As a rule, the evergreen daylilies perform best in hot climates, while the deciduous types prefer cooler locations, although there are exceptions.

Species and older daylily cultivars are known for their ease of culture. Propagation is by division; fall is the ideal time to divide and reset existing clumps. Division is necessary to maintain the growth and vigor of newer cultivars, but the species and early types described here can go many years without being disturbed. Like most plants, they respond favorably to good, well-drained soils and garden culture, but the luxuriant stands of daylilies flourishing along countless roadsides, in cemeteries, and at abandoned homesites attest to this perennial's ability to cope with less than ideal conditions.

Daylily foliage is attractive all season long, and the flowers appear with onset of our late spring and summer heat—in other words, just as the flowers of most other perennials and spring annuals are fading. Surely these privy lilies deserve a better spot in Southern gardens.*—*WCW*

Special thanks to the late Florence P. Griffin and the Cherokee Garden Library of Atlanta for their assistance in researching the heirloom daylilies. I also appreciate the assistance and support of Nell Crandall of Houston and the American Hemerocallis Society.

Hibiscus mutabilis (and related species)

Confederate Rose, Cotton Rose
Family: Malvaceae (Mallow)
Size: 12–15 ft
Zones: 7–11
Perennial or small tree (in tropical zones)
Showy white, pink, bicolor flowers in fall

Confederate rose (*Hibiscus mutabilis*)
(Photo by William C. Welch)

A native of South China, the Confederate rose (*Hibiscus muta-bilis*) was once a highly popular plant throughout the South. Sometimes known as "cotton rose" because its flowers, foliage, and growth habit recall those of the cotton plant, the Confederate rose will form a large shrub or even a small tree in areas where winters are not severe. It is root hardy in colder areas of the South and performs in the garden as a large perennial. Although still common in Southern gardens, the Confederate rose is rarely seen in nurseries.

There are several forms of Confederate rose, including

Texas star hibiscus (*Hibiscus coccineus*)
(Photo by Greg Grant)

'Peppermint Flare' rose mallow (*Hibiscus moscheutos* 'Peppermint Flare') (Photo by Greg Grant)

'Rubrus,' which has deep pink flowers; 'Plena,' which has double white flowers that turn pink or red the second day; and the species type, which bears single pink flowers. All the forms are showy landscape plants with flowers that frequently measure six inches in diameter. They bloom most heavily in late summer and early fall.

Propagation is by cuttings, which root easily in soil or water during spring and summer. Confederate roses are not particular about soil and tolerate a wide range of moisture conditions. Cotton root rot can be a problem in alkaline soils where cotton has been cultivated.

The common rose mallow (*H. moscheutos*) is native to wetland areas of the South and has also been used as a perennial. It is root hardy as far north as zone 5 and provides a long season of garden color. Breeders have developed giant flowering forms of the rose mallows that are available today from seed or plants. The cutting grown clones are generally superior, including the hot pink 'Flare,' the gorgeous light pink 'Lady Baltimore,' the red

'Lord Baltimore' rose mallow (*Hibiscus* × 'Lord Baltimore') (Photo by Greg Grant)

'Lord Baltimore,' and Greg's own flecked 'Peppermint Flare' and big pink 'Jackie Grant.'

Another popular native species is the Texas star hibiscus (*H. coccineus*). This bears single, red flowers about three inches in diameter atop branches of palmately lobed leaves with three to seven segments. Propagation is from seed or by cuttings, and Texas star hibiscus thrives in most any garden soil. Like *H. moscheutos*, the Texas star hibiscus freezes back in winter and should be cut to ground level after the first hard freeze.

All four of the hibiscuses mentioned were formerly common in Southern landscapes, especially in cottage-type gardens where they were often mixed with other perennials and annuals.—*WCW*

Hibiscus syriacus

Althea, Rose of Sharon
Family: Malvaceae (Mallow)
Size: 8–12 ft
Zones: 5–11
Medium-sized deciduous shrub or small tree
White, pink, or purple flowers in summer

The Rosedale Nurseries (Brenham, Texas) catalogue from 1899 includes this description of althea: "These beautiful shrubs have been neglected and their advantages for lawn decorations, as single plants or in clumps or hedges, overlooked. They bloom from May till fall, during our hottest, driest weather, when flowers are scarce. They do not require watering, and demand little attention. They are decided acquisitions to any flower garden."

A native of India and China, *Hibiscus syriacus* has been cultivated in the latter nation for as long as records exist. In China, both its flowers and leaves were used as food. In 1597, the English herbalist John Gerard recorded that he had planted seeds of the "Tree Mallow," and in 1629, John Parkinson, one of the first English garden writers, mentioned that he had cultivated this plant. In the 1759 edition of his monumental *Gardener's and Florist's Dictionary,* Philip Miller described seven kinds:

> The most common hath purple flowers with dark bottoms, another hath bright purple flowers with black bottoms, a third hath white flowers with purple bottoms, a fourth variegated flowers with dark bottoms, and a fifth pale yellow flowers with dark bottoms but the last is very rare at present in the English gardens; there are also two with variegated leaves which are by some much esteemed.

In 1778, John Abercrombie, author of *The Universal Gardener and Botanist,* called the plant "the greatest ornament of the

Althea (*Hibiscus syriacus*) (Photo by Greg Grant)

Althea (*Hibiscus syriacus*) (Photo by Greg Grant)

autumn season, of almost any of the shrubby tribe." Double-flowered forms are not mentioned until 1838, when J. C. Loudon described them as common in his *Arboretum et Fruticetum Brittanicum.*

This "greatest ornament" has been equally as popular in the American South—altheas have been in Southern gardens from the beginning of our gardening heritage. Thomas Jefferson planted althea seeds at all his homes—at Shadwell in April 1767, at Monticello in March 1794, and at Poplar Forest in December 1812.

Altheas were sold in almost all the early Southern nurseries dealing in ornamentals. In a survey of catalogues from nineteen nurseries covering the years 1851–1906, I found that sixteen of them offered altheas. That makes it the most popular Southern nursery plant; it ranked just ahead of arborvitae, honeysuckles, and roses. Typical of the listings was that of Thomas Affleck's Southern Nurseries in Washington, Mississippi, which advertised "fine new double Althaeas, a dozen sorts" in the 1851–52 catalogue. Rosedale Nurseries, founded in 1860, listed althea in that year's catalogue. It was one of the first commercial nurseries in Texas, and by 1901 was advertising that "we can supply about twenty named varieties in Single and Double; White, Pink, Red, Purple, and all their modifications and combinations; also the Variegated-leaved, with purple flowers."

Altheas, in all their forms, are still supremely adapted to today's gardens, and the future holds promise of even better things. In the 1960s, the late Donald Egolf, of the National Arboretum in Washington, D.C., and well known for his work with crapemyrtle hybrids, developed a series of sterile triploid altheas that have larger, earlier flowers yet develop little or no seed. Sterility ensures that the plant's energy is spent on flower production instead of seed. The Egolf altheas are 'Diana' (white), 'Helene' (white with maroon throat), 'Minerva' (lavender), and 'Aphrodite' (pink). These new types have grown just as well for me as the old standards. They seem to bloom a bit earlier, have slightly larger flowers, and are more compact in height. I have observed some seed development, however. Sam McFadden of Somerville,

Althea (*Hibiscus syriacus*) (Photo by Greg Grant)

Althea (*Hibiscus syriacus*) (Photo by Greg Grant)

Tennessee, has also developed improved altheas, including the beautiful 'Bluebird' and 'White Angel.'

Altheas are very easy to cultivate in just about any soil that is well drained and located in part to full sun, preferably the latter. They are, however, susceptible to cotton root rot in areas with alkaline soils. They can be grown as either shrubs or limbed up to make small trees. Propagation is by seeds (if you aren't particular about the quality of the offspring) or by cuttings rooted under high humidity.

Most people have quit using altheas today in favor of the more popular crapemyrtle. In this new era of plant diversification and with the renewed popularity of old-fashioned plants, it's time for the rose of Sharon to obtain its rightful place as the queen of the Southern garden—or at least as a princess.—*GG*

Hippeastrum × johnsonii

St. Joseph's Lily, Johnson's Amaryllis
Family: Amaryllidaceae (Amaryllis)
Size: 2–3 ft
Zones: 7–11
Perennial bulb
Showy red flowers with white stripes in late spring

Written in German, Henry Nehrling's treatise on the amaryllis, *Die Amaryllis* (1909), describes his first encounter with the St. Joseph's lily and Southern gardens. It started a love affair that would change his life, for he moved to Houston and then Florida and became the father of modern amaryllis breeding.

> I shall never forget the impression which the first amaryllis made on me. It was on a wonderful day in April of the year 1879, as I, aimlessly observing only the half-tropical vegetation, wandered about in the idyllically situated town of Houston in Texas. . . . The splendor of the tea roses, the bloom of the charming Gloire de Dijon, Marechal Niel, Lamarque, Chramotella and other climbing roses on the wide veranda were to me quite overwhelming, since I had just recently quit the raw climate of Chicago. . . . The song of the mockingbird resounded out of all the gardens and the red cardinals slipped chirping through the thick, evergreen loquat trees, *Eriobotrya japonica,* the myrtle bushes and the profusion of red and Cherokee roses. . . . While I wandered in there half dreaming, half in joyful rapture, I suddenly saw in the distance a great, beautiful garden, long, glowing red strips of such wonderful beauty, that I accelerated my steps involuntarily. . . . The low house stood in the background, surrounded by magnolias and other evergreen trees. At the broad veranda, which extended the length of the house, bloomed roses and jasmines, and on both sides of the broad path, leading to the house, there appeared broad

beds with great, beautiful, trumpet-shaped flowers, which glistened and shone in the light of the southern sun as if strewn with gold dust. There was not a hundred, no, a thousand of the flowers, which arose about two feet high over the somewhat short strap-shaped leaves that came forth in thick masses. The flowers showed a broad white stripe on every flower petal, and gave off a very lovely aromatic fragrance. Young palms, *Cycas revoluta,* pampas grass, and gardenias together with roses appeared in lovely groups near the blooming red mass and in union with the short green grass plot heightened the loveliness quite effectively. . . . This first view made a deep and lasting impression on me. No flower appears to me so beautiful, so delightful, so rare in beauty as these, the one characterized here as the red or paradise lily, which I, however, recognized immediately as Johnson's amaryllis, *Hippeastrum Johnsonii,* the first hybrid, which has been raised. It is an old garden flower of the south of our land. . . . I must say that no flower either before or after has so inspired me as this beautiful Amaryllis. Later, I tended and raised many more colorful, more gleaming, and more completely formed amaryllis, but these old favorites recall

Johnson's amaryllis (*Hippeastrum* × *johnsonii*) (Photo by Greg Grant)

the most beautiful time in my life and are still quite my especial joy. I still raise and propagate them today with particular pleasure.

As soon as I had become settled in Houston, I procured *Amaryllis Johnsonsii* and planted them in my garden. I found them later as a favorite garden flower in New Orleans and in all of southern Louisiana, especially plentiful in Mobile and Tallahassee, in Macon and Savannah, and in Charleston, South Carolina.

When I was growing up, the amaryllis was my favorite flower. Each year my mother would give me a Christmas present fit for a budding horticulturist. One year this gift was a boxed Dutch amaryllis. I'll never forget the magic as the stalk emerged from the seemingly lifeless bulb. I was so impressed that each year thereafter I requested and got a new amaryllis. Once I found out my childhood hero, George Washington Carver, also liked (and painted) them, I was even more smitten. Eventually, the collection grew so large that I had to have a greenhouse in which to keep it, for the amaryllis bulbs weren't cold hardy at my home in northeast Texas. Every penny I had ever saved (plus the half my parents paid) went into buying that greenhouse. Before moving off to college, I had to plant my entire amaryllis collection in the yard because I knew no one would look after them for me. Unfortunately, a devastating freeze killed them all.

I quickly noticed, however, that there was an amaryllis blooming in many of the yards in the country that was not killed by the freeze. It was a spring-blooming plant that bore narrower trumpets than those of the Dutch amaryllises. They were bright red and striped white on the inside. I began asking nurserymen what this flower was and where I could buy it. Nobody knew. Finally, my grandmother secured some bulbs from a friend and shared them with me. I'm still multiplying that stock today.

Only when I went to work for Texas A&M did I found out what the plant truly is. Incredibly, it is the first hybrid amaryl-

Johnson's amaryllis (*Hippeastrum × johnsonii*) (Photo by William C. Welch)

lis ever produced, a plant developed by an English watchmaker named Johnson sometime around 1790. A cross between *Amaryllis vittata* and *A. reginae,* it is known scientifically as *Hippeastrum × johnsonii* (formerly *A. johnsonii*) and is commonly referred to as Johnson's amaryllis or the St. Joseph's lily. As is typical of a first-generation hybrid, this plant is a very strong grower and sets no seed when self-pollinated.

Without a doubt, Johnson's hybrid is the finest amaryllis for garden culture in the South. The combination of the brilliant red flowers, the spicy fragrance, and its unbelievable toughness makes it a bulb without equal. Although many early nurseries and catalogues offered this plant, it is available only from specialty sources today. It still thrives, however, in many gardens and cemeteries in the South, and the persuasive gardener should be able to secure a stock (as my grandmother did) from those sources. It's not uncommon to find both of the St. Joseph's lily's parents and other related crosses in Southern gardens as well, particularly as one gets closer to the coast.

Sprekelia formosissima (*A. formosissima*), another member of the amaryllis family, is an even older garden flower than the St. Joseph's lily. This odd-looking native of Mexico was described in John Parkinson's *Garden of Pleasant Flowers* as *Narcissus jacobeus flore rubro* ("The red Indian Daffodil") in 1629 and in Gerard's 1633 herbal as *Narcissus jacobeus indicus* ("the Indian or Jacobean Narcisse"). Bernard M'Mahon, an early American nurseryman, sent Thomas Jefferson "6 roots of the *Amaryllis formosissima*" in 1807 and for cultural information referred Jefferson to his *American Gardener's Calendar,* where the *Sprekelia* is referred to as the "Scarlet Amaryllis." On December 24, 1834, William Prince and Son of Flushing, New York, sent "six splendid scarlet Amaryllis or Jacobean Lily" to Rosedown Plantation in St. Francisville, Louisiana. Today it is commonly called the Aztec or Jacobean lily. It is unfortunately difficult to bring into bloom reliably in the garden.

Yet another amaryllis relative that can be found in older gardens is the oxblood lily (*Rhodophiala bifida,* formerly *A. advena*). Supposedly introduced into the United States by the German Texan botanist Peter Heinrich Oberwetter around the turn of this century, this miniature red "amaryllis" from Argentina has naturalized throughout the German-settled areas of Texas. It blooms in the fall much like *Lycoris* and tolerates all types of soils. It is an excellent naturalizing perennial for beds, lawns, and even roadsides. Texas bulb expert Scott Ogden says, "No other bulb can match the fierce vigor, tenacity, and adaptability of the oxblood lily."

Amaryllis and its relatives are of easy culture. Although not particular about conditions, they grow and multiply best in a well-drained, loose soil with at least part to full sun. Propagation is by division and occasionally seed. —GG

Hyacinthus orientalis albulus

Roman Hyacinth, French Roman Hyacinth
Family: Liliaceae (Lily)
Size: 6–10 in
Zones: 7–9
Perennial bulb
Heavenly scented blue or white (rarely pink) flowers in late winter or early spring

Roman hyacinths (*Hyacinthus orientalis albulus*) were one of the first flowers I ever grew. I dug them from the old Wheeler place in Arcadia where my dad kept his cows. There were both blue and white hyacinths there. I also got my first Byzantine gladiolus from the same site. All were growing beneath a mimosa tree along with 'Grand Primo' narcissus. Those hyacinths have been a favorite of mine since the first time I smelled them.

They are not the flowers you see in the Dutch bulb catalogues. Dutch hyacinths do not perform as true perennials in most of the South and often have to be replanted yearly. In the upper South, Dutch hyacinths may return for a number of years, but each time they will be smaller.

The fragrant, smaller-flowered Roman hyacinth I grew is native to southern France. It is a dependable perennial for the South, the only kind of hyacinth that is. In our region it perennializes both in flower beds and in the grass. And though they are not as showy as the oversized Dutch hyacinths, you'll have to plant Roman hyacinths only once in your lifetime.

Hortus Third says the flowers of Roman hyacinths are white to bright blue. I've also seen a pale pink form, which is very rare today but still persists here and there; people often recall it was in their mother's or grandmother's garden. The blue-flowered form is much more common in old gardens of East Texas and seems to be the most vigorous. Bill comments on Roman hyacinths:

Roman hyacinth (*Hyacinthus orientalis albulus*) (Photo by Greg Grant)

Roman hyacinth (*Hyacinthus orientalis albulus*) (Photo by William C. Welch)

The white form has been most vigorous for me. There were a few naturalized in the garden at Mangham, Louisiana, when I first went there in 1989, and I also received some from an old garden in Fayette County, Texas. Although I have always thought that Roman hyacinths thrive best in relatively dry, sunny locations, the white ones have reproduced quickest where they have more moisture, almost to the point of being overly wet. The particular site where they have done best is a little knoll where the windmill at Fragilee often overflows. The white form also blooms earlier, sometimes at Christmas.

The white form seems to be more common in the black alkaline soils of Central Texas. Lindie Wilson sent Bill three bulbs of pink Roman hyacinths from Elizabeth Lawrence's garden the winter of 2007–8. It is sometimes difficult to tell if a hyacinth is a true Roman hyacinth or just a Dutch hyacinth that has degenerated. Whatever these three bulbs are, Bill says they bloom nicely in late winter.

Liberty Hyde Bailey's *Standard Cyclopedia of Horticulture* (1917) offered three illustrations of Roman hyacinths, including one portrait that covers a full page. In the accompanying text, the book observes that "instead of one large truss from each bulb, the Roman Hyacinth produces three or four smaller but more graceful flower-spikes. By reason of its beauty and exquisite fragrance, its earliness and easy culture, the white Roman hyacinth is the most popular of winter-blooming plants. Several millions of these bulbs are grown annually by the florists of the large cities for winter cut-flowers." Elsewhere, the *Standard Cyclopedia* mentions *Dutch* Roman hyacinths, which it describes as "smaller sized bulbs of the ordinary Dutch hyacinths."

My good friend, the late Flora Ann Bynum of Winston-Salem, North Carolina, was the queen of Roman hyacinths. She devoted a considerable amount of her time to researching them and to the hunt for a double-pink form. Any project she took up, she pursued with religious dedication.

Roman hyacinths bloom outdoors in late winter in the South and are very easy to grow in a well-drained soil. The blue-flowering form requires no care at all. Older gardeners say that the white, and especially the pink, need to be fertilized annually and divided from time to time, and perhaps that is why they have tended to disappear. I started with mostly whites and a few blues. Now I have mostly blues and a few whites. The white blooms first, followed by the blue. Propagation is by division.

These bulbs were widely advertised in Victorian bulb catalogues, not only for outdoor use but also (and especially in the case of the white form) as a forcing bulb for use at Christmas. During the early part of the twentieth century, the name "French Roman hyacinth" began to be used in catalogues, perhaps because the bulbs came from France. They are very rare in the trade today but well worth seeking out. —*GG*

Pink Roman hyacinth (*Hyacinthus orientalis albulus*) (Photo by Cynthia W. Mueller)

Hydrangea macrophylla

Hydrangea, French Hydrangea, Hortensia
Family: Saxifragaceae (Saxifrage)
Size: 2–8 ft
Zones: 7–10
Deciduous shrub
Showy white, pink, or blue flowers in spring and summer

My grandfather Emanis's favorite plant was the big blue hydrangea near the end of the porch by the swing. Now that he is gone, I've grown to cherish hydrangeas as well. My oldest brother, who lives in the house where we grew up, wants to cut his down because it looks messy. I told him he couldn't cut down Momma's hydrangea; people in most parts of Texas would do anything to be able to grow hydrangeas.

The showy shrub we call the "French" hydrangea is not from France, or at least not originally. In fact, *Hydrangea macrophylla* is a native of Japan. The French were responsible, however, for

Lacecap (*Hydrangea macrophylla*,
unknown cultivar) (Photo by Greg Grant)

Oakleaf hydrangea (*Hydrangea quercifolia*)
(Photo by Greg Grant)

much of its breeding around the turn of the twentieth century. The results have been divided into two distinct groups, the hortensias and the lacecaps. The two types of *macrophylla* hydrangea are easy enough to distinguish. Hortensias bear clusters of showy, mostly sterile flowers, which give them their large "mophead" look. Lacecaps have a center of nonshowy, fertile flowers surrounded by a ring of showy, sterile flowers. There are many cultivars of both types, but hortensias are by far the most common in Southern gardens and are also popular as a source of fresh and dried cut flowers.

I could not find a date for the introduction of *H. macrophylla* into American gardens, although I did learn that the species was in Europe before 1800. However, my nursery catalogues gave some indication of what was available locally by the late nineteenth century. An 1881–82 Langdon Nurseries catalogue (near Mobile, Alabama) listed *H. hortensis* ("an elegant well-known plant"), *H. imperatrice eugenia* ("a new variety"), *H. paniculata grandiflora* ("new, from Japan"), and *H. japonica*. Frank Vestal

"Mophead" hydrangeas (*H. macrophylla*) are deservedly popular southern heirloom plant. (Photo by William C. Welch)

of Little Rock, Arkansas, listed *H. paniculata* in 1896. A 1906–7 Fruitland Nurseries catalogue (Augusta, Georgia) listed the hortensia cultivars 'Japonica,' 'Otaksa,' 'Otaksa monstrosa,' 'Ramis Pictis' or 'Red Branched,' 'Rosea,' and 'Thomas Hogg.' This nursery also advertised *H. paniculata grandiflora*. Known as the "pee gee" hydrangea, this species with large, white flowers is frequently cultivated in gardens of the upper South today.

The first hydrangea in the South, if not in Southern gardens, was *H. quercifolia,* the oakleaf hydrangea, a native of southeastern North America. This plant was named by William Bartram and introduced into English gardens in 1803. In addition to the showy white flowers it bears in summer, this shrub's foliage colors well in the fall. The most beautiful specimens I have ever seen are at the Birmingham Botanic Garden. A number of cultivars of oakleaf hydrangea are available today, including one with double flowers, another with golden foliage, and even a dwarf one. They all make spectacular specimens in partly shaded gardens and, like all hydrangeas, produce beautiful cut flowers, either fresh or dried.

"Mophead" hydrangea (*H. macrophylla*) prefer partially shaded locations and moist soils. (Photo by William C. Welch)

Oakleaf hydrangea (*Hydrangea quercifolia* 'Snowflake') (Photo by William C. Welch)

Hydrangeas require a loose, well-drained organic soil and plenty of moisture to thrive. These shrubs should be pruned back annually to keep them from looking "messy," but make your cuts right after the bushes bloom, for pruning later in the season or especially in wintertime removes the buds that make the following season's flowers. Hydrangeas are not nearly as pretty without the flowers, although I always thought the foliage smelled good. The hortensia is unique in that it serves as a sort of living litmus paper: acidic soils cause it to bear blue flowers, while alkaline soils turn the flowers pink. Shades between the two are often seen as well. Aluminum sulfate, a soil acidifier, may be added to the soil to obtain blue flowers, and lime may be added to create pink ones. Make them any color you want; just don't cut them down.

The Ruby Mize Azalea Garden, part of the Stephen F. Austin State University Mast Arboretum in Nacogdoches, Texas, has an extensive collection of hydrangeas. Go see them if you can. You are guaranteed to fall in love.—*GG*

Oakleaf hydrangea (*Hydrangea quercifolia*) (Photo by William C. Welch)

Ilex spp.

Holly
Family: Aquifoliaceae (Holly)
Size: 3–60 ft
Zones 7–11
Evergreen (occasionally deciduous) shrubs or trees
Attractive evergreen foliage and red (sometimes orange or yellow) berries for cutting and wildlife

One of the earliest favorites in Southern gardens was the native American holly (*Ilex opaca*). Its bright red berries, evergreen foliage, and handsome pyramidal form made it a favorite holiday decoration, and settlers either collected cut foliage from the woods or dug entire young trees to bring to their gardens. There were a number of forms, and this plant soon took the place of the familiar English holly in the garden plans of early America. It can serve as a specimen or used as a large, evergreen hedge. The English holly is not very adapted to the cold of Northern areas of the United States or the intense heat of the Southern states.

American holly (*Ilex opaca*) (Photo by Greg Grant)

Possumhaw holly (*Ilex decidua*) (Photo by Greg Grant)

Colonists in the Carolinas used dahoon holly (*I. cassine*) as a tea substitute after noticing that Native Americans set great store by it. Dahoon holly is a native found throughout the South, especially on moist soils. As with all hollies, plants of both sexes are needed to produce berries, which are excellent bird and wildlife food.

Possumhaw holly (*I. decidua*) loses its leaves in the winter, and its decorative berries shine in the landscape. Variations in berry color and tree shapes were common in the wild, and early settlers often dug these and transported them into the home garden. The small leaves are easily pruned into shapes, and multistemmed specimens are often used as accent plants. Once again, only the female plants have berries, but there is usually plenty of male pollen in the area to allow for fruit set. Fruit color varies from bright yellow to orange and dark red. The red berries on bare stems against a blue winter sky are one of the most beautiful sights of the native Southern landscape. Late in the winter or early spring cedar waxwings and other birds strip the fruit from its stems. Recent years have seen cutting-grown selections of possumhaw hollies like 'Warren's Red' become popular.

Dwarf yaupon holly (*Ilex vomitoria* 'Nana') (Photo by Greg Grant)

Yaupon holly (*Ilex vomitoria*) (Photo by Greg Grant)

Topiary of yaupon holly (*Ilex vomitoria*)
(Photo by Greg Grant)

Possumhaw holly (*Ilex decidua*) (Photo by
William C. Welch)

Yaupon holly (*I. vomitoria*) is said to have the highest caffeine content of any plant in North America and was also utilized by Native Americans to make tea and stronger, ceremonial drinks. This is one of our most important hedges or shrubs, very drought resistant once established and little bothered by pests. Dwarf forms of yaupon (*I. vomitoria* 'Nana') are popular and useful as hedges in Southern gardens. They are more tolerant of poorly drained soils than boxwood and also more drought tolerant.
—*WCW*

Iris spp.

Iris, Flags, Fleur-de-lis
Family: Iridaceae (Iris)
Size: 3–5 ft
Zones: 5–9
Perennial bulb or rhizome
Showy flowers in all colors of the rainbow in spring

Among the most beautiful and cosmopolitan perennials in the world, bearded iris thrive throughout the South except in those areas that lie within a hundred miles or so of the coasts, although some of the older types may succeed there, too. As with daylilies and roses, the older forms of iris, those favored by our ancestors, are easier to grow and longer lived than the hundreds of new hybrids that fill catalogues today.

All of the irises discussed here are rhizomatous and have swordlike foliage. The flower-bearing stalks appear mostly in springtime, and the blooms are very showy, six-petaled, and

Cemetery whites (*Iris × albicans* (Photo by Greg Grant)

Cemetery whites (*Iris × albicans* (Photo by William C. Welch)

often fragrant. The three upright petals are known as standards, and the lower three, as falls. Their form is the pattern of the fleur-de-lis, known as the symbol of French royalty. In bearded irises, brightly colored hairs (the whiskers of the "beard") emerge from the falls and serve as attractants to pollinating insects. The name *Iris* is for the Greek goddess of the rainbow and suggests the iridescent colors found in the flowers of this genus.

Probably the most common bearded iris grown in the South is the cemetery white (*I. × albicans*). These irises are a naturally sterile hybrid and extremely hardy, often marking abandoned homesites and old cemeteries, where for several weeks each spring they command the attention of all passersby. Originally from Yemen, cemetery whites have naturalized so extensively in the South and become such a fixture of our rural landscape that many people consider them native.

Another iris commonly found on old homesites and cemeteries in Texas and the Gulf South are the early purples. These are thought to be a form of *I. × germanica*. Both these and the cemetery whites thrive over a broad area, even in areas close to the coasts where excessive humidity and moisture limit success with other bearded irises.

Bearded irises are drought tolerant but resent poorly drained soils. They perform best when their rhizomes are only partially covered by well-drained soil and prefer a spot where the sun bakes their roots for at least half of each day in summertime. Dividing plants every three to five years helps keep them vigorous and flowering while providing a source for more plants. Each division should have a growing point and fan of foliage.

Probably the first iris imported from the Old World to America was the yellow flag (*I. pseudacorus*). This was commonly grown during the seventeenth century, and early American gardeners are known to have secured stock from Europe. Part of their appeal was their supposed medicinal value, for this plant was used in the treatment of "weak eyes" and ulcers. Undoubtedly, though, colonial gardeners prized this plant for its beauty as well, for the

Louisiana iris (*Iris* spp. and hybrids) (Photo by William C. Welch)

bright yellow flowers appear in April, displaying the classic fleur-de-lis form.

The yellow flag's foliage is much taller than that of the bearded irises and may reach four to five feet under ideal conditions. Unlike the bearded irises, yellow flags thrive on wet sites and naturalize along the edges of ponds and streams, in much the same fashion as the native Louisiana irises. Yellow flags prefer the moisture and humidity of the coast but will thrive anywhere in the South. Unfortunately, it has proven invasive in Southern wetlands.

Louisiana irises can be grown successfully in every area of the South. The source of this adaptability no doubt lies in their parentage, for the Louisiana irises were bred from species found native in Arkansas, Louisiana, and Texas. Their historic use as garden plants outside their native range was minimal until recent years. But in the last generation, modern breeding methods and a strong national support group have produced hundreds of new cultivars.

The flower stalks of the Louisiana irises may vary considerably, from one to six feet, and the flowers may measure from three to seven inches across. Because all the primary colors are inherent in the various species that contributed to this group, there is no limit to the color range. The Louisianas, for example, include the purest form of red of any iris.

Louisiana irises prefer an acidic soil in the range of pH 6.5 or lower. They like large quantities of both fertilizer and water, but their greatest need for both of these comes during the naturally cool, moist fall and winter seasons. They are among the few irises that will thrive in poorly drained soils. Louisiana irises can be effectively used along streams and lakes in areas that are inundated periodically by changing water levels. Their foliage is lush and requires heavy fertilization to remain healthy and productive. Some cultivars go dormant during the heat of summer, leaving dead foliage that should be cut back or removed. New foliage will appear again in the fall.

Fall is the best season for transplanting. Beds should be well tilled and amended with large amounts of compost, peat, or pine bark. Rhizomes should be planted just below ground level and kept moist until well established. Clumps spread quickly, and individual rhizomes should be spaced several feet apart to avoid the need for annual division.

The Historic Iris Preservation Society (HIPS) was founded in 1988 to provide dates of introduction and other pertinent information relating to heirloom irises. —*WCW*

Jasminum spp.

Jasmine, Jessamine, Confederate Jasmine, Star Jasmine
Family: Oleaceae (Olive)
Size: 2–6 ft
Zones: 8–11
Tropical or semitropical shrubs and vines
Most with very fragrant white (sometimes yellow) flowers in spring or summer

The overpowering scent of jasmine has proven so alluring throughout the ages that anything that smelled or looked like jasmine was generally called such. Sometimes the plant in question *was* a jasmine: the vine that George Washington called "Persian Jessamine" in his diary was *Jasminum officinale,* more popularly known as the poet's, white, or common jasmine. Lady Skipwith, another colonial Virginian, also grew "white jasmine," and Thomas Jefferson grew both "jasmine white" and "jasmine yellow." This last was not in fact a true jasmine. What is popularly called Carolina or yellow jasmine is actually a native species of *Gelsemium*—lovely, but not related to jasmine.

Climbing jasmine (*Jasminum polyanthum*), a fragrant, spring-flowering climber (Photo by William C. Welch)

Confederate or star jasmine
(*Trachelospermum jasminoides*) (Photo by
Greg Grant)

Confederate or star jasmine
(*Trachelospermum jasminoides*) (Photo by
William C. Welch)

Jasmines weave their way through the history of Southern gardens, appearing in our earliest handbooks and catalogues. Bernard M'Mahon made numerous references to jasmines in his *American Gardener's Calendar.* An invoice dated February 27, 1837, from nurserymen William Prince and Son showed that Martha Turnbull received the following at Rosedown Plantation: "Spanish or Catalonian Jessamine, *Jasminum revolutum, Jasminum gracile,* and *Jasminum undulatum.*" Thomas Affleck's Southern Nurseries catalogue (Mississippi) listed "Hardy Jessamines, several varieties" in 1851–52, and Arnold Puetz's "Lily Nursery" (Florida) offered "Cape, Arabian, Grand Duke, and others" in 1881—the cape jasmine, however, is a gardenia. Langdon Nurseries (Alabama) offered *J. officinale* and *J. nudiflorum* in 1881–82.

Jasminum nudiflorum was a gift of the famous plant explorer Robert Fortune, who brought this sprawling shrub back from China between 1843 and 1861. Arnold Puetz's Arabian jasmine was undoubtedly *J. sambac,* which seems to be the species most commonly cultivated in the coastal South today. Its cultivars, 'Maid of Orleans' and the double, buttonlike 'Grand Duke of Tuscany,' are especially popular for their heady fragrance.

Confederate or star jasmine
(*Trachelospermum jasminoides*) (Photo by
Greg Grant)

Other jasmines cultivated in the South include the primrose jasmine (*J. mesnyi*) Florida jasmine (*J. floridanum*), and winter jasmine (*J. polyanthum*). A host of unrelated jasmine imposters have traditionally been part of the Southern garden: Confederate or star jasmine (*Trachelospermum jasminoides*), the heavenly scented night-blooming jasmine (*Cestrum nocturnum*), crape jasmine (*Tabernaemontana divaricata*), and orange jasmine (*Murraya paniculata*).

Jasmines, and most of the imposters, are generally very easy to grow under most conditions. Some are cold-tender and best grown in pots, some are vines, and some are fairly hardy shrubs. Propagation is by rooting cuttings or layering.

The heavy scent of jasmine is like that of paperwhites: tawdry and overpowering. Some lust after it, while others gasp for air. Personally, I fall in the lust category, especially when the jasmine scent is drifting through a garden. Not surprisingly, the extraction of perfume from jasmine flowers is an ancient industry—though today it is an artificial jasmine scent that we splash on everything from potpourri to the upholstery in cars. Unfortunately, it smells like melted plastic to me. There's just no substitute for the real thing.—*GG*

Juniperus virginiana

Cedar, Red Cedar, Eastern Red Cedar
Family: Cupressaceae (Cypress)
Size: 40–50 ft
Zones: 3–10
Evergreen tree
Attractive green foliage for cutting and blue berries (on females) for the birds

What we all call cedar is not a true cedar but a juniper. True cedars belong to the genus *Cedrus,* in the pine family, while our native red "cedar" belongs to the cypress family that includes baldcypress, which isn't actually a cypress at all. An honest, true cypress belongs to the genus *Cupressus.* See why you're a gardener and not a botanist?

How many cedars are there marking abandoned homesites, lining avenues, and standing guard at cemeteries in the South today? They are everywhere. The fence-post guys haven't even made a dent in them. The cedar ranks right up there with the magnolia and the live oak as a popular evergreen tree in the South. Although it may be less popular in urban gardens, it is probably the king of evergreens in rural areas, especially old cemeteries and homesites. Rachel's Garden in Tennessee has a fine example of a cedar allée.

It was king especially at holiday time, when traditionally it supplied the Christmas tree for rural families. When my dad was in charge of cutting a "Charlie Brown" tree for the Grant family, it was what we always had. Thanks to the affection of its needles for my mom's carpet, we switched to loblolly or shortleaf pine. But now that she's in a different house with a tile floor, the cedar is again welcome. One year when I wasn't around to cut us a tree, my mother went into town to the Christmas tree farm to get our first bought tree. She looked for hours but couldn't find one as ugly as we were used to and came home empty-handed. It was

Red cedar (*Juniperus virginiana*), the Grants' Christmas tree (Photo by Greg Grant)

just like old times because my dad was sent out to the pasture again to make an "acceptable" emergency selection.

In addition to its ornamental value, the red cedar provides outstanding aromatic wood that has traditionally been used for pencils, chests, closets, rustic furniture, and any structure that calls for weather resistance. I use red cedar for making my plethora of untreated bluebird houses.

In a letter to the editor of the *Natchez Daily Courier* on October 28, 1854, Thomas Affleck tried my same futile bit of botanical education, writing that "the cedars are very beautiful. And, by the way, what we know as the Red Cedar, is a Juniper." He went on to add some advice that is just as good today:

> The Junipers, headed by our own beautiful native, the so-called Red Cedar (*J. virginiana*), are indispensable. In the "Red Cedar" there is a great diversity of foliage and habit of growth; some being open and loose in habit, others upright and compact. The latter I have always selected from the seed-bed. They should have room to grow, and be allowed to sweep the

Red cedar (*Juniperus virginiana*) (Photo by Greg Grant)

ground with their branches; not pruned up into the likeness of a gigantic broom!

Most of the early nurseries in the South carried the red cedar. The ones that didn't probably knew that their customers would just dig them from the wild. Early Southern nursery catalogues in which I have found mention of this tree include Affleck's Southern Nurseries of Washington, Mississippi, 1851–52; Langdon Nurseries near Mobile, Alabama, 1881–82; Denison Nurseries of Denison, Texas, 1885–86; Mission Valley Nurseries of Nursery, Texas, 1888; Waldheim Nursery of Boerne, Texas, 1895–96; and Frank Vestal–Florist and Nurseryman of Little Rock, Arkansas, 1896.

I'm sure everybody realizes that our native "cedars" are very easy to grow, since they flourish along fence rows throughout the South. Propagation is from seed, or you may dig the young trees from the woods or the fence rows, with permission of course. Remember that they come in male and female. The males make the yellow pollen in the winter and spring that causes "cedar fever" for some. I'm more partial to the females, which make the somewhat showy blue berries in the fall and winter for the birds and Christmas decorations. —*GG*

Kerria japonica 'Pleniflora'

Kerria, Japanese Rose
Family: Rosaceae (Rose)
Size: 3–6 ft
Zones: 4–9
Deciduous shrub
Showy yellow flowers in spring

William Kerr first brought the double-flowered form of this plant from China to Kew Gardens in England in 1805, so perhaps it is only fair that it was named for him. The form brought back to the United States was typically referred to as *Kerria japonica pleniflora,* although in point of fact, the kerria was already known in Europe from descriptions written by Engelbert Kaempfer in 1712 and Carl Peter Thunberg in his *Flora Japonica* in 1784. If the *K. japonica* was a novelty to Westerners, however, it was thoroughly familiar to the gardeners of temperate Asia. A native of China, it had by the eighteenth century been long cultivated in Japan.

Toward the end of the nineteenth century, kerrias with gold and silver variegated foliage were discovered and soon became a common sight in American gardens. Peter Henderson remarked in 1890 that kerria was "an old favorite in the garden, with both single and double flowers, to which has lately been added a very pretty variety with variegated leaves."

The plant form is that of a spreading shrub, three to six feet tall. The stems are green year-round and are an asset to the winter garden, but the kerria's flowers are the feature that popularized this plant. The individual blossoms are about one and one-half inches in diameter and are borne singly at the ends of short stems produced during the previous year's growth. The kerria's heaviest period of bloom lasts for two or three weeks in April or early May, though flowers also appear sporadically throughout the growing season. In the garden of the late Bob McDonald

Kerria (*Kerria japonica*) (Photo by William C. Welch)

in Mangham, Louisiana, kerria is mixed with mock orange and white Lady Banks roses, creating a spectacular spring display for several weeks each year.

Kerria flowers are sometimes confused with those of the yellow Lady Banks rose. Both plants thrive in our region, and since both are members of the rose family, the flowers have a superficial similarity. But the kerria bears flowers of a much more golden color than the pale straw yellow blossoms of the Lady Banks rose. There are variations, however. Ryan Gainey shared a paler yellow single-flowering type that is thriving in my north Louisiana garden. Propagation is from cuttings in summer or fall. Pruning should be carried out immediately after the spring flower season. Kerrias prefer well-drained loamy soils that are neutral or slightly acidic. High fertility can result in excessive growth and little flowering. They much prefer a location with protection from the afternoon sun—the flowers burn otherwise—and kerrias will actually bloom well in the shade.—*WCW*

Lagerstroemia indica

Crapemyrtle, Lilac of the South
Family: Lythraceae (Loosestrife)
Size: 3–30 ft
Zones: 7–11
Deciduous shrub to small tree
Showy white, pink, red, lavender, or purple flowers all summer

A knowledgeable expert and garden writer suggested that lilacs be included in this book. Lilacs as in "the North," I asked? He quickly quoted historic examples of lilacs in the South. I responded by pointing out that most plants have been grown in the South somewhere by somebody at sometime, but that doesn't make them Southern. Anyway, we have our own "lilac of the South," the crapemyrtle. According to Gilbert Onderdonk's 1989–99 Mission Valley Nurseries catalogue (Nursery, Texas), crapemyrtle is "deservedly one of the most popular shrubs in America. In the South it takes the place of the lilac of the North, but is far more beautiful."

Crapemyrtle (*Lagerstroemia indica*) (Photo by Greg Grant)

Every self-respecting gardener knows that you grow lilacs in the North and crapemyrtles in the South. Even the famed Michigan horticulturist Liberty Hyde Bailey knew this. In his 1917 *Standard Cyclopedia of Horticulture* he stated, "The crape myrtle, *Lagerstroemia indica,* is to the South what the lilac and the snowball are to the North—an inhabitant of nearly every home yard." Saying the lilac is a Southern heirloom plant is like saying "Yankee Doodle" is the state song of Georgia.

The crapemyrtle received its common name for its superficial resemblance (although no relation) to the true myrtle (*Myrtus*) and for its crapelike flowers. The Latin name of the genus, *Lagerstroemia,* was given to the tree in 1759 by the Swedish botanist Linnaeus in honor of his friend Magnus von Lagerstroem (1696–1759), director of the Swedish East Indies Company and an avid naturalist. The species name *indica* is a misnomer, for the

Crapemyrtle (*Lagerstroemia indica*) (Photo by Greg Grant)

Crapemyrtle (*Lagerstroemia indica*) (Photo by Greg Grant)

crapemyrtle is not native to India but to China. Many early plants made it to the West from China through India, leading to the nomenclature confusion.

According to *Hortus Third*, there are about fifty-five species of *Lagerstroemia*, all native to Asia and the Pacific Islands. Of these, only four are cold hardy through most of the South: *L. indica*, *L. fauriei*, *L. subcostata*, and *L. limii*. Traditionally, *L. indica* has monopolized the attention of Southern gardeners, but this is changing. *Lagerstroemia fauriei*, a species native to Japan, is the parent of a breeding program carried out at the National Arboretum in Washington, D.C. This tree boasts small but fragrant white flowers and an incredible, cinnamon-colored exfoliating bark, but its resistance to disease was of greatest interest to the National Arboretum's breeder, the late Donald Egolf. From *L. fauriei* he bred a strain of mildew-resistant hybrid crapemyrtles, which he named after American Indians ('Natchez,' 'Tuscarora,' 'Muskogee,' etc.). The North Carolina State University Arboretum (now the J. C. Raulston Arboretum) introduced a cultivar of *L. fauriei* named 'Fantasy,' which has proven cold hardy in that

'Catawba' crapemyrtle (*Lagerstroemia indica* 'Catawba') (Photo by Greg Grant)

'Dynamite' crapemyrtle (*Lagerstroemia indica* 'Dynamite') (Photo by Greg Grant)

‘Siren’ crapemyrtle (*Lagerstroemia indica* ‘Siren’) (Photo by Greg Grant)

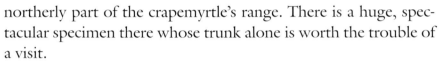

Crapemyrtle (*Lagerstroemia indica*) (Photo by Greg Grant)

northerly part of the crapemyrtle's range. There is a huge, spectacular specimen there whose trunk alone is worth the trouble of a visit.

Very few folks are aware that the first hybrids between *L. fauriei* and *L. indica* came from the yard of Bill Basham in Houston, Texas, not the National Arboretum. In 1965, the legendary Lynn Lowery introduced the first ones through his nursery there and also sent them to Donald Egolf. Of those early chance hybrids, the vigorous lilac-colored ‘Basham's Party Pink’ is still available today. It's my opinion that Egolf got the idea to start his hybrid breeding program from these trees in Texas because he did not start hybridizing with *L. fauriei* until after he received ‘Basham's Party Pink.’ ‘Tuscarora,’ one of his very first introductions, was a 1967 cross between ‘Basham's Party Pink’ and ‘Cherokee.’

Lagerstroemia subcostata is a native of Taiwan and China. It apparently was used in breeding the National Arboretum hybrids as well. It has very small white flowers and an extremely attractive smooth, tan-colored bark. Its bark color looks like a mixture of cinnamon and sugar. There is a very nice specimen just inside the entrance of Louisiana State University's Burden Research Plantation in Baton Rouge. Otherwise, it's very uncommon.

Crapemyrtle (*Lagerstroemia indica*) (Photo by Greg Grant)

Lagerstroemia limii is an odd duck with pink flowers and furrowed nonexfoliating bark. We have one in our "drive-through" crapemyrtle collection at the Stephen F. Austin Mast Arboretum in Nacogdoches, Texas. The queen's crapemyrtle (*L. speciosa*) is widely cultivated in tropical regions for its large clusters of huge flowers in shades of purple, pink, and white. It's a sight to behold

Crapemyrtle (*Lagerstroemia indica*) on the campus of Texas A&M University, College Station (Photo by William C. Welch)

but unfortunately not cold hardy. When I lived in San Antonio, there were a few root-hardy specimens in a yard near the botanic garden that I admired for the individual flower size alone.

Of course, *L. indica* is the queen of Southern gardens. It is very likely the most popular small flowering tree in the entire South. It has been cultivated in its native Southeast Asia for thousands of years. Our crapemyrtle was supposedly introduced to the Royal Botanic Gardens at Kew, England, in 1759. Its exact date of introduction into the United States is unknown. Credit is often given to André Michaux, who established a nursery near Charleston, South Carolina, around 1786. Apparently George Washington was one of the first to attempt to grow the crapemyrtle here. Records at Mount Vernon show that a ship arrived in Philadelphia in April 1799 carrying two plants and seeds of *L. reginae*, as well as seeds of *L. indica*. Bernard M'Mahon mentioned *L. indica* in his *American Gardener's Calendar* in 1806. Crapemyrtle was listed among the plants cultivated in 1811 at the famous Elgin Botanic Garden in New York. Records at Prince

Crapemyrtle (*Lagerstroemia indica*) in the Heights area in Houston (Photo by William C. Welch)

Crapemyrtle (*Lagerstroemia indica*) trunks at the Dallas Arboretum (Photo by William C. Welch)

Crapemyrtle (*Lagerstroemia indica*) (Photo by William C. Welch)

Crapemyrtle (*Lagerstroemia indica*) trunks
(Photo by William C. Welch)

Nursery in New York show that it was offering the crapemyrtle for sale in 1827, and soon it began to spread across the South. Martha Turnbull ordered a number of different plants from the Prince Nursery for Rosedown Plantation in St. Francisville, Louisiana. Thomas Affleck mentioned the crapemyrtle in a letter to the editor of the *Natchez Daily Courier* in 1854, but it was not listed in his 1851–52 Southern Nurseries catalogue in Washington, Mississippi. Other nurseries began to offer crapemyrtle in their catalogues: Montgomery Nurseries of Montgomery, Alabama, in 1860; Langdon's Nurseries near Mobile in 1881–82 (four varieties: pink, purple, crimson, and white); in Texas, T. V. Munson's Denison Nurseries in 1885 (pink, crimson, and purple), and in Frelsburg J. F. Leyendecker's Pearfield Nursery in 1888, noting that it was "too well known to require description."

Almost every abandoned early homesite in the South is marked by at least one surviving crapemyrtle. It always fascinated me as a child to see the large-trunked crapemyrtles, jonquils, and garlic growing by themselves in the middle of the pastures. This toughness and survivability have led to their use as a frequent cemetery ornamental and a common street tree.

Crapemyrtles are very easy to cultivate in any type of soil as long as they have direct sunlight. If the highway department can grow them remarkably well, the rest of us have an overwhelming chance of success. Unfortunately, they are often overpruned and in this way horribly disfigured. My friends and I call this "crape murder." Actually, the only pruning they require is to remove unwanted suckers to show off their beautiful bark and branching structure. Green seed pods may also be trimmed off on smaller trees to promote reblooming. Why on earth people want to pay somebody money to trim off all the dry seed pods on their dormant trees I'll never understand. We don't do it to any other tree. I actually think the pod clusters are kind of attractive. They are certainly natural. The smart thing to do is plant crapemyrtle cultivars that grow the same height as your landscape situation calls for.

When looking for crapemyrtles at nurseries, you will find various plants described as "mini," "dwarf," "semidwarf," "standard," and "tall." In fact, crapemyrtles are available in all sorts of sizes, with different cultivars stopping at heights of anywhere from three to thirty feet. Carl Whitcomb of Oklahoma is actively introducing a plethora of novel *L. indica* cultivars, including some with true red and maroon flowers along with those with burgundy foliage. These may be improvements over the often overly vigorous and heavy seed setting of National Arboretum hybrids.

Crapemyrtle propagation is by seed, dormant cuttings, or leafy cuttings under mist. Though they may be a bit overplanted, they certainly are adapted, attractive, and historic. —*GG*

Laurus nobilis

Greek Laurel, Cooking Bay, Bay Tree, Sweet Bay
Family: Lauraceae (Laurel)
Size: 10–30 ft
Zones: 9–11
Large evergreen shrub or small tree
Aromatic foliage

Many plants have the name of laurel, but this is the only one properly so called. Many other common names have attached themselves to *Laurus nobilis,* reflecting the plant's long history of varied uses. Thus, over the years it has been called sweet bay, cooking bay, and spice laurel—names that all reflect the leaves' use as a culinary spice—as well as Greek laurel, poet's laurel, or victor's laurel—names that reflect the ancient Greek custom of weaving its branches into the wreaths used to crown a victor.

This beautiful evergreen shrub or small tree is a native of southern Europe. Although grown throughout the world as a container plant, the laurel is cold sensitive and freezes back occasionally even in zone 9. Because of their agreeable flavor, the leaves are popular in cooking and in various confections. One source (Peter Henderson, 1890) indicates that in the last century the dried figs imported into this country were usually packed with bay leaves.

In the garden, the bay is valued for its tolerance to shearing. The leathery, evergreen foliage responds well to clipping, and the plant is popular as a topiary specimen. It shapes well into cones, pyramids, standards, or hedges. The dark green leaves are typically two to four inches long, and the plant has a compact, tapering form. Frances and Milton Parker's beautiful garden in Beaufort, South Carolina, has a bay hedge about eight feet tall that separates their landscape into two "rooms." This planting is reported to be at least 150 years old and only occasionally suffers damage from cold.

Greek laurel (*Laurus nobilis*) (Photo by Greg Grant)

Large old specimens of treelike proportions are rumored to exist in Brenham, Texas, and a very old plant at the Gideon Lincecum homesite at Long Point, Texas (Washington County), may date back to the year of the house's construction, 1843. Though neglected for many years, the Lincecum bay continued to prosper until its recent exposure to a large bulldozer. Even that experience has not caused its demise, for bay trees sprout readily from the roots and form clumps.

Since I have never seen fruit on *L. nobilis,* I surmise that all the plants I have grown and seen were propagated from male stock. The flowers are described as yellowish, and the fruit black or dark purple, the size of a small cherry. References describe the bay's fruit as a source of essential oils from which laurin ointment, a remedy useful in human and veterinary medicine, is made. These berries are also used to create sweat-inducing aromatic baths and are distilled to make the liqueur Fioranvanti.

Probably the best-known decorative use of this plant is the

Greek laurel (*Laurus nobilis*) (Photo by Greg Grant)

one referred to in many of the common names: the weaving of its leaves and branches into wreaths for crowning heroes and scholars. The term "laureate" refers to that tradition. This plant was considered a medicinal cure-all until the eighteenth century, and according to Nicholas Culpeper's *English Physician Enlarged, or the Herbal* (1653), it "resisteth witchcraft very potently."

The bay is not fussy about soil but does require good drainage. It is quite drought tolerant, although it grows best where it receives some afternoon shade during the hot summer months. Propagation is by division of the root parts, cuttings, or seed. Cuttings are not easily rooted, but nurserymen experienced with mist systems and semihardwood cuttings during the summer report some success.

Bay plants are available from nurseries specializing in herbs and unusual plants. Although susceptibility to cold limits their use, bays are otherwise easily grown and an interesting and useful plant for containers.

Southern nurseries seventy-five or one hundred years ago often offered bay trees to their customers. Fruitland Nurseries, Augusta, Georgia, in its 1906–7 catalogue describes the plant well: "*Laurus nobilis* (Bay tree, Apollo's or Spice Laurel). A beautiful evergreen with long, narrow, glossy green leaves, which are very aromatic. . . . There is a growing demand for these beautiful trees. We offer a nice lot of standard and pyramid bays in tubs."

Greg indicates that when settlers first arrived in the South and didn't have access to true bay, they used red bay (*Persea borbonia*), sweet bay magnolia, also called white bay (*Magnolia virginata*), and wax myrtle (*Myrica cereifera*) as substitutes. —*WCW*

Leucojum aestivum

Summer Snowflake, Snow Drops, Dew Drops
Family: Amaryllidaceae (Amaryllis)
Size: 1 ft
Zones: 6–9
Perennial bulb
Delicate white flowers in late winter or early spring

Leucojums are among the most persistent of the spring-flowering bulbs that grow in the South. Their ability to naturalize is comparable to that of the hardiest of the *Narcissus*. The three-fourths-inch fragrant flowers generally appear in late winter, are bell shaped, and are marked with a distinctive green spot on the margin of each petal. Beginning in February or March in the South, the leucojums' bloom lasts for several weeks. The dark green foliage the snowflakes produce is among the most attractive of any spring bulb foliage, and it is outstanding for several months from late fall through winter.

Summer snowflake (*Leucojum aestivum*)
(Photo by Greg Grant)

Summer snowflake (*Leucojum aestivum*)
(Photo by Greg Grant)

Leucojums—or snowflakes, as they are commonly known—show to best advantage in the landscape when planted in large clumps of bulbs. They also combine well with other spring-flowering bulbs and thrive in sun or shade of deciduous trees. Clumps may be left undivided for many years without sacrificing flowers, but division is an easy means of propagation. Mature clumps may be divided in late spring after the foliage has yellowed. Snowflakes thrive even in heavy clay soils.

I have recently combined snowflakes with blue plumbago (*Plumbago auriculata*) in my garden (zone 8). After the first hard freeze in fall I cut back the plumbago and enjoy the dark green foliage of the snowflakes all winter. By the time the flowers have faded in spring, the blue plumbago is beginning to flower and conceals the dying snowflake foliage. It is interesting to note that snowflakes are often found growing at the base of deciduous trees like pecans, where they receive some sun in winter but little at other seasons. They are also well adapted to areas where moisture is scant. They seem to thrive on summer dryness, making them perfect for the natural rainfall in most of the South. Both plants like some protection from the hottest afternoon sun. 'Gravetye Giant' is a cultivar that has noticeably larger flowers than those of the species form. It has done equally well as the species form in my garden, and the flowers are definitely larger and showier. It blooms a little later, however. Greg notes that it's actually quite common in the trade now.

One of the nicest landscape uses of *L. aestivum* I have observed is their placement as a one-foot-wide border between the walks and a large panel of turf in the main parterre of Robert Smith's garden in Breaux Bridge, Louisiana. Robert has created a beautiful setting for his home and his Au Vieux Paris Antiques business with a garden that features many Southern heirloom plants. Snowflakes are natives of central and southern Europe and are often found along stream banks in southern France. The name is derived from the Greek *leukos,* meaning "white," and *ion,* a "violet." According to Peter Henderson (1890) snowflakes were first introduced in 1596 and are dedicated to St. Agnes, the patron saint of young virgins, for their loveliness and purity and hence are sometimes called St. Agnes' flower. In Parkinson's time they were also known as the great early bulbous violet.

The summer snowflake (*L. aestivum*) is often confused in the trade with the spring snowflake (*L. vernum*), a species less well adapted to gardens of the lower South. One source of this misidentification may be that the so-called summer snowflake actually blooms in the spring and dies back in the summer, at least in the South. But if in doubt about the identity of your snowflakes, wait until they bloom, for the two species are easily distinguished then: *L. vernum* bears solitary flowers on each of its arching stems, whereas *L. aestivum* bears multiple flowers on each stalk.

In *A Southern Garden,* Elizabeth Lawrence wrote about her experiences with growing both the spring and summer snowflakes. Her North Carolina experiences are similar to those I have had here in Texas. When comparing the two, she says of *L. aestivum* that it is "a much more robust plant, with stems to two feet, larger and broader bells, and longer, thicker leaves. The summer snowflake is much handsomer."

In another of her books, *The Little Bulbs,* Lawrence commented on a different source of confusion about the identity of the snowflake: "Nearly everyone in the South calls a snowflake a snow-drop. No matter how often Southerners are told that *Leucojum aestivum,* found in every dooryard, is a snowflake, they go on calling it snowdrop, just as they go on calling camellias japonicas, and daffodils jonquils."

I have not been able to establish a date for the introduction of snowflakes to Southern gardens, but they are definitely not newcomers. They are frequently found at cemeteries and abandoned homesites at least one hundred years old. I have had reasonably good luck in ordering bulbs from commercial sources, but it is hard to go wrong with those collected from old naturalized plantings. — *WCW*

'Gravetye Giant' leucojum (*Leucojum* 'Gravetye Giant') (Photo by William C. Welch)

Lilium spp.

Garden Lilies
Family: Liliaceae (Lily)
Size: 2–6 ft
Zone: 7–11
Perennial bulbs
Showy white, orange, pink, or yellow flowers in spring or summer

Lilies are considered to be the oldest garden flower in cultivation. The Madonna lily (*Lilium candidum*), native to Asia Minor, is depicted in ruins of Egypt and Crete. The large white, tubular flowers appear in midspring. They prefer limestone soils like those in the Hill Country of Texas, parts of North Texas, and the mid-South. The shallow-growing bulbs produce attractive rosettes of foliage much like those of hosta through the winter, before bolting in spring to produce their sweet-scented flowers.

The foliage dies down soon after flowering and remains dormant until early fall, when the growth cycle begins anew. Transplanting and dividing should be done in late summer or early fall. Bulbs should be set in a sunny location, only one to two inches below the soil surface. Few other garden lilies return as perennials in the South. Many cultivars are late blooming and last only a few days in our intense late spring and summer heat. While teaching and touring in the Tuscany region of Italy in June 2008, I was fascinated by naturalized stands of Madonna lilies growing on abandoned homesites as well as in well-tended gardens. It was exciting to see these in the beautiful Renaissance paintings of the Madonna and Child and then see the exact thing growing in the gardens of Tuscany.

Tiger lily (*L. × lancifolium*), Easter lily (*L. longiflorum*), and Philippine or Formosan lily (*L. formosanum*) are all excellent choices for Southern gardens. Tiger lilies grow to about four feet and bear many pendulous flowers of orange spotted with black.

Madonna lily (*Lilium candidum*) (Photo by William C. Welch)

Philippine lily (*Lilium formosanum*) (Photo by Greg Grant)

Tiger lily (*Lilium × lancifolium*) (Photo by Greg Grant)

Philippine lily (*Lilium formosanum*) (Photo by William C. Welch)

The tiger lily is believed to be a natural hybrid, reproducing by bulblets formed at the point where the leaves meet the stems rather than by seed. These are known as "bulbils" and look like pea-sized bulbs. They may be planted in late summer or fall. The double-flowering tiger lily 'Flore Pleno' was introduced in 1870 and is still available.

Tiger lilies are vigorous and thrive in acidic soils of the South. In the Far East, they have been cultivated for many centuries. Tiger lilies were in our Mangham, Louisiana, garden when it was acquired in 1989 and appear to have been there for many years. Garden lilies require well-drained soil, and their flowers last longer if they receive protection from the hot afternoon sun. Remove faded flowers, but wait until stems and leaves have turned yellow before cutting them back nearly to the ground. With care, lilies can be transplanted at any time, even when in flower, but spring and fall are ideal. They need constant moisture while growing and blooming but withstand dry periods after they have flowered. Mulch is advised to keep moisture even, reduce weed growth, and keep the soil cool.

Lilium longiflorum is a dependable perennial in zones 8 and 9. For many years commercial production of Easter lilies was in

Philippine lily (*Lilium formosanum*) (Photo by William C. Welch)

South Louisiana but moved to the state of Washington in the 1940s. Florist forms will usually thrive as garden perennials, but some of the older forms are particularly vigorous. My grandmother Menke and Aunt Bern always had them in their gardens in Yoakum (south-central Texas). I currently have a nice planting of them that came from Pam Puryear's grandmother's garden in Navasota, Texas. Although they don't bloom right at Easter, they are usually at their peak by early to mid-May.

Lilium formosanum is a superb garden plant for most of the South. Although one of its common names is "Philippine lily," it is actually native to the island of Taiwan (formerly Formosa). George L. Slate was a research associate at New York State University when he published *Lilies for American Gardens* in 1927. He was enthusiastic, and wrote extensively, about the lily he knew as *L. philippinse* var. *formosanum*. He stated that it was first discovered in 1858; in 1880 the English firm Veitch received bulbs, which they flowered. It passed out of cultivation but was reintroduced in 1918 by E. H. ("Chinese") Wilson, the famed "plant hunter." It was given the Award of Merit of the Royal Horticultural Society in 1921. Slate further extolled the virtues of "Price's variety," which differed mainly in being shorter and more dwarf. This second form received the Royal Society's Award of Merit in 1929. Slate went on to stress the importance of growing seedling crops of Philippine lilies to reduce incidence of virus. He also spoke of the production of blooming-size bulbs in a year from seed.

Flowers appear in mid-July and usually continue through mid-August. Like all the lilies these do best if planted where they receive some afternoon shade. The seed pods are handsome as dried florist material. Seeds ripen in September and germinate easily. If kept in a greenhouse or cold frame, the seedlings will grow quickly and can even flower the summer following their planting, although by the second year the bulbs are larger and flowers more prolific. Bulbs should be planted in well-drained soil five to six inches deep.

Philippine lily (*Lilium formosanum*) (Photo by William C. Welch)

Philippine lily (*Lilium formosanum*) (Photo by William C. Welch)

Easter lily (*Lilium longiflorum*) (Photo by William C. Welch)

My introduction to Philippine lilies came as a gift from friend and horticulturist Tom LeRoy of Conroe, Texas. Tom sent me a plant in the late 1970s, and I was able to identify it soon after. Greg was impressed with a large, naturalized planting he chanced upon in East Texas while still a student at Texas A&M University. The lilies had naturalized in large numbers in a semishaded area surrounding an old home. Greg and I agree that Philippine lilies are great garden plants that should be much more widely used. The late E. H. Wilson was probably responsible for their introduction into American gardens about 1925.

Other garden lilies for our region include the regal lily (*L. regale*), discovered by E. H. Wilson in 1903 growing in limestone soil of western China. The white trumpets on tall stems resemble Easter lilies and are more cold hardy than most lilies. They are also the parents of the Olympic and Aurelian hybrids and grow well in the central South. 'Golden Splendor' is probably the best known of the Aurelian hybrids. Garden lilies are beautiful additions to our gardens and treasured as cut flowers in our homes. — *WCW*

Philippine lily (*Lilium formosanum*) (Photo by William C. Welch)

Lonicera spp.

Honeysuckle, Woodbine
Family: Caprifoliceae (Honeysuckle)
Size: 10–15 ft
Zones: 7–11
Evergreen (occasionally deciduous) vines or shrubs
Creamy white, yellow, or red trumpet-shaped flowers in winter, spring, or summer

The sweet perfume of honeysuckle is an inseparable part of Southern memories, and both the native and introduced honeysuckles are important garden vines and shrubs. Perhaps the most important species horticulturally is the native coral, or trumpet honeysuckle (*Lonicera sempervirens*). Indigenous from Connecticut to Florida and westward to Nebraska and Texas, trumpet honeysuckle is adapted to a wide variety of soils and growing conditions. It will grow in sun or shade, though it blooms better in a brighter site.

'Pam's Pink' honeysuckle (*Lonicera* × *americana* 'Pam's Pink') (Photo by Greg Grant)

'Sulphurea' trumpet honeysuckle (*Lonicera sempervirens* 'Sulphurea') (Photo by Greg Grant)

Trumpet honeysuckle (*Lonicera sempervirens*) (Photo by Greg Grant)

Trumpet honeysuckle flowers vary in color from a beautiful pure yellow—in the cultivar 'Sulphurea'—to bicolored blossoms that are orange-red or red on the outside of the tubular corolla and yellow to yellow-orange inside. The twining vines are vigorous but not invasive, and the new foliage is red-purple, turning bluish green at maturity.

Since this attractive vine is native to much of the South, it found use on trellises and arbors early on. It is propagated easily from cuttings or seed from the one-fourth-inch red fruit that ripens in fall. Fruit production is unpredictable, but cuttings may be taken from April throughout the growing season.

Japanese honeysuckle (*L. japonica*) was introduced from East Asia and has become a serious weed in the South—it can be found invading woodlands throughout the region. The creamy white flowers are highly fragrant—the perfume is noticeable even from a passing car—and this vine has, over the years, covered many trellises, arbors, and fences. Hall's honeysuckle (*L. japonica* 'Halliana') is the best-known form in cultivation and may be used as an aggressive ground cover or vine. *Lonicera japonica* 'Purpurea,' a shrubby vine that may be used as a low-maintenance shrub or ground cover, has purplish foliage. It, too, has become naturalized.

Winter honeysuckle (*L. fragrantissima*) is another of the many plants brought back from China in 1845 by Scottish plantsman Robert Fortune. This species, curiously, has never been found in the wild. It is another very easily grown plant, forming a deciduous shrub rather than a vine. The small, creamy white flowers open in mid- to late winter and are extremely fragrant, although not very showy. The lemonlike scent permeates the air in the vicinity of the plant, and on warm winter days, the result is almost shocking, since that is not a season when one looks for flowers. Small, bright red fruits sometimes form during May and June, but they remain hidden beneath the foliage and are not conspicuous.

Winter honeysuckle is one of the toughest and easiest-grown shrubs imaginable. I have seen it thriving from Amarillo to Beau-

'Pam's Pink' honeysuckle (*Lonicera* × *americana* 'Pam's Pink') (Photo by Greg Grant)

mont in Texas and throughout the South. It can reach six to ten feet tall, and almost as wide, and is useful as a specimen planting or as a background shrub or hedge. Every garden should have at least one!

Best of all, this shrub requires very little maintenance, though it keeps a neater appearance if some of the old canes are removed at ground level each winter. This can be done when the branches are in flower so that the prunings may be enjoyed as cut material inside the home. I have also seen old specimens trimmed up and effectively used as small, multitrunked trees.

Many old-time nurseries listed winter honeysuckles; for example, W. A. Yates of Brenham, Texas, advertised this plant in the 1906–8 catalogue. Some of the finest old specimens I have seen are located in the Mt. Holly Cemetery in Little Rock, Arkansas. Personally, I have fond memories of a large old specimen that grew by my grandmother's gate in Yoakum, Texas.

Although its origins are a bit obscure, 'Gold Flame' honeysuckle (*L.* × *heckrottii*) is thought to be a hybrid of *L. sempervirens* and *L. americana*. Whatever its parentage, the plant is a genuine

Winter honeysuckle (*Lonicera fragrantissima*) (Photo by William C. Welch)

Trumpet honeysuckle (*Lonicera sempervirens*) (Photo by William C. Welch)

antique, for it is known to have been introduced onto the market prior to 1895—Fruitland Nurseries in Augusta, Georgia, listed *L. × heckrottii* along with four other honeysuckles in the 1906–7 catalogue.

'Gold Flame' honeysuckle is a vine that remains evergreen except in severe winters. The flowers start opening early and recur during spring, summer, and fall. With its carmine buds that open to blossoms yellow on the outside that gradually change to pink, it is surely one of the most handsome of the climbing honeysuckles. Flowers occur simultaneously with new growth all season, and the fragrance is pleasant, though slight.

Although it is fairly vigorous in growth, I describe the 'Gold Flame' honeysuckle as a "mannerly" vine. Cuttings root readily, and new plants often begin flowering the second year. I have noticed that this vine is susceptible to powdery mildew in some areas; it appears to me that this honeysuckle's vigor and flowering are better a hundred or more miles inland from the Gulf of Mexico.

Greg and I introduced an interesting honeysuckle that Pam Puryear shared with us from her grandmother's garden. Greg identified it as *L. × americana* (one of the parents of 'Gold Flame' honeysuckle) and named it 'Pam's Pink.' It, too, is a mannerly vine, or even a shrub, with showy blue-gray foliage, purple stems, and pink and white flowers. We have seen it surviving in a number of Central Texas gardens as well as the Texas Hill Country and Europe.

Several years ago I also observed a strikingly beautiful blue-green-foliaged honeysuckle in Rachel's Garden at the Hermitage near Nashville. Jane Symmes identified it as *L. prolifera* and grew it at her nursery, Cedar Lane Farms, near Madisonville, Georgia. *Hortus Third* describes the flowers as pale yellow marked with purple. It is a summer bloomer and native from Ohio to Tennessee. Plant form is a shrubby vine.—*WCW*

Lycoris radiata

Spider Lily, Guernsey Lily, British Soldiers, Naked Ladies
Family: Amaryllidaceae (Amaryllis)
Size: 1–2 ft
Zones: 7–9
Perennial bulb
White, yellow, pink, or red showy blooms in late summer or fall

Among the flowers that I first cherished as a child was what I knew as the spider lily. There is something about flowers that magically spring forth after long, hot, dry periods that still mesmerizes me. If there is any true magic in horticulture, this seems to be it.

Of course, determining the true identity of my spider lilies proved to be no child's play. To begin with, there is the usual confusion that comes with common names. In the South, "spider lily" always seems to apply to members of the Amaryllis family, but depending on where you live, which genus you tag with that

Spider lily (*Lycoris radiata*) (Photo by Greg Grant)

Spider lily (*Lycoris × haywardii*) (Photo by Greg Grant)

name changes. Had I grown up near the Gulf Coast, I would have cultivated *Hymenocallis* as spider lilies. But since I grew up inland, I, like other gardeners of the mid- and upper South, used the name to describe the bulbs that botanists today call *Lycoris*.

Not that botanists don't make mistakes, too. By now, it has been determined that *L. radiata,* which is naturalized widely in the South, is a native of Japan. Yet from the day this bulb arrived in the United States, botanists insisted that it had come from South Africa, and for decades thereafter they misidentified it as Guernsey lily (*Nerine sarniensis*). How this mix-up occurred is anyone's guess, but no one noticed until 1936.

In that year, W. M. James of California and Wyndham Hayward of Florida contributed an article to the bulletin of the American Amaryllis Society, pointing out that the Japanese bulb was different from the South African one. But it was up to Elizabeth Lawrence to trace the real history of spider lily, which she did in *A Southern Garden* (1942):

In North Carolina we might have wondered before, if we
thought at all about the flowers that grow in our gardens,
about the name nerine. For the nerine is a South African genus,

Spider lily (*Lycoris* × *incarnata*) (Photo by Greg Grant)

and the first red spider-lilies in North Carolina (and probably in this country) came directly from Japan to a garden in New Bern. They were brought to that garden nearly a hundred years ago by Captain William Roberts who was with Commodore Perry when he opened the port of Japan. The Captain brought three bulbs which were, his niece Mrs. Simmons says, in such a dry condition that they did not show signs of life until the War between the States. The original bulbs have increased and been passed on until they have spread across the state.

Henry Nehrling also helps to clear up the matter. He writes in *My Garden in Florida* (1944):

In 1888 Mrs. Thompson of Spartanburg, South Carolina, an ardent flower lover, sent me about 50 fine bulbs of another species, *L. radiata.*

L. radiata, often called *Nerine japonica,* is an old garden plant, for it was noted by Kaempfer in 1712, and cultivated in England around 1750. It is a native of China and Japan, where it is commonly cultivated in gardens, and offered by nurserymen at about 75 cents/100. It is very like a nerine. Thunberg mistook it for the Guernsey Lily (*Nerine sarniensis*), which it resembles.

In addition to a huge population of *L. radiata*, there are other less common species of *Lycoris* blooming across the South. The real naked lady, or surprise lily (*L. squamigera*) is common only in the upper South and farther north, as it apparently needs a period of winter chilling to bloom. *Lycoris aurea* (*L. africana*), the yellow spider lily or hurricane lily, is common only in the lower South, as it does not tolerate frost well. This flourishes in large numbers in Florida and had the distinction of being included (under the name *Amaryllis aurea*) in *Les Liliacees,* the famous collection of watercolors that the French floral artist Pierre Joseph Redouté finished in 1816. Finally, the observant gardener occasionally meets creamy white forms of *L.* × *albiflora.*

All of these are available commercially, although Scott Ogden

Spider lily (*Lycoris* × *jacksoniana*) (Photo by Greg Grant)

Spider lily (*Lycoris radiata*) (Photo by William C. Welch)

of Austin tells me that the bulb sold as red spider lily is different genetically from the form found naturalized in old gardens. The naturalized form is a sterile triploid—that is, it has three sets of chromosomes rather than the usual two so cannot reproduce by seed. But if slower to propagate, it is stronger growing, so if you can get the naturalized form, plant that.

Gardening friends and specialty bulb nurseries are often a good source of unusual spider lilies. The late Cleo Barnwell of Shreveport gave me bulbs of *L. × incarnata, L. × elsiae, L. × jacksoniana, L. × houdyshelii,* and *L. × caldwellii* that I grow. She got them from the late Sam Caldwell of Tennessee, the most famous collector and breeder of spider lilies in the United States.

Specialty nurseries and collectors are also great sources for unusual *Lycoris*. Friend Tony Avent's Plant Delights Nursery provided me with such treasures as *L. sprengeri, L. longituba, L. × haywardii,* and several other interesting hybrids.

Spider lilies are very easy to grow in sun or shade. They thrive and multiply best in a somewhat acidic, loose, and well-drained soil. Propagation is by division. Although summer is the preferred time for division, they will survive transplanting at any time of the year. I often moved them immediately following their bloom when it's on my mind.

One of the most beautiful sights I have ever seen was in the Grace Episcopal Church cemetery in St. Francisville, Louisiana. It was covered with red spider lilies—what Virginians called British soldiers—in full bloom. Knowing that Martha Turnbull, the mother of the beautiful gardens at Rosedown Plantation, lay buried there, I couldn't help thinking that she would approve of resting in a beautiful moss-draped Southern garden with hundreds of British soldiers standing at attention.—*GG*

Magnolia grandiflora

Southern Magnolia, Bull Bay, Sweet Bay
Family: Magnoliaceae (Magnolia)
Size: 60–80 ft
Zones: 7–11
Evergreen tree
Large, fragrant, creamy white flowers in spring and summer

> The finest and most superb evergreen-tree that the earth
> produced.
> —Alexander Garden, Charleston, South Carolina, 1757

> The monarque of the Southern forest, and needs no descrip-
> tion.
> —Gilbert Onderdonk's Mission Valley Nurseries, Nursery,
> Texas, 1898–99

> *Magnolia grandiflora!* The most beautiful tree in the world; no
> picture and no painting can do thee justice; no description, and
> be it ever so glowing, can give an idea of thy natural and noble
> beauty.
> —Henry Nehrling, *My Garden in Florida,* 1944

No other flower, perhaps no other plant, evokes images of the South the way the magnolia does. It is the emblem of the Southern Garden History Society and the state flower of both Louisiana and Mississippi. This stateliest of the evergreen trees is native from Texas to North Carolina and can reach an immense size (up to one hundred feet!) on deep soils in the wild. For the early naturalists and gardeners, to see this tree, with its large glossy leaves and huge fragrant flowers, was to fall in love. William Bartram made numerous references to the "glorious magnolia" in the chronicles of his travels through the Southeast in the 1780s.

Southern magnolia (*Magnolia grandiflora*)
(Photo by Greg Grant)

Southern magnolia (*Magnolia grandiflora*)
(Cynthia Mueller)

According to Alice Coates in *Garden Shrubs and Their Histories* (1964), huge native specimens were regarded by Frenchman André Michaux, early American explorer and botanist, as some of the finest productions of the vegetable kingdom. Coates adds: "It is said that the Indians would not sleep under such a tree when in bloom, because of the overpowering scent of its flowers—one of which, if kept in a bedroom, could cause death in a single night." All early Southern nurseries carried this tree, and almost everybody in the South grew it.

The genus is named for Pierre Magnol (1638–1715), professor of medicine and director of the botanic gardens in Montpelier, France. Of course, *grandiflora* refers to the huge flowers. Southern gardeners soon added to this species a number of fine varieties, including *gloriosa,* which bears larger flowers; *angustifolia* and *lanceolata,* which have narrow leaves; *rotundifolia,* a rounded-leaf form; and *praecox,* which is early flowering. I'm not aware that any of these still exist, though there are now many named cultivars and patented selections. The southern magnolia was introduced into England around 1734 but never thrived there as in its home. This fits a rule that I have developed over the years: if it thrives in England, it won't grow in the South, and if it sulks in England, send it home to Dixie!

Actually, some magnolias from our region did succeed reasonably well in European gardens. The first American magnolia to make the trip to the Old World (and the plant from which the genus was named) was the sweet bay, white, or swamp magnolia (*M. virginiana*), a native of the Southeast. Formerly known as *M. glauca,* it was listed as such in John Bartram and Sons' 1792 catalogue with the description "charming—the neat white rosette blossom possesses an animating fragrance." According to Coates, this species was introduced into England as early as 1688.

Saucer magnolia (*Magnolia* × *soulangiana*) (Photo by William C. Welch)

William Cobett, who wrote *The English Gardener* in 1833, was obviously a fan of *M. virginiana.* He said that its fragrance was "the most delightful that can be conceived, far exceeding that of the rose; in strength equaling the jasmine or tuberose, but more delightful. . . . None of the other magnolias are nearly so odiferous as this; all but this are somewhat tender; this might be in every shrubbery in England with the greatest of ease, and I cannot help expressing my hope that it may be one day as common as the lilac." Those are heady words—I think he stayed in the bedroom sniffing it a little too long.

Other magnolias cultivated in the early South included three more southeastern natives: the cucumbertree magnolia (*M. acuminata*), the umbrella magnolia (*M. tripetala*), and the magnificent bigleaf magnolia (*M. macrophylla*). In fact, an amazing selection of these trees was available to our ancestors. Bartram and Sons' Nursery carried *M. acuminata* and *tripetala,* while Prince's Nursery of Flushing, New York, listed Thompson's magnolia, a cross between the sweet bay and the umbrella magnolia, in its 1823 catalogue. In *Breck's Book of Flowers* (1851), Joseph Breck, a Boston nurseryman, listed *M. glauca, M. acuminata, M. auriculata, M. fuscata, M. conspicua, M. soulangiana, M. purpurea,* and *M. gracilis.*

By the mid-nineteenth century, magnolias from the Orient were arriving in the South to further enrich our native selection. Two Chinese species—the yulan magnolia (*M. heptapeta* [formerly *M. denudada* and *M. conspicua*]); and *M. quinquapeta* (formerly *M. liliflora* and *M. purpurea*)—crossed to produce the early-blooming, deciduous saucer magnolia (*M. × soulangiana*). A mainstay now of our Southern gardens, this plant—which I knew as the "tulip tree"—was another of my childhood favorites. Anyone passing by the Louisiana State University campus in Baton Rouge should pause to see the beautiful specimens there.

Prince's catalogue was listing *M. × soulangiana* by 1832, and since that nursery had many Southern customers, we can assume this tree was current in our region by then. In the case of many other oriental magnolias, it is difficult to establish exactly when they arrived in the South, though the date of introduction into England provides a clue. Joseph Banks introduced the white-flowered yulan magnolia into England from China around 1879; there are also very nice specimens of this tree scattered around Baton Rouge. Carl Peter Thunberg introduced the purple-flowered *M. quinquapeta* into England from Japan in 1790. Samuel Parson (another New York nurseryman who shipped to the South) listed *M.* × *soulangiana* 'Lennei' and the star magnolia (*M. stellata*) in his 1876–77 catalogue. Dave Creech and the Stephen F. Austin Mast Arboretum in Nacogdoches, Texas, have a large, diverse collection of deciduous magnolia cultivars to ogle.

Magnolias require deep, acidic, well-drained soils. Otherwise, they are easy to grow. Propagation is from stratified seed, by cuttings (which are somewhat difficult to root), or by grafting. Even if just for the fragrance, everybody in the South should have a magnolia. I think it's a law. — *GG*

Malvaviscus arboreus drummondii

Turk's Cap
Family: Malvaceae (Hibiscus)
Size: 3–5 ft
Zones: 7–11
Perennial
White, pink, or red flowers that attract hummingbirds in summer and fall

Plants native to the South that were showy and easy to propagate quickly became a part of our ancestors' landscaping palette. One such example is the Turk's cap. In an 1891 copy of a Pearfield Nurseries catalogue from Frelsburg, Texas, the plant is listed by its botanical name and state *"Malvaviscus drummondii*—A native of Texas, producing during summer a profusion of scarlet flowers. 40 cents each." It doesn't just produce a profusion of small, twisted, turbanlike flowers but a multitude of hummingbirds, sulfur butterflies, and small red-orange fruit as well. I have always considered the miniature tomato-looking fruit palatable, but some might disagree. A 1933 Otto M. Locke Nursery catalogue from New Braunfels, Texas, is on my side, however. It lists *"Malvaviscus drummondii.* This has large broad leaves . . . and produces a small fruit which some people call Mexican Apples. The fruit is sweet and edible. 10c each, $1.00 per dozen." Locke's Nursery once laid claim to the oldest nursery in Texas, having started in 1856. Unfortunately, when the last Locke died in 1994, the nursery died with him. It was famous for its animal menagerie, including a prairie dog "town," and for supplying the United States with most of its tuberose bulbs. I had the fortunate experience of getting to meet Locke when I was the Bexar County horticulturist in nearby San Antonio. On one visit he told me some man tried to buy the property from him for one million dollars, but he wouldn't sell it to him because the buyer planned to do away with the nursery. His dad and granddad had owned and oper-

ated that nursery and he couldn't bear the thought of it not being there. Unfortunately, the property was immediately adjacent to the interstate in a rapidly growing area. Luckily, Turk's cap still grows up and down the nearby Comal and Guadalupe rivers.

My first experience with Turk's cap was around the back steps of a friend's house. His family rented the home from my next-door neighbors Autry and Marie Daly. I would sit on the back steps waiting for him, watching the hummingbirds visit the flowers as I nibbled on the small, sweet fruit. At the time I feared Marie Daly, as I was told she was an evil, mean old witch. It turned out just the opposite, and she later became one of my dearest friends. She loved flowers (and me!), and Turk's cap was just one of her many treasures. People are like plants. You just have to get to know them and know what time of the year to be around them!

Thanks to prodding early in my career by the late rosarian, historian, and queen of the eclectic, Pam Puryear, I began a breeding project with Turk's cap when I started work at Stephen F. Austin State University. I first crossed a pink-flowered, tropical

Turk's cap (*Malvaviscus drummondii*)
(Photo by Greg Grant)

'Pam Puryear' Turk's cap (*Malvaviscus* ×
'Pam Puryear') (Photo by Greg Grant)

M. arboreus with a red-flowered *M. drummondii*. The intent was to transfer the larger flowers from the tropical species to the more cold-hardy, but smaller-flowered Turk's cap. Unfortunately, a big rat in the greenhouse ate most of my seed-bearing fruit. I managed to salvage only one, and then only two seeds germinated. One plant was a dwarf, fuzzy-leafed Turk's cap look-alike, but the other was a perfect intermediate cross with attributes of both species. I named it 'Big Momma' after my great-grandmother (Dee Smith) and because it also became the large-growing mother of my next introduction. I used a white *M. drummondii* as the pollen parent to produce the salmon pink–flowered 'Pam Puryear.' I hope to eventually introduce others as well, including an improved red and a more vigorous white. Though Turk's cap is often considered by many horticulturist and upscale gardeners as a common "weed," I beg to differ. After all, Turk's cap will grow in sun or shade, wet or dry, acidic or alkaline soils; is resistant to deer and glyphosate herbicide; attracts swarms of hummingbirds and sulfur butterflies; has edible fruit; and is native. Does that

Turk's cap (*Malvaviscus drummondii*)
(Photo by Greg Grant)

sound like a bad plant to you? The days of not wanting plants because they are easy to grow should end. Only a gardening fool would fill the yard with plants craving water, fertilizer, pesticides, and attention.

Like many "passalong" plants (plants shared or given away to friends and neighbors), Turk's cap has garnered other names as well. When I was the county horticulturist in Cherokee County, Texas, the locals called it "bleeding heart." My heart certainly bleeds for it. —*GG*

'Pam Puryear' Turk's cap (*Malvaviscus* ב× 'Pam Puryear') (Photo by Greg Grant)

Michelia figo

Banana Shrub
Family: Magnoliaceae (Magnolia)
Size: 10–15 ft
Zones: 8–11
Large evergreen shrub or small tree
Banana-scented flowers in spring

Originally known as *Magnolia fuscata* and still called that by many Southerners today, the evergreen banana shrub provides one of the most distinctive fragrances in our Southern gardens. The pale, creamy yellow blossoms it bears in the spring are not showy—but when you smell like ripe bananas, you don't have to be.

The banana shrub is a native of China and according to *The Hillier Manual of Trees and Shrubs* was introduced into Europe in 1789 as a greenhouse plant. Like many European greenhouse plants, it found itself right at home in gardens of the Deep South. I couldn't locate a date of introduction into American gardens, although Philadelphia nurseryman Robert Buist listed it among the greenhouse plants in his *American Flower-Garden Directory* in 1860. Early nursery catalogues in which I found advertisements of "*Magnolia fuscata*" included Affleck's Central Nurseries near Brenham, Texas (1860), Mission Valley Nurseries near Victoria, Texas (1898–99), Rosedale Nurseries, Brenham, Texas (1901), Fruitland Nurseries, Augusta, Georgia (1906–7), and W. A. Yates Nursery, Brenham, Texas (1906–8).

I am sure there were many other sources of this plant in the southeastern states. The 1917 edition of Liberty Hyde Bailey's *Standard Cyclopedia of Horticulture*—the foremost American garden reference of the time—calls *M. fuscata* "one of the most popular garden shrubs in the southern states." Bailey also lists *M. champaca* as being cultivated in the Southern states—a less cold-hardy species.

A recently introduced banana shrub (*Michelia maudiae*) (Photo by Greg Grant)

Banana shrub grows best in an acidic, deep, sandy loam soil and was historically pest-free. It is presently being plagued by a mysterious defoliating leaf spot disease in many southeastern states. It may also occasionally suffer freeze damage, especially in or near zone 7. Banana shrub may be grown as a medium-sized shrub or pruned to make a small tree. I have trained one at my parents' home in East Texas as a small tree to shelter a Carlos Cortez *faux bois* bench—the effect is quite nice.

Dave Creech at the Stephen F. Austin Mast Arboretum in Nacogdoches, Texas, has amassed one of the most diverse collections of *Michelia* species in the South. He has had success with *M. maudiae* (huge, floppy white flowers in late winter that smell of honeysuckle), *M. foggi #2, M. yunnanensis, M. foveolata, M. platytypetala, M. martini, M. compressa, M. maclurei, M. chapensis, M. skinneriana,* and *M. wilsonii.* Sniff them out if you get a chance. —*GG*

Mirabilis jalapa

Four-o'clock, Marvel of Peru
Family: Nyctaginaceae (Four-o'clock)
Zones: 7–11
Perennial or reseeding annual
Sweet night-scented flowers (plants that give off scent at night to attract pollinators such as moths) in summer and fall that can be white, yellow, pink, or combinations

Felder Rushing, coauthor of *Passalong Plants,* calls four-o'clocks a "can't fail perennial." Actually, gardeners in colder climates must grow them as annuals, but in most of the South they develop fleshy tubers that persist from year to year and seem to last forever. *Hortus Third* says that these tubers may eventually grow to a weight of forty pounds in warm climate regions.

Alice Le Duc, now at Texas State University, wrote her doctoral thesis on four-o'clocks and found that the Aztecs had grown them and even developed strains with different flower colors many years before the Spanish conquest of the Southwest. The conquistadors were struck by this achievement, apparently, for they sent four-o'clocks back to Spain sometime during the sixteenth century. Within seventy-five years, this plant had turned up in English gardens, and it had been in cultivation in Europe for about two hundred years before Linnaeus first described the species in 1753.

The specimens that Linnaeus described were those of cultivated plants. Curiously, although four-o'clocks are often found on old garden sites in Mexico (and the Southern United States), they are no longer found in the wild there.

Plants are lush and bushy to three feet. The tubular flowers come in colors ranging from iridescent purple to white, red, yellow, and striped. Their name derives from the fact that their flowers open in the late afternoon and stay open until the next morning—on cloudy days, four-o'clocks may open somewhat earlier. The fragrance of the flowers is a strong plus and a major reason for their popularity. Four-o'clocks attract hummingbirds and moths to the garden.

This is a very heat- and drought-tolerant plant and one that blooms well in sun or fairly dense shade. I remember visiting a cemetery on a ranch near Yoakum, Texas, where four-o'clocks were the only reminder of a once well-tended plot. They had escaped the small fenced area under a great live oak tree and were happily flowering in profusion during the hottest time of the summer.

Thomas Jefferson grew what he referred to as the "fragrant Marvel of Peru" at Monticello; he also cultivated *M. longiflora,* a creamy white–flowering species native to West Texas and Mexico. A few years ago we secured seed of this plant and sent it to Peggy

Four-o'clock (*Mirabilis jalapa*) (Photo by William C. Welch)

Four-o'clock (*Mirabilis jalapa*) (Photo by William C. Welch)

Cornett, director of the Historic Plant Collection at Monticello, so *M. longiflora* is again blooming in that garden. Currently, seed is available through the Monticello mail-order catalogue.

Four-o'clocks may be easily started from seed or tubers. In colder parts of the country the tubers may be dug in the fall and stored until spring. This plant tends to produce a great deal of seed and can become a garden pest, although the young seedlings are easily pulled or hoed. One year I planted a number of magenta-colored four-o'clocks at our farm, and they reseeded prolifically by early fall, covering an area of about 120 square feet. It was an unusually dry year, and the young plants received no irrigation. They remained wilted and stunted until the first good fall rain, whereupon they miraculously freshened, covering themselves with flowers in just a few days. They were as showy as azaleas that autumn, and I developed a new appreciation that year for this plant's old name, "Marvel of Peru."—*WCW*

Myrtus communis

Myrtle, Sweet Myrtle, Bride's Myrtle
Family: Myrtaceae (Myrtle)
Size: 3–10 ft
Zones: 9–11
Evergreen shrub
Scented foliage with white flowers in summer

If your garden lies on the Gulf Coast, then this densely foliaged, aromatic evergreen is the plant for you, for myrtles thrive in seaside locations. They also tolerate alkaline soils and intense heat and, when planted outdoors, may grow into a shrub fifteen feet tall. They do not tolerate cold well, however, which means that through most of the South, *Myrtus communis* must be grown in a pot and moved indoors in wintertime. But such plants make fine specimens for setting out on a terrace or lawn in summertime, and because myrtle tolerates clipping well, potted specimens lend themselves to topiary. In midsummer, too, they bear white flowers that give way to purple-black berries.

Compact myrtle (*Myrtus communis compacta*) (Photo by William C. Welch)

Compact myrtle (*Myrtus communis compacta*) (Photo by William C. Welch)

Myrtle was a prized plant in ancient Roman gardens and provided the material for the garlands worn by generals who had won bloodless victories. Later on this shrub featured prominently in Spanish gardens, and by 1562 it had been introduced into England, where it ranked with such highly esteemed imports as lemons and pomegranates.

In classical mythology, the myrtle was the plant of Venus, the goddess of love, who is said to have worn a garland of myrtle when she rose from the sea. Small wonder, then, that the distilled water of myrtle flowers was regarded as a beautifier and aphrodisiac. The berries have been used as an ingredient for sauces to accompany meat. At one time myrtle was a common component of bridal bouquets. The flowers were very popular for cutting in Europe, especially in the 1700s.

Dwarf forms such as 'Microphylla' have smaller leaves and are more compact in form. Various common names include "German," "Greek," and "Roman" myrtle. In coastal areas of the South myrtles were sometimes used as a substitute for boxwood because they were better adapted to salty and sometimes alkaline conditions. They root readily from semihardwood cuttings and have few insect and disease problems.

Langdon Nurseries, Mobile, Alabama, described and offered myrtles in its 1881–82 catalogue: "*Myrtus communis,* Sweet myrtle, Pretty shrub, very desirable for ornamental hedges. 50 cents. *Myrtus angustifolia,* Narrow leafed, a pretty variety of myrtle with smaller leaves than the above. 50 cents." Fruitland Nurseries, Augusta, Georgia, describes and offers two forms in its 1906–7 catalogue: "*Myrtus communis,* double, A dwarf evergreen, with small, glossy green leaves. Flowers double, pure white and very fragrant. *Myrtus communis,* single, a very desirable evergreen, bright glossy green leaves larger than those of the double myrtle. Flowers single: very fragrant."

I am currently growing both a large- and a small-leaved form of *M. communis.* The large-leaved form came from Mrs. Ripper in Schulenburg, Texas, who brought it "to town" with her from her farm at High Hill about fifty years ago. The cuttings rooted readily, and I used four plants as sheared mounds in the parterre at Fragilee (reflecting the 1870s period). These were planted in 2001 and have been quite satisfactory. The dwarf form was used as a hedge in the potager garden and planted the same year. Cynthia Mueller rooted both sets of cuttings. The dwarf form quickly formed a compact hedge but has developed some chlorosis (yellowing of the foliage) and some die-back in the past several years. The dwarf form came from Mary Anne Pickens in Frelsburg. Both forms have been referred to as "German myrtle."—*WCW*

Nandina domestica

Nandina, Heavenly Bamboo
Family: Berberidaceae (Barberry)
Size: 2–6 ft
Zones: 7–9
Evergreen shrub
Small, white flowers in spring; red (rarely yellow) berries in fall and winter

Sometimes when a plant becomes a cliché, there's good reason. Or many reasons, as in the case of nandina. This is an exotic-looking plant with a down-home toughness. As the common names suggest, nandinas have the look of a bamboo—where they are happy, nandinas form clumps of long, erect, unbranched stems topped with feathery, compound green leaves. And nandinas seem to be happy just about everywhere. They adapt easily to a range of soil types and shrug off all but the most extreme heat and drought. Nandinas thrive in full sun or partial shade, and they are troubled by few insects or diseases.

Small wonder that this plant was perhaps the most popular landscape plant in the South during the first half of the twentieth century. In fact, nandinas used to be a common housewarming gift in rural regions—when a couple built a new home, neighbors, friends, or family divided their mature clumps to start a foundation planting that often consisted of little else.

Even if they weren't so tough and adaptable, nandinas would still deserve their popularity, for they provide an unusual amount of garden color, and at a time of year when it is most precious. The leaves, which remain purple tinged all year, may actually intensify in color with the onset of cold weather, turning bright red or purple in winter. This seasonal coloring is most dramatic on plants growing in sunny, exposed areas. Complementing this dormant-season foliar show is the nandinas' colorful fruits. Pea sized and typically bright red (there is a yellow-berried form),

Nandina (*Nandina domestica*) (Photo by William C. Welch)

these are borne in bold clusters in the fall but commonly last all winter, right through to spring. Nandinas are attractive when in bloom, too; plumes of small white flowers open at the stem tips in summertime. Whether in flower or fruit, however, nandinas are hard to miss, for the typical height is four to six feet, with an occasional specimen reaching seven or eight feet.

As their appearance suggests, the nandina is of exotic origin. It is native to China and Japan but was well established in the American South by 1890. In that year, Peter Henderson wrote in *Henderson's Handbook of Plants* that this was "also a favorite ornamental plant in the Southern States where it is now thoroughly domesticated." In part this popularity may have been due to the ease with which nandinas are propagated. New plants may be started from semihardwood cuttings or from seeds, but the method most often practiced by rural home owners in search of a housewarming present is division. A many-stemmed clump of nandina is dug from the ground with a sharp spade and split into two clumps, each of which, if replanted promptly, provides the start of a new clump.

Because of nandinas' vigorous growth, some gardeners think they require periodic pruning, and this can be a puzzling process for the uninitiated. If the gardener follows the common impulse and uses his or her hedge clippers to shave off the top foot or so of a clump's stems, the result will be a woody, awkward, and generally unattractive plant. A more pleasing, natural look is achieved by removing whole stems: cut out at ground level about one-third of each clump's oldest canes each year. New sprouts and plants will soon emerge to make a denser, more compact plant.

Nandinas make good material for container planting, especially in the dwarf forms that have begun to appear in recent years. These, of course, also lend themselves to planting in smaller gardens. My favorite of the dwarf nandinas is one that I acquired sometime around 1970. The late Mrs. U. B. (Jo) Evans of Ferriday, Louisiana, a well-known and respected horticulturist, gave me a nice, one-gallon-size plant of *Nandina domestica* 'Nana Purpurea,' a cultivar that was then new to the nursery trade. 'Nana Purpurea' has since proven to be a great popular success, and I certainly treasure my plant. It thrives in a difficult location where it receives little water and much radiated heat. Each winter the foliage turns a magnificent red-purple, and the clump has slowly spread to cover an area about two feet in diameter. Yet this plant doesn't exceed a height of eighteen inches.

Unfortunately, this particular dwarf has proven to be rather finicky about soil type and requires good drainage. But other dwarf forms, such as 'Harbor Dwarf,' appear to adapt well to a broader range of growing conditions. They, however, lack the spectacular fall color of 'Nana Purpurea.' None of the dwarf nandinas, I should add, has ever flowered or set fruit in my garden, which is the reason I will continue to grow the larger, heirloom type as well. It offers not only history but berries.

Unfortunately, the common nandina has proven to be invasive in some parts of the South. Consult with local experts about where the plant might be a problem, and consider using the fruitless forms if it is. —*WCW*

Narcissus spp.

Daffodil, Narcissus, Jonquil
Family: Amaryllidaceae (Amaryllis)
Size: 1–2 ft
Zones: 5–11
Perennial bulbs
Showy white or yellow flowers in winter and spring

> But now, regarding the Daffodil from an artistic standpoint
> rather than as a mathematical problem, or as an achievement,
> have they not gone far enough with its development? Should
> not there be a halt called in this race for bigger and better Daf-
> fodils? It is essentially a simple and friendly flower, gay, grace-
> ful, appealing, and when it is made bold, and huge, and brazen,
> it has been called out of character, degraded not improved.
> —Louise Beebe Wilder, *Adventures with Hardy Bulbs,* 1936

I'm afraid I have to agree with the famed garden writer Louise Wilder.
Ethereal, springtime displays of graceful yellow and white narcissus
are synonymous with abandoned homesites throughout the South,
serving as annual reminders of this flower's popularity and tenacity.
Because they are so long-lived, daffodils, narcissus, and jonquils can
be an invaluable tool for garden restorers—for enduring patterns of
these flowers often provide excellent evidence of garden designs and
site orientations that have otherwise vanished.

According to *Hortus Third,* there are some twenty-five to
thirty species of *Narcissus,* most from Central Europe and the
Mediterranean region. Because *Narcissus* have been cultivated
for a thousand years in this homeland, distinguishing between
stands of truly wild, native bulbs and those that were once cultivated but naturalized perhaps centuries ago is a difficult or
impossible task.

To confuse the matter still further, gardeners from a very
early date were tinkering with every wild narcissus they could get

Greg's late Jack Russell terrier, Buckeye,
along with snowflakes (*Leucojum aestivum*),
(*Narcissus tazetta* 'Grand Primo'), and
campernelle jonquils (*N. × odorus*) (Photo
by Greg Grant)

Hoop petticoats (*Narcissus bulbocodium bulbicodium*) from Cousin Celia (Photo by Greg Grant)

hold of. A number of these early plants often proved to be natural hybrids from the wild. In 1629, John Parkinson described ninety-four distinct kinds of narcissus in *A Garden of Pleasant Flowers*—and interestingly, his list includes many of the forms commonly found naturalized in the South today. These and many other types of *Narcissus* were introduced into Southern gardens by the earliest settlers. Thomas Jefferson was among the colonial admirers of this flower, bringing what he called simply "Narcissus" into bloom at Shadwell in 1766. Entries from his diary reveal that later he cultivated "daffodils, jonquils, and narcissus" at Monticello.

Narcissus proliferated in America's first gardening books. Bernard M'Mahon's *American Gardener's Calendar* in 1806 mentioned jonquils, double jonquils, narcissi of sorts, double-narcissus (daffodils), and polyanthus-narcissus. By 1833, H. Bourne's *Florist's Manual* was citing the daffodil, jonquil, poetic or poet's narcissus, primrose daffodil, fragrant narcissus or great jonquil, and polyanthus narcissus.

'Golden Dawn' narcissus (*Narcissus ×
intermedius* 'Golden Dawn') (Photo by
William C. Welch)

Jonquil (*Narcissus jonquilla*) (Photo by Greg
Grant)

Campernelle jonquils (*Narcissus × odorus*) in front of Greg's barn (Photo by Greg Grant)

Chinese sacred lily (*Narcissus tazetta orientalis*) (Photo by William C. Welch)

Although there are many species and cultivars of *Narcissus*, historically the most commonly cultivated ones in the South were *N. pseudonarcissus* and its somewhat grotesque double form, as well as *N. × odorus, N. tazetta, N. × intermedius, N. × medioluteus,* and *N. × incomparabilis.*

Little *N. pseudonarcissus* is known as the Lent lily but also as the early daffodil here, as it blooms around February. It is the forerunner of today's large-flowered daffodils such as 'King Alfred.' It is small, very early blooming, and has typical wide, bluish gray-green foliage. The petals of the early daffodil are pale yellow, while its trumpet is golden yellow. Its odd-looking double form—named *N. pseudonarcissus telemonius plenus* or 'Van Sion'—is often encountered, although not near as frequently as the species type. Many consider the double form's ragged combinations of yellow and green petals downright homely. My great-grannies had it in their yards, and I think it is pretty cool, especially just as the fat buds start to open. Some call it the "scrambled eggs" daffodil. I can't help thinking of green eggs and ham when I see it.

Sweetly scented *N. jonquilla* is the true wild jonquil, occasionally referred to as the "johnny-quill." The late, dear Cleo Barnwell of Shreveport called them "sweeties." *Narcissus jonquilla* bears clusters of small, yellow, fragrant flowers held above deep green, rushlike foliage. Jonquils also bloom around February and naturalize fairly prolifically by seed. *Narcissus × odorus* is a natural hybrid, a cross between *N. pseudonarcissus* and *N. jonquilla*. It is known as the campernelle jonquil and occasionally as the giant or great jonquil. It's probably my favorite of all the *Narcissus*. It is exactly intermediate—in foliage and bloom characteristics— between the two parents, as all good little hybrids should be. It has two to three "giant," fragrant, yellow jonquil flowers held above foliage that looks like jonquil foliage on steroids. The large rushlike leaves are somewhat concave, and they have inherited a touch of the daffodil's bluish gray tint. It blooms alongside the early daffodils and jonquils. Typical of many first-generation hybrids, it is very strong growing and is sterile, setting no seed.

Narcissus tazetta is considered the oldest cultivated narcissus. It was known in ancient Egypt and Greece and cultivated in

Naturalized narcissus (Photo by Greg Grant)

'Grand Primo' narcissus (*Narcissus* 'Grand Primo Citroniere') (Photo by Greg Grant)

'Grand Primo' narcissus (*Narcissus* 'Grand Primo Citroniere') (Photo by Greg Grant)

Britain before 1597. In 1851, Boston nurseryman Joseph Breck proclaimed this species the most desirable of all the *Narcissus*. Its many forms and offspring, which are officially classed together as tazetta narcissus, are also known as polyanthus narcissus and are often what most gardeners mean when they refer simply to "narcissus."

The often-forced paperwhite (*N. tazetta papyraceus*) belongs in this group. Except for a few yellow types like 'Grand Soleil d'Or,' tazettas are mostly white with white, cream, or yellow cups. They bear clusters of many small flowers, which are intoxicatingly fragrant. As a matter of fact, my grandmother Emanis, with her rural East Texas tact, frequently told me to "get those stinking things out of the house!"

Because they bloom so early in the season, tazettas often suffer from frost damage. Many a bouquet has been picked the day the "norther" blew in. As a rule, the true paperwhites are very, very early blooming (opening at Christmas or New Year's even), bearing pure white, delicate flowers with a scent somewhere between that of cotton candy and fresh manure. You either love it or run for fresh air. True paperwhite foliage is wide and grayish green. Paperwhites perennialize most readily along the Gulf Coast where the winters are mild.

Another tazetta frequently found along the Gulf Coast is the Chinese sacred lily (*N. tazetta orientalis*). This plant has very wide, robust foliage and is also very early blooming. There is a double form that goes by the name of 'Romanus' or 'Constantinople.' Paperwhites and Chinese sacred lilies are frequently sold for indoor forcing. It appears, however, that most of the bulbs available from commercial sources are infected with virus.

As you move farther in from the coast, you begin encountering later-blooming types of tazetta narcissus. The earliest blooming of these is the delicate but somewhat "rag-tag" *N. tazetta italicus*. It has narrow, twisting petals and small, pale yellow cups.

Narcissus × *intermedius* (Photo by Greg Grant)

Because it is early flowering (usually in January here), it often blooms above stunted, freeze-nipped foliage.

The most often found tazetta narcissus in the South is a vigorous, sterile selection known as 'Grand Primo,' which blooms around late February to early March here. It has creamy white flowers with pale yellow cups and a strong pleasing (to me) fragrance. There are other enduring cultivars of *N. tazetta* surviving in Southern gardens as well. There were once hundreds of different kinds available, making identification of these surviving clones very difficult.

Narcissus × intermedius is a natural hybrid between *N. jonquilla* and *N. tazetta*. I've never heard this form referred to as anything but jonquils, although my ever-cheerful cousin Celia Jones of Gibsland, Louisiana, says her bulb-farming grandmother called them "Texas star" jonquils. This is the lowest growing of the commonly found narcissus. As a matter of fact they usually look like somebody stepped on them.

The foliage is dark green and flattened, and the clusters of flowers are pale yellow and delightfully fragrant. The short-stemmed flowers occur right among the foliage. Bulb expert and good friend Scott Ogden of New Braunfels, Texas, says they are "homely," but most people mistake them for regular jonquils. Bloom time is around February, along with its kin.

The late-blooming *N. × medioluteus* (formerly *N. biflorus*) goes by the names of primrose peerless, April beauty, and twin sisters. It is supposedly a natural hybrid between *N. tazetta* and *N. poeticus*. It bears two flowers per stem, and each has white petals and yellow cups. I don't see this one that often, but Celia Jones has a great many and the late Flora Ann Bynum said it's frequently found around North Carolina. My only problem with this particular narcissus is that I'm partial to the early-blooming types. Their foliage matures the quickest, allowing me to mow by Mother's Day.

The double-flowering forms of *N. × incomparabilis* give us the best names of the group. Cultivars of this hybrid have been cultivated through the years under such names as butter and eggs, eggs and bacon, codlings and cream, milk and honey, orange phoenix, golden phoenix, and primrose phoenix. Some have considered these flowers abominations, while others consider them charming. *Narcissus × incomparabilis* is supposedly a hybrid of *N. pseudonarcissus* and *N. poeticus.* It is found quite commonly throughout the South, blooming in February or early March. I call the double form my ancestors grew "butter and eggs." It is quite common but blooms best when divided every decade. It got its name back when fresh butter was pale yellow and yard eggs were orange-yellow. Today butter is artificially colored, and commercial chicken house eggs are pale yellow. Thankfully the reversed colors still fit. The single forms are even more wonderful and have the charm of wildflowers.

Most of the old-fashioned, early-blooming Narcissus are of very easy culture. As a rule, those that bloom in clusters and those with smaller flowers tend to be the best performers in the South. Those with larger flowers and those that bloom late are almost always less successful. Even the well-adapted types grow and multiply best, however, in situations with at least half to full sun and well-drained, sandy loam soils. Propagation is by division. Although the best time to divide narcissus is after the foliage has died down, I have found that just about anytime works as long as you are dealing with the old-fashioned, tougher types. I frequently divide and move them in full foliage and even full bloom. If the temperature is cool and moist, they often don't even realize they were transplanted.

If I had my way, many historic roadways of the South would be lined with naturalized plantings of our antique, easy-to-grow *Narcissus.* They are much easier than the so-called wildflowers many states are planting, they finish blooming before it's time to mow, they never die, and they get better every year. Even the highway departments couldn't mess this up. Garden clubs, civic groups, students, and the like could add some each year until the effect was truly Arcadian. —*GG*

Greg's beloved terrier, Rosie, with "sweeties" or wild jonquils (*Narcissus jonquilla*) in the foreground and campernelle jonquils (*N. × odorus* in the background (Photo by Greg Grant)

Nerium oleander

Oleander, Rose Bay, Rose Laurel
Family: Apocynaceae (Dogbane)
Size: 6–12 ft
Zones: 8–10
Evergreen shrub
Showy white, yellow, pink, or red flowers in summer

> The genial kindness of our climate assimilates the most pre-
> cious plants of other countries to itself, and exotics like the
> Camellia, the Oleander, the Gardenia, the Tea Roses, are rap-
> idly becoming indigenous in the milder portion of our State.
> When these beautiful genera were first introduced among us,
> they were treated in Carolina and Georgia as they were treated
> in England and the Northern States, nursed and protected into
> feebleness and ugliness. By and now the Gardenias and the Tea
> Roses are as much at home in all lower and middle Georgia
> as in any portion of the world, and the Oleander and Camel-
> lias are rapidly becoming weeds in the Eastern counties of the
> State.
> —Rev. Stephen Elliot Jr., first Episcopal bishop of Georgia,
> addressing the Southern Central Agricultural Society, 1851

Maybe oleanders aren't true weeds, but if the Texas Highway
Department can grow them, anybody can! No other flowering shrub that I know of can tolerate as much abuse as the oleander and still flourish. I was surprised to find out that in its
native Mediterranean habitat, the oleander is a water-loving plant
found in wet sites only. I have always thought of it as a drought-
tolerant, xerophitic plant. I guess it's like baldcypress, crinums,
and hymenocallis—they all can grow in standing water or in the
middle of an unirrigated parking lot.

I became a fan of oleanders after moving to San Antonio,
where they flourish in the heat, drought, and rocky limestone

soils. After a tour of Galveston, "The Oleander City," with the late Kewpie Gaido, along with Elizabeth Head, Sherry Brahm, and Jerry Parsons, I became an even bigger fan.

The following information is taken from *Oleanders, Guide to Culture and Selected Varieties on Galveston Island* published by the International Oleander Society in 1991.

Oleanders grow in the wild in Asia and countries of the Mediterranean area and have been in cultivation since ancient times. Holy forests of oleanders were maintained by the ancient Greeks and altars were decorated with their blossoms to honor

Oleander (*Nerium oleander*) (Photo by Greg Grant)

the sea-god Nereus and his fifty daughters, the Nereides. Chinese literary men grew them as a hobby. They liked them for their fragrance and recognized them as an emblem of grace and beauty. The oleander was planted in Roman gardens during the time of Cicero, 106–103 B.C. In mural paintings excavated from homes in Pompeii, the oleander was the flower most often pictured in 79 A.D.

Plants with single odorless pink or white flowers were the only known varieties in Europe until about 1683. At this time, a cultivated plant with a strong, sweet scent was introduced from India. Subsequently a French nursery developed many new cultivars in the late 1800s. Today, oleanders are a favorite for planting in gardens of tropical and subtropical countries.

The first oleanders came to subtropical Galveston in 1841. Joseph Osterman, a prominent merchant, brought them aboard his sailing ship to his wife and to his sister-in-law, Mrs. Isadore Dyer. Mrs. Dyer found them easy to cultivate and gave them to her friends and neighbors. The familiar double-pink variety that she grew has been named for her. Soon these plants were growing throughout the city.

As early as 1846, note was taken of the yards in Galveston with oleanders and roses in full bloom and the contribution they made to the beauty of the city. Oleanders flourished in these early days of the city and were able to withstand the subtropical weather, alkaline soil, and the salt spray. Therefore, it was logical for oleanders to be chosen as one of the predominant plants to be used in the replanting of the city following the destruction of the 1900 hurricane and grade raising that covered the existing vegetation with sand. Concerned ladies of the city soon organized the Woman's Health Protective Association (WHPA) with the mission to beautify the island and improve the health conditions of the city. They planted along Broadway, the entrance to the city, and on 25th street, the path to the beach front, and in a few years oleanders made a spectacular display of blooms for citizens and visitors. Although the name of the WHPA was changed to the Woman's Civic League, planting continued for many years up and down city streets, in parks, in yards, around public buildings and schools and soon the whole city became a garden of oleanders. As early as 1908, an editorial in the *Galveston Tribune* observed that the oleander was emblematic of Galveston and that people came from all over to see them. In 1910, The *Galveston Daily News* also reported that Galveston was known throughout the world as "The Oleander City" and in 1916 an article named it one of the most beautiful cities in the South.

In 1806 in the greenhouse section of his book, Bernard M'Mahon gave instructions for cultivating oleanders. Early nursery references to the oleander include Langdon Nurseries' 1881–82 catalogue listing of "*Nerium splendens,* the double rose oleander," and "*Nerium alba,* the white oleander." The 1904 Royal Palms Nurseries (Oneco, Florida) catalogue offered "14 sorts of this old favorite," including 'Single Pink,' 'Double Pink,' 'Lilian Henderson,' 'Single Cream,' 'M. Leon Brun,' and 'Cameum.' In 1906–7, Fruitland Nurseries (Augusta, Georgia) listed in its catalogue 'Carneum,' 'Mme. Peyre,' 'Savors,' and 'Single White.'

Oleanders are very easy to cultivate in all types of soils. They grow and bloom best in areas with full sun. They are easy to propagate from seeds and cuttings and will even root in water, a trick I learned from the good folks in Galveston. Oleanders make great low-maintenance landscape plants, and the new dwarf, everblooming types are superb when grown as container plants. —*GG*

Opuntia spp.

Prickly Pear, Indian Fig
Family: Cactaceae (Cactus)
Evergreen succulent
Size: 2–12 ft
Zones: 8–11
Evergreen plant
Showy yellow, orange, or red flowers in spring or summer

Of all the plants the Spanish discovered in the Americas, they considered the prickly pear one of the most valuable. This cactus was valued for its fruit, of course, but even more for an insect parasite that infested the plant, the cochineal insect (*Dactyopius cacti*), the source of a rich scarlet dye. This is extracted from the female insect, which the dye makers scraped from the plant and dried in ovens.

Franciscan missionaries learned of this process from the Aztecs and sent specimens of the prickly pear back to Spain as part of the loot seized after Hernán Cortés conquered Mexico. Soon the processed bugs were selling for the equivalent of two thousand dollars per ton, and the Spanish were establishing prickly pear plantations not only in Mexico but also in New Granada and the Canary Islands. Today, though cochineal is no longer a commercially important crop, the prickly pear is still featured in the coat of arms of the Mexican Republic.

Modern gardeners are more likely to value the prickly pear for its flowers, which appear from midspring to early summer on the outermost parts of the plant. Vigorously growing plants may continue to bloom over several weeks and are very showy with their bright yellow, orange, or red tulip-shaped flowers. The fruit that follows the flowers ripens from mid- to late summer and is variable in size and shape but often does resemble an elongated pear. Its color changes from green to red as it ripens, with a final change to purple, announcing maturity. Although often covered

Prickly pear (*Opuntia* sp.) (Photo by Greg Grant)

with spines, the fruit is edible and some consider it a delicacy. The bold texture of the stems, the attractive flowers and fruit, and its ability to withstand very hot and dry conditions makes prickly pear useful as a landscape plant. Some forms of the plant are more shrublike and may reach ten or twelve feet tall, while others are in the two- to three-foot range. Spiny forms may be

Spineless prickly pear (*Opuntia* sp.) (Photo by Greg Grant)

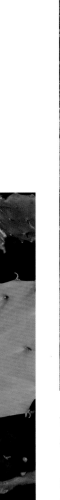

Prickly pear (*Opuntia* sp.) (Photo by William C. Welch)

useful where vandalism occurs or traffic control is wanted, but spineless types are available and much more "user-friendly."

More than 250 species of prickly pear have been identified, and this plant ranges naturally from the tropics to the northern-most parts of the continental United States. There are forms of prickly pear native as far north as New England, but the most attractive and useful ones come from Mexico and Texas.

Both the fruit and pads of prickly pear are often found in the produce sections of southwestern grocery stores or in areas with large Latin American populations. The pads (which are actually stems) are eaten as a green vegetable, somewhat like green beans, and various cultivars are considered superior for the quality of pads they produce. The flesh of the fruit is very sweet and may be eaten fresh or preserved.

Propagation is from seed or by cuttings. To root a cutting, cut a whole pad from an existing plant, set it in a sunny, relatively dry area, and partially cover it with soil. Roots soon sprout from the pad's base, and the plant that grows from it will usually bloom the second year.

Prickly pears flourish in containers since they require little, if any, irrigation and add interesting color and texture to the garden. In ranching areas of the Southwest where prickly pear is plentiful, it has sometimes performed a role as cattle feed during times of drought. Ranchers use flamethrowers to burn off the spines, and the cattle eagerly consume the pads. In addition to their long spines, prickly pear have numerous small, hairlike structures called glochids arranged in clusters on the pads. Although not as dangerous as the spines, they can be quite irritating. My favorite selection came from the California breeding work of Luther Burbank by way of horticulturist Scott Ogden. It still has irritating glochids, but the pads have a nice bluish green color and plants grow in a mannerly way. Pad-marring cactus bugs can be persistent pests but rarely kill the plants.—*WCW*

Osmanthus fragrans

Sweet Olive, Tea Olive, Fragrant Olive
Family: Oleaceae (Olive)
Size: 8–15 ft
Zones: 8–11
Evergreen shrub or small tree
Very fragrant, small flowers in fall, winter, or spring

The flowers of the sweet olive, which are borne in early spring and sometimes fall and winter, are small and white, but their perfume is powerful, one of the most distinctive of garden fragrances. Originally from China, the sweet olive has been cultivated in temple and home gardens there for so long that its origins are uncertain. Following the usual route west, sweet olives were brought to England in 1771, and from there to America. This plant forms a shrub or small tree and can reach a height of twelve to fifteen feet in coastal areas of the South. Its evergreen foliage, and a fairly dense form, make this plant valuable as a specimen, hedge, or mass. In areas where winters are too severe to grow

Sweet olive (*Osmanthus fragrans*) (Photo by Greg Grant)

them as landscape plants, sweet olives are sometimes grown as container specimens and taken into greenhouses during winter.

Propagation is usually by cuttings, although Peter Henderson in his 1890 *Henderson's Handbook of Plants and General Horticulture* suggests that grafting them onto privet is quicker. Sweet olives prefer moist, deep, acidic soils, but they adapt fairly well to less favorable growing conditions. An orange-flowering form, known as *aurantiacus,* is sometimes found in Southern gardens.

Records from Rosedown Plantation in St. Francisville, Louisiana, show that its owners, the Turnbulls, purchased three "Chinese fragrant olives (used to scent their tea)" from the New York nursery William Prince and Son in 1836. Today the scent of huge descendants from those plants permeates the entire garden.

Most of the older catalogues list sweet olive as *Olea fragrans.* Affleck's Central Nurseries, near Brenham, Texas, offered it in the 1860 price list. Fruitland Nurseries, Augusta, Georgia, in its 1906–7 catalogue offers the following: "*Olea fragrans* (Tea, or Sweet Olive). One of the most desirable flowering shrubs of

Sweet olive (*Osmanthus fragrans*) (Photo by William C. Welch)

Southern gardens. The white flowers, although small, are produced in clusters and emit the most pleasing fragrance. It is well said that 'each individual bloom has more sweetness than the most fragrant lily.' As a conservatory shrub for northern florists it will be found invaluable and of ready sale. The blooming period begins in the fall and lasts for several months. It is of easy culture and especially desirable as a window plant."

W. A. Yates, in his Brenham, Texas, catalogue of 1906–8 lists the holly leaf tea olive: "*Osmanthus* (Holly-leaved Tea Olive) A beautiful evergreen shrub with dark green spiny-toothed leaves resembling the holly [most probably *O. fortunei*, introduced in 1862]. Delightfully fragrant flowers produced in the fall in great profusion. These trees attain a height of 25–30 feet, very attractive, Hardy to New York."—*WCW*

Paeonia spp.

Peony
Family: Paeoniaceae (Peony)
Size: 2 ft
Zones: 8 and north
Perennial
Showy white, pink, or red flowers in spring

One of the best-loved (and most beautiful) of cultivated flowers, peonies have played an important role in American gardens for more than a century. Unfortunately, they are not adapted to the climate of the Deep South. But a number of the older cultivars flourish in the upper South, and peonies are an important element of historical gardens in that region.

I remember clearly my own introduction to peonies, which came when I left my boyhood home in Houston to enroll at Southwestern University in Georgetown, Texas, in the fall of 1957. When assigned the task of buying floral decorations for a

Peony (*Paeonia* × *hybrida*) (Photo by William C. Welch)

Peony (*Paeonia × hybrida*) (Photo by
William C. Welch)

fraternity function, I went to a home-operated small florist and
greenhouse. The owner gathered from her garden bouquets of
double-pink blossoms that amazed me with their size and richness; they were peonies, which she was growing in a spot where
the plants were protected from the hot afternoon sun.

Those peonies have remained in my mind as a beautiful memory, but I didn't try to grow this flower myself until recently. In
1991, though, Bertie Ferris in Dallas, knowing of my interest
in heirloom plants, graciously offered me roots of peonies that
had been in her family's possession for more than seventy-five
years. Bertie's gift grew all right in College Station but was much
happier when I moved it to our garden in Mangham, Louisiana,
where it bloomed well. I identified it as 'Festiva Maxima,' one
of the oldest cultivars of *P. albiflora*. It is probably the most frequently found peony in old Southern gardens and is still among
the most popular and available peonies. *Paeonia albiflora* was
introduced by the French grower Miellez in 1851. This cultivar
blooms early, producing fragrant, double white flowers that are

streaked with crimson at the center. Still, the fact is that peonies are generally better adapted to the region north and east of a line drawn from Dallas, Texas, to Shreveport, Louisiana, and Jackson, Mississippi.

This flower is well rooted in classical mythology and was named *Paeonia* (the botanical name for the genus) by the ancient Greeks because of the plant's supposed connection with a youth named Paeon. He was the pupil of Aesculapius, the first doctor, and Paeon's fame comes from the fact that he was so rash as to outshine his master. According to legend, when the hero Hercules wounded the god of the underworld, Pluto, Paeon used a peony root to heal the injured god. This aroused Aesculapius's jealousy, and the healer killed the too-successful pupil. Even the god of the underworld could not restore Paeon to life, but as a gesture of gratitude, he changed him into a flower, the peony.

Actually, there was a certain basis for this story, because peony roots contain an alkaloid with a sedative effect, and an infusion of the seeds acts as an emetic and purgative. Indeed, peonies originally found their way into gardens as a source of medicines rather than as a source of flowers. But by the seventeenth century, John Parkinson was extolling the aesthetic virtues of peonies in his pioneering gardening book, *Paradisi in Sole*. Today, all parts of the peony are considered poisonous to some degree, and the plant is cultivated only for its visual appeal.

The older peonies found in Southern gardens are usually varieties of either *P. officinalis* or *P. lactiflora*. *Paeonia officinalis* in particular is a venerable garden plant. First described around 300 BC by the Greek scientist Theophrastus in his *Enquiry into Plants*, *P. officinalis* had traveled as far as England before the beginning of the sixteenth century, when a double-flowered form was cultivated. These flowers were greatly admired because of the luminescent quality of the blossoms. Closer to home, it is known that *P. officinalis rubra* grew in the gardens of Old Salem, North Carolina, from the early days of that settlement, where it has been handed down as an heirloom in the Winkler family. White and pink forms are also said to be still growing in many American gardens.

Paeonia lactiflora came into the garden from Siberia near the end of the eighteenth century. It was known earlier as *P. albiflora* and was widely used by peony hybridists of the 1800s, who admired this species for the creamy color of its flowers and their outstanding perfume.

The tree peony (*P. suffruticosa*) is not a common Southern heirloom plant, but it has a rich history in the Orient and is highly prized by modern gardeners. Tree peonies were described in Chinese literature over fifteen hundred years ago, and the first varieties date back at least to the T'ang dynasty in AD 640. Japanese botanists created forms with enormous semidouble blooms and thick stems to better hold the weight of the flowers. In 1804, William Kerr successfully sent tree peonies from Canton to England, and live plants also arrived in France, where they created a "peonie mania" in 1814. When the Royal Horticultural Society sent Robert Fortune to China in 1843, he found that each district boasted its own varieties, and he succeeded in bringing home some thirty to forty different kinds. These were introduced into the United States about the turn of the twentieth century, and the American Peony Society was formed soon afterward.

Southern nurseries have been offering peonies to their customers from early days. Thomas Affleck's Southern Nurseries of Washington, Mississippi, stated in its 1851–52 catalogue that it had for sale "a few of the finest phloxes, paeonies, amaryllis, hyacinths, etc." Fruitland Nurseries, Augusta, Georgia, was more specific in its 1906–7 catalogue: "Peonies, Herbaceous—After trying many varieties we have at last succeeded in securing a collection of these beautiful plants which succeed admirably in this section. We offer 12 best sorts."

Mrs. K. M. Colby of Monroe, Louisiana, specifically addressed the cultivation of peonies in the South in an October 1966 article in the *Peony Quarterly*. There, she stated that there is no magic to growing peonies in the South, but the culture is different from

Peony (*Paeonia × hybrida*) (Photo by William C. Welch)

that in colder climates. She noted that at one time she had been growing over a hundred different peonies and had found that the early- and midseason-blooming varieties were best in the South since they flower before our weather becomes too hot. The peak flower season in her garden in Monroe ran from April 15 through mid-May. In her article she also mentioned having found thirty-year-old plants of 'Festiva Maxima' in a nearby garden.

Her recommendations for peony cultivation called for planting in a site away from competing roots of heavily feeding trees, shrubs, and hedges, where the peonies would receive a half to a full day's sun. According to Mrs. Colby, it is important to purchase good-quality plants and to plant them in the fall. The plants should be spaced about two feet apart in very well-prepared holes—as she noted, it is the digging process that separates the coffee drinkers from the serious gardeners! She called for holes about three feet in diameter and two feet deep. Any good topsoil excavated from the hole should be saved, but any hardpan or subsoil should be replaced with good, loamy soil. Before replacing soil in the hole, mix in about a pound of bone meal. Then refill the hole to within eight inches of its top, and thoroughly tamp down the soil fill—if necessary, add more soil and pack it in sufficiently so that you are satisfied winter rains will not cause settling.

The next step is to mound soil in the center of the hole so that when the dormant peony is set on the mound's top, the peony's "eyes"—its crown—rest an inch or two above ground level. Fill the remainder of the planting hole, gently shaking the peony from time to time to make sure that the soil settles in around the roots and fills any air pockets. When the planting is completed, the peony's eyes should be covered with about three-fourths inch of soil. Water well, and after the water has drained away, add soil if necessary to re-cover the peony's eyes.

Do not mulch at this time, since in the South peonies relish exposure to winter cold. In summertime, however, a mulch of pine straw or bark helps to conserve moisture and prevent weeds. Remove the mulch in the fall, and cut the dead stalks to the ground when the plant goes dormant. Otherwise, the only care necessary is to water occasionally during dry spells and to administer an annual feeding of one cup of bone meal per plant.*—*WCW*

Special thanks to Greta Kessenich, secretary of the American Peony Society, for providing information for this profile. The Society was formed in 1904 and is active in collecting and distributing educational information about peonies to the membership.

Passiflora incarnata

Maypop, Passionvine, Passionflower
Family: Passifloraceae (Passionvine)
Size: 10 ft
Zones: 7–9
Perennial vine
Intricate lavender flowers and edible fruit in summer and fall

Like pawpaws, the maypop is a member of a tropical fruit family and serves as a specific host for a pretty tropical butterfly as well. These temperate-zone members of otherwise tropical families are supposed remnants from the days when the South was even more tropical and mild. Most of the other beautiful passionvines are cold tender and will freeze in all but the coastal parts of the South.

Passionvines got their name from early Spanish priests who wove each part of the amazingly intricate flowers into the story

Maypop (*Passiflora incarnata*) (Photo by Greg Grant)

Maypop (*Passiflora incarnata*) (Photo by Greg Grant)

of the Passion of Christ. And intricate they are. At least in the South, I know of no other flower with such an array of floral parts.

The maypop has beautiful, fragrant, fringed, pale lavender flowers highlighted with purple, green, and white. Occasionally plants have all-white flowers. It blooms repeatedly throughout the warm season with the delicate flowers giving way to green goose-egg-shaped fruit. When the fruit start to turn color, shrivel, and look like they are going to ruin, they are ready for harvest. Around each seed (somewhat like a pomegranate) the clear pulp has a wonderful bit of tropical juice and flavor. One can either eat them as is (spitting out the seed) or press them into a sieve to retrieve the precious juice. A little juice goes a long way. I've made "passion-ade" with sugar and water as well as adding it to fruit punch to truly make it tropical. Some also harvest and dry the flowers and leaves to make a soothing tea.

Maypop vines occur along the edges of woods and roadsides and will either climb trees, fences, and other structures or sprawl about the ground as they do in open prairies. The maypop is virtually indestructible but performs best in full sun with good drainage. Propagation is from seed or cuttings. Once you obtain a plant, the real show starts.

All summer long, showy Gulf fritillary butterflies dance about the vines, looking for leaves where they can lay their solitary golden yellow eggs. The gray and orange larva feed exclusively on passionvine foliage before becoming a chrysalis nearby. They can occasionally eat all the foliage, but as maypops are very vigorous, they quickly recover to host even more. Maypop vines sucker profusely. I think it's an evolved mechanism to stay one step ahead of the Gulf fritillaries. The chase is certainly worth watching.—*GG*

Petunia × hybrida

Old-fashioned Petunia
Family: Solanaceae (Nightshade)
Size: 1–2 ft
Zones: 6–10
Annual or short-lived perennial
Fragrant white, pink, lavender, or violet flowers in spring, summer, and fall

If you travel around any rural area of the South, you are sure to see bouquets of small-flowered petunias poking out of everything from old dishpans to Crown tire planters. They're everywhere—they even naturalize in the grass—and nobody pays them any mind. Called a "hybrid swarm" by the botanists, this unruly crew with its pastel shades of purple, pink, and white represents the parents of our large-flowered, brightly colored modern petunias. Although the old-fashioned petunias are rarely sold in the nursery trade, they are still very common in gardens—partially

Old-fashioned petunia (*Petunia × hybrida*)
(Photo by Greg Grant)

Old-fashioned petunia (*Petunia* × *hybrida*)
(Photo by William C. Welch)

because they are pretty and fragrant, and partially because they keep coming back whether you want them to or not.

When I was a kid staying with my grandparents in Arcadia, I remember a stray white petunia popping up and blooming near the woodpile. At the time I could not believe a pretty petunia could just appear without planting one from the nursery (where I wasn't allowed to shop, by the way). When I asked Grandmother Emanis where it came from, she said she didn't know. After thinking about it later, she said her grandmother used to grow petunias in the same garden and it came from those! How on earth, I thought, could petunias skip a generation and then show up again?

The two parents of these old-fashioned petunias are the white-flowered and night-fragrant *Petunia axillaris* (formerly *P. nyctaginiflora* and *Nicotiana axillaris*) and the purple-flowered *P. violacea* (formerly *Salpiglossis integrifolia*), both perennials from southern South America. The large white petunia was introduced from Brazil in 1823; the smaller-flowered violet petunia was introduced in 1831 from Argentina.

Violet petunia (*Petunia violacea*) (Photo by William C. Welch)

In the early 1990s I noticed that the Atlanta Botanic Garden was growing a cute little small-flowered petunia labeled *P. integrifolia*. I had never heard of this species, and Bill was later able to obtain a plant for us to observe and use to propagate other plants. Later in the season I made a trip to Germany and saw a large bed of what was labeled *P. violacea* growing beneath a wisteria at the horticulture exposition in Stuttgart. I brought back three seeds, and after growing the German petunia beside the Georgian one, I realized that the two were the same species. (By the way, *P. integrifolia* is the latest name assigned to it by the ever-meddling botanists. I refuse to use it, however, as *P. violacea* is so much prettier.) The German clone, however, had darker, slightly larger flowers and was more floriferous. I introduced it to the nursery trade in San Antonio as 'VIP' petunia ("violet in profusion"). The refined nature and pretty little flowers made this species popular again in today's gardens. Later, a white-flowered form was introduced into the trade. By crossing these with old-fashioned petunias, I eventually developed a small-flowered strain with pink, white, and purple flowers. Also, by crossing it with one of Bill's white old-fashioned petunias, Jerry Parsons and I developed what he named the 'Laura Bush' petunia. It has larger flowers that are violet like its father and is a vigorous reseeder.

Old-fashioned petunias can be propagated by cuttings or seed. Though they tolerate heat, they prefer cool weather and often germinate a crop of seedlings in the fall (which may or may not overwinter) and again in the spring. They are easily transplanted when it's cool and moist.

Once breeders get started on "improving" a plant, they often go too far, and that's just what they have done, in my opinion, with the petunia. Despite all the hoopla we hear each spring about new and vigorous, heat-tolerant "miracle petunias," "perennial petunias," and "super petunias," it's time that people realize we already have such flowers—and have had for a long time.—*GG*

Philadelphus spp.

Mock Orange
Family: Saxifragaceae (Saxifrage)
Size: 8–10 ft
Zones: 7–9
Deciduous shrub or small tree
White flowers in spring

Mock orange is found in many Southern gardens, but its use there is primarily a twentieth-century phenomenon. These multistemmed shrubs bear bright white, single or double, dogwood-like blossoms in April and May after the foliage emerges from the bare stems. At maturity, the height of mock oranges can be eight to ten feet, and some bear flowers that are extremely fragrant, while others bear blossoms with no scent at all.

Philadelphus coronarius appears to have been the most important species in the South. This species came to Europe from Turkey in 1562, when Ogier Ghiselin de Busbecq, ambassador from Emperor Ferdinand to Suleiman the Magnificent, brought it back to Vienna. The lilac, another Middle Eastern flowering shrub introduced into the West around the same time, belongs to an entirely different genus than the mock orange, but the two plants were lumped together under the name of *syringa*. This mislabeling seems to have originated not in the shrub's appearances (the flowers and foliage are quite different) but in a practical application; both mock oranges and lilacs produce hollow stems, which the Turks used to make pipes.

The many species of the genus *Philadelphus* hybridize readily, which makes the plant breeder's work easier, but the mock oranges' promiscuity makes the identification and maintenance of distinct cultivars difficult. Complicating the task of distinguishing the different mock oranges is their sheer numbers; the Lemoine Nursery in Nice, France, crossed *P. coronarius* with *P. microphyllus* and *P. coulteri* and introduced a host of hybrids and named selec-

Mock orange (*Philadelphus coronarius*)
(Photo by William C. Welch)

tions in the years from 1894 to 1927. There is also one native American species in cultivation, *P. inodorus,* whose name reflects the flowers' lack of scent. Mark Catesby discovered and described this species in South Carolina in 1726.

In addition to the cascades of white flowers they produce, a major reason for the mock oranges' popularity is their ease of

Mock orange (*Philadelphus coronarius*)
(Photo by William C. Welch)

culture. Though they prefer slightly acidic soils, they thrive in a wide variety of soils both moist and dry, and in sun or partial shade. Pruning should be done after spring bloom, and new plants may be started from cuttings, division of mature plants, or seedlings that often sprout in the garden. They are sometimes known as English dogwood, and although quite different from the flowering dogwood, the mock oranges are valuable for their comparatively easy culture; their tolerance to cold, heat, and drought; their late spring flowering; and the powerful scent of some cultivars. —*WCW*

Phlox spp.

Phlox
Family: Polemoniaceae (Phlox)
Size: 1–3 ft
Zones: 5–10
Perennials and annuals
Flowers colorful purple, pink, white, red (many with contrasting "eyes")

Phlox is an extensive and interesting genus of perennials and one annual that are exclusively North American. The perennial phlox are mostly forms of *P. paniculata,* which is commonly native from Pennsylvania and Illinois southward. They bloom in mid- to late summer with immense terminal heads of white, pink, purple, and crimson flowers.

Phlox drummondii is the only annual species and is native to Texas, where it was discovered in 1835 by Thomas Drummond, a botanical collector sent out by the Glasgow (Scotland) Botanical Society. Seeds were sent home, but soon the discoverer fell victim to a fever in Cuba and died. For this reason W. J. Hooker named the plant *P. drummondii* that it might serve as a "frequent memento of its unfortunate discoverer."

There can be no stronger proof of the value and beauty of this species than the extent to which it is grown. For many years new varieties were added. Some have pure white eyes, and many have interesting color markings. From the Rio Grande Valley to deep East Texas, drifts of various colors appear in sandy soils. (In South Texas and the Hill Country it is generally blood red.)

Phlox paniculata sometimes goes by the common names "standing phlox" or "summer phlox." Since there are native forms quite common to northeast Texas, these hardy perennials have been popular in Texas and Southern gardens for many generations. They are easily grown but can be subject to powdery mildew. The most common color is a pink-purple form. Greg

Drummond phlox (*Phlox drummondii*)
(Photo by Greg Grant)

'John Fanick' phlox (*Phlox paniculata* 'John Fanick') and "magenta" (Photo by Greg Grant)

'Forest Frost' phlox (*Phlox pilosa* 'Forest Frost') (Photo by Greg Grant)

introduced 'John Fanick' in the early 1990s, which has become highly popular. It is pale pink with a darker eye and particularly attractive when combined with the common solid pink-purple type. My experience has shown it to be the most vigorous of all the summer phlox, and it is also highly fragrant. Greg says that it is one of the best butterfly-attracting plants available, especially swallowtails. It is a long-lasting and wonderful addition to summer bouquets. Mildew resistance adds another really good characteristic.

Summer phlox benefit from fairly frequent division. Fall or winter is the ideal time to dig the clumps about every two years and reset the individual plants. They thrive in sunny, well-drained locations but will tolerate up to about half shade. Since the flowers come at a really hot time of year, they last better with some afternoon shade. 'David' is a dependable white-flowering form, and 'Victoria' adds a slightly different color to the common lavender-purple type. Bloom height is two to three feet.

Another great phlox for the garden is prairie or downy phlox (*P. pilosa*). It spreads vigorously, making spreading clumps or edging with blooms at about twelve to sixteen inches tall. My start of this plant came from Ruth Knopf, who lives in Sullivan's Island, South Carolina. Ruth got her start from Elizabeth Lawrence, the famous garden writer and plant aficionado from Charlotte, North Carolina. I included it in my garden near Winedale, Texas, then took some to the Mangham, Louisiana, garden, where it has been passed along among many friends and neighbors. It has wider leaves than the typical southeastern native form. 'Forest Frost' is a nice pure white selection from Mississippi introduced by horticulturists Peter Loos and Gale Barton. Prairie phlox is best divided in early to midfall. I like it bordering azaleas or massed in large drifts. It blooms from about April 1 into late May or early June.

Two other phlox have been traditionally useful in Southern gardens. Moss pink (*P. subulata*) is a mat-forming, prostrate phlox to six inches tall with exceptionally showy early spring blooms. Foliage is fine textured and mossy in appearance. It is evergreen and fairly drought tolerant, preferring well-drained, sunny locations. It sometimes rots in highly humid, moist conditions. The

Summer phlox (*Phlox paniculata*) (Photo by William C. Welch)

'John Fanick' phlox (*Phlox paniculata* 'John Fanick') (Photo by William C. Welch)

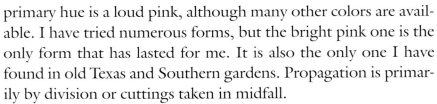

Prairie phlox (*Phlox pilosa*) (Photo by William C. Welch)

primary hue is a loud pink, although many other colors are available. I have tried numerous forms, but the bright pink one is the only form that has lasted for me. It is also the only one I have found in old Texas and Southern gardens. Propagation is primarily by division or cuttings taken in midfall.

Louisiana phlox or blue phlox (*P. divaricata*) combines well with spring-flowering bulbs and thrives in semishady borders. The long spring flowering season, showy flowers, and ease of culture make it a popular choice. The twelve- to fifteen-inch height is good as a border or in drifts combined with azaleas, perennials, or bulbs. The blue-purple form is most popular, but 'Fuller's White' is sometimes available. Fall is the ideal time to divide existing plants or set out new ones. — *WCW*

Platycladus orientalis

Oriental Arborvitae, Chinese Arborvitae, Arborvitae
Family: Cupressaceae (Cypress)
Size: 10–15 ft
Zones: 6–9
Large evergreen shrub or small tree
Attractive flat, green foliage

I know everybody is conditioned to hate arborvitae these days, but we can't hide from its historical use in Southern gardens. And of course there is hardly a cemetery in the South without this common evergreen in it. According to my late grandmother Ruth and great-aunt Ruby Dee, arborvitaes lined the walk up to my great-grandmother's house. "Big Momma," as we all called her, had a number of pretty things in the yard.

I once looked through my collection of old Southern nursery catalogues to see what plants were the most popular. In a stack of nineteen catalogues from 1851 to 1906, arborvitae was offered by fifteen of them! *Platycladus orientalis* was formerly known as *Thuja orientalis* and *Biota orientalis*. According to *The Hillier Manual of Trees and Shrubs,* this native of China was introduced into Europe around 1690. In America, John Bartram and Sons' Nursery carried it in 1792. By 1854 it was a standard feature of Southern gardens. In the letter he wrote to the *Natchez Daily Courier* on October 28 of that year, nurseryman Thomas Affleck said: "The Arbor Vitae is well known—that is, the Chinese, (orientalis), the sort common here. And to form a pretty screen hedge, I know of nothing more beautiful."

The Chinese arborvitae was listed in Affleck's 1851–52 Southern Nurseries catalogue as *T. orientalis.* Langdon Nurseries of Alabama listed this shrub as B. *orientalis* in its 1881–82 catalogue and included the related species *B. aureus, B. hybrida, B. meldensis,* and *B. filiformis pendula.* The Mission Valley (Texas) catalogue of 1898–99 offered *B. aurea, B. aurea nana, B. orientalis,*

Oriental arborvitae (*Pladycladus orientalis*)
(Photo by Greg Grant)

B. pyramidalis, Arbor Vitae Compacta, and the Rosedale Arbor Vitae. This last is a dwarf juvenile-foliaged type introduced by Rosedale Nursery of Brenham, Texas, and afterward sold in many early nurseries across the South.

The 1906–7 Fruitland Nurseries (Georgia) catalogue listed three introductions of its own—*B. orientalis, Aurea conspicuua, A. nana* (Berckmann's Golden Arborvitae), and *A. pyramidalis*—

Oriental arborvitae (*Pladycladus orientalis*) and bluebonnets (*Lupinus subcarnosus*) (Photo by Greg Grant)

Oriental arborvitae (*Pladycladus orientalis*) (Photo by Greg Grant)

together with the varieties *Japonica filiformis,* Intermedia Green, and the Rosedale arborvitae.

Though these shrubs have moved in and out of fashion, their toughness has ensured that many old established plantings have survived in Southern gardens, even if often in an overgrown and neglected condition. According to Bill, an effective way of utilizing such survivors is to limb them up into attractive multitrunked small trees. I've had others tell me they make good kindling! When and if I get around to wrapping Christmas presents, I often used the flat foliage of arborvitae on them. You can also use them to spray-paint evergreen silhouettes of snow white, gold, or silver.

Arborvitae is a plant that doesn't deserve all the grief we give it. —*GG*

Prunus caroliniana

Carolina Cherry Laurel, Wild Peach, Mock Orange
Family: Rosaceae (Rose)
Size: 10–20 ft
Zones: 7–11
Large evergreen shrub or small tree
White flowers in spring

I'm willing to bet that most people don't realize what an important role our native cherry laurel has played in our Southern gardening history. Found wild from Texas to North Carolina, this native tree was traditionally used as an evergreen hedging material in the gardens of the early South. But it often played a more important role, helping farmers and planters choose the site for their operations.

In her book *Texas,* published in 1836, Mary Austin Holley explained:

Carolina cherry laurel (*Prunus caroliniana*)
(Photo by Greg Grant)

Carolina cherry laurel (*Prunus caroliniana*)
(Photo by Greg Grant)

The undergrowth of the best land . . . is cane and a species of
laurel, the leaves of which taste like the kernel of a peach stone.
. . . The leaves of the laurel resemble those of the peach tree.
Hence it is called by the colonists the wild peach. This tree is
an evergreen, and grows to the height of twenty or thirty feet
though usually not exceeding ten. It is regarded as a certain
indication of the best soil. Hence when a colonist wishes to
describe his land as first rate, he says it is all peach and cane
land.

"Wild peach" referred to the cherry laurel, while cane referred to
our native bamboo (*Arundinaria gigantea*) or "switch cane"; the
presence of these two plants on a virgin site indicated excellent
soil for farming and production.

I can't be sure, but it appears that this expression apparently
morphed into "peachy keen" as an expression for something nice.
Another interesting bit-o'-trivia is that when crushed, the new
growth of the cherry laurel smells like maraschino cherries or
almonds.

At one time cherry laurel was such a standard part of Southern horticulture that its presence on a site today as a naturalized tree is a good indication that the land was once developed as a garden. We find evidence of this popularity in the incredible garden diary of Martha Turnbull. The mistress of Rosedown Plantation in St. Francisville, Louisiana, she made numerous references to her cherry laurel hedges. In her entry for June 14, 1837, for example, she noted that she had that day "trimmed wild peach and rose hedge"; on January 22, 1849, she "trimmed down the wild peach hedge to 14 inches." Sounds like she needed the compact selection available today.

To sidetrack for a moment, I'd like put in a word here for Martha Turnbull's sixty-year garden diary, which is preserved in the special collection of the Hill Memorial Library at Louisiana State University. It has also been published in paperback form. It is a fabulous source of information, as well as a heart-touching story. It tells a fascinating tale of a newly married woman going from a position of wealth and stature to that of a postwar, single pauper, while never losing her overwhelming and undying love of gardening. As far as I'm concerned, this diary is the most important and complete source of historic garden documentation in the South. Martha was an incredible gardener and plant lover.

Martha Turnbull wasn't the only one who grew cherry laurel. In his letter to the *Natchez Daily Courier*, Mississippi nurseryman Thomas Affleck wrote, "Nothing can be more beautiful than the Laurier Amandier, (Cerasus Caroliniensis), Cape Jessamine, Arbor Vitae, some of the Viburnums, Pittosporums, Euonymus, and Myrtles; yet, there is a sameness in our lawns and dooryards, from the general and almost exclusive use of these."

Langdon Nurseries near Mobile, Alabama, listed *Cerasus caroliniensis* in the 1881–82 catalogue and called it "mock orange," "carolina cherry," and "lauramundi." The description noted that it was "beautiful for hedges, screens, or single specimens."

Fruitland Nurseries listed it among its ornamental hedge plants in a 1906–7 catalogue. They called it "wild orange" and

Carolina cherry laurel (*Prunus caroliniana*)
(Photo by Greg Grant)

"mock orange of the South." And in a 1901 catalogue from Rosedale Nurseries in Brenham, Texas, it is listed as *C. caroliniana* or "wild peach."

Today the cherry laurel is much maligned and underused in Southern gardens, particularly as a hedge—an indication of what it can do in that line may be found in the Georgia garden of the talented Ryan Gainey. The compact selection on the market today is particularly suited for this purpose. The old-fashioned, wild-type cherry laurel will make an excellent small evergreen tree as well.

This plant is very easy to grow, particularly in acidic, well-drained soils. Propagation is by seed or by rather difficult to root cuttings under high humidity. The compact variety is occasionally available from nurseries and garden centers, while the standard type is a frequent volunteer in many Southern gardens, as its fruit is relished by robins, cedar waxwings, mockingbirds, and my beloved bluebirds.—*GG*

Prunus glandulosa

Flowering Almond
Family: Rosaceae (Rose)
Size: 4–5 ft
Zones: 4–9
Deciduous shrub
Showy pink (or white) flowers in early spring

Flowering almond is a welcome ornament in early spring, when the bare branches burst into bloom even before the leaves open. The plant's form is that of a multistemmed, deciduous shrub that reaches a height of four feet, spreading to a width of about three feet. Single-flowered forms exist and may produce one-half-inch dark pink-red fruit, but double-flowered strains are most commonly found in Southern gardens.

The cultivar 'Sinensis' has one-fourth-inch blossoms that are bright pink, very double, and tightly spaced in the stems. 'Alboplena' bears double flowers of the purest white. S. Millar

Flowering almond (*Prunus glandulosa*)
(Photo by Greg Grant)

Gault in his *Dictionary of Shrubs in Colour* lists 1774 as the date of introduction for 'Sinensis' and 1852 for 'Alboplena.' Native to China and North China, flowering almonds have long been cultivated in Japan.

Its early-flowering habit also makes this shrub a valuable source of cut flowers; its branches can fill a vase most gracefully at a time of year when little else is in bloom. Indeed, in Europe

Flowering almond (*Prunus glandulosa*)
(Photo by Greg Grant)

Flowering almond (*Prunus glandulosa*)
(Photo by William C. Welch)

flowering almond is commonly grown and forced for the floral trade.

For healthy, compact growth and the heaviest crop of flowers, prune the plants back severely during or just after bloom. Landscape uses range from single planting as specimens, or in groups as masses, or even in hedges. New plants are started from cuttings or from the suckers that spring up around the mature plants.

Flowering almond was popular in Edwardian and Victorian gardens and is easily grown and long-lived. A characteristic that makes it especially valuable for Southern gardeners is that this shrub requires only a very short period of chilling to induce flowering. I grew up admiring flowering almond in a neighbor's garden in Houston and have enjoyed growing both the white and pink forms at our home in Washington County, Texas. My plant of 'Alboplena' came from the Childress garden in Mangham, Louisiana, and has grown and bloomed beautifully for the past three years.

A century ago, many nurseries listed flowering almonds in their catalogues. For example, Langdon Nurseries of Mobile, Alabama, listed both the double white and pink forms in its 1881–82 catalogue; Rosedale Nurseries of Brenham, Texas, advertised both forms in 1901, as did Fruitland Nurseries of Augusta, Georgia, in 1906–7.

This plant is less generally available today. You may wish to check the bargain counter of packaged deciduous shrubs at local discount stores, since the flowering almond often finds itself there. The white form is more difficult to locate than the pink.
—WCW

Punica granatum

Pomegranate
Family: Punicaceae (Pomegranate)
Size: 10–15 ft
Zones: 8–11
Deciduous shrub or small tree
Orange (occasionally white, pink, red, or yellow) flowers in spring; edible fruit in summer

Native to China and Japan and countries long known as Arabia, Persia, and Bengal, pomegranates may prove hardy in favored spots as far north as Washington, D.C., but are best adapted to the Deep South. They have a long history there, for the plant was introduced into North America by Jesuit missionaries following in the footsteps of Hernán Cortés. From Mexico, pomegranates were carried northward to missions in California and possibly east to Texas. They were also thought to have been planted by Spanish settlers in St. Augustine, Florida. At any event, they thrive along the Gulf Coast and long ago escaped from gardens there to establish themselves in the wild. The plant form is that of a small deciduous tree or large shrub to twenty-five feet tall, and pomegranates typically are multistemmed unless pruned to a single trunk. This makes them good material for hedges—the foliage is dark green, and the stems are somewhat thorny. Though most commonly grown for their fruit, pomegranates are also remarkable for the beauty of their flowers, which are borne over a period of several months in spring and early summer. Most commonly these blossoms are red-orange, but white, pink, and variegated flowers may also be found.

Pomegranates appear very early on in the history of Western gardens. The ancient Roman encyclopedist Pliny considered pomegranates to be among the most valuable of ornamental and medicinal plants. Theophrastus provided an early description about 300 BC, and many Asian legends concerning the pomegranate have been handed down through the centuries. The numerous seeds are supposed to be a symbol of fertility. In Turkey there is a custom that a bride throw a ripe pomegranate to the ground; then by counting the number of seeds that fall out of the fruit, she can divine the number of children she will bear. Legend also says that the pomegranate was the "tree of life" in the Garden of Eden, and from this belief it became the symbol of hope and eternal life in early Christian art. The erect calyx lobes of the fruit were the inspiration for Solomon's crown, so for all subsequent crowns.

Peter Henderson's *Handbook of Plants and General Horticulture* (1890) recommends the dwarf form. Henderson says that this plant, *Punica nana,* although naturalized in the Southern United States, is native to the East Indies and was introduced into England in 1723. I recall seeing beautiful three- to five-foot specimens of *P. nana* in flower and fruit in August as a part of the foundation planting near the main house at Filoli Gardens near San Francisco.

In a monograph titled *The Pomegranate: A Southern Tradition,* Jack E. Rice of Laurinburg, North Carolina, states: "The pomegranate (*Punica granatum*) was once a proud tradition in the South and graced many gardens with their beautiful flowers and fruit. I fondly remember the fall ripening fruit as a young boy [in the 1940s] and the wide variety of sizes, colors, and tastes. Most of these have vanished along with the traditional farming communities. I have never lost my taste or affection for the pomegranate and it remains one of my favorite fruits."

For a period in the early 1900s pomegranates were grown in commercial quantities in California, Arizona, Georgia, Alabama, Nevada, and even Utah. American consumers have, however, really never developed much appreciation for the pomegranate fruit, though in Mexico they are very popular. Recent years have seen a resurgence of interest with large commercial plantings being established in California. This has been spurred by research demonstrating the antioxidant value of the fruit and juice. The

Pomegranate (*Punica granatum*) (Photo by William C. Welch)

beauty of the fruit alone is sufficient for many consumers to purchase it. Varieties like 'Cloud' and 'Spanish Beauty' fruit well in Texas. The search for varieties that could be grown commercially in the South has also begun.

Jack Rice blames the lack of popularity of the pomegranate fruit in this country on the prevalence of one cultivar, 'Wonderful.' This is an old clone, discovered by a Mr. Bears of Porterville, California, in 1896 as one of a group of cuttings he received from Florida. Jack Rice insists that despite the name, 'Wonderful' bears poor-quality fruit, though if aged at room temperature for a month or two after picking, the 'Wonderful' pomegranates do develop the rich, sweet taste characteristic of better-quality cultivars.

Although of very easy culture, pomegranates prefer a sunny location and deep soil. They thrive in acidic or alkaline soils and tolerate heavy clay as long as there is sufficient drainage. Many forms exist, but not all fruit well. Generally, double-flowering types provide little, if any, fruit. Mature specimens withstand drought well, but fruit often splits after rainy spells following extended dryness. Plants are often long-lived with some trees in France recorded as having fruited for over two hundred years.

Double-flowering types have carnation-like flowers. Propagation is by seed or cuttings, with cuttings being necessary to perpetuate specific cultivars. Dormant hardwood cuttings root well, as do softwood cuttings kept under mist in the summer.

Though most commonly eaten fresh, pomegranate fruits may also be processed into syrups, such as grenadine, fermented into alcoholic beverages, or cooked into jellies. Plants of the dwarf and large-growing forms are sometimes available in the southern half of Texas. In all but the warmest zones, plants may freeze back to the ground. Fruit specialists are conducting interesting trials in the Houston area with pomegranates from Iran and Russia because some of these plants may have superior fruiting, growth, and hardiness characteristics.

Pomegranates were often found in nineteenth-century Southern gardens and nurseries. In his *Southern Rural Almanac, and Plantation and Garden Calendar* for 1860, Thomas Affleck listed them as grown in his Washington County, Texas, nursery and noted, "The pomegranate grows, thrives and bears most admirably." By the late 1800s, they were being advertised in other catalogues, such as those of Langdon Nurseries (Mobile, Alabama, 1881–82) and Mission Valley Nursery (Victoria County, Texas, 1898–99)—*WCW*

Quercus virginiana

Southern Live Oak
Family: Fagaceae (Beech)
Size: 50–60 ft
Zones: 8–11
Spreading evergreen tree
Dense shade and evergreen foliage

> As a shade and ornamental tree, there is none will compare
> with our magnificent Water oak, and Live oak. The latter is
> more beautiful and permanent. . . . Suppose that, instead of
> the China tree, your streets and pleasant Bluff promenade, had
> been lined and shaded with these oaks! By this time, you would
> have had ornamental trees such as few cities can boast of. The
> Mobilians were alive to the beauty of the Live Oak as a shade
> tree for their streets and squares, and see the results now!
> —Thomas Affleck, Mississippi nurseryman, in a letter to the
> editor of the *Natchez Daily Courier,* October 28, 1854

It is impossible to discuss the gardens of the Deep South and
ignore the "evergreen" live oak. Almost every early visitor to

Southern live oak (*Quercus virginiana*) at
Oak Alley, Vacherie, Louisiana (Photo by
Greg Grant)

Southern live oak (*Quercus virginiana*)
(Photo by Greg Grant)

the Gulf Coast sent home a marveling description of the great, spreading live oaks with their Spanish moss–bedecked limbs.

This tree, *Quercus virginiana,* is widely adapted to Southern conditions, for it is native from Texas all the way to the Carolinas. Throughout this region, the live oak's broad-reaching form and dense, persisting foliage made it the shade tree of choice, the premier material for lining the streets and allées of early Southern towns and gardens. It's not hard to understand the appeal—all it takes is one visit to an old plantation home with an allée of live oaks to be smitten. Two of my favorite examples are Oak Alley and Rosedown plantations in southern Louisiana. In that state there is actually a live oak society, which has named and recorded the most cherished specimens.

Live oaks are easy to grow in most types of soil. They are, however, prone to ice and freeze damage in the upper South. Nor does *Q. virginiana* thrive in the drier, alkaline soils of the Texas Hill Country—but there you can substitute the smaller live oak species native to that region, *Q. fusiformis.* Unfortunately, the live oaks there are battling a crippling vascular disease known as oak wilt. Let's hope that oak wilt never gets to the Deep South.
—*GG*

Rhododendron spp.

Azalea, Wild Honeysuckle
Family: Ericaceae (Heath)
Size: 6–10 ft
Zones: 6–9
Evergreen or deciduous shrubs
Showy white, yellow, pink, red, or purple flowers in spring (and sometimes fall)

Whereas the magnolia blossom once served as the floral symbol of the South, today that honor most likely belongs to the evergreen azaleas. Historically, though, members of the other major group of azaleas, the deciduous azaleas, were important in the early gardens of the South because the first azaleas to be cultivated in America were our own native species, and these are deciduous.

In early days, the selection of azaleas available to American gardeners was slim. In a letter to James Madison in 1791, Thomas Jefferson noted that "I find but two kinds, the *nudiflora* and *viscosa* acknowledged to grow with us." This situation had changed dramatically, however, by the middle of the nineteenth century, as exotic and American species were crossed to create a host of hybrids suited to Southern conditions. The 1851–52 catalogue of Thomas Affleck's Mississippi nursery, for instance, offered "fifty named varieties of the new Ghent Azaleas, hardy hybrids, between *Rhododendron Ponticum* and *Azalea Nitida*, the latter the beautiful, fragrant Wood Honeysuckle of the South." Affleck was also offering at this time "*Azalea Ponticum*, very much like the Wood Honeysuckle, but with larger corymbs of bright yellow, highly fragrant blossoms."

Although their parentage was half American, the Ghent hybrids originated with the nurserymen of the Belgian city of Ghent. This was a substantial contribution that these growers made to Southern gardening, for as Alice Coates noted in her

Native azalea (*Rhododendron canescens*)
(Photo by Greg Grant)

Azaleas (*Rhododendron* spp.) at Stephen F.
Austin Mast Arboretum, Nacogdoches,
Texas (Photo by Greg Grant)

book, *Garden Shrubs and Their Histories* (1964), there were by
1850 were some five hundred types of these deciduous "Ghent
Azaleas" in commerce. Later, these same growers were to present
the South with another gift when they developed the evergreen
"Belgian indicas."

However, the real story of the evergreen azaleas belongs to
the Orient, mainly China and Japan. In Japan, the cultivation
and breeding of evergreen types had been a fashionable hobby
for hundreds of years. Evidence of the azaleas' popularity can be
found in the fact that as early as 1692, a Japanese expert named
Ito Ihei had published a monograph on these plants, discussing
in it every major azalea species of Japan, plus those introduced
from China and Korea.

The appearance of evergreen azaleas in Southern gardens, by
contrast, is a relatively modern occurrence. George Stritikus, late
horticulturist for the Alabama Extension Service and the Birmingham Botanical Gardens, found an article in the May 1859 issue
of *American Cotton Planter and Soil* (published in Montgomery)
that points this out. Written by Robert Nelson, a horticultural

editor and nurseryman from Columbus, Georgia, the article "Chinese Honeysuckle, (*Azalea indica*)" begins by remarking, "It is surprising, indeed, that this magnificent shrub—the beauty and glory of the Northern greenhouses in the early spring—is hardly ever to be met with in the South. True, a few specimens in pots may now and then (though seldom) be seen, in a very poor condition. But why keep them in pots? Turn them out of doors, into the open ground; give them but one-tenth of the attention which you bestow on the plant, while in a pot, and you will have the most beautiful blooming shrub in your garden, during March and April, that your eyes ever beheld."

Nelson ended his article with an exhortation: "Two of the most brilliant varieties I ever had were the two old, well known kinds, *A. phoenicea* and *A. Hibbertia purpurea;* but in fact all the *Azalea indica* will thrive well in this latitude."

Actually, a few perceptive Southerners were already experimenting with the evergreen Asian species. Martha Turnbull of Rosedown Plantation in St. Francisville, Louisiana, had been investing in Chinese azaleas for more than twenty years when

Azaleas (*Rhododendron* spp.) at Stephen F. Austin Mast Arboretum, Nacogdoches, Texas (Photo by Greg Grant)

Azaleas (*Rhododendron* spp.) at Stephen F. Austin Mast Arboretum, Nacogdoches, Texas (Photo by Greg Grant)

Nelson's article hit the press. In the Hill Memorial Library of Louisiana State University there is an invoice dated February 8, 1836, from the New York nursery firm William Prince and Son, billing Turnbull for four "Chinese scarlet flowering azaleas," four "Chinese white flowering azaleas," four "Chinese superb cerulean azaleas," one "Chinese blue flowering azalea," and one "Chinese Young's splendid new flowering azalea." Another bill dated February 27, 1837, records Turnbull's purchase of one "blue or cerulean azalea," one "splendid hybrid or cerulean azalea," and one "scarlet or Indica azalea." On February 15, 1847, Turnbull noted, "Azaleas put in ground." There's no mention of the variety she was planting, however. And whatever she may have used to enrich the Turnbull plantation, Southern gardeners as a whole did not follow suit until the twentieth century.

The tender "Indian azaleas" (a group that includes the Belgian indicas) were the first evergreen azaleas to gain wide acceptance in the South. These large-flowered beauties are hybrids derived from *R. indicum, R. simsii,* and others. They were developed in Europe, primarily Belgium, Holland, Germany, and England, where they were grown in greenhouses. When the indicas reached the mild climate of the Southern United States, though, they proved well suited to cultivation outdoors.

Subsequently, a race of Southern indica hybrids sprang up in the Carolinas in the latter half of the nineteenth century. According to Harold Hume (*Azaleas and Camellias,* 1936), "Had it not been that many found a place in the gardens of the Lower South and that the old nursery firm of P. J. Berckmans Co. [Fruitland Nurseries, Augusta, Georgia] became interested in them as

Kurume azaleas (*Rhododendron obtusum* 'Kurume') (Photo by William C. Welch)

Drifts of southern Indian azaleas (*Rhododendron indicum*) (Photo by William C. Welch)

garden plants, they would have made little impression on the gardens of America." The Southern indicas remained the only evergreen azaleas grown outdoors in the United States until the importation of the kurumes directly from Japan to California in 1915.

This event occurred when Japanese nurseryman Kojiro Akoshi entered twelve plants in the Panama Pacific Exposition of 1915, held in California, according to Christopher Fairweather in *Azaleas* (1988). A more significant introduction was brought about by Ernest "Chinese" Wilson of the Arnold Arboretum, who had seen some small plants of these azaleas in bloom in Japan in 1914 and returned in 1918 to select fifty cultivars for importation to the United States. The "Wilson fifty" reached the Arnold Arboretum April 24, 1919, in time to cause a considerable sensation at the Massachusetts Horticultural Society's annual flower show in the spring of 1920 (Hume, *Azaleas and Camellias*).

From there the evergreen azaleas moved south, inspiring famous displays at Magnolia Gardens, Middleton Place, and The Oaks, near Charleston, South Carolina; Pinehurst at Summerville, South Carolina; Belle Isle at Georgetown, South Carolina; Wormsloe Plantation near Savannah, Georgia; the Whitney Estate at Thomasville, Georgia; the Brewer Garden, Winter Park, Florida; Airlie at Wilmington, North Carolina; and Rosedown Plantation at St. Francisville, Louisiana.

The evergreen azalea craze spread eventually to Houston, at the western edge of azalea country. According to information from Sadie Gwin Blackburn and her garden club's archives, the River Oaks Garden Club in Houston held its first Azalea Trail in 1936 with an attendance of over three thousand. A 1937 *Houston Chronicle* editorial explains the evolution of this event:

> In the past several years thousands of Houstonians have made pilgrimages to Southern Louisiana and Mississippi, and some gone farther eastward in the South, following the Azalea Trail. Only in the past few years have any great number of these plants been set out here, but already it has become evident there is no need of leaving Houston to enjoy the sight of these exquisite blossoms. Doubtless the day will come when people from all over the country will come to Houston to see the azaleas and camellias, just as they now go to Natchez and Charleston.

Great numbers indeed. A March 1937 article in the *Houston Chronicle* mentioned "the marvelous garden of Mrs. H. R. Cullen, which has over eight thousand Camellias and Azaleas—the largest known planting outside the famous Bellingrath Gardens of Mobile, Alabama."

Although the azalea did not reach commonplace status in the South until the era of the Azalea Trail, one couple had obviously started planting much earlier. A 1937 *Houston Press* article, headlined "Hanszen Garden Has Four Acres: 2000 Tulips: Rare Azaleas," states: "Mr. Hanszen has collected some of the finest azaleas to be found in Louisiana. Among these, his Rosedown Orchid, over 60 years old, and the Salmon Pink, over 40 years of age, dominate the planting."

Azaleas (*Rhododendron*) massed along a creek bank in a Tyler, Texas, garden (Photo by William C. Welch)

Azaleas require acidic, well-drained, organic soils for successful cultivation. They generally need at least some shade to protect them from burning in summertime. Most gardeners prefer to grow them directly under trees, although this may increase the need for watering, which is considerable anyway; azaleas have very shallow roots and require frequent irrigation during dry periods. Although not considered easy to propagate, they can be layered or rooted with cuttings kept in conditions of high humidity. In the old days, gardeners fertilized them immediately after bloom with cottonseed meal; however, today commercial azalea-camellia-gardenia food is generally used. —*GG*

Rosa spp.

Rose
Family: Rosaceae (Rose)
Size: 2–30 ft
Zones: 7–10
Evergreen shrubs or climbers
Showy blooms in all colors in spring, summer, fall

The most aristocratic of flowers, roses also rank among the most democratic, at least in the South. Roses have been a fixture in the gardens of the rich and mighty throughout our history, and a century ago no plantation was complete without its beds of tea roses or Noisettes. Because of their popularity with the well-to-do, roses are the best documented of heirloom flowers, and the titled names of the more fashionable roses—the types named for European aristocrats that came to us from nurseries in France and England—appear constantly in old diaries and historic garden plans.

Yet if roses have been the flowers of elegance in the South, they have also been just as much a fixture of our rural cottage gardens. Indeed, it was often the more modest gardeners who kept alive the splendid heirloom varieties. Whereas wealthy gardeners might follow fashion by rooting out old favorites and replacing them with the latest introductions, poorer gardeners could not afford such extravagant gestures. Not only did cottage gardeners keep their old roses but they commonly helped to keep them in circulation after they had dropped out of nursery catalogues. Roses are, for the most part, easy to propagate by cuttings, and cottage gardeners used to pass along starts of their favorite types to friends and family members. As a result, modern rose collectors commonly find the finest specimens of eighteenth- and nineteenth-century roses in the humbler neighborhoods. The owners of these glorious antiques may not know the name of what they have been preserving, but they know a special beauty when they see it.

'Cramoisi Superieur' rose (*Rosa chinensis* 'Cramoisi Superieur') (Photo by Greg Grant)

'Cramoisi Superieur' rose (*Rosa chinensis* 'Cramoisi Superieur') (Photo by Greg Grant)

For the collector, part of the appeal of the heirloom roses lies in their authenticity. As with other plants grown from cuttings, grafting, or tissue culture, roses are not re-creations of past artifacts but are in fact a piece of the original plant, a part of the original creation. But if the old-fashioned roses are a Southern tradition, they are also very timely plants because the old roses have all the virtues we cherish in heirloom plants.

They offer a special and very different kind of beauty. There is tremendous variation in the form and size of the flowers, and the perfumes are typically richer and more varied than those of modern roses. The colors of the heirloom roses tend toward pastels of pink, purple, yellow, white, and rose, so they blend more easily into garden and interior settings than the eye-catching bright reds, oranges, and yellows of the modern hybrids. Old roses often bear handsome foliage and attractive hips (fruit) that help round out their seasonal interest. And finally, these floral antiques are tough. Often these roses are found flourishing on the site of abandoned homesteads and cemeteries, where they carry on without pruning, spraying, fertilization, or irrigation.

These roses are beautiful, but they are survivors, too, survivors from an era when garden plants had to thrive without the help of sprinkler systems, pesticides, and all the other aids of modern horticulture.

Some idea of the role that these heirloom roses played in yesterday's landscape can be gained from an observation of a nineteenth-century tourist named Harriet Martineau. In *Retrospect of Western Travel,* while describing a visit in 1837 to the site of the Battle of New Orleans, Martineau noted, "Gardens of roses bewildered my imagination. I really believed at the time that I saw more roses that morning than during the whole course of my life before."

Today, the same roses that charmed Harriet Martineau are beginning to play an important part in the Southern landscape once again. Modern gardeners are rediscovering their charms and strengths, and organizations and nurseries are forming to provide educational information and sources of plants. Nostalgia has a part in this "old rose revival," but practicality is more of a spur to those bent on recovering the forgotten treasures of the flower's fame.

More complete information on the classes and varieties as well as culture and landscape use of these fascinating plants is available in my book *Antique Roses for the South.* In this present volume, varieties from each class that have shown the best adaptability and potential as assets in the landscape will be listed along with their dates of introduction, if known, so these living antiques can be used authentically in garden restorations.

Landscaping with Heirloom Roses

Using old roses authentically—and effectively—is easy. All that is necessary is that you combine a touch of imagination with patient reflection on how roses were used in our ancestors' gardens. Trellises, espaliers, arches, pillars, and pergolas are all appropriate means of displaying old roses, and you may also introduce them (as our ancestors did) into mixed borders or plant them as specimens or in hedges. When designing with old roses, keep in mind that these shrubs make their most spectacular displays during spring in the South. Many, however, will bloom again during summer and fall, and tea roses, in particular, seem to reach their peak in the fall.

When I first fell in love with antique roses, I strongly favored those that rebloomed, the types usually known as "everblooming" in the South. However, after observing some of the "spring only" bloomers in Europe and in old gardens of the South, I came to the realization that although these varieties may flower for only three to six weeks each spring, they often produced more flowers during that period than their everblooming cousins do in a whole year. For lavish effect I consider some of these spring bloomers—roses such as Lady Banks, 'Veilchenblau,' 'Tausendschon,' 'Carnea,' *Rosa* × *fortuniana,* "Cherokee," 'Cl. American Beauty,' "Swamp Rose," and "Seven Sisters"—to be indispens-

'Duchesse de Brabant' rose (Photo by Greg Grant)

'Cl. American Beauty' rose (Photo by William C. Welch)

able for my garden. In addition to their exuberant spring display, these roses commonly prove more disease and drought tolerant than the everbloomers. Besides, there is enjoyment in expectation: I look forward to the spring bloomers' season of display, and the flowering ends before I can grow satiated.

Yet it is important to recognize how exciting the everbloomers were when they first made an appearance in our gardens.

Few events in horticultural history equal the importance of the arrival of the first everblooming roses from China in the eighteenth and nineteenth centuries. Until that time only two fairly minor types of roses, the musk rose and the autumn damask, had ever bloomed after springtime in the West, and even those two rebloomed only sparingly. When the first truly everblooming roses did arrive from China, rose breeders (especially those in France) immediately began crossing them with Western roses to produce a flurry of new types and classes.

Though spectacular as flowers, many of the new roses proved too frost sensitive to thrive in northern Europe, or the northern half of North America, since the Chinese everbloomers were natives of warm-weather regions. But experience has shown these old-timers to be ideally suited to the climate of the Southern states. The classes we know today as tea and China roses are especially well adapted to the South and were cherished by our gardening ancestors. They are just as welcome and appropriate in a modern garden as a restoration, and thanks to the renewed interest in antique roses, they are widely available from mail-order sources, if not at most local garden centers.

Antique Roses by Class

It has been estimated that more than ten thousand rose varieties were introduced in the period between 1804 and 1935. This, coupled with the fact that roses can, and frequently do, mutate spontaneously (this is called "sporting"), helps us to understand why it is difficult to identify the roses we find growing in old cemeteries and gardens. Of all the thousands of roses that were introduced (and which may still be growing unrecognized on some abandoned homestead), only a small fraction are commercially available today. Further limiting the average gardener's choice of roses is the fact that of the choice band of old roses still offered in nursery catalogues, many prefer the cooler temperatures of the North.

We have chosen to concentrate on the old roses that will perform well in modern Southern gardens, so the photographs included represent those types of roses most commonly found enduring benign neglect in our Southern cemeteries and gardens. We list many other roses as well, but we believe that when nature chooses to send a message, the gardener ought to listen. If a rose commonly flourishes on its own, then it is truly "time tested" and is a good choice for new or restored gardens.

As you look through the recommendations, you will find the roses listed together in "classes." Developed originally by rose nurserymen and refined by generations of rose growers, the class system is simply a convenient way to organize roses into groups of plants that are similar in appearance and in need. Members of the various classes commonly share a similar parentage—they descend from similar crosses of species or types—so have many characteristics in common. In my coverage of each class I have included a list of varieties with which I have been successful and, therefore, recommend to other Southern gardeners.

Following the name of each rose is the approximate date of its introduction (the date it first appeared on the market), if known. Knowing the date of introduction is important when you are planning a garden that you want to reflect a specific period of time. You would not want, for example, to plant a rose that was introduced in 1870 in a colonial-era garden. In addition, I have included in the description of each rose variety the approximate size the plant will attain when mature.

Climbing 'Cramoisi Superieur' rose (*Rosa chinensis* 'Cramoisi Superieur') (Photo by William C. Welch)

Species and Related Hybrids

Species roses may be defined as those types found growing in wild populations in nature. Most of the roses listed here are species, but I have included a number of hybrids as well, hybrids that retain many species characteristics. All the roses in this section, both species and specieslike hybrids, tend to be of excellent vigor and are for the most part disease resistant. They are good choices

Cherokee rose (*Rosa laevigata*) (Photo by William C. Welch)

for naturalizing and will often grow well without regular maintenance if planted properly and given some care during the first year or so. Species roses work particularly well with plantings of native shrubs, perennials, and wildflowers since they all tend to thrive with minimal attention.

Besides their carefree quality, species roses are desirable for the natural elegance they impart to the landscape and fit well into a wide range of settings. Most bloom only in the spring and spend the rest of their energy producing healthy, abundant foliage. Some species roses also produce handsome fruit that add to their attractiveness in the landscape and have value as food for wildlife. Most grow to a large size and look their best when given ample room in which to expand. Although many are climbers, with a minimum of training and pruning, these, too, can be grown as large shrubs.

Though we tend to think of an interest in native plants as a new trend, in fact the enthusiasm for species roses is well rooted in Southern garden history. For example, in 1858 a visitor to Natchez extolled the beauty of Laurel Hill, owned by a man considered to be of great culture and wealth. The gardens at Laurel Hill included a hedge, "miles upon miles of Cherokee Rose," described as having a breadth of ten feet. Natchez at this time, according to this correspondent, was the "Persia of roses. In no other part of the Union have we ever seen them attain such perfection and beauty." The rose in question, *R. laevigata,* is a species rose (Hedrick).

Recommended species and varieties
Rosa moschata, Musk Rose, 1540, 6–10 ft, white
Rosa eglanteria, Sweetbrier, prior to 1551, 8–10 ft, pink
Rosa palustris scandens, Swamp Rose, 1726, 6–8 ft, pink
Rosa laevigata, Cherokee, 1759, 5–15 ft, white
Rosa multiflora 'Carnea,' 1804, 15–20 ft, pink
Rosa virginiana, Virginiana, before 1807, 3–6 ft, pink
Rosa banksiae 'Alba Plena' (white), 1807, and 'Lutea' (yellow), 1824, Lady Banks Rose, 10–20 ft
Rosa setigera, Prairie Rose, 1810, 4–6 ft, pink
Rosa roxburghii, Chestnut Rose, prior to 1814, 5–7 ft, pink
Rosa multiflora 'Platyphylla,' 1817, 12–15 ft, cream, carmine, mauve
Rosa multiflora 'Russelliana,' Russell's Cottage Rose, prior to 1837, 5–7 ft, magenta-pink
Rosa × *odorata pseudindica,* Fortune's Double Yellow, 1845, 6–10 ft, yellow

Rosa × *fortuniana*, Fortuniana, 1850, 8–10 ft, white
Rosa multiflora 'Tausendschon,' 1906, 10–15 ft, dark pink
Rosa multiflora 'Veilchenblau,' 1909, 10–15 ft, lavender-purple

China Roses

A thousand years before the birth of Christ, the Chinese had bred a single-flowering native rose (*R. chinensis*) into true garden types. These new garden plants had a revolutionary characteristic: they bloomed not just in the spring but repeatedly through the growing season. The impact of this ancient innovation persists even today, for all the modern everblooming roses descend from those first Chinese shrubs.

The influence of *R. chinensis* has been especially strong in the American South. One testimony to this is the inspirational book *Everblooming Roses* written by Georgia Torrey Drennan in 1912. Georgia Drennan was a Southerner born in 1843 at her parents' plantation, Round Hill in Holmes County, Mississippi, and her book, in its wealth of firsthand experience, reveals that she was a knowledgeable horticulturist as well. "Turn where I may," she wrote, "I cannot find, nor remember, any roses that are more hardy, healthy, long-lived and everblooming than these old Bengals [Chinas]."

Individual blossoms of the China roses are not likely to win "Best of Show," but their profusion of flowers, their disease resistance, and the long, healthy life they typically live more than compensate. Undoubtedly the best testimony to the China roses' hardiness and vigor is the fact that they are the roses most commonly found surviving without care in Texas and the South.

Chinas serve well as material for hedges, specimen plants, or borders. If pruned severely, most of them can be easily maintained as small, rounded plants. They respond well to heavy pruning in winter but seem to resent it in summer. If pruning is limited to the removal of dead or weak wood, these shrubs will slowly attain a large size.

My own interest in old roses began when I was a child, back in the mid-1940s as I watched my aunt Edna carefully planting a hedge of the China rose 'Old Blush' with plants she had grown from cuttings at her home in Rosenberg, Texas. In this hedge she alternated 'Old Blush' (which she called "The Fisher Rose," in honor of the dear friends and neighbors who had given it to her) with bridal wreath spirea, to create a living wall that enclosed two sides of her garden. The effect was memorable.

Actually, though Aunt Edna had gotten her start of 'Old Blush' from a neighbor, she was familiar with the rose from her grandmother's garden, and including it in her own garden was like welcoming an old friend. When Aunt Edna moved back to her hometown of Yoakum, Texas, in 1951, she took starts of her bridal wreath spirea and "Fisher Rose" with her and repeated the display at her new home. Although Aunt Edna is gone, both the plantings in Rosenberg and Yoakum bloom and make a cheerful spectacle each spring.

"Martha Gonzales" rose (Photo by William C. Welch)

Another experience of mine associated with 'Old Blush' has to do with the way in which I acquired its climbing form. Cleo Barnwell of Shreveport, Louisiana, was one of the most expert horticulturists I have known; when she became aware of my interest in old roses, she said that I must have a cutting from the 'Climbing Old Blush' she had obtained many years ago from her friend Elizabeth Lawrence of Charlotte, North Carolina. I eagerly accepted the cuttings and shared them with the newly established Antique Rose Emporium near Brenham, Texas.

A few years later I noticed beautiful specimens blooming on trellises in front of the Nimitz Hotel in Fredericksburg, Texas, and was pleased to know that they were descendants of the cuttings I had been given by Cleo Barnwell. These large, trellised specimens were literally stopping traffic when I photographed them.

The story doesn't end at the Nimitz Hotel. In the spring of 1993 I was pleased to participate as a speaker in the "Winghaven Symposium," an annual event sponsored by friends of Winghaven Gardens in Charlotte, North Carolina, a private foundation dedicated to educational endeavors centered around birds

"Natchitoches Noisette" rose (Photo by William C. Welch)

and gardens. Attached to the foundation are the beautiful gardens that the Clarksons developed and left in trust. These gardens are found on the same street, just a few houses down, from the Elizabeth Lawrence home and garden. Apparently the Clarksons and Elizabeth Lawrence enjoyed sharing gardening experiences and, of course, plants.

This is how what was originally a Texan rose found its way into the Lawrence garden: during my stay in Charlotte I learned that Elizabeth Clarkson was actually a native of Uvalde, Texas. The 'Cl. Old Blush' she had planted at her home in Charlotte was a cutting she had taken from a rose at her childhood home, a rose that she knew as "Mama's Rose." The cutting that Elizabeth Clarkson planted in Charlotte is thriving still, as is the cutting from it that she gave to Elizabeth Lawrence (it grows by a tree near the entrance to her home). It was a treat to know that in setting out my plant of 'Cl. Old Blush' I was merely returning a Texan rose to its native soil.

Another instance of the China rose's durability occurred during an unscheduled visit I made with several Southern Garden History Society members who (like myself) were attending the May 1994 annual meeting in Colonial Williamsburg. Peggy Cornett, a good friend and horticulturist for Monticello, was with me at our stop at the Dora Armistead garden on Duke of Gloucester Street. According to the present owner, Robert T. Armistead, the home was built in 1890 on the foundations of a 1715 home where, it is said, George Washington once slept. Dora Armistead was a noted gardener in her day, and her nephew, a botanist. Today, this late Victorian structure, one of only a handful remaining in the historic district, had lost much of its original splendor and was moved away a few years later, but the remnants of the garden included some true gems.

Several roses throughout the property were in full bloom; one of these I considered to be a major find. For years I had searched for the climbing form of 'Cramoisi Superieur,' a robust dark red China rose. The bush form is frequently found on old homesites, cemeteries, and similar locations throughout the South. Although I had seen references to the climbing form, it had always eluded me—until then.

Quite often the old roses found at abandoned sites survive in less than ideal conditions. The magnificent specimen I found in the Armistead garden, however, had been carefully trained to shade the large front porch of the house. Armistead testified that this rose is so vigorous, it sometimes climbs well on to the roof of the porch, although a freeze several years ago had cut it back. He speculated that Dora Armistead planted this particular specimen in the 1890s.

Although I had never encountered this rose in the flesh before, I had come across it in print in articles published in the *San Antonio Express* (September 2, 1934) and the *Dallas Morning News* (December 16, 1934) by Adina de Zavala. She was chair of the Texas Centennial Commission and was encouraging Texans to plant roses to celebrate the state's upcoming centennial celebration in 1936. In the article she related her memories of conversations with her grandmother, Emily West de Zavala, and visits to her garden, which dated to the early 1830s.

Grandmother Emily had begun her garden shortly after her husband Lorenzo returned to Texas from a stint as ambassador to France—he had also served as vice-president for the newly formed Republic of Texas. While in France, Lorenzo reported receiving gifts of new China roses to take back to this home in Texas. One of the roses mentioned by Adina de Zavala was 'Cramoisi Superieur,' although according to rose records the early 1830s was too early for this particular rose to be present in Texas. Greg Grant's files on red China roses include two climbing forms of 'Cramoisi Superieur': 'Rev. James Sprunt,' introduced by Sprunt in 1858, and 'Cl. Cramoisi Superieur,' introduced by the Coutourier nursery of France in 1885.

Peter Henderson, a well-known horticultural author and plantsman of the period, introduced both roses through his nursery in New York, and they were also listed by two early Texas nurseries: Gilbert Onderdonk's Mission Valley Nurseries in 1888 and William Watson's Rosedale Nurseries of Brenham in 1899. These two forms may be the same, both being climbing sports of the same well-known shrub ('Cramoisi Superieur').

In his book *Shrub Roses of Today,* Graham Stuart Thomas wrote, "The climbing form 'Cramoisi Supérieur Grimpante' is a magnificent plant for a sunny wall." And in his catalogue of 1912, nurseryman Tom Smith noted that he had "seen the whole front of a two-story house completely covered with the Climbing Cramoisi," whose flowers "are continually produced all the season through."

But my enthusiasm for this rose goes beyond its unique beauty. There are few truly red heirloom roses and even fewer climbers. Because China roses usually rebloom profusely, it is a very useful plant for period or modern gardens. Certainly, it was not difficult to infect Southern Garden History Society members Steve Wheaton, Peggy Cornett, and Peter Schaar with my enthusiasm for this rose. Cuttings were secured, and this interesting rose is again available to Southern gardeners. It appears to be a "borderline climber."

There are many useful roses in the China class, most of them being red or pink. Red Chinas are probably the most commonly found old rose in the South. Most appear either to belong to the varieties 'Louis Philippe' or 'Cramoisi Superieur.' 'Louis Philippe' is common in Louisiana, particularly in the New Orleans area, where it is sometimes referred to as the "Creole Rose." Also of special interest is the China rose known as "The Green Rose," which some describe as beautiful, while at least one rose authority has dismissed it as "an engaging monstrosity." Flower arrangers find the bronzy green flowers useful and long-lasting subjects. It is easily grown and often found in old gardens. An old specimen survives at Grace Episcopal Church in St. Francisville, Louisiana.

Recommended varieties
'Old Blush,' 1752, 5–6 ft, pink
'Cl. Old Blush,' date unknown, 15–20 ft, pink
'Cramoisi Superieur,' 1832, 4–6 ft, red
'Louis Philippe,' 1834, 3–5 ft, red
'Archduke Charles,' prior to 1837, 3–5 ft, red, pink, and white
'Hermosa,' 1840, 3–4 ft, pink
Rosa chinensis 'Viridiflora,' The Green Rose, prior to 1845, 3–4 ft, green
'Ducher,' 1869, 3–4 ft, white
Rosa chinensis 'Mutabilis,' The Butterfly Rose, prior to 1896, 4–7 ft, pink, red, yellow

Tea Roses

Tea roses are exceptionally well suited to Southern climates and are often found as large bushes marking old homesites where they have thrived with no care whatsoever for decades. The blossoms themselves are large and memorable, the kind people speak of with nostalgia. Tea roses inherited their fragrance and large blossoms from the wild tea rose, *R. gigantea,* a native of the eastern Himalayan foothills. Their everblooming character comes from *R. chinensis,* their other parent.

Many old tea roses resemble in form the typical high-centered hybrid teas of today, so are generally admired as cut flowers as well as garden plants. This class was very popular from the 1830s until its own more cold-hardy descendants, the hybrid teas, superseded it at the turn of the century. As a rule, teas have an upright habit, forming tall and sometimes narrow bushes with bronzy red new foliage. In the Southern states, they bloom profusely in the spring and fall, with scattered summer flowers. Blossoms are spectacular and large in pastel pinks and yellows, with some reds and a few whites. Fragrance is distinctive, cool, and somewhat similar to that of dried tea leaves.

"Peggy Martin" rose (Photo by William C. Welch)

In *Everblooming Roses,* Georgia Torrey Drennan extolled the virtues of tea roses above all others: "Nothing in the history of the rose has been of greater importance than the creation of the Tea. Its introduction to the Occident ranks with the bountiful best gifts of the nineteenth century."

Most teas have good resistance to black spot and seem to thrive in the heat of the South, although they are occasionally damaged by cold in northerly areas of our region. Though susceptible to frost, tea roses bloom until the arrival of very cold weather. Accounts of early Southerners gathering bouquets for Christmas and other midwinter events indicate that tea roses were considered an essential part of the garden at that time. The flower stems are weak and often bow gracefully with the weight of the large flowers; though this might be seen as a defect today, it was considered an elegant trait during Victorian times. It is still admired by those who enjoy the many distinctive and easily grown roses that comprise the tea class.

Recommended varieties

'Bon Silene,' prior to 1837, 4–6 ft, pink
'Safrano,' 1839, 5–7 ft, yellow-apricot
'Sombreuil,' 1850, 6–10 ft, white
'Duchesse de Brabant,' 1857, 3–5 ft, pink
'Perle des Jardins,' 1874, 3–5 ft, yellow
'Monsieur Tillier,' 1891, 3–6 ft, rose-salmon
'Maman Cochet,' 1893, 3–5 ft, pink
'Souvenir de Mme. Leonie Viennot,' 1898, 15–20 ft, pink
'Mrs. B. R. Cant,' 1901, 5–7 ft, rose
'Mrs. Dudley Cross,' 1907, 4–6 ft, yellow-pink

Noisette Roses

The Noisettes are of special interest historically because they are the first class of garden roses to have originated in the United States. John Champneys, a rice planter from Charleston, South Carolina, raised the first of the class by crossing the musk rose (an old garden rose that reblooms in the fall and so has been popular since Shakespeare's day) with 'Old Blush.' Champneys named the result for himself: 'Champneys' Pink Cluster.' A few years later, a friend of Champneys, a florist from Charleston named Philippe Noisette, raised a seedling from Champneys' rose. In 1817, Noisette sent his rose to his brother Louis in Paris, who named it 'Blush Noisette.' The French eagerly received and expanded the new rose class because of its heavy clustering bloom, musky scent, and strong, healthy growth. The early Noisettes that they produced bear flowers in small clusters; later varieties, those that resulted from crosses with tea roses, have larger blossoms with fewer flowers per cluster.

Although considered more susceptible to cold than most classes, the Noisettes are well adapted to the Southern states and found immense popularity here. Their musk rose ancestry ensures a good floral display in the fall and the spring. As a rule, however,

Noisettes are not as resistant to black spot and mildew as are the teas and Chinas.

Many of the Noisettes have the ability to create a landscape effect unique among roses. Whether grown on walls, fences, arbors, or even trees, the climbing varieties are valuable to a garden in which a period effect is desired. Noisettes are not found as frequently as teas and Chinas on abandoned homesites and cemeteries, but many of them are easily grown, long-lived garden plants.

Recommended varieties
'Champneys' Pink Cluster,' circa 1811, 4–8 ft, pink
'Jaune Desprez,' 1830, 15–20 ft, apricot
'Lamarque,' 1830, 8–10 ft, white
'Chromatella,' 1843, 12–20 ft, yellow
'Jeanne D'Arc,' 1848, 5–8 ft, white
'Marechal Niel,' 1864, 10–15 ft, yellow
'Rêve d'Or,' 1869, 10–12 ft, apricot
'Mme. Alfred Carrière,' 1879, 15–20 ft, white
'Nastarana,' 1879, 3–4 ft, white
'Mary Washington,' 1891, 6–8 ft, pink

Old European Roses

Included in this section are roses from a variety of classes that are sometimes found in old Southern gardens and that deserve the heirloom gardener's consideration. Since the European roses were developed primarily for shorter growing seasons and colder winters, in the South they may lack the vigor and disease resistance of roses from areas more like our own. However, they are significant historically because of their long association with major events of Western history. Moreover, their beauty and fragrance have inspired great art and literature.

"Peggy Martin" rose (Photo by William C. Welch)

Recommended varieties

Rosa gallica officinalis, Apothecary Rose, prior to 1500, 3–4 ft, rose

Rosa gallica versicolor 'Rosa Mundi,' prior to 1581, 3–4 ft, variegated rose/white

'Celsiana,' prior to 1750, 3–5 ft, pink

'Autumn Damask,' prior to 1819, 4–6 ft, pink

'Madame Plantier,' probably an Alba/Moschata cross, 1835, 4–6 ft, creamy pink

'Salet,' a moss rose, 1854, 3–4 ft, pink

Bourbon Roses

Bourbon roses resulted from a natural cross between 'Old Blush' and 'Autumn Damask,' both of which had been planted as hedges on the French island then called Bourbon and now called Reunion. An alert resident noticed this spontaneous hybrid and sent the plant to France, where breeders further perfected the class. Redouté painted the first cultivar in 1817. There are about forty varieties still in commerce today.

Bourbons produce some of the most beautiful flowers ever developed. They often have old-fashioned, cupped or quartered blossoms, generally in pastel pinks, on large, robust plants. Due to their damask influence, Bourbons tend to be more cold hardy than Chinas or teas. Only a few varieties reliably repeat-flower in summer and fall in the South. These roses also tend to be more susceptible to black spot and mildew than Chinas or teas. Bourbon flowers are, in general, highly fragrant and beautifully formed, which accounts for their popularity in spite of their sometimes sparse and short bloom period and lack of disease resistance.

In all my hunting, I have found and identified only three Bourbons on old Southern homesites. These are 'Souvenir de la Malmaison,' 'Kronprinzessin Viktoria,' and 'Zéphirine Drouhin,' all excellent and fairly tough garden plants. Actually, though, I may have found a fourth Bourbon, and that is the rose I call "Maggie," which was the first old garden rose I found and propagated. Judging by various characteristics, this is very possibly a Bourbon.

I had noticed this rose during several visits to my wife's grandmother's farm near Mangham, Louisiana. The plant always seemed to be in bloom, and the flowers were very full and highly fragrant—they left an intriguing scent of black pepper lingering on my hands when I picked them or handled a stem. Finally, during the Christmas season of 1980, I decided to take cuttings. I took cuttings of "Maggie" and another rose growing nearby that we later identified as the "swamp rose," and wrapped them all in a plastic bag. After several days in the bag, the cuttings were stuck in an east-facing flower bed in our College Station garden.

They rooted and began blooming later that very same spring. They have grown vigorously and were shared with the Antique Rose Emporium, the Huntington Botanical Garden, and Joyce Demits of Heritage Roses in Ft. Bragg, California.

Greg obtained his "Maggie," the identical rose, from a different source, a specimen growing in his great-grandmother's garden in East Texas. He once noted during a plant-collecting trip to Belize that it was the most common dooryard rose in that former British possession. "Maggie" has since been found in numerous other old gardens and cemeteries. It is sometimes trained as a climber, but most often as a large bush. It seems odd that a rose so fine and popular remains unidentified. There must be a healthy dose of China in its parentage, though, since it reblooms as well as any China rose I have grown.

Recommended varieties
'Souvenir de la Malmaison,' 1843, 3–4 ft, pink
'Zéphirine Drouhin,' 1868, 6–15 ft, cerise-pink
'Mme. Isaac Pereire,' 1881, 6–7 ft, deep rose
'Kronprinzessin Victoria,' 1888, 3–4 ft, white
Variegate di Bologna,' 1909, 4–7 ft, variegated rose/white

Hybrid Perpetuals

The hybrid perpetual class includes some of the most beautiful flowers ever developed. Typically, hybrid perpetual blossoms are very large, full, and heavily scented, and some make outstanding cut flowers. The bushes tend to be tall and sometimes ungainly, but they can be shaped to become usable landscape plants. They are considered forerunners of today's hybrid tea roses and are related to Bourbons and damasks.

Southerners often referred to hybrid perpetuals as "cabbage roses," although that name more accurately applies to another class of roses. 'Paul Neyron' is among the best known in the class and as such was often described as a cabbage rose. Probably the hybrid perpetual most often found in old Southern gardens is 'Cl. American Beauty.' All the members of this class that I have grown bore powerfully fragrant flowers.

"Peggy Martin" rose (Photo by William C. Welch)

An interesting way to grow hybrid perpetuals is to "peg" them. This involves fastening the ends of the canes to the ground with stakes or wire pins: the lateral buds along the canes then "break"—that is, they start growing—and the result is a shrub with a beautiful fountainlike effect.

Recommended varieties
'Baronne Prevost,' 1842, 4–6 ft, pink
'Marquise Bocella,' 1842, 3–5 ft, pink
'Comte de Chambord,' 1860, 3–5 ft, pink
'Reine des Violettes,' 1860, 4–5 ft, rich violet

'Paul Neyron,' 1869, 5–6 ft, pink
'Ulrich Brünner Fils,' 1881, 4–6 ft, dark pink
'Frau Karl Druschki,' 1901, 4–6 ft, white
'Cl. American Beauty,' 1909, 12–15 ft, dark pink

Polyantha Roses

Polyantha roses were created by crossing the Chinas with the rambling Japanese multiflora rose. The goal was to create a group of roses that could be massed together in borders or other similar types of landscape displays. In fact, the result of the cross was a group of roses that blooms prolifically, is compact in size, and bears large clusters of relatively small flowers. The fragrance of the blossoms varies from almost nonexistent to some of the finest ever created. Some of the polyanthas also inherited their China rose parents' everblooming habit.

This class contains several of our favorite roses for Southern gardens. 'Cécile Brünner,' better known as the "sweetheart rose," is most appreciated for its vigorous climbing form. 'Marie Pavié' is occasionally found in old gardens and has wonderful fragrance. It is nearly thornless and makes a great three- to four-foot hedge or container specimen. 'La Marne' is often found in cemeteries and is a real survivor. Perle d'Or is very similar to 'Cécile Brünner' but with more salmon or orange in its coloration.

Recommended varieties
'Cécile Brünner,' 1881, 3–4 ft, pink
'Perle d'Or,' 1884, 3–4 ft, apricot-pink
'Marie Pavié,' 1888, 2–4 ft, palest pink
'Clotilde Soupert,' 1890, 3–4 ft, pink
'Cl. Cécile Brünner,' 1894, 15–20 ft, pink
'La Marne,' 1915, 4–6 ft, dark pink, white
'The Fairy,' 1932, 3–4 ft, pink
'Marie Daly,' 2000, 2–3 ft, pink

'Red Cascade' rose, a relatively new miniature climber from the late Ralph Moore that is vigorous, blooms repeatedly, and fits in well with antique and old garden roses (Photo by William C. Welch)

Roses from Miscellaneous Classes

There are a number of *wichuraiana* ramblers introduced around the turn of the century that have since naturalized throughout the South. 'Excelsa' and 'Dorothy Perkins' are probably the most common of these, although they are usually plagued with powdery mildew.

'Silver Moon' (1910) is a once-blooming climber with healthy foliage that bears semidouble white flowers with good fragrance. 'New Dawn' (1930) claims the distinction of having U.S. Plant Patent No. 1, the first plant ever patented under federal regulations. It is an everblooming sport of the well-known 'Dr. W. Van

Fleet' and exceeded the popularity of its parent. Some of the early hybrid teas such as 'La France' (1867), 'Radiance' (1908), and 'Red Radiance' (1916) are still found in old gardens and passed on locally as rooted cuttings.

Another interesting plant that Southern gardeners have traditionally viewed as a rose is the "blackberry rose," also known as the "Easter rose" or "coronation rose." Actually it belongs to the genus *Rubus* and is listed in *Hortus Third* as *R. coronarius*. Although rarely mentioned in gardening literature, it was commonly traded about among Southern gardeners. My plant came from Zada Walker, a longtime friend who lives near Kirbyville, Texas. It grows and blooms prolifically in my country garden and suckers freely. This spreading habit has not been a problem, since gardening friends have eagerly "rustled" the divisions. Double-white blossoms are less than two inches in diameter and appear around Easter each year. Its foliage looks more like that of a blackberry than of a rose.

Once-blooming roses that appear to belong to the Gallica class are often found in old cemeteries throughout the South.

They are spring-only bloomers and tend to sucker, sometimes forming small thickets. Most are very fragrant and occur in interesting shades of dusty purple and pink.

Found Roses

Some of the most interesting roses are among this group. Upon locating an interesting rose, you make a major effort to identify it. After researching the art and literature, sometimes it just isn't possible to be sure what you have found. Fortunately, many of the best of these have been picked up and propagated by the rose nurseries.

Following are a few of my favorites. Their names are usually put in double quotes rather than the single ones used for cultivar names.

"MAGGIE"

"Maggie" was the first of these and was first commercially propagated by the Antique Rose Emporium in Independence. "Maggie" was in the garden of my wife Diane's grandmother's home near Mangham, Louisiana. I first noticed it in about 1970 and decided to root cuttings in about 1980. "Maggie" is a deep rosy red color with a lot of petals and a wonderful fragrance. Although vigorous and spreading as a shrub-climber, "Maggie" does get blackspot, usually overcoming the difficulty without spray. It has proven to be a popular rose; although there have been many attempts at identification, most still use the study name.

ROSA PALUSTRIS SCANDENS 'SWAMP ROSE'

Growing beneath some small slash pines about a hundred feet from "Maggie" in Diane's grandmother's garden was an interesting foliaged rose I had watched for several years but never seen blooming. I decided that it was in too much shade to flower, so I took a few cuttings back to College Station and noticed that they rooted easily. The following year there were a few blooms in May that looked a bit like 'Old Blush' (loosely double and pink). I began looking at catalogues and books that might provide a clue to the identity. Among my rose books was one that had color images of the roses painted by the famous botanical illustrator Redouté. He painted the 'Swamp Rose' at Empress Josephine's famous rose garden at Malmaison, outside Paris. The foliage is willowlike, and branches arch in a fountainlike form. Upon further investigation I learned that my rose had been described by Marshall in 1726 and later by Michaux (as *R. pennsylvanica*). The plant that I found was described as *R. palustris scandens* and differs from the species form in that it has double flowers. I further learned that it was native from Louisiana throughout the Southeast and north to Minnesota and Canada. I provided cuttings to the Antique Rose Emporium, who found them easy to root and included the rose in its earliest offerings. Most roses like well-drained soils, but this one thrives in boggy places and even partially submerged, making it a useful shrub for the edges of ponds or streams. Flowers appear in May for about a month and are sweetly fragrant. Stems are nearly thornless and rarely bothered by black spot. About the only restriction in growing conditions I have observed is a preference for neutral to acidic soils. Highly alkaline conditions result in poor growth and iron chlorosis (yellowing foliage).

'RUSSELL'S COTTAGE ROSE'

My start of this rose came from longtime friend Lynn Lowrey from Houston. I planted it at the first Washington County farm property we purchased in 1979. Lynn had no idea about the identity but said it was disease resistant and hardy. After observing how well it grew, I became more interested in the plant and saw one that looked similar while attending a meeting on old roses at the Huntington Botanical Garden in California. While I was observing the similar plant, Joyce Demits, a California producer of old roses, told me that one way to tell for sure about it is to rub your fingers on the new foliage. If it smells like pine, it is 'Russell's Cottage Rose.' Joyce is a lovely person, and it was a thrill to feel certain about my plant.

Shortly after learning the identity of my plant, I presented a program to a group at Winedale. Among the audience was an elderly woman who brought a sample of rose foliage and flowers and asked if I could identify it for her. When I did, she burst into tears, saying she had wondered for years about it and was delighted to learn the "real" name.

No one seems to be sure about the origins or date of introduction, although it seems certain that it was prior to 1837. It is known for its ability to withstand, heat, cold, drought, and pests. It is strongly and pleasantly fragrant and blooms for a month or more each spring with clusters of double two- to three-inch flowers that fade from magenta to crimson. It's unusual in that its fragrance lasts for a long time in potpourri. These roses tend to flower later than the first spring roses and make quite a spectacle of themselves. 'Russelliana' may be used as a shrub or a modest-sized climber.

'Zéphirine Drouhin' rose (Photo by William C. Welch)

Close-up of 'Cl. American Beauty' roses at the Antique Rose Emporium in Independence, Texas (Photo by William C. Welch)

"NATCHITOCHES NOISETTE"

While visiting with my wife's grandmother in Natchitoches, Louisiana, I wandered into the old cemetery in search of roses. I found one in a partially shaded area of the graveyard that wasn't close enough to a headstone to relate it to a particular individual. It seemed a bit like 'Old Blush,' but there were subtle differences in its fragrance, foliage, and the coloration of the flowers. I liked it and took cuttings, which rooted easily and were shared with the Antique Rose Emporium. Since then, it has stood the test of time well and remains a favorite. There is a four- to six-foot specimen to the right of the entrance at the Mangham house that gets good sun and blooms almost continuously from midspring till hard frost. Its healthy foliage, fragrance, and vigor are welcome in my garden and make me wonder about its past. I have never been tempted to adopt a "real" name for it by anything I have seen or read in the literature. Thankfully, it is available from several commercial sources. To Greg, it has always seemed much more a China than a Noisette, and he agrees that it is a great rose.

'Buff Beauty' roses are easily grown and colorful possibilities for massing in the garden. (Photo by William C. Welch)

"MCCLINTON TEA"

A few blocks from my wife's grandmother's home I noticed an old-fashioned garden with lots of roses. When I looked more closely, I realized that most of the roses were the same one. I knocked on the door, and a friendly woman was pleased at my interest and offered cuttings. There was similarity to the well-known tea rose 'Duchesse de Brabant,' but this plant was even more fragrant. In fact, I believe it to be the most fragrant of all the tea roses I have grown. Like many of its kin, "McClinton Tea" is a bit slow to get started. It seems to resent heavy pruning and takes several years to build a good-sized, productive plant. It tends to be healthy and fairly disease resistant, but the fragrance is what makes it a continuing favorite for me.

"GEORGETOWN TEA"

I spent my first two years of college at Southwestern University in Georgetown, Texas, and always enjoyed the older neighborhoods there. I return occasionally to explore these neighborhoods and try to get there each spring when the "Georgetown tulips" are in bloom. I first noticed these tulips while walking to the campus one day. There was a patch about five or six feet in diameter with large, red tulips blooming in a lawn. Since then they have increased, and I have seen them in other communities, learning that they are *Tulipa praecox,* a species tulip well adapted to the area. The tulips had already bloomed and were fading when I noticed the rose in an older neighborhood. The house had been converted to a childcare center, and no one was there. The shrub was six or seven feet tall and as big around. It was healthy and full of tealike flowers. I took a few cuttings and shared them with the Antique Rose Emporium, where it has been a popular item ever since. Like most of the other tea roses, it is a little slow to root and develop but finally becomes a productive and worthwhile addition to the garden.

"PEGGY MARTIN"

Peggy Martin has been a mainstay in the New Orleans Old Garden Rose Society (NOOGRS) for many years. She and her husband, M. J., lived in Plaquemines Parish a few miles across the Mississippi River from the city. We were her guests several years ago when I accepted a speaking engagement for the NOOGRS.

Peggy's garden included a wonderful collection of old roses assembled with love and care over the years. There were many specimens that appealed to me, but one rambler in particular caught my eye. I am always interested in thornless roses, and Peggy was particularly enthusiastic about a large, healthy specimen she had collected in New Orleans in 1989. According to Peggy, "I was given cuttings of the thornless climber in 1989 by Ellen Dupriest, who had gotten it from her mother-in-law, Faye Dupriest. Faye had gotten her cuttings from a relative's garden in New Orleans, and it was in full bloom and smothered the eight-foot wooden fence in Ellen's back yard. It took my breath away! I had never seen a rose so lushly beautiful with thornless bright green foliage that was disease free. All along the canes there were clusters of roses that resembled perfect nosegays of blooms."

I departed New Orleans in late summer of 2003 with several cuttings of Peggy's thornless climber. I was pleased that the cuttings rooted quickly and immediately set one on the fence that encloses the air-conditioning equipment at Fragilee, our weekend home in Washington County, Texas. I was a little dubious of the site I had selected because the soil was less than ideal. My concern soon disappeared as I saw the cutting quickly mature into a vigorous specimen that spans most of the twelve to fifteen linear feet of the four-foot-tall picket fence.

I did not allow myself to get overly excited about the plant because I assumed that it would be a "once bloomer" with a fairly short flowering season in the spring. On a subsequent visit with Peggy she indicated that my plant would rebloom in the fall after it had been established for a couple of years. I must admit that I had some doubt about the rebloom in our hot and sometimes very dry Texas climate. The third year after planting, Peggy's rose rewarded us with a nice bloom from September through November. Even though it was covered by ice for two days during December 2005, we had some scattered bloom all winter.

HURRICANE KATRINA

As the news about Hurricane Katrina became more and more frightening in late August 2005, we opened our College Station home to some families fleeing southeast Texas. We then decided to drive to Birmingham, Alabama, to attend an annual meeting at *Southern Living* magazine. Our home in Mangham, Louisiana, is about halfway to Birmingham from College Station, so we stopped there to determine whether our cotton and soybean crops and home had sustained damage. We were relieved to find little damage to the crops; the old pecan trees in our yard had suffered little more than the loss of a few limbs and most of the current crop of pecans because Katrina had veered more to the east.

Upon arrival in Birmingham, we checked into our hotel, which was close to the *Southern Living* headquarters. Early the next morning we went to breakfast and were seated adjacent to two couples who sounded like they had New Orleans accents. After introducing ourselves, we learned that they were from Plaquemines Parish and had lost their homes. Birmingham was the first place they were able to find shelter. I asked them if they knew Peggy Martin and her family. They knew them well and wondered if we were familiar with the tragedy of their losses. It seems that Peggy lost both her elderly parents, her home, and commercial fishing boat that her husband used to supplement their income.

AN INSPIRATIONAL SURVIVOR

It took a couple of months for me to reestablish communication with Peggy. She and her family have moved to Gonzales, Louisiana, near Baton Rouge. Peggy told me the house and garden were under about twenty feet of salt water for two weeks following the hurricane. When she was finally able to return to visit their property, she was heartened to see the lush growth of her thornless climber, a testament to its toughness and status as a true survivor. This rose and one crinum were all that remained of the once beautiful garden.

I had already been convinced that this rose deserved to be widely available and enjoyed by gardeners in other locations. Its disease resistance, thornless stems, and colorful displays of bright pink flowers along with a graceful vining form make it a logical choice for creating beautiful garden pictures. My specimen is literally covered with clusters of dark pink flowers each spring from mid-March through May. It starts blooming again in late summer and repeats until a hard frost slows it down for the winter.

A WAY TO HELP

In mid-January 2006, I was pleased to receive notification that my friend Nancy Godshall, a member of the Garden Club of Houston and currently zone 9 director for the Garden Club of America (GCA), had given a donation in my name to a recently established Zone IX Horticulture Restoration Fund. The fund was established for the purpose of restoring parks, gardens, and green space in New Orleans; Laurel, Mississippi; and Beaumont, Texas, following Hurricanes Katrina and Rita. I learned that Nancy Thomas, also from Houston and a former GCA president, was closely involved in selecting projects for the restoration fund.

An idea came to me early on "in the middle of the night" about growing the "Peggy Martin" rose as a fund-raiser for the Zone IX Horticulture Restoration Fund. First, I checked with Peggy to see if she would be in agreement; then I went to Mike Shoup, owner of the Antique Rose Emporium. Mike was enthusiastic—the first small crop of cuttings we provided quickly increased into a good supply. Nancy Godshall agreed to help establish a separate fund through the Greater Houston Community Foundation.

A hedge of 'Old Blush' roses provides almost continuous color through the growing season. *Iris albicans* provides an early spring show and nice blue-gray foliage at other seasons. (Photo by William C. Welch)

Jason and Shelley Powell, owners of Petals from the Past Nursery in Jemison, Alabama, were impressed with the rose while visiting here in late October 2005 and took quite a few cuttings at that time. Jason received his master's degree from Texas A&M and was an early recipient of my scholarship sponsored by Texas Garden Clubs. Shelley, also a horticulture graduate from Texas A&M, is a talented propagator.

Mark Chamblee, owner of Chamblee Rose Nursery in Tyler, Texas, was enthusiastic about marketing the rose, as was Aubrey King, owner of King's Nursery in Tenaha, Texas, and Heidi Sheesley, who owns Treesearch Farms in Houston, which serves as a wholesale source for large orders and a supplier to landscape contractors. Ready-to-sell "Peggy Martin" roses are now available commercially. Each of these growers has pledged a donation of one dollar to the Garden Restoration Fund for each plant sold. Reduced or wholesale prices may be available for garden club plant sales, Master Gardener events, and so on. This will allow more opportunity for contributions. Awards from the fund, now administered by the Greater Houston Community Foundation, will be made periodically.

A beautifully written article by Gene Bussell, garden editor for *Southern Living* magazine, and photographed by Ralph Anderson appeared in the September 2007 issue. This article, along with supporting articles that have appeared in most of the major newspapers in the South, have resulted in creating a large awareness and demand. Production of plants has finally caught up with requests. Many thousands of plants have been sold, and "Peggy Martin" is well on the way to creating beautiful pictures and lasting memories across the nation. Peggy Martin herself has been speaking to rose societies and gardening groups all over the South about the value of her rose and other old garden roses that are so much a part of our gardening heritage.

This has become a fun and worthwhile project. A great rose and a great cause—a hard combination to beat! I am fully convinced that the resilience and fortitude of our friends and neighbors in New Orleans, Beaumont, and Mississippi are matched by the beauty and toughness of the "Peggy Martin" rose. This rose is a beautiful symbol of survival on the Gulf Coast.

Some of Greg Grant's "Found Roses"

"Big Momma's Blush": Greg got this old pink tea rose from his great grandmother's garden in Arcadia. His relatives told him it was brought from Tennessee when they first settled the area.

"Canary Island Gallica": This once-blooming old European rose came from a San Antonio garden during Greg's famous "Search for the San Antonio Rose" that Pam Puryear and I helped him with when he was the county horticulturist there. Canary

Islanders immigrated to San Antonio early in the city's history and evidently brought some mementos from their earlier home with them.

"Lemon Tea": Greg got his start of this pale yellow thornless tea rose from a seventy-year-old plant in a San Antonio garden during the same contest.

'Marie Daly': This was a pink-flowered sport of 'Marie Pavié' from Greg's mother's garden in Arcadia. He named it for a late dear friend.

'Nacogdoches' ("Grandma's Yellow"): Greg found this popular yellow rose at the Old Stone Fort motel in Nacogdoches and shared it with Jerry Parsons.

"Queenie": I obtained this thornless but unnamed hot pink rambler from an Austin, Texas, garden. Greg likes it so much he has named it for my late wife, Diane, and sells it at the Stephen F. Austin Mast Arboretum plant sales.

"Speedy Gonzales": This was a vigorous climbing sport from the red China "Martha Gonzales" that Greg found in a San Antonio hospital parking lot. It has showy purple new foliage and is often sold as "Cl. Martha Gonzales."

The current renewal of interest in old roses, and their reappearance in nursery catalogues, is much more than a symptom of nostalgia. Old garden roses are practical garden plants and are especially appropriate for the environmentally aware age in which we seem to be entering. Humans and roses seem to be eternally linked, especially in the South, where climate and soils encourage a flowering of so many beautiful types. — *WCW*

Rosmarinus officinalis

Rosemary
Family: Labiatae (Mint)
Size: 1–5 ft
Zones: 8–11
Evergreen aromatic shrub and herb
Blue (occasionally white) flowers in winter and spring; highly scented foliage

As long as the drainage is good, rosemary will thrive even on poor, dry, rocky soils. Indeed, in its native range around the Mediterranean Sea, rosemary flourishes in coastal regions so arid that a significant part of the plant's moisture comes from the dew absorbed through the foliage.

But though tolerant of drought, this plant is not always cold hardy, which limits its use as a landscape plant, even in the South. Milder winters have resulted in fairly reliable hardiness through zone 7. However, rosemary is an ideal candidate for container cultivation, in which case the plant can be moved to a protected spot during the coldest parts of winter. It's worth the trouble, for this is a most decorative plant. Rosemary tolerates clipping and responds well to training; it's a good subject for bonsai or topiary and through these techniques can adopt an endless variety of forms. Whatever the shape, rosemary preserves the same virtue: rosemary is evergreen, so the needlelike foliage looks good year-round—and smells even better.

The genus name *Rosmarinus* means "dew of the sea" (a reference to the plant's preference for seaside conditions); the species name *officinalis* indicates that the plant has been used for medicinal purposes. Indeed, early herbals devoted considerable space to the properties (both curative and magical) of this plant. One American authority, Samuel Stearns, noted in his book *The American Herbal* (1801), "It strengthens the brain, helps the memory."

Prostrate rosemary (*Rosmarinus officinalis* 'Prostratus') (Photo by Greg Grant)

Lady Rosalind Northcote's comprehensive treatment of rosemary in *The Book of Herbs* (London, 1903) identifies it as among the most important of all herbs:

Rosemary has always been of more importance than any other herb, and more than most of them put together. It has been employed at weddings and funerals, for decking the church and for garnishing the banquet hall, in stage-plays, and in "swelling discontent," of a too great reality; as incense in religious ceremonies, and in spells against magic: "in sickness and in health," eminently as a symbol, and yet for very practical uses.

Rosemary (*Rosmarinus officinalis*) (Photo by
Cynthia W. Mueller)

An aromatic oil used in perfumery and medicine is still distilled
from rosemary's fresh needles. And anyone who had the good
fortune to participate in the politically incorrect English classes
of a generation ago surely remembers Ophelia's speech in Shakespeare's *Hamlet:* "There's rosemary, that's for remembrance; pray,
love, remember."

Today, this marvelous, memory-strengthening herb is mostly
used for culinary and decorative purposes. This, too, is a matter of tradition. Rosemary was an essential ingredient of earliest
herb and kitchen gardens and is almost always present in English cottage gardens. There it is often planted close to the front
door, where people brush against it as they pass, releasing some
of the foliage's clean, rich scent. The foliage is popular, fresh or
dried, for seasoning various dishes and is particularly good (in
this writer's opinion) with meats and potatoes.

An interesting note concerning the landscape use of rosemary
comes from Gertrude Jekyll, who recommends in her book *Wood
and Garden* (1899),

> bushes of Rosemary, some just filling the border, and some
> trained up the wall. Our Tudor ancestors were fond of Rose-
> mary-covered walls, and I have seen old bushes quite ten feet
> high on the garden walls of Italian monasteries. Among the
> Rosemaries I always like, if possible, to "tickle in" a China Rose
> ('Old Blush') or two, the tender pink of the Rose seems to go
> so well with the dark but dull-surfaced Rosemary.

Gertrude Jekyll's advice, while excellent, represents just one way
to use this plant in the landscape. Gardeners have developed
many distinctive forms of rosemary, so it is an exceptionally ver-
satile plant. There are, for example, prostrate rosemaries that fur-
nish an unusual ground cover and make an attractive detail as
they spill over retaining walls. Upright forms, by contrast, provide materials for a compact hedge or elegant container plants,
and the mature heights of these may vary from eighteen inches to

four feet or more, depending upon the cultivar and the growing conditions. Rosemary flowers, while not spectacular, are attractive, and they vary from lavender-blue to dark blue and white, appearing intermittently through winter and spring.

Gardeners looking for an upright form of rosemary should consider 'Lockwood de Forest,' which is also reported to tolerate cold particularly well. This cultivar bears dark blue flowers and tends to rebloom better than most cultivars. Said to be a hybrid of *R. prostratus* and *R.* × 'Tuscan Blue,' this, like all rosemaries, thrives in dry, calcareous soils. 'Tuscan Blue' is an upright, rigid rosemary with blue-violet flowers; 'Collingwood Ingram,' a bright, blue-violet flowering cultivar, has graceful, curving branches. 'Prostratus' is a low, spreading form that rarely exceeds two feet in height. It is not as cold hardy as the upright forms but is worth moving or covering for a few nights each winter. For white flowers, try 'Albus.' *Rosmarinus corsicus* is pine scented but similar in its lack of cold hardiness to the prostrate forms.

The late Madelene Hill, a well-known herb authority from Round Top, Texas, found a cold-tolerant rosemary in 1972 in Arp, Texas, that is said to be hardy to Washington, D.C. The National Arboretum has given this plant the name *R. officinalis* 'Arp.' More recently a sport or seedling of 'Arp' has been found and named "Hill Hardy."

Rosemary is propagated from pencil-sized cuttings taken in fall or early winter. Remove the leaves from the bottom half of the stems, and then stick the cuttings in moist garden soil, where they will root by summer. In moist climates where rosemaries often prove short-lived, it is a good idea to root new plants periodically to maintain a supply of replacements.

Rosemary has flourished in Southern gardens ever since the arrival of European colonists on these shores—and in each colony, for this plant was precious to every group that settled here. In *A New Herbal* by D. Rembert Dodoens (London, 1619), in a section titled "Of Rofemary," the author states, "Rofemary groweth naturally and plentifully in divers places of Spaine and France, as in Provence and Languedock: they plant it in this country [England] in gardens and maintaine it with great vigilence." Maintain yours with vigilance, and rosemary will flourish for you, too.*

—WCW

Special appreciation is extended to the late Florence P. Griffin of Atlanta for her assistance in researching rosemary. The sharing of her library resources and those of the Cherokee Garden Library in Atlanta has been most helpful.

Ruscus spp., *Danae racemosa*

Butcher's Broom, Ruscus, Box Holly, Jew's Myrtle
Family: Liliaceae (Lily)
Size: 2–3 ft
Zones: 8–11
Evergreen shrub
Glossy green foliage (sometimes with red berries) for cutting

Butcher's broom is a name with an ominous sound to it, yet in truth it is only an acknowledgment of this shrub's humblest service to humans. *Ruscus* is evergreen, and the branches are flattened, leathery, and oval shaped—like prickly leaves. A handful of these branches, apparently, was formerly a butcher's standard device for sweeping clean his cutting block.

Quite apart from its utility, this is an attractive shrub, albeit one with an odd habit of flowering: because of the form of the branches, the flowers that spring from them seem to be sprouting from leaves. These are followed by red, or sometimes yellow, berries up to half an inch in diameter. The combination of evergreen foliage and bright fruits makes this a popular choice for holiday decoration, as well as for florists' winter bouquets.

Though native to Europe, ruscus, especially the species *R. aculeatus*, was often found in old Southern gardens. An old planting

Alexandrian laurel (*Danae racemosa*) (Photo by William C. Welch)

of this species exists at Elm's Court Plantation (c. 1835–40) in Natchez, Mississippi, where it was planted in large clumps about twenty feet apart to flank the wide walkway that serves as the axis from the rear entrance of the main house to the garden. Originally the masses of ruscus were alternated with shade trees. Some of the latter have died, however, and as the garden's owner, Grace MacNeil, pointed out, this has exposed the ruscus to full sun that is burning the foliage—a point to keep in mind when choosing a site for this plant.

My own ruscus came from Felder Rushing's garden in Jackson, Mississippi, and is planted in our herb garden in Washington County, Texas. I have never seen berries on this plant, but I believe the reason is that ruscus is dioecious. That is, the male and female flowers are borne on separate plants, and what Felder shared with me is a male (and so fruitless) plant. Watch for this problem—Elizabeth Lawrence wrote in *A Southern Garden* that she never had fruit on her plants in North Carolina.

She gave butcher's broom its due, however, noting that it "is one of the most reliable shrubs for troublesome places. It will grow in the driest places, even under trees, and in all degrees of shade. It does need a good mulch of cow manure in the fall. When the plants are starved some of the new spring shoots become colorless by summer."

I have found that, as suggested by those at Elm's Court, butcher's brooms prefer to grow in shady situations under the drip of trees, which is useful since few other plants thrive in such a situation. Propagation is by division of suckers from the root mass that are thrown up in abundance.

Another interesting ruscus is *R. hypoglossum*. It is not prickly and bears leaves about four inches long and one and a half inches wide. My plants were given to me by Herb and Betty Langford, who had grown it for many years in their Texas City, Texas, garden, where Betty used it frequently in her flower arrangements. It has grown well for me under the shade of some giant live oaks.

Danae racemosa is a native of Asia Minor and Persia that was once classified as a ruscus but now is placed in a separate genus. (*Hortus Third* gives a useful hint for the pronunciation of the generic name

Danae: it has three syllables.) It is similar to the nonspiny forms of ruscus but has much glossier foliage, although like ruscus, what appear to be leaves on this plant are in fact leaflike branches. *Danae racemosa* is commonly known as Alexandrian laurel and is said by some sources to be the true laurel used to wreathe the brows of poets. This plant's cherrylike berries appear singly on the new shoots and redden in November, hanging on until spring. As with the butcher's broom, the combination of red berries and shiny evergreen foliage makes this a popular choice for floral arrangements.

This lovely plant is sometimes found at very old Southern homesites. Steve Wheaton, formerly horticulturist for Barnsley Gardens in Georgia, discovered large plantings of *D. racemosa* at the old Westover Plantation along the James River in Virginia. The owners shared some of their plants (seedlings) with Steve, who in turn provided me with two small transplants. I gave one to my friend Frances Parker in Beaufort, South Carolina, since I knew it was high on her "want list" of plants (that had been all the encouragement I needed to place it on my own).

Fine masses of *D. racemosa* also flank the tree-shaded gates of the Governor's Palace at Colonial Williamsburg. However, I first became interested in this plant when a fellow faculty member at Texas A&M brought me pictures of stems and fruit in her mother's garden in Tyler, Texas.

No one had been able to identify the plant, which her mother had carried with her for many years as she moved from Virginia to several other states and finally to Texas. It was thriving in her Tyler garden. After identifying the shrub, I learned that it is not a difficult plant to grow but that it much prefers a good, moist soil and at least partial shade.

Just because the brooms—*Danae* and the two species of *Ruscus*—were once fairly common in Southern gardens, don't expect to find them at your local garden center or discount store. Indeed, these plants are difficult to find in the nursery trade at all. That's unfortunate, for they appear to be long-lived with few cultural problems. They deserve more widespread use, especially in heirloom gardens. —*WCW*

Salvia greggii and others

Cherry Sage, Autumn Sage
Family: Labiatae (Salvia, Sage)
Size: 2–3 ft
Zones: 7–10
Evergreen shrub or perennial
White, pink, or red flowers in spring, summer, and fall

Salvia greggii is one of the toughest and most beautiful plants for our gardens. It is native to dry, sunny sites in southern and western Texas and New Mexico. *Salvia greggii* is also found in the Mexican states of Coahuila, Sonora, and Durango and actually classed as a sub-shrub, since it does not normally die back in winter. Till recently modern nurserymen largely ignored it, but it was frequently found in the cottage gardens of early Texas.

'Henry Duelberg' mealy sage (*Salvia farinacea* 'Henry Duelberg') (Photo by Greg Grant)

Salvia spp. (Photo by William C. Welch)

Recent years have seen much better availability and use across the South.

Colors range from pure whites, rich reds, pinks, salmons, and bicolored forms like 'Hot Lips' with its popular combination of red and white. Once established, *S. greggii* will usually thrive on existing rainfall, but more flowering occurs with supplemental irrigation and fertilizing. Periodic light pruning during the growing season keeps the plants more attractive and productive. This can be done with hedge shears, removing the top four to six inches of spent flowers and growth. Sunny locations are best, but partial shade will also work. Few plants offer so much for so little care.

One of the more common native salvias to Texas is mealy or blue sage (*S. farinacea*), which is native to alkaline soils of Central, West, and South Texas. Typically the spikes of blue or blue-purple flowers occur periodically after a major spring flush. Greg discovered a form at a cemetery near La Grange, Texas, that is proving to be outstanding. He named it after Henry Duelberg, the name

'Indigo Spires' salvia (*Salvia* × 'Indigo
Spires') (Photo by William C. Welch)

Mexican bush sage (*Salvia leucantha*)
(Photo by William C. Welch)

on the headstone where it was growing. A white form was on the adjoining gravesite of Augusta Duelberg. Both have become available in the nursery trade. 'Henry Duelberg' reseeds prolifically and is the best-performing salvia in my garden. 'Augusta' is nice but is not a pure white.

Mexican bush sage (*S. leucantha*) is a spectacular late summer–fall bloomer. A native of Mexico, it is a fairly recent introduction to gardening. Well-drained soils work best, and sunny locations produce four- to six-foot rounded mounds of solid purple or purple and white spikes. Cold hardiness is marginal beyond zone 8.

Salvia × 'Indigo Spires' is a fairly recent introduction from the Huntington Botanical Garden in California. It is very vigorous and makes four- to six-foot mounds of foliage and ten- to twelve-inch spikes of dark purple flowers throughout the warm seasons. It is so vigorous that pruning heavily in midsummer is needed to keep it in bounds. Another useful salvia is *S. guaranitica* with its magnificent dark blue to violet-blue flowers. A native of Brazil, Paraguay, and Argentina, it is often cultivated as an annual since it is not very cold tolerant. *Salvia* × 'Anthony Parker' was introduced by Frances Parker in Beaufort, South Carolina, and has vibrant blue-purple spikes in the fall atop handsome foliage. Another semitropical salvia is forsythia sage (*S. madrensis*). It is distinguished by twelve- to eighteen-inch spikes of yellow flowers produced in mid- to late fall. Pineapple sage (*S. elegans*) is often grown for its culinary as well as its ornamental value. Bright scarlet flowers occur periodically during the growing season. It is a native of Mexico and prized for the pineapple or fruit scent to the dried or fresh foliage.

Salvia officinalis is the salvia that is important as a culinary seasoning. It is also an attractive plant and comes in a purple-foliaged form as well as one with creamy yellow and green variegated foliage. The various forms of *S. officinalis* prefer sunny, well-drained sites and tend to be short-lived. Propagation of all the salvias mentioned is usually from cuttings. Cutting them back after first frost and mulching is recommended. — *WCW*

Cherry sage (Salvia greggii) (Photo by William C. Welch)

Saponaria officinalis

Bouncing Bet, Soapwort
Family: Caryophyllaceae (Pink)
Size: 1–2 ft
Zones: 3–9
Perennial
Pink and white flowers in summer

Upon visiting a historic house in England a few years ago, we noticed that some of the tapestries were being taken down. When we asked why, the attendant informed us that they were to be cleaned with an agent containing *Saponaria officinalis.* I was aware that the plant contained a soaplike substance that was often used in the nineteenth century and earlier to wash new cloth but did not know that it was still being employed for this purpose today.

Some say that the name "bouncing bet" originated in England where barmaids, often called "Bets," cleaned ale bottles by filling them with water and a sprig of this plant and then shaking vigorously. Southerners who have grown the plant argue that the name derives from the fact that once planted, *S. officinalis* bounces all about their gardens.

Since bouncing bet tends to outlast the homes around which it was planted and because it has naturalized freely along streams throughout the South, some people think that it is native to North America. Actually, it is indigenous to Europe and Asia and was brought to this country by early settlers.

Certainly this perennial exhibits an immigrant's toughness. But it is also highly ornamental, bearing showy, fragrant pink or white flowers for several months during the summer. Foliage and stems usually remain at a height of less than a foot until flowering begins, whereupon they may reach two feet or more. Both single- and double-flowering (*S. officinalis* 'Flore Plena') forms occur, the double one generally being preferred for ornamental purposes.

Bouncing bet (*Saponaria officinalis*) (Photo by William C. Welch)

Soapwort remains attractive throughout most of the year if it is cut back after it blooms in late summer. I have been known to trim mine with a lawn mower in the fall. This plant spreads by underground rhizomes and is quite aggressive when grown in well-prepared soil; it may become a pest. It flourishes equally well in either partial shade or full sun, but in sunny locations plants may suffer some leaf and flower sunburn in midsummer. Propagation is by division of rhizomes, preferably in fall, winter, or early spring. I collected my first plants of bouncing bet from the Sam Houston homesite at Independence, Texas. It was surviving there in a partially shaded spot, and it may well have been a survivor of the original 1830s garden. I have also found it on numerous other old homesites in Texas. It tolerates dry or rather wet conditions and is susceptible to few, if any, insect or disease problems. — *WCW*

Spiraea spp.

Bridal Wreath, Spirea
Family: Rosaceae (Rose)
Size: 3–6 ft
Zones: 6–9
Deciduous shrubs
White flowers in spring

Although they rank as relative latecomers to the American garden scene, spireas have been an important shrub in the South since the mid-1800s. The types most often found in our region are *Spiraea prunifolia* 'Plena,' *S. thunbergii*, *S. cantoniensis* (*S. reevesiana*), and *S. vanhouttei*. All are white-flowering, deciduous shrubs with a graceful fountainlike form.

Reeve's spirea (*S. cantoniensis*) has an English name and has been grown in that country since 1824, but like most *Spiraea* species it is Asian in origin, having been cultivated since early times in Japan. Although once popular in the United States, it has largely been superseded by *S.* × *vanhouttei*, a hybrid produced

Popcorn spirea (*Spiraea prunifolium*) (Photo by Greg Grant)

Popcorn spirea (*Spiraea prunifolia*) (Photo by Greg Grant)

Baby's breath spirea (*Spiraea thunbergii*) (Photo by Greg Grant)

Popcorn spirea (*Spiraea prunifolium*) (Photo by Greg Grant)

prior to 1866 by crossing *S. cantoniensis* with another Asian species, *S. trilobata*. Both Reeve's spirea and its hybrid offspring bear dense umbels (umbrella-shaped seed-holding structures) of pure white flowers along the branches in April and May, and for this reason they were commonly planted together with spring-blooming azaleas and roses. These two spireas were valued not only for their flowers but also for their ease of cultivation.

The pure white, double flowers that burst open in stalkless clusters along its branches in March and April earned *S. prunifolia* 'Plena' the common name "popcorn spirea" in the South. Discovered by the Scottish plant explorer Robert Fortune in a Chinese garden in 1844, popcorn spirea is a long-lived, low-maintenance plant that can live unattended for many years. When mature, it makes a graceful shrub of fountainlike branches five to seven feet tall.

Baby's breath spirea (*S. thunbergii*) was introduced into England from Asia about 1863. Numerous clusters of small, white flowers appear very early in the season, sometimes in midwinter in the lower South. The overall effect is very airy, providing

Baby's breath spirea (Spiraea thunbergii)
(Photo by Greg Grant)

Reeve's spirea (*Spiraea cantoniensis*)
(Photo by William C. Welch)

fine texture with or without leaves. When mature, this shrub may reach a height of six to seven feet with a similar spread. It is often confused with its close relative *S. × arbuta,* which differs, however, in having fewer teeth on the margins of its leaves. *Spiraea thunbergii* has been a Southern garden favorite for many years. Like all the spireas described here, it is of easy culture but prefers a neutral to slightly acidic soil rather than highly alkaline soils, where it tends to develop iron chlorosis. — *WCW*

Taxodium distichum

Baldcypress
Family: Cupressaceae (Cypress)
Size: 50–70 ft
Zones: 5–9
Deciduous conifer
Bronze fall color

Baldcypress is an interesting conifer, for unlike most of its ever-green cousins, it is deciduous, hence the name "bald." It's not really a true cypress (*Cupressus*) but more related to redwoods. Baldcypress is one of the South's most impressive and distin-guished natives, with a range from Central Texas to Florida and up to Illinois and Delaware. Baldcypress trees can live to be over one thousand years old, maturing into towering specimens. Although they do not have to live in water, baldcypress trees are most associated with swamps and rivers in the South. South Louisiana and Florida are both famous for their cypress swamps. The first cypress swamp I ever saw was as a child at Caddo Lake in northeastern Texas. Caddo Lake is the only natural lake in Texas and straddles the border with northwestern Louisiana. I'll never forget the unusual protruding cypress knees (technically known as pneumatophores) and all the Spanish moss (*Tillandsia usneoides*) eerily draped from them. Continuing the misleading name game, Spanish moss is not a true moss but a bromeliad, related to pineapples. Though Spanish moss does not have to grow on baldcypress or even in swamps, it is certainly associated with both of them.

In a cruel twist of fate, the baldcypress has long been associated with its long-lasting and easily worked wood. It is even known as "the eternal wood" for its rot-resistant characteristics. Many Southern mansions, roof shingles, boats, docks, greenhouses, and the like were constructed from native baldcypress. Because of the value placed on its amazing wood, almost all cypress swamps in the South were harvested, many by draining. Instead of having primeval monstrous trees living among us, we are now left with young regrowth. Even the regenerated baldcypress faces pressure today from the cypress mulch industry. Quickly renewable mulches like pine straw or chipped power line right-of-way trimmings are a much better option in my opinion.

Early Spanish explorers named the Sabine River that divides Texas and Louisiana for the baldcypress (*sabina*). Unfortunately, few are to be seen there now. When I cross the river at Logansport, Louisiana, I get to see "Sprawlmart special" Bradford pears from China instead.

Baldcypress did not become popular landscape trees until fairly recently, though several early nurseries offered them. Thomas Affleck's 1851–52 Southern Nurseries catalogue from Washington, Mississippi, offered "Great Southern or Swamp Cypress, four to six feet high, seedlings grown on upland, 50 cents each." A 1933 Otto M. Locke Nursery catalogue from New Braunfels, Texas, listed "Cypress, Native (*Taxodium distichum*), A grand, stately tree. Needs plenty of moisture. 4 ft. $1.00 each."

Baldcypress (*Taxodium disticum*) at Caddo Lake (Photo by Greg Grant)

Locke's Nursery was established in 1856 on the western fringe of the range of baldcypress. The Comal River and Guadalupe River near the nursery site are still home to beautiful native baldcypress lining the banks. The baldcypress trees of the Texas Hill Country are more alkaline tolerant and don't form knees. Baldcypress trees from the southeastern United States form knees on wet sites and get iron chlorosis (turn yellow) when planted on high pH, alkaline soils. Unfortunately, the alkaline-tolerant Central Texas form is rarely available in the trade. The Mexican and South Texas native, Montezuma cypress (*T. mucronatum*), is occasionally available. It possesses tolerance to alkaline soils and drought and does not form knees. The Montezuma has a somewhat weeping appearance, hangs onto its needles longer into the winter, and often has multiple trunks. Sometimes the narrow-leaved, columnar, pond cypress (*T. ascendens*) is available. It makes a beautiful, fine-textured, narrow tree in the landscape. Thanks to work by David Creech at Stephen F. Austin State University in Nacogdoches, Texas, hybrids between these different species are beginning to make their way around horticultural circles, from their breeders in China. The hybrids seem to possess salt tolerance as well, while apparently not forming knees.

The baldcypress, the state tree of Louisiana, is finally beginning to become a common landscape tree. It is long-lived, has beautiful reddish bronze fall color, has few pests, and is adapted to a range of soils, either wet or dry. The biggest misconception about this tree is that it has to grow in wet soils. It doesn't but will if you want it to. Since so many of our legendary Southern swamps have been destroyed, I'm on a one-man mission to create as many as I can. I have planted cypress trees, along with some water tupelos, in every little shallow pond and swamp I own. They're no substitute for the real thing but certainly better than none at all. Perhaps in a thousand years, ivory bill woodpeckers will come back and call them home. —*GG*

Viola odorata

Violet
Family: Violaceae (Violet)
Size: 8–10 inches
Zones: 6–11
Perennial
Purple flowers in late winter or early spring

This is an *old* garden flower—it was already in commercial cultivation long before the birth of Christ, not so much for use as an ornament as for sweetening food and making perfume. Still, the modest beauty of the flower has earned it many admirers along the way, including the warlike Napoleon Bonaparte. Just before his exile, Napoleon is said to have picked a few blooms from the grave of his beloved Josephine and placed them in a locket that he was wearing on his deathbed.

Violet flowers were also widely used for medicinal purposes as remedies for a variety of complaints, including headaches, melancholy, and sleeplessness, and were even used in the treatment of cancer (violet leaves were used until fairly recent times in Wales and Ireland as a cure for external cancers). In *The Little Herball*, author Anthony Ascham wrote in 1525: "For they that may not sleep, seep this herb in water and at even let him soak well his feet in the water to the ancles, and when he goeth to bed, bind of this herb to the temples and he shall sleep well by the Grace of God."

Until fairly recent times, chemists were still using blue syrup of violets, though for a more mundane purpose. It served as a sort of natural litmus paper, turning red when brought in contact with acid, and green when in contact with alkali.

Violet blooms, both dried and crystallized, have been used for cake decoration and sweetmeats since medieval times; they are still utilized today for that purpose as well as to decorate chocolates. Candied violets may be made by dipping the flowers in a solution of rose water and gum arabic followed by a sprinkle of fine sugar. After drying in a warm oven, the candied violets are ready to serve.

The fragrance of violets is a major factor in their popularity, yet it has often been described as fleeting and of short duration. Actually, it isn't the perfume that is fleeting but the sense of smell when it is exposed to violet fragrance. It contains a substance known as ionine (*ion* is the ancient Greek word for "violet") that dulls the olfactory sense after a few sniffs. One's ability to enjoy the violet scent soon returns, but the presence of the ionine makes sure that the flower fancier never overindulges, at least in the case of violets.

These flowers were a major florist crop well into the early twentieth century. Their fragrance, rich colors, and relatively easy culture contributed to national and worldwide popularity. They are, however, a very labor-intensive crop, which is the reason violets are rarely found in today's florist shops.

Although several species of violets are native to the South, the violet of choice for most Southern gardens was *Viola odorata,* which is of European, Asian, and African origins. Dark blue or purple is the predominant color of this species' flowers.

Violets prefer a rich, moist, but well-drained soil high in organic content and slightly acidic. Partially shaded locations are preferred, but full sun and full shade can also produce good results. Their natural season of bloom is late winter and early spring. Although evergreen, garden violets become semidormant during our long, hot summers. They can, however, endure considerable drought and heat stress, usually resuming lush, healthy growth with the onset of cooler, moister fall and winter conditions.

The landscape uses of violets include borders and ground covers. Large container shrubs can be enhanced by planting a mass of violets around their bases, for the violets provide attractive foliage, fragrance, and color in winter and early spring, seasons when few other plants are at their peak. The rounded foliage is quite attractive even when the plants are not in bloom. Spider mites

Violet (*Viola odorata*) (Photo by William C. Welch)

are an occasional problem but may be controlled with insecticidal soaps or chemicals labeled for such use.

Propagation is usually by division of mature clumps during early to midfall. Seeds can also be used to produce new plants but require considerable attention during the early stages. Borders and masses of garden violets may still be found in many old Southern gardens. They can be long-lived and relatively low-maintenance perennials. Heirloom hybrids include 'Royal Elk,' with long-stemmed dark purple flowers; 'Royal Robe,' a dark purple–flowered cultivar that is a garden favorite in the South; and 'Charm,' a white cultivar.

Violets naturalize well in wooded gardens, and the native species are especially suitable for this use. These include bird-foot violet (*V. pedata*), primrose-leaf violet (*V. primulifolia*), Brainard violet (*V. affinis*), and Walter's violet (*V. walteri*).

One of my favorite violets is *V. tricolor.* Known in the nursery trade as violas, these plants are available as seed in a range of forms with flowers of various colors. They perform well as cool-season annuals, but the old form, the one known as Johnny-jump-ups, is the only viola to reseed each year in my garden. Its flower is purple and yellow, measuring about one-half to three-quarters inch across.

Like miniature pansies, Johnny-jump-ups can cover the ground with their neat foliage and small, fragrant blossoms. Since this plant is very cold tolerant, its bloom often begins in December or January and continues until late May or early June. It is not uncommon for Johnny-jump-ups to move into lawn or other areas adjacent to where they were originally planted. They prefer full sun or partially shaded locations. A good way to introduce Johnny-jump-ups into your garden is to purchase started plants the first year. If conditions are right, they will reseed each year thereafter.

In *A Southern Garden,* Elizabeth Lawrence says of *V. tricolor:* "They will tolerate considerable shade and the meanest conditions. The prune purple of the flowers is the perfect color contrast with spring yellows, and dark, velvet petals are effective with white."—*WCW*

Vitex agnus-castus

Chaste Tree, Hemp Tree, Sage Tree, Indian Spice
Family: Verbenaceae (Vervain or Verbena)
Size: 12–15 ft
Zones: 6–9
Deciduous large shrub or small tree
Lavender, blue, or purple (occasionally white or pink) flowers in summer

This plant thrives so well in Texas and the South that many regard it as a native of that region. It is even considered invasive in West Texas. In fact, the chaste tree originated in China and India, though it is now naturalized widely in the Southern United States. Peter Henderson, writing in 1890, stated that *Vitex* has been in cultivation since 1670.

Preferring sunny sites, it adapts well to a variety of soils, thriving in just about any as long as it is reasonably well drained. The chaste tree is exceptionally tolerant of drought, which makes it

Chaste tree (*Vitex agnus-castus* 'LeCompte') (Photo by Greg Grant)

Chaste tree (*Vitex agnus-castus*
'LeCompte') (Photo by William C. Welch)

Chaste tree (*Vitex agnus-castus*
'LeCompte') (Photo by William C. Welch)

one of the best large shrubs (twelve to fifteen feet) or small trees for hot, dry sites.

Vitex foliage is palmate, having five to seven aromatic leaflets. The common name "hemp tree" refers to the resemblance of chaste tree leaves to those of marijuana. Steve Bender, coauthor of *Passalong Plants,* speculates concerning the "chaste tree" name: "Perhaps the tree was often planted on the grounds of monasteries. This makes sense, because a group of men living celibate lives need all the chastity they can muster." Actually, the name originated centuries ago in Europe where the ancient Greeks believed that its aromatic flowers reduced the passions of lust.

The aromatic blossoms of the chaste tree emerge from May to September and are borne in terminal spikes that range from four to twelve inches long. Flower color ranges from purple to lavender, off-white, and pale pink. The fruit ripens in fall and is brown or black and one-eighth to one-sixth inch long. Beekeepers like to plant chaste trees because the flowers are very attractive to their favorite insects. Insect and disease problems are few.

To keep chaste trees neat and attractive, remove all dead wood on a regular basis and prune back in wintertime, cutting back the previous year's growth by several feet. I prefer removing some of the lower branches to expose several feet of trunks near the base. Propagation is from cuttings in summer or winter. Lower branches can easily be ground-layered, and seed collected in fall will usually germinate the next spring.

Greg has done some useful breeding and selecting with vitex that has resulted in extending their usefulness. 'LeCompte' has large, blue-purple spikes and was collected in LeCompte, Louisiana. 'Montrose Purple' is similar and fairly widely available in the nursery trade. Greg also has selected an attractive pink-flowering form he has named 'Flora Ann'. — *WCW*

Vitis spp.

Muscadines and Grapes
Family: Vitaceae (Grape)
Size: 15–30 ft
Zones: 6–9
Deciduous vine
Edible fruit in summer

As the Bible and countless other ancient texts bear witness, grapes are among the plants longest cultivated by humans. Certainly, they have always been staples in the South. Native Americans were known to preserve wild muscadines as dried fruit (as John Bartram noted in 1791), and wine, raisins, and jellies, as well as the fresh fruit of cultivated vines, have been important food sources to Southerners since colonial times. Likewise, grape vines and the arbors that support them have also been significant components of Southern gardens from early times. This group of plants is also a must for gardeners with an interest in wildlife, since grape vines of cultivated or wild varieties are a food source for numerous species of birds and animals.

The many grapes native to the South have been the ones used chiefly for food and landscape in our region, since the cultivated grapes of Europe tend to be short-lived here. *Vitis rotundifolia,* better known as muscadines or scuppernongs, is by far the most important species in the South. Indigenous populations may be found throughout the southeastern United States, except in mountainous areas. They are most abundant in coastal plains of the Atlantic Ocean and the Gulf of Mexico. Muscadines tend to be insect and disease resistant and are easily grown, preferring acidic, well-drained soils.

Captain John Hawkins reported in 1565 that Spanish settlements in Florida were making large quantities of muscadine wine (Hedrick, 1908). In fact, winemaking with muscadines continued to be a viable industry in the South until Prohibition. The last twenty or so years have seen an increase in muscadine plantings, but today they are grown mostly for juice and jellies, although there is new interest for their use in wines.

Though the early harvests were no doubt taken from wild vines, Southern gardeners wasted no time in improving on the native species. Indeed, the very first grape cultivar developed in North America was one selected by Isaac Alexander of Tyrrel County, North Carolina, sometime around 1760. Originally this grape was known as the "big white grape" or "Hickman's grape," but it was later called "scuppernong" for the area in which it was found. The naming probably occurred in 1810 and is credited to Calvin Jones, a noted naturalist and editor of the *Star,* a Raleigh newspaper. Like many common names, however, this one can be misleading, because over the years all bronze-colored muscadines have come to be known generically as "scuppernongs."

There are also many dark-colored muscadines, sometimes known as "bullis," "bullace," "bullet grapes," or "bull grapes." Bartram wrote in 1802 (Hedrick, 1908) that the name "Bull Grape" was an abbreviation of "Bullet Grape" and that it was so called because the

'Champanel' grape (*Vitis* 'Champanel')
(Photo by William C. Welch)

fruit is the size of a musket ball. Other lore suggests that "bull" refers to comparisons of the berries with cow or pig eyes.

Native muscadines and some of the improved cultivars are functionally dioecious (male and female flowers on separate plants), with male vines making up about three-fourths of the populations. This means that a majority of any random planting will be naturally fruitless. However, female vines and self-pollinating types are available from nurseries specializing in muscadines, and the gardener can ensure better harvests simply by ordering from these sources.

Propagation of improved cultivars is done through cuttings or layering. Muscadine grapes do not root easily, though, which accounts for the fact that the relatively primitive technique of ground layering remains a popular method for starting new plants. Muscadines were first transplanted into the garden because of their fruit, but it wasn't long before gardeners came to appreciate the beauty of the vines and use them as landscaping material. As grape arbors became a part of eighteenth- and nineteenth-century Southern landscapes, muscadines, with their attractive foliage and ease of culture, became popular for clothing them. Muscadine vines also contribute to the autumn display, for their leaves turn bright yellow just before dropping off in the fall. An additional, and very welcome, virtue of muscadines is their longevity; their vines may live for generations, and individual specimens are a part of the gardening heritage of many Southern families.

In Texas, muscadines are native to the eastern part of the state and are the important grape for that region but are gradually replaced by other species to the west, as conditions become drier and more alkaline. Most important among these western grapes is the mustang grape (*V. candicans*). Mustangs are naturally abundant from Central Texas westward, and although the fruit is highly acid, are a logical choice within this range for shading arbors and making wine and jelly. Thomas Affleck experimented with making wine from *V. candicans* in the 1850s. This grape is still a popular plant among Texans.

The most important date in Southern viticulture is April 1876, when T. V. Munson arrived in Denison, Texas, and settled on a rough piece of timbered land on the bluffs of the Red River. Munson had trained as a chemist at Kentucky State Agricultural College and while doing so, had been fascinated by the vineyards of one of his professors, Robert Peter. Located near Lexington, this planting included nearly all the cultivars of American grapes then being grown.

Thus, Munson was delighted to discover upon settling in Denison that the ravines and uplands of his Texas home abounded in numerous vines of mustang grape, the sour winter grape or frost grape (*V. cordifolia*), post oak grape (*V. lincecumii*), and sweet winter grape (*V. cinerea*). The area was also the western limit of the southern muscadine (*V. rotundifolia*). Munson found there at least six or eight good native species, several of which he had never before seen. In his own words, "I had found my grape paradise!"

Munson drew on the experiences of Gilbert Onderdonk of Victoria County, Texas, a veteran experimenter with and writer on grapes, and Onderdonk's experiences confirmed his own observation that the traditional grapes of vineyard and table, cultivars of the European species *V. vinifera* and of the northern American native *V. labrusca,* were prone to disease in Texas and tended to be short-lived. Thus, he was excited to discover the native Texas species that were perfectly suited to the soils and climate of the region.

Munson began a breeding program, crossing native species with valuable but less hardy exotic grapes. His work first attracted national attention in 1885 when he presented a display of herbarium specimens and live vines grown in pots in the Horticultural Hall of the Cotton Centennial Exposition at New Orleans. He presented a written report on this exhibit to the American Horticultural Society in February of the same year and included a new botanical classification of grape species in that document.

‘Champanel’ grape (*Vitis* ‘Champanel’)
(Photo by William C. Welch)

Subsequently, Munson published many further articles on hybridization and varieties of grapes in journals across the United States and France. The exhibit of American and Asiatic grape species he displayed at the Columbian exhibition in 1893 was hailed as the most complete botanical display of the grape genus ever made. In this Munson included not only live plants of every species but also specimens of roots, sections of young and mature vines, pressed leaves in all stages of development, flowers, and clusters of ripe fruit, even life-size photographs—and all were identified according to Munson's own system of nomenclature.

As generous as he was learned, Munson distributed seeds and sets of live plants of American grape species without charge to researchers and grape growers throughout the world. These activities helped materially in saving the vineyards of France, which in the late nineteenth century were falling prey to a small root insect, the phylloxera, which had been accidentally imported from America. Acting on the belief that native American grapes must be resistant to this native pest, Munson collected fifteen wagons of dormant stem cuttings and shipped them to southern

France via three boats. When Munson's gifts were used as root-stock, and the French wine grapes grafted onto them, they did indeed produce resistant plants. This discovery saved the French wine industry and the hundreds of villages that depended on it for their economic survival.

By the turn of the century, the T. V. Munson and Son Nursery of Denison had become the largest fruit nursery in Texas and was one of the largest in the nation. Through it, Munson introduced a series of more than three hundred grape cultivars well adapted to growing conditions in the South and the southwestern United States. To accomplish this, Munson traveled over seventy-five thousand miles in forty states, mostly by horse, to collect breeding material and pollinated by hand thousands of grapes in his ten vineyards in Denison. Munson's breeding program focused on natural disease resistance and adaptation to climate, goals that placed him far ahead of his time and make his grapes of enduring value, even today.

The most famous of Munson's creations is probably 'Champanel,' which he released as a Champini-Lambrusca hybrid in 1893. Munson recommended 'Champanel' for its ability to thrive even in the black, waxy clay soils of the South. In fact, it has proven an unusually vigorous, productive, and useful grape. Long life, great vigor, and resistance to Pierce's disease make it particularly good for arbors and other landscape uses. 'Champanel' is also used as a rootstock for other cultivars because it has demonstrated a resistance to cotton root rot.

Munson recognized the landscape value of grapes and extolled their use in the home garden. In his book *Foundations of American Grape Culture* (self-published in 1909), he included a chapter titled "The Grapevine for Home Adornment, Shade, Fruit and Health." In this he advised:

> The humblest cottager and the millionaire may engage with pleasure and success in producing handsome clusters, luscious berries, and comforting shade. The plebian is the more likely

to succeed best and enjoy the fruits most, for he works with his head and hands in partnership, while the aristocrat depends on his gardener, and has such a multiplicity of other cares that he has few moments to spend in his "pergola" that has cost hundreds of dollars where the simple arbor of the toiler has cost cents.

At least one other grape will be mentioned here because of its long and successful cultivation as a source for wine, juice, and jellies in Texas and other Southern areas. 'Black Spanish' (also known as 'Lenoir') is a cultivar of mysterious origin that has been grown for at least two hundred years. The Qualia family's Val Verde Winery of Del Rio, Texas, the oldest continuously operated winery and vineyard in the state, bases its production on the 'Black Spanish' grape, from which they have been producing wines since 1883.

The fruit of this cultivar is small, dark in color, and sweet when ripe. Since about 1900, when Pierce's disease eliminated all other *V. labrusca* and *V. vinifera* grapes from the South, 'Black Spanish' (together with 'Herbemont') has become the predominant bunch grape for winemaking throughout our region. In particular, 'Black Spanish' is the premium grape for production of port wines because of its unusual acidic strength.

With our abundance of native grapes, and thanks to the inspirational work of T. V. Munson, Southerners can easily grow grapes to shade our arbors and fill our vineyards. Muscadines, 'Champanel,' 'Black Spanish,' and other heirloom varieties are available for today's gardeners. With minimum care they can produce handsome, prolific vines. Proper pruning is essential for vineyard plantings and helpful for arbors. When planting dormant, bare-root, or container-grown grapes, cut the stems back to one or two buds. Pruning of established vines is necessary to prevent overcropping and shading of the fruiting buds. —*WCW*

Wisteria frutescens

American Wisteria
Family: Fabaceae (Pea)
Size: 20–30 ft
Zones: 5–10
Deciduous vine
Lavender or purple (occasionally white) flowers in spring

Since childhood I've always had a "running" love affair with wisteria. The genus was named by Thomas Nuttall in memory of Caspar Wistar of the University of Pennsylvania. Although Nuttall spelled the genus *Wisteria,* nurserymen spelled it *Wistaria* for many years. The species first introduced to Europe (1724) and the nameplant of the genus was *W. frutescens,* our own American wisteria, which is native from Texas to Virginia and Florida. Thomas Walter in South Carolina, John Bartram in Pennsylvania, and Lady Skipwith in Virginia all grew it in their colonial gardens. American wisteria is becoming more common in cultivation as a wider range of cultivars are introduced and more gardeners appreciate its noninvasive habit. Selections available today include 'Amethyst Falls' (short, dark purple flowers), 'Nivea' (short, white flowers), 'Dam B' (medium, lavender flowers), 'Delta Blues' (longer lavender flowers), and 'Clara Mack' (longer white flowers). Although American wisteria doesn't have the strong scent of Chinese wisteria (*W. sinensis*), it certainly belongs in Southern gardens for its beauty, its history, and its restraint.

According to *The Hillier Manual of Trees and Shrubs,* Chinese wisteria was introduced to Europe in 1816 from a garden in Canton. And Julia Morten writes in *America's Garden Heritage* that it reached America via England "after 1825." In *The Flower Garden* (1851), Joseph Breck refers to Chinese wisteria as "one of the most magnificent climbing shrubby plants in cultivation" and mentions that "a new variety, with white flowers, was brought to

'Amethyst Falls' wisteria (*Wisteria frutescens* 'Amethyst Falls') (Photo by Greg Grant)

'Delta Blues' wisteria (*Wisteria frutescens* 'Delta Blues') (Photo by Greg Grant)

'Delta Blues' wisteria (*Wisteria frutescens* 'Delta Blues') (Photo by Greg Grant)

England from China, by Mr. Fortune." In addition to the purple and the white, there is also a double variety.

An 1860 catalogue from Montgomery Nurseries (Wilson's Nursery) of Montgomery, Alabama, offered Chinese glycene (Chinese wisteria). The 1881–82 Langdon Nurseries (near Mobile) catalogue listed both the purple and the white varieties; the 1906–7 Fruitland Nurseries (Augusta, Georgia) catalogue listed all three varieties along with *W. frutescens magnifica*.

Chinese wisteria (*Wisteria sinensis*) (Photo by William C. Welch)

Chinese wisteria (*Wisteria sinensis*) (Photo by Greg Grant)

In addition to the Chinese wisteria cultivated all over the South, the Japanese wisteria (*W. floribunda*) is sometimes grown. It has more leaflets and longer bloom racemes (hanging/drooping bloom spikes). The famous plant explorer Ernest "Chinese" Wilson claimed to have seen some in Japan with blooms over five feet long! The Japanese wisteria has forms with purple, white, pink, double, and longer flowers. *The Hillier Manual of Trees and Shrubs* states that Philip von Siebold introduced it to Europe in 1830.

Wisteria is very easy to grow (it's a relative of kudzu, you know) in almost any kind of soil. It is, however, susceptible to iron chlorosis in alkaline soils. Wisterias need a strong support to be grown as a vine. They eat wooden trellises for snacks. Luckily, our American wisteria is far less aggressive than its Chinese counterpart. Wisteria can be propagated from seed or cuttings from improved forms and blooms best in full sun.

Unfortunately, the Asian wisterias are considered invasive in many parts of the United States and are frowned upon in numerous gardens. It's wonderful though that the first wisteria cultivated in the West, our own native *W. frutescens,* is now becoming available again for all Southerners to enjoy. —*GG*

Zephyranthes candida

Rain Lily, Zephyr Lily
Family: Amaryllidaceae (Amaryllis)
Size: 1 ft
Zone: 7
Perennial bulb
White flowers in summer and fall

The flowering bulbs we call rain lilies actually belong in several genera, mostly *Zephyranthes* and *Habranthus.* Complicating the situation is that there are numerous native rain lilies that brighten our prairies, but the most gardenworthy come to us from Argentina. The reason for including them in this book is that they are wonderful plants and some have been around a long time, definitely fitting the mold of being almost indestructible as well as

Rain lily × 'Labuffarosa,' a species cross
(Photo by William C. Welch)

Giant prairie lily (*Cooperia pedunculata*)
(Photo by William C. Welch)

Giant prairie lily (*Cooperia pedunculata*)
(Photo by William C. Welch)

beautiful additions to our gardens. Rain lilies are useful in the landscape for borders or mass plantings and require little attention once planted. Seeds of rain lilies, like those of other amaryllids, should be sown as soon as they are gathered.

Two of the oldest and most commonly used rain lilies are the *Z. candida* (white) and *Z. grandiflora* (pink). The white rain lily is said to be native to the shores of the Rio de la Plata, the Silver River, in Argentina, which takes its name from this white-blooming fairy lily. Flowers appear from late summer well into the fall, usually beginning with late summer or early autumn showers. Foliage, dark green at first glance, looks somewhat like monkey grass (*Ophiopogon japonicus*). Flowers are six petaled, starlike, and about two inches in diameter. Although they will grow just about anywhere, white rain lilies prefer a sunny location and moist soils. In fact, they will grow partially submerged.

According to Scott Ogden in *Garden Bulbs for the South* (Timber Press, 2007), Peter Henry Oberwetter, who came to Texas in the 1840s from Germany, was among the early advocates for bulbs. He settled near Comfort and collected seeds and rain lilies on his farm to send around the world. During the Civil War Oberwetter moved to Mexico, collecting and exporting bulbs while there. After the war he settled in Austin and introduced oxblood lilies (*Rhodophiala bifida*) and native rain lilies (*Cooperia pedunculata*) to the nursury trade. He worked with Arnold Puetz in Jacksonville, Florida, in 1881 marketing Easter lilies and the Easter lily–like Florida variant, atamasco (*Z. treatae*). The Cherokees called these small flowers "culowee." Puetz sold them for twenty-five cents per dozen, or five dozen for a dollar.

Elizabeth Lawrence, who gardened in Raleigh and later in Charlotte, North Carolina (zone 7), left us many interesting anecdotes about bulbs that Southern gardeners could grow successfully. She corresponded with women across the South through state Market Bulletins (where individuals could market plants, livestock, and other agricultural produce for sale or trade) and personal communications. Through her newspaper columns

Rain lily (*Habranthus robustus*) (Photo by William C. Welch)

and later books she began corresponding with plant enthusiasts such as Caroline Dorman (famous gardener and plant illustrator from Louisiana) and Eudora Welty (author) in Mississippi. She ordered and attempted to grow many of the rain lilies and referred to them as "Fairy lilies." B. Y. Morrison, a well-known horticulturist in the 1950s and 1960s who gardened and retired to Pass Christian, Mississippi, wrote, "I like to have them surprise me with their small and sudden flowers—they make no demands and take up so little space."

Another gardener of note from this period was William Lanier Hunt of Raleigh and Chapel Hill, North Carolina. He donated the land for the Hunt Arboretum at Chapel Hill and was a noted gardener and lecturer both here and abroad. Working closely with the late Flora Ann Bynum from Old Salem, North Carolina, Hunt helped found the Southern Garden History Society. He had a lifetime interest in bulbs and a particular interest in rain lilies, citing that "the bulbous flowers were a relief from all the big round zinnias and marigolds of summer but also bringing the element of surprise that is always a joy in the garden" (Hunt,

Rain lily (*Habranthus robustus*) (Photo by William C. Welch)

Southern Gardens, Southern Gardening, Duke University Press, 1982). Bill Hunt loved the way the little zephyranthes suddenly came from nowhere, overnight, and bloomed in the hot summer garden.

Zephyranthes grandiflora is one of the largest and showiest of the rain lilies. Although its origins are obscure, it is known to have been introduced very early to gardens in warm countries and has escaped frequently throughout the subtropics.

The atamasco lily or wild Easter lily (*Z. atamasco*) is a beautiful southeastern native and differs from other rain lilies by preferring shady, woodsy places and blooming early in the spring. Its large, funnel-shaped white blooms put on a good show and are compatible with other acid-loving plants such as azaleas and Louisiana phlox. I have not been able to successfully grow them in alkaline soils. Another really beautiful native rain lily is *Z. drummondii* (*Cooperia pedunculata*), the giant prairie-lily, which has large, white flowers and is native to Central Texas. The primrose-scented evening blooms appear from April through midsummer and sporadically into the fall. I have observed these growing on rocky, well-drained soils of Central Texas.

Habranthus robustus doesn't have a common name but truly lives up to the species name. Another native of Argentina, *H. robustus* is the most useful rain lily I have grown. I first obtained some bulbs from Cynthia Mueller about ten years ago, and they have reseeded and multiplied profusely in my College Station garden. Periodically blooms occur in great profusion with large, pink, funnel-shaped flowers. They thrive in sun or partial shade and bloom five or six times during the growing season from late spring till early fall.

Equally as gardenworthy is *Z.* × 'Grandjax,' a cross between *Z. candida* and *Z.* × 'Ajax.' It is a vigorous grower, multiplier, and bloomer, repeat-flowering many times through the warm seasons. Flower color is pink with tones of apricot. There is currently quite a bit of breeding under way with rain lilies. I believe they are not only wonderful as heirlooms but will continue to be a source of new and useful garden plants. The repeat flowering, insect and disease resistance, and water efficiency make them great choices for almost any garden. — *WCW*

Zinnia elegans

Common Zinnia, Old-Maids
Family: Asteraceae (Sunflower)
Size: 1–4 ft
Zones: NA
Warm-season annual
Summer flowers in all colors

I consider zinnias to be the easiest, showiest, and best cut flowers that can be home grown in Southern gardens. They haven't always been so showy, though. The original wild zinnias from Mexico were red and had just a single circle of petals with a protruding cone in the middle.

According to Peggy Cornett's *Popular Annuals of Eastern North America 1865–1914* (1985), the zinnia was introduced in 1796; the first double forms appeared in the mid-1800s. In *The American Gardener's Calendar* (1886), Bernard M'Mahon mentioned sowing zinnia seeds. In *The Flower Garden* (1851), Joseph

Common zinnia (*Zinnia elegans*) (Photo by Greg Grant)

Common zinnia (Zinnia elegans) (Photo by Greg Grant)

Breck included *Zinnia elegans,* remarking that the "colors are white, pale to dark yellow, orange to scarlet; shades from rose to crimson, from crimson to light purple, lilac, &c." He continued, "The flowers are handsome when it first commences the process of blooming; the central part of it, which contains the florets, as they begin to form seed, assume a conic shape, and a brown husky appearance, which gives a coarse, unsightly look." In the *American Flower-Garden Directory* (1860), Robert Buist included notes on the varieties *coccinea* (scarlet), *alba* (white), and *pauciflora* (yellow).

Of course, today zinnias come in a multitude of colors, sizes, and flower shapes. Some cultivars have been bred for cut flowers, while others were developed as summer bedding plants. All are easily grown from seed during warm weather.

Besides *Z. elegans,* several other species of zinnias are cultivated. *Zinnia angustifolia* (*Z. linearis*), the narrow-leaved zinnia from Mexico, is commercially available today in both white- and orange-flowered forms. It is a low-growing annual that bears multitudes of small, daisylike flowers. It is an excellent summertime

Zinnias (*Zinnia* spp.) (Photo by William C. Welch)

bedding plant. The Mexican zinnia (*Z. haageana*) is commercially available as well. It is known for its red and yellow bicolored flowers. I have seen the cultivars 'Old Mexico' and 'Persian Carpet' listed in various catalogues.

Everybody should have some zinnias to cut in the vegetable garden. Besides, they're prettier than okra and peas. —*GG*

Zizyphus jujuba

Chinese Date, Jujube
Family: Rhamnaceae (Buckthorn)
Size: 12–30 ft
Zones: 6–9
Deciduous small tree
Edible fruit in late summer

Chinese date (*Zizyphus jujuba*) (Photo by Jason Powell)

Chinese dates are among the most persistent and long-lived imported trees in the South. Thickets of root sprouts often mark old home and orchard sites throughout Texas and the South. Although thorny and somewhat aggressive, jujubes are drought tolerant and pest free. Interest in growing them for their fruit has increased with migration of more Asians into Texas and other areas. Some sources indicate that Robert Chisholm first introduced Chinese dates from Europe in 1837 in Beaufort, South Carolina. However, they have also been claimed as part of the planting at early Spanish missions in California so may have been brought to America at an even earlier date.

The Chinese date may be, as its common name suggests, a native of China, but some botanists have proposed Syria as the species' original homeland. What is certain is that they are widely distributed now through the warmer parts of Europe, South Asia, Africa, and Australia. The Chinese have cultivated this plant for hundreds of years and have developed as many as four hundred different cultivars. They have a great fondness for the fruit, which they sometimes process with honey and sugar and sell as a dessert confection. Most of the Chinese cultivars are not commercially available in the United States, but Roger Meyer of the California Rare Fruit Growers is attempting to identify sources for some of the best jujubes.

Jujubes can reach a height of fifty feet but are often maintained as much smaller plants through pruning and training. The stems may be thorny, and the foliage is shiny, deciduous, and

Jujube Butter

6 pints jujube pulp

½ teaspoonful cloves

5 pints sugar

1 lemon

2 teaspoonfuls cinnamon

¼ pint vinegar

1 teaspoon nutmeg

The fruit should be boiled until tender in sufficient water to cover it. It should then be rubbed through a sieve or colander to remove the skin and seeds. Cook slowly until thick, put in jars, and seal while hot.

dark green; the small, inconspicuous flowers appear in the axils of the leaves. The fruit ranges from half an inch to two inches long and changes from green to reddish brown as it matures in late summer and early fall.

These fruits were at one time believed to have medicinal properties and were turned into pastes, tablets, and syrups that were supposed to have demulcent (soothing to mucous membranes) characteristics. Research on the nutritional and culinary uses of jujube fruit was done in the Food Science section of Texas A&M's Horticultural Sciences Department in the 1940s. Homer Blackhurst, Emeritus Professor of Horticulture, remembered that the vitamin C content of the fruit was found to be very high. He also recalled experiments where the seeds were removed and the fruit cooked with water, sugar, and seasonings. The resulting product was similar in appearance and flavor to apple butter, and in taste tests of the two, the jujube butter was selected as superior.

I have been able to locate numerous recipes for preparing the fruit that appear to be interesting. Following is one recipe taken from USDA publication B-1215, *Methods of Utilizing the Chinese Jujube.* —WCW

Part Five

HOW OUR GARDENS GREW

*Creating Your Own
Garden Traditions*

A Country Cottage Garden

Fragilee

WILLIAM C. WELCH

Jayme and Harley Ponder had just purchased a thirty-acre parcel adjoining their ranch near Burton, Texas, and it included a dilapidated house that was calling out to me. They said the house would be torn down as soon as the purchase was final, but we could have it if we would move it off the property. I have always been attracted to old houses and liked this one in particular. It had the simplicity consistent with early Texas houses from the 1850s but was in very bad condition. We owned several acres in Round Top, Texas, and I thought about moving it there.

My wife, Diane, and I had sold our last house in the area several years before, and I thought we might not really be ready to take on another project. Diane was more specific. The house was filled with junk, including an old electric range in the kitchen. When I opened the oven door, an opossum came out. Then, as we ascended the stairs to the two loft bedrooms, several vultures were surprised by our intrusion and noisily flew away. That was enough for Diane. She said that if I wanted this house, it was going to be my project. She suggested that the house was so fragile we should name it "Fragilee," and Greg Grant seconded the suggestion. The Ponders had offered to sell us four acres on the corner of their ranch that already had a well, a barn, and a small outbuilding. It seemed more sensible to move the house a few hundred yards to this site rather than the eight miles or so to Round Top.

I contacted Larry Schroeder, a well-respected local house mover for his opinion about whether the house could withstand a move and asked for an estimate. Larry declared that "the porch was going

Stonemasons rebuilt the chimney, and the front porch was rebuilt soon after Fragilee was moved. (Photo by William C. Welch)

to fall off anyway" but he thought that the house could stand the move—if we would "ask the termites to hold hands!"

On the day of the move, I held my breath while the "termites held hands," and Larry and the termites made it to the new site. We had a good supply of lumber harvested from cypress trees on Diane's family property in Louisiana, and we decided to utilize it for new columns on an enlarged front porch as well as for decking, railings, and a gazebo I envisioned for the garden. We also had enough cypress to provide picket fencing for the garden that I was planning. Enlarging the front porch was actually the only change we made in the footprint of the house. Inside we added an opening from the master bedroom into what was to become a bathroom and closet (there were no bathrooms or closets originally in the house), exposed the raised ceiling in the kitchen, and added a half bath upstairs. As these renovations became reality, I was getting very anxious to begin work on a garden.

The Garden Begins

Moving Fragilee to a new location offered a real opportunity for us to site it to take advantage of existing views. I loved the openness of the landscape, with just a few trees and a view of the lake on the Ponders' ranch, as well as rolling hillsides, wildflowers, cattle, and pastures. The garden had to be low maintenance since this was not a full-time residence and our time for working there was limited. The soil was less than ideal from years of row-crop farming and grazing. Restraining my inclination to have a large plant collection and a large garden was a major challenge. My concerns about water conservation and about creating a garden appropriate for the period of the house (1860–80) were also important considerations. As costs escalated on restoring the house, I realized more than ever that the garden must be very practical.

Vertical structures seemed a logical way to design a small garden that would not have to depend upon plants for all its impact. I decided

to repeat the gable lines of the house with simple arches, arbors, and fences. A four-foot-high cypress picket fence enclosed the rear and side garden, and the front lawn met a low stone retaining wall. An additional low stone wall was capped by cypress pickets about two feet high on the south side, creating a small *potager*, or kitchen garden. Japanese persimmons, a couple of tangerine trees, and blackberries trained on the fence provided fresh fruit in season. Two raised boxes (each five by twelve feet) made a good environment in the back area for growing vegetables. There was no lawn inside the fenced area. Decomposed granite gravel served as the paving material except where stone walks led to the stone steps at the rear and front of the house.

A climbing red China rose drapes the rear entrance with verbenas at the base. (Photo by William C. Welch)

The Garden Takes Shape

My interest in roses, perennials, and heirloom native plants would be satisfied with cuttings and plants from friends across Texas and the South. A white Lady Banks rose, rooted from a cutting from Elizabeth Lawrence's garden in Charlotte, North Carolina, adorns the gazebo on one end, while 'Mme. Alfred Carriere' and a 'Champanel' grape share the other. A fifteen-foot-wide specimen of "Peggy Martin" rose covers the fence surrounding the air-conditioning equipment, while a climbing red China rose (thought to be 'Cramoisi Superieur') from Frances Parker in Beaufort, South Carolina, drapes the arch near the back door. I believe the red China rose at the back entrance (also thought to be 'Cramoisi Superieur') is the one that Peggy Cornett, horticulturist at Monticello, and I found in a Williamsburg garden a number of years ago where I first obtained cuttings. The one on the right side is younger and was a gift from Peggy Martin in New Orleans. (These two red Chinas may be the same rose.) A small specimen of 'Ducher,' the old white China rose, is just inside the garden fence. Also along that fence is a very vigorous clump of Philippine lilies (*Lilium formosanum*).

A large specimen of bay (*Laurus nobilis*) is thriving and becoming treelike. Just over the fence is a nice specimen of winter honeysuckle from the garden of Frances Parker's mother. I have memories of winter honeysuckle at my grandmother's back gate at her home near Yoakum, Texas. The wonderful January fragrance comes at a

Philippine lilies (*Lilium formosanum*) provide fragrant white trumpet-shaped flowers in late summer. (Photo by William C. Welch)

time when little else is blooming. It is one of the few plants that grows literally all over the South.

A touch of formality comes from the four clipped specimens of large leaf myrtle (*Myrtus communis*) rooted by Cynthia Mueller from an old specimen in Schulenburg, Texas. A four-foot-tall obelisk in the center is surrounded by "Martha Gonzales" roses collected by Pam Puryear. The roses are edged with 'Grandjax' rain lilies from Scott Ogden, and the dwarf myrtle hedge in the *potager* came from cuttings supplied by Mary Anne Pickens near Frelsburg, Texas. Easter lilies thrive in two locations within the garden and came from Pam Puryear by way of Cynthia Mueller. Two 'Republic of Texas' orange trees were a gift from Heidi Sheesley in Houston, and Greg Grant supplied 'Pam's Pink' and 'Big Momma' Turk's cap hibiscus as well as numerous other plants. Aubrey King of King's Nursery in Tenaha, Texas, provided the handsome 'LeCompte' vitex, with its really large, blue-violet blooms, along with several figs and pomegranates.

Fruiting plants have always interested me as long as they do not require extensive spraying or other care. Pomegranates and figs do really well and are an important part of our Texas and Southern gardening heritage.

Bulbs have been fairly successful at Fragilee. I was able to "liberate" several bulbs of Johnson's amaryllis from the original homesite, and they have multiplied in the raised bed at the front gate. In addition, *Narcissus tazetta* 'Grand Primo' and Chinese sacred lily (*N. tazetta orientalis*) along with snowflakes (*Leucojum aestivum* 'Gravetye Giant') and the 'Grandjax' rain lily thrive in the soils there. Gladiolus byzantinus and Roman hyacinths (*Hyacinthus orientalis*) provide early spring color and unmatched fragrance. My favorite crinum is 'Mrs. James Hendry,' which does well at each corner of the front planting area along with Greg's 'John Fanick' selection of summer phlox and the "gaudy pink" form. Pots of *Sedum potosinum* and hen and chicks (*Graptopetalum paraguayense*) work well with the low-water routine. Mexican buckeye (*Ungnadia speciosa*), red yucca (*Hesperaloe parvifolia*), Texas mountain laurel (*Sophora secundiflora*), and

Four heirloom myrtles (*Myrtus communis*), perennials, and bulbs surround a wheelbarrow filled with pumpkins. (Photo by William C. Welch)

"Martha Gonzales" roses surround an obelisk in the parterre garde. (Photo by William C. Welch)

Metal "tuteurs" provide vertical structure and interest. Coral honeysuckle (*Lonicera sempervirens*) is evergreen and blooms periodically during the growing season. (Photo by William C. Welch)

Perennial marigolds (*Tagetes lemmonii*) provide low-maintenance fall blooms. (Photo by William C. Welch)

desert willow (*Chilopsis linearis*) are Texas natives that thrive under the inconsistent natural rainfall along with two forms of the spineless prickly pear.

Reseeding annuals are a welcome addition to the garden. Old-fashioned petunias, nicotiana, poppies, violas, celosia, bachelor's buttons, purple-leaved castor beans, and French hollyhocks return reliably, as do bluebonnets, Texas bluebells, and numerous other wildflowers in the pastures.

The forty-by-fifty-foot barn and an eight-by-ten-foot tool shed and well house were on the property. These have been painted a gray-beige color that blends with the stain on the house, fences, gazebo, and arches at the gates. It is actually a fairly close match to the color of the soil. The windows and trim are wine red. The leaves of heirloom castor beans provided by Cynthia Mueller are an exact match of the trim color.

The front of the sheet metal barn faces west and really gets hot during the summer. I decided to take a hint from Texas' German heritage and plant a grape arbor to provide shade and grapes for jellies and wines. I designed a simple structure of treated pine posts and two-by-eights, creating an eight-by-forty-foot arbor that I covered with cattle panels. I planted two 'Champanel' grape vines, which the legendary Texas viticulturist T. V. Munson developed near the turn of the twentieth century. 'Champanel' is extremely vigorous and fruitful. The vines covered the structure in less than two years and produce abundantly. The biggest advantage, however, is the cooling shade provided on that hot west side.

Planting by the road at the entrance has been an interesting learning experience. In free-form beds on each side of the gate, raised and contained by native stone, Central and West Texas natives have done well. These include Texas mountain laurel, desert willow, Mexican buckeye, red yucca, eastern red cedar (*Juniperus virginiana*), and one of Luther Burbank's ornamental opuntias.

Red China shrub roses along with rose 'Clair Matin' provides color through the seasons. Hardy bulbs such as 'Grand Primo' narcissus and Byzantine glads (*Gladiolus byzantinus*) join the Johnson's amaryllis that was rescued from the original homesite. Four-o'clocks come back readily, as do the tiny narcissus 'Hawera.' Autumn asters provide a dependable source of fall flowers. A large specimen of lavender has been recently pruned back and seems to be thriving. The specimen of 'Fuyu' Japanese persimmon is bearing nicely.

Part of the learning experience in this area has been the susceptibility of some plants to cotton root rot, a legacy of the former cotton fields that once covered the region. Hardy hibiscus has been victims of this disease, as have several fig trees, such as the 'South Carolina Lemon' and 'Texas Everbearing.'

Rosa banksiae 'Alba Plena' needs a heavy structure for support. This white form is especially known for its violet-like fragrance. (Photo by William C. Welch)

Like all gardens, the landscape at Fragilee is continuing to evolve. The dwarf myrtle hedge in the *potager* garden had become chlorotic (yellowish foliage) and had some dieback. Greg suggested that I remove it and plant dwarf Barbados cherries (*Malphigia glabra*). The raised beds for vegetables are being replaced with an edging of the succulent *Graptoveria* × 'Vera Higgins.' The soil in the boxes should work for a hedge of dwarf myrtle. Masses of *Gladiolus byzantinus* and *Tulipa* praecox provide spring color.

The list of plants that have failed is long, but so is the list of those that thrive. I continue to enjoy sharing plants from my garden and adding new ones from gardening friends.

A Sense of Place

Emanis House

GREG GRANT

My original garden in Arcadia was unfortunately a temporary one. It was only designed to last until I could afford to have the house restored. I was determined to have some sort of simple landscape there. Actually, simplicity relates better to the style of the house and the history of its use.

The old farmhouse belonged to my maternal grandparents, Marquette and Eloy Emanis (to us grandchildren, my grandparents were "Grandmother" and "Papaw") and never had much of an ornamental garden. I have been in love with my grandparents' house since I was a child, not because the house was anything special but because I loved them so, and they made me so feel special when I was there. I begged to spend each holiday and summer vacation with my grandparents in the country. They were poor and had to work all the time (especially my grandmother), but that did not stop me from thinking it was the grandest place on earth. There were chickens to feed, eggs to gather, gardens to plant and harvest, tractors to drive, birds and numerous other wild animals to watch, fish to catch, and much more. To make things even better, everything in Arcadia seemed to be a generation behind my little everyday world, not itself exactly cutting edge in East Texas. Therefore, I got a small, but fascinating taste of days gone by, including syrup making, quilting, old country stores, home food production and storage, hunting, cisterns, dogtrot houses, and other such elements of rural Southern life.

When I was young, my grandparents owned the little country store in Arcadia, M&E Grocery. Although the community has withered on the vine and no longer has any businesses, historically

The "Peggy Martin" rose graces the front of the hen house. (Photo by Greg Grant)

there was always a small store there providing goods to its residents. Before my grandparents' store was the Lou Wheeler store. I now own Lou Wheeler's old Creole cottage-style house and hope to restore it as well someday as my "retirement" home. Jim Walker, who owned a store before Lou Wheeler's, originally owned my grandparents' house. I don't know whether he built it, but he sold the store and house to my great-great grandparents, Bob and Mary Pate. It was originally a dogtrot house, with the open "dog run" through the middle of it. Dogtrot houses were of course designed to pull a breeze through the house in the days of no fans or electricity. They were called such because the dogs could literally trot or run right through the middle of them.

With a total of twelve acres, I have divided the property into different use areas. The beautiful "Ozarklike" West Creek runs through the back of the property, with its steep banks and large rocks. We used to sit on the big flat rock that sticks out over the creek, while Grandmother told us about the world. We even called it "Grandmother's Creek." Near the creek grow native switch cane (*Arundinaria gigantea*), pawpaws (*Asimina triloba*), southern sugar maples

(*Acer barbatum*), large loblolly pines (*Pinus taeda*), and many others, so I have left it completely natural.

I planted eight acres in loblolly pine with the intent to harvest the pines for timber and use the proceeds to help restore the house. My plan was to reconstruct an eight-acre prairie of native grasses and wildflowers after the pines were harvested. But I fell in love with my little pine woods that the nephews call "the black forest" and decided to never cut it. I will let it grow into a natural pine savannah with an understory of native grasses and wildflowers, similar to what the early East Texas settlers found when they arrived. Each spring, I conduct a controlled burn to eliminate any bushy understory and to encourage grasses and perennials. Maybe in a hundred years or so, an endangered red cockaded woodpecker will call it home. Back when I left home, I never anticipated a love affair with pine trees. But after living in College Station, Dallas, and San Antonio without any pines, I soon realized that I had to have them. I love the way they look, the way they smell, the way the wind sounds when it blows through their branches, and the wonderful pine straw mulch they provide.

The front of the property has the last two remnants of Arcadia's past as a real community, an active Masonic lodge and the last store building that went out of business in the 1970s. Neither is very

Thebreezeway of the old dogtrot house was closed in the 1940s but will be reopened. (Photo by Greg Grant)

Greg started with five Byzantine gladiolus (*Gladiolus byzantinus*) corms from the old Wheeler homeplace nearby when he was a boy and has been multiplying them ever since. (Photo by Greg Grant)

attractive, the lodge a small brick building, and the store a metal one, but I use the store for storage and the front of it to advertise the Arcadia name and our population of fifty-seven. I've naturalized an assortment of locally propagated heirloom bulbs on the acre behind the store building. It also has a small pond where I planted baldcypress (*Taxodium distichum*) and Louisiana iris (*Iris* spp. and hybrids) to create a little cypress swamp like the ones I saw while living in Baton Rouge. In the South, they were all drained and cut down for the valuable long-lasting wood, so I'm doing my part to restore them for the future. I once had a collection of catalpas planted where the bulbs are, which I dedicated to my dear friend Flora Ann Bynum as the Flora Catalpa Arboretum. It was the largest collection of catalpa species and cultivars in the world as far as I knew. However, when she died, they made me so sad when I looked at them that I cut them all down. I planted one lone northern catalpa (*Catalpa speciosa*) instead. I do love the big showy white catalpa flowers. Papaw was a big fisherman, and I used to help him collect catalpa worms for bait. The catalpa tree is the lone host for the catalpa sphinx moth. Although some folks get excited about the worms eating the leaves, it's completely natural and does not kill the tree. The caterpillars get toxic alkaloids from the tree, making them distasteful to birds. Like I was to my elderly neighbors, my tree will be a young friend to the two old catalpas on the adjacent properties. Papaw said the one across the street grew from a sprouted fence post that one of my late distant cousins put in when building a pen for his cows.

The gardened areas around the house are fairly limited. It's a good thing that they are because I can no longer maintain three landscaped gardens, vegetable and sugarcane plots, and a bulb farm like I used to. My grandparents' old vegetable garden lies to the east of the house. It's where I first started rowing out local heirloom bulbs to experiment with commercial production. It later became the Byzantine gladiolus (*Gladiolus byzantinus*) plot. I never intended to become a commercial bulb farmer. I just wanted to identify the old-fashioned bulbs that grew so wonderfully in the South and to figure out how to produce them. It became obvious that the feeble back was not going to tolerate yearly digging, division, and planting, so I sold the whole lot to friend Chris Wiesinger at the Southern Bulb Company. I never told him, but after they dug all my plots of bulbs, I wandered through the empty plowed patches and cried like a baby. Each of the plots started as a few bulbs I dug as a child from old homeplaces in Arcadia. I especially missed the screaming magenta spikes eight rows of Byzantine glads provided, so I immediately divided some from along the front yard fence and replanted them in their rows. I don't have any intention of ever digging them again. I just feel more comfortable with them standing at attention guarding the house. I have always kept every other row empty where I grow sweet corn and tomatoes in the spring and okra and peas in the summertime. These are the very same rows where Papaw taught me how to plow, and Granny, how to pick, shuck, and cut corn. There is nothing more satisfying than producing your own food and certainly nothing that tastes better.

As a matter of fact, the little back yard is probably the world's only Crown tire vegetable parterre. I made a dozen of the tire planters

Fragrant milk and wine lilies (*Crinum × herbertii*) scent the air after summer rains. (Photo by Greg Grant)

myself while friend and "Crown Tire King," Felder Rushing, made one that an unappreciative Austin nursery didn't want. Two are made with the wheels left intact as pedestals. These are fine for dry-loving Mediterranean herbs and look statelier, but they dry out too quickly for most other plants. The rest sit on the ground so the plant roots can go down into the ground when the weather is dry or proliferate in the aerated potting soil inside the tire when wet and rainy. I normally give them two coats of white latex paint, but I have seen all sorts of other artistic expression gracing them. I also have one horse watering trough along the side where I grow spinach during the winter and sweet potatoes during the summer, as well as one large planter made from an old butane tank in the middle. I usually grow Irish potatoes in the tank in the spring and assorted herbs the rest of the year. I use the recycled tires for just about any kind of vegetable, including tomatoes, peppers, onions, squash, carrots, broccoli, and lettuce. I used to hand-water them, but I eventually installed drip irrigation that connects to the water faucet along with an inexpensive timer. It makes watering a snap. When the house is restored, the Crown tire parterre will come out, as the back bedroom that my great-aunt and great-uncle added will be removed and the back and side portions of the dogtrot will be opened up again. When I move back into the house, I will probably fashion some sort of small vegetable garden there again, as I can't fathom not gardening. Ever since I was a little tyke, feeding the extended family has always been my job. The lone ornamental plant back there is a night-blooming jasmine (*Cestrum nocturnum*) that scents the whole house during the fall. In San Antonio I have heard it called flore de noche, "the flower of the night."

My front little garden there has always been my pride and joy. When I was a boy, it was mostly St. Augustine grass with several clumps of nandinas (*Nandina domestica*) and crinum lilies across the front of the porch. The nandinas always had yellow jacket (paper wasps) nests in them. I would swat them with a stick or broom and run like the wind while they tried to catch me. Now I can't even run from the slugs! There were chairs and a swing on the old porch that we would all sit in while the fragrance of the crinums bathed us. I believe Grandmother said the crinums came from Papaw's aunt and uncle. There was also a big mimosa (*Albizzia julibrissin*) in the front yard. The pink powder-puff flowers smelled like heaven when they covered the tree in the summer, attracting swarms of humming-birds. Appropriately, it's called the "tree of happiness" in the field of Chinese herbal medicine and used as an antidepressant. It sure made me happy. However, it's no longer recommended for planting because of a wilt disease and because it is invasive and now natural-ized throughout the Southeast. According to my uncle Ronnie, the front yard was once bordered with another invasive exotic, Chinese privet (*Ligustrum sinense*). His job, which he hated, was to keep it

Greg's Grandmother Emanis's favorite crinum was 'Ellen Basarquet.' (Photo by Greg Grant)

'Grand Primo' narcissus march in rows at Greg's former bulb farm. (Photo by Greg Grant)

trimmed. He eventually decided to scatter rock salt on the plants, which led to their "mysterious" demise. The county agent even came out to try to figure out why Papaw's hedge was dying. He went to his grave not knowing.

When I moved into the house, the first thing I did was cut all the trees in the front yard and kill the St. Augustinegrass. Grandmother, who was legally blind at the time, noticed the dead grass instantly from the highway fifty yards away at sixty miles per hour! She chastised me about how long it took her to get that grass to grow. It was always pretty, even with no fertilizer and water, especially when the little lavender and purple prairie nymphs (*Herbertia lahue*) popped up. I normally try to keep my grandmother happy. After all, it was her house and her grandmother's house. But in this case, I was determined to make a pretty old-fashioned cottage garden out front. The silty loam soil there was nice, so after the grass died, I put a layer of composted black pine bark on top and was ready to plant. Then I put a double-loop wire fence around it to keep the occasional marauding cows and goats out. I acquired a matching gate from a family nearby. I also collected old bricks from family homesites in the community and used them for my walkway. My intent was to create a garden that consisted of old-fashioned plants primarily from family, friends, and local sites. Since the house had been in the community for so long and inhabited by so many family members, I felt it deserved plants with local and familial roots. To me a powerful sense of place implies a powerful sense of duty and respect. Using local heirloom plants around a historical piece of architecture easily provides the design element of unity.

I got rid of the nandinas and divided the crinum bulbs so that the canvas was clean and ready to paint. "Painting" a landscape is very much the same thing as painting a picture. The famous English landscape designer Gertrude Jekyll certainly knew that. In staying with an inherited theme, I lined the front porch with crinums. I used my grandmother's favorite, the dark pink 'Ellen Bosanquet,' for the bulk of the bed, with the light pink 'Cecil Houdyshel' on the ends. When I lived in San Antonio, my landlady allowed me to dig a start from one of her properties. I have always tried to put a piece of each place I've lived into my landscape, even if it's not noticeable to others. I

The local native perennial morning glory or "man of the earth" (*Ipomoea pandurata*) covers the fence around purple sugarcane and castor beans. (Photo by Greg Grant)

then lined the fence with 'Grand Primo' narcissus (*Narcissus tazetta* 'Grand Primo Citroniere') on the inside and Byzantine gladiolus on the outside. I punctuated the outside front corners of the fence with Grandmother's old milk and wine lilies (*Crinum × herberti*). They were a gift from Papaw's aunt and uncle years ago. After finding many an abandoned garden's original design surviving in a pattern of eternal heirloom bulbs, I decided I would preserve mine the same way. Gardens are so fleeting that it's truly amazing how these bulbs, along with some of their owner's ideas, last almost indefinitely, as long as the green foliage isn't mowed regularly. I erected two bottle trees that served as sentinels in the front corners. They stood in white Crown tire planters festooned with old-fashioned petunias. I stuck with white paint for the planters as well as the house. In the early days, white for houses and red for barns were about the only colors

Old-fashioned purple crapemyrtles, propagated from the old Wheeler homeplace nearby, line the drive. (Photo by Greg Grant)

available. For several years the bottle trees were all green, mimicking my great-grandmother's ("Big Momma") long-gone arborvitaes just down the road. My grandmother Ruth, who lived nearby, never threw away anything, allowing me to scavenge all the bottles from her place. Later I changed the bottle trees to a mix of colors to display my old bottle collection that I have worked on since childhood. I placed a collection of antique white clay pots, also from Granny Ruth's, on the front steps. Early on, they displayed my amaryllis collection, but they eventually held drought-tolerant, durable succulents.

The front garden itself has gone through several changes. The first treatment consisted of reseeding double red poppies from Johnson City, blue larkspur from San Antonio, and Queen Anne's lace from the roadside during the spring, and Flora Ann Bynum's tall cockscomb from North Carolina during the summer and fall. Then I decided I wanted a traditional swept yard, so I carved out two diamond-shaped beds on each side, which I lined with brown root beer bottles. I wanted to use snuff bottles but couldn't find enough, and they weren't tall enough to embed in the soil. In the days before metal and plastic edging many country folks used discarded bottles. I put two of Grandmother Emanis's pink flowering quince in the back corners, two of Big Momma's blush tea roses on each side of the walk at the steps, and two of Granny Ruth's cape jessamines (*Gardenia jasminoides*), which she got from her grandmother, on each side of the walk as you came in the gate. I kept them sheared into round globes to add a touch of formality and to keep them from overgrowing the fairly limited spaced. Inside the bottle-bordered diamonds I would plant a different "bedding" scheme, including cool-season plants during the winter and heat-tolerant plants during the summer. It's quite fun to be able to express yourself in a different style each year. I planted different annual vines on the fence itself each year, including sweet peas and hyacinth beans. The rest of the area was kept hoed and raked like the swept yards of old. My greatest compliment came when a lady stopped and said, "Your yard looks just like my grandmother's did in Mississippi." Another fellow stopped and said, "This doesn't look like a man's yard; it looks like a little old lady's yard." I thanked him for what he probably did not intend as a compliment, not realizing I was gardening in my granny's granny's yard.

After multiple surgeries, and preparing to move out of the house for its long-awaited restoration, I removed everything from the front yard except the fence and walk and put in what I refer to as an "all-American border." There is a chance everything will need to be removed and a new fence installed, so I decided to play around a bit with a perennial border composed of nothing but Texas and American native flowers and grasses. The side fence is now covered with the wild perennial morning glory (*Ipomoea pandurata*) and the front fence draped with the native passionvine, or maypop (*Passiflora incarnata*). All summer long it dances with Gulf fritillary butterflies. The brick path is bordered with butterfly weed (*Asclepias tuberosa*) for both the color and the monarch butterflies. Depending on what the restoration involves, I'm not sure how long this current border will last, but it sure has been fun exploring the world of native American perennials.

On the west side of the house where my grandmother's favorite tree, the grancy graybeard fringe tree (*Chionanthus virginicus*), once stood, I originally planted a mixed herbaceous border, concentrating heavily on perennials. The color theme for this border, along with the little display beds in the front yard, was "anything but yellow." I yanked yellow from the palette in honor of my beloved jonquils (*Narcissus jonquilla*) and their kin. As the ruler of this little Arcadian horticultural domain, I banished yellow each year when they finished blooming, not to be seen again until the "little sweeties" (as late friend Cleo Barnwell dubbed them) opened early next spring. After the sight and heavenly scent of the jonquils each year, it was very apparent to me that no other flower could do justice to that color but a jonquil. The beauty of designing one's own garden is that every inch of it paints a picture and tells a story. If visitors don't like the picture you have painted, send them home to look at their own! It's great to have admirers visit your garden, but I have a

A bouquet of old-fashioned flowers graces the front gate. (Photo by Greg Grant)

disdain for garden critics. After all, the only thing better than people entering your garden is people exiting your garden. There is nothing like the peace alone in one's garden where you can hear every hummingbird buzz, every cricket chirp, and every bluebird warble. I installed a cistern to catch rainwater from this house, which stood in the border along with a collection of different pink rain lilies in antique white clay pots. My rebellious spine has since caused me to remove this border with a simpler plan to replant another native grancy graybeard in my grandmother's memory.

My uncle Noel Grant restored my grandparents' barn for me and moved in my great-grandfather's log corncrib from Granny Ruth's old place. I hired friend Larry Shelton to restore the crib for me. Larry is an incredible woodworker and an active environmentalist and naturalist. I begged him to restore Granny's dogtrot house, and he agreed. I promised her as a little boy sitting on the rock at the creek that I would look after her house when she was gone, and I fully intend to do so.

Next to the pump house I moved an old outhouse and planted my 'LeCompte' vitex (*Vitex agnus-casti* 'LeCompte') for the showy indigo-blue flowers, the fragrance, and the butterflies. Both of my grandmothers grew vitex next to their chimneys. I filled this area with a mixture of naturalizing bulbs that go dormant as the vitex begins to bloom each year. Although the rest of the yard formerly contained "commercial" blocks of bulbs, I have since changed my campernelle jonquil (*Narcissus* × *odorus*) patch to sugarcane, the oxblood lily (*Rhodophiala bifida*) patch into a tallgrass prairie, and the 'Grand Primo' patch into an evaluation garden for my breeding projects.

I had the randomly curved driveway straightened so that it would be perpendicular to the house. Although the dogtrot had long since been closed in, I planted along the drive an allée of lilac-purple crapemyrtles propagated from the old Wheeler place nearby, so when the middle of the house is opened up again, you will be able to look straight down the tunnel of crapemyrtles and right through the house. I also framed either side of the house with pink crapemyrtles from my Emanis great-grandparents' homesite. In addition to accenting and framing the house, all the crapemyrtles will help block the look of the less-than-appropriate brick Masonic lodge nearby. The crapemyrtles have never been topped or pruned and never will be. I want to show off their beautiful natural branching pattern. I also need them to be full-sized trees to be in scale with the size of the twelve-acre property and the open countryside. Other people can cut off the limbs or bind the feet of their crapemyrtles, but I just want them to know they don't have to.

Like most gardens, this landscape will be a lifelong project. I am tied to it by my genetics, geography, and heartstrings. A passage from my favorite book, *Land of Bears and Honey: A Natural History of East Texas* by Joe C. Truett and Daniel W. Lay, sums up my relationship with it quite effectively: "Traditions are the last legacy. After grandparents' trees, turkeys, and teakettles have run out, they alone remain. One cannot be robbed of them, even should one want to be. They hang on, like a song you can't unlearn."

Index

Abelmoschus esculentus, 28
acanthus, 61
accessories, garden, 147–48
Acer spp., 154–58
Acer barbatum, 154–55
Acer buergerianum, 158
Acer grandidentatum, 156
Acer leucoderme, 155
Acer palmatum, 156, 158
Acer palmatum 'Crimson Queen,' 155
Acer rubrum, 157
Acer rubrum drummondii, 157
Acer rubrum rubrum, 157
Acer rubrum trilobum, 157, *158*
Acer saccharum 'Caddo,' 156, *158*
Acer skutchii, 156–57
Acer truncatum, 158
acorns, 8
Affleck, Thomas, 163, 244
African influence, 22–30
agriculture: Native American, 5–6;
    Spanish influence in Texas, 16
Akoshi, Kojiro, 410
Alabama, Spanish influence in, 15
Albizzia julibrissin, 517
Alexandrian laurel, *455*, 456–57
Allen, C. L., 231
Allium spp., 8
althea, 62, 270–73
amaryllis, 274–76
Amaryllis formosissima, 278
American box, 164
American ginseng, 8
American holly, 286
American wisteria, 485–88
Andropogon gerardii, 219
Andropogon glomeratus, 219
Andropogon ternarius, 219
annuals: bachelor's buttons, 256–58;
    cockscomb, 192–94; petunia, 379–
    81; phlox, 385–88; zinnia, 494–96

Antique Rose Emporium, San Antonio,
    Texas, 85
antique roses. *See Rosa* spp.
antiques, 143–45
apple, 110
April beauty, 358
Arabian jasmine, 294
arbors, 11–12, *42*, 43, 55–56
arborvitae, 389–91
architecture, 16, 17, 50
Aristolochia serpentaria, 8
Armistead garden, Colonial Williams-
    burg, 425
art elements, *57*, *59*, 133–41, 149
Arundinaria gigantea, 393
Asclepias tuberosa, *122*
Asian influence, 62–71
Asimina triloba, 114, 159–61
asymmetrical vs. symmetrical balance,
    128
atamasco lily, 490, 492
Aucuba japonica, 67
autumn sage, 458–61
Avent, Tony, 330
Avery Island, Louisiana, 177
azalea, *64*, 405–12
Azalea Trail, Houston, Texas, 411

baby's breath spirea, *465*, 466–67
bachelor's buttons, 256–58
Baker, Marvin, 221
balance principle in landscape design,
    127–29
baldcypress, 49, 468–70
banana shrub, *67*, 340–41
Baptisia alba, 218–19
Barbados cherry, 90
Barnwell, Cleo, 238, 355
Basham, Bill, 304
Bayou Bend Gardens, Houston, Texas,
    18, *140*, 175

bay tree, 310–12
beans, 5
bearded iris, 50, 289–92
beebalm, 8
Belamcanda chinensis, 162–63
Bellingrath Gardens, Mobile, Alabama,
    176
Bender, Steve, 152
Berckmans Fruitland Nurseries,
    Augusta, Georgia, 174–75
berries, 7
big bluestem, 219
bigleaf magnolia, 334
"Big Momma's Blush" found rose, 448
Bignonia capreolata, 180, 182–83
Bignonia capreolata 'Helen Fredel,' *180*,
    183
Bignonia capreolata 'Tangerine Beauty,'
    183
big tooth maple, 156
birdbaths, 148
bird-foot violet, 473
birds in the garden, 118–20, *121*
Birmingham Botanic Garden, 71
blackberry, 107–8
blackberry lily, 162–63
"blackberry rose," 438
Blackburn, Sadie Gwin, 177–78
blueberry, 108, *109*
bluebonnet, *391*
blue flag iris, 8
blue phlox, 388
"blue rose" (*Rosa* 'Veilchenblau'), *45*
blue sage, 459–60
bottle gourds, 5, 29
bottle trees, 25–26, 520–21
bouncing Bet, 462–63
Bourbon roses, 432–34
Bouteloua curtipendula, 219
box holly, 455–57
boxwood, 17, 164–66

Bradbury, Joe, 214
Brainard violet, 473
Brazilian skipper butterfly, 184
bridal wreath, 464–67
bride's myrtle, 345–47
British soldiers, 326–30
Brown, Lancelot "Capability," 31, 32
Buist, Robert, 248
bulbs/corms/rhizomes: amaryllis,
    274–78; Byzantine gladiolus, 253–
    55; daffodil, 8, 95–101, 351–59;
    daylilies, 259–66; harvesting, 79,
    86; iris, 289–92; jonquil, *87, 96, 97,
    353, 354,* 355, *359;* narcissus (daf-
    fodil), 8, 95–101, 351–59; natural-
    izing, 95–105; paperwhite, 356–57;
    Roman hyacinth, 279–81; sumtmer
    snowflake, 313–15. *See also* lilies
bull bay, 331–35
bull grape/bullet grape/bullis, 479–80
Burbank, Luther, 230, 264
bushy bluestem, 219
Bussell, Gene, 448
butcher's broom, 455–57
butterflies in the garden, 120–22, 161,
    184, 378, 386
butterfly weed, *122*
button blazing star, 218
Buxus japonica, 166
Buxus microphylla, 166
Buxus sempervirens, 17, 164–66
Buxus sempervirens 'Arborescens,' 164
Buxus sempervirens 'Suffruticosa,' 164,
    165
Bynum, Flora Ann, 193, 200, 281
Byzantine gladiolus, 253–55, *514*

"cabbage" roses, 434–36
Caddo maple, 156
Calamagrostis spp., 215
calamondins, 211
Caldwell, Sam, 330
Calycanthus floridus, 167–68
Camassia esculenta, 7
Camassia scilloides, 46
Camellia spp., 169–79
Camellia japonica, 172

Camellia japonica 'Delores Edwards'
    [Need decision, looks like from
    Welch, on japonica or sinensis for
    species], *170,* 175
Camellia japonica 'Duchess de Cazze,'
    171, 175
Camellia japonica 'Red Survivor,' *169*
Camellia japonica 'Rose Dawn,' *82, 176*
Camellia japonica 'White Empress,'
    173, 175, 178
Camellia sasanqua, 172–73
Camellia sinensis, 65, 170, 172
campernelle jonquil, *87,* 96, *97, 354,*
    355, *359*
Campsis grandiflora, 182
Campsis radicans, 180–83, *181*
Campsis radicans 'Flava,' *181*
Campsis × tagliabuana 'Madame Galen,'
    182
Canada wildrye, 219
"Canary Island Gallica" found rose,
    448–49
Canna spp. and hybrids, 184–87
Canna × generalis 'Cleopatra,' *185*
Canna × generalis 'Tropicana,' *184*
Canna × iridiflora 'Ehemanii,' *186,* 187
canna lilies, 184–87
cape jasmine/cape jessamine, 247–49
caper, 61
Capparis spinosus, 61
Carolina allspice, 167–68
Carolina cherry laurel, 392–95
Carolina jessamine, *78,* 250–52
Carolina larkspur, 218
Carya spp., 8
Carya illinoiensis, 8
castor bean, *26,* 29
catalpa, 188–91
Catalpa bignonioides, 188–91
Catalpa bignonioides 'Variegata,' *189*
Catalpa speciosa, 190–91
cedar, 296–98
cedars of Lebanon, 58
Cedrus libani, 58
Celosia argentea, 193
Celosia cristata, 192–94
cemeteries, heirloom plants for, 81–85

cemetery whites, *289,* 290
Cercis canadensis, 79
ceremonial plants, Native American, 8
Cestrum nocturnum, 295
Chaenomeles lagernaria, 201
Chaenomeles speciosa, 195–202
chalk maple, 155
Chamblee, Mark, 447
Chasmanthium latifolium, 216, 217–18
chaste tree, 475–77
Cheiranthus varieties, 61
Cherokee rose, *420,* 421
cherry laurel, 392–95
cherry sage, 458–59, 461
Chilopsis linearis, 49, 203–5
China roses, 422–28, *504, 510*
Chinese arborvitae, 389–91
Chinese (evergreen) azaleas, 405–8
Chinese date, 49, 114, 497–98
Chinese fringe tree, 66, 67, 206–7
Chinese privet, 17–18, 63
Chinese quince, 197
Chinese sacred lily, 95, *100, 354,* 357
Chinese snowball, 67
Chinese wisteria, 65, 485, *487*
Chionanthus spp., 206–8
Chionanthus retusus, 66, 67, 206–7
Chionanthus virginicus, 206, *208*
cigar tree, 188–91
citrus, *13,* 61, 209–14
Citrus spp., 209–14
Citrus aurantifolia, 214
Citrus/Citrofortunella mitis, 211
Citrus limon, 214
Citrus 'Republic of Texas,' *213, 214*
Citrus reticulata, 211
Citrus reticulata 'Changsha,' *210, 212,*
    213
Citrus sinensis, 210
Citrus unshiu, 214
clay pots, 148–49
climbing jasmine, *293*
climbing roses: "Cherokee" *(Rosa
    laevigata), 420,* 421; "Peggy Mar-
    tin" found rose, *429, 432, 435,* 444,
    445–48, *503, 512;* recommenda-

tions list, 421; *Rosa banksiae* × 'Alba Plena,' 67, *508, 510*; *Rosa chinensis* 'Cl. Cramoisi Superieur,' *419*, 425–27; *Rosa chinensis* 'Cl. Old Bush,' 424–25; *Rosa chinensis* 'Cramoisi Superieur,' *413–14*; *Rosa* 'Cl. American Beauty,' *417, 434, 442*; *Rosa* 'Cl. Cécile Brünner,' *436*; *Rosa* 'Rêve d'Or,' *438*; *Rosa* 'Silver Moon,' *437*; *Rosa* 'Veilchenblau,' *45*; *Rosa* 'Zéphirine Drouhin,' *441*; "Speedy Gonzales" found rose, 449

cockscomb, 192–94

color element in landscape design, 133–36

compact myrtle, *345–46*

coneflower, "purple," 218

Confederate jasmine, *11, 15*, 68, *294*, 295

Confederate rose, 267–69

containers/container planting, 12, 14, 148–49

contrast principle in landscape design, 133

Cook, Alistair, 242

cooking bay, 310–12

Cooperia drummondii, 489–90

Cooperia pedunculata, 492

coral honeysuckle, 321–22, *324, 508*

corms. *See* bulbs/corms/rhizomes

corn (maize), *4*, 5

Cornett, Peggy, 343–44, 425

Cornus florida, 76–78

"coronation rose," 438

Cortaderia selloana, 215–19

cottage garden, *36, 38*, 501–10, 518–21

cotton rose, 267–69

cow-itch, 180–83

crabapple, 110

crape jasmine, 295

crapemyrtle, *68*, 301–9, *520*

Crataegus opaca, 220–22

cream peas, 27

Creech, David, 68–69

Crinum spp., 29–30, *93*, 223–31

Crinum americanum, 225

Crinum americanum 'Elsie,' 229

Crinum × 'Bradley,' *228*, 229

Crinum bulbispermum, 225

Crinum × 'Carroll Abbott,' *224*

Crinum × 'Cecil Houdyshel,' *224*, 227

crinum/crinum lily, 29–30, *93*, 223–31

Crinum × *digweedii*, 230

Crinum × *digweedii* 'Royal White,' 230

Crinum × 'Ellen Bosanquet,' 229, *517, 519*

Crinum × *gowenii*, 226–27

Crinum × *herbertii*, 225, 226, 227, *515*

Crinum × *herbertii* 'Caroll Abbott,' 226

Crinum jaegus ratrayii, 230–31

Crinum × 'J. C. Harvey,' 228–29

Crinum macowanii, 230

Crinum macowanii × 'White Queen,' 230

Crinum × 'Mardi Gras,' *227*, 229

Crinum × 'Mrs. James Hendry,' *227, 229*, 230

Crinum × *powellii*, 227

Crinum × 'Sangria,' *228*, 230

crookneck squash, 5

crossvine, 180–83

crowder peas, 27

cucumbertree magnolia, 334

Cucurbita spp., 5

Cucurbita maxima, 5

Cucurbita moschata, 5

Cucurbita pepo, 5

Cupressus sempervirens, 58

cut flowers, 117–18

cuttings, rooting from, *79*, 87–89

Cydonia oblonga, 197, 199–201, 202

Cymbopogon citratus, 216

daffodil, 8, 95–101, 351–59

dahoon holly, 287

Dallas Arboretum, *19*

Danae racemosa, 455, 456–57

daylilies, 259–66

Delphinium caroliniana, 218

Demits, Joyce, 440–41

desert willow, 203–5

deutzia, 232–33

Deutzia gracilis, 232, 233

Deutzia scabra, 232–33

dew drops, 313–15

Diospyros kaki, 112–13, 234–37

Diospyros texana, 234–37

Diospyros virginiana, 7, 112, 114, 234–37

dominance principle in landscape design, 132, *133*

Downing, Andrew Jackson, 35, 63, 201–2

downy phlox, 386–87

"drifts" of massed color, 36–37, *64*, 133

Drummond, Thomas, 385

Drummond phlox, *385*

Dumbarton Oaks, Georgetown, Washington, DC, 31, *35*

Dutch box, 164, *165*

Dutch hyacinth, 279

dwarf box, 164, *165*

dwarf nandina, 350

Easter lily, 316, 318–19, *320*

eastern catalpa, 188–91

eastern gamagrass, 219

eastern redbud, *79*

eastern red cedar, 8, 296–98

"Easter rose," 438

Echinacea purpurea, 3, 7

Echinacea sanguinea, 218

edging box, 164, *165*

edible landscaping, 106–7, 115–16

Egolf, Donald, 272, 303

Elymus canadensis, 219

Elymus virginicus, 219

Emanis House, 511–25

Engelmann, George, 44

English influence, 21, 31–38, 134–35

Eragrostis trichodes, 219

Erianthus ravennae, 216

Eriobotrya japonica, 107

espalier, 18, 21

Eulalia grass, 216, *217*

Evans, U. B. (Jo), 350

everblooming roses, 416–18, 422, 437–38

evergreen azaleas, 405–8

Evergreen Plantation, Wallace Louisiana, *28*

Exochorda racemosa, 67, 238–39

false indigo, 218–19

Fanick, Eddie, 230

faux bois art form, 147, *148*

feather reed grass, 215

feijoa, 114

Feijoa sellowiana, 114

Ferris, Bertie, 372

Ficus carica, 10, 61, *110,* 240–46

Ficus carica 'Celeste,' *110, 241, 243–44,* 245

Ficus carica 'Magnolia,' 243–44, 245–46

Ficus carica 'White Marseilles,' *10,* 242

field pumpkin, 5

fig, *10,* 61, 109, *110, 111,* 240–46

fishbait tree, 188–91

flags, 289–92

fleur-de-lis, 289–92

floral design, Asian influence, 69–70

Florida, Spanish influence in, 9–11

Florida jasmine, 295

flower forms in garden design, 138

flowering almond, 90, 396–98

flowering dogwood, *76–78*

flowering quince, 195–202

flowering willow, 49

food crops: German settlers, 40; importance of in home gardens, 115–16; propagating fruit trees from pits, 90–91; Roman/Italian, 53, 55; vegetables, *4,* 5, 115–16, *117. See also* agriculture; fruiting plants

formal vs. informal balance, 128

form element in landscape design, 138

Formosan lily, 316, *317, 318,* 319–20

forsythia, 67

forsythia sage, 461

Forsythia viridissima, 67

Fortune, Robert, 63–65, 67–68

Fortunella spp., 211, 212–13

Fortunella japonica, 66, *107*

Fortunella margarita, 66, *209,* 212

Fortunella margarita × *japonica,* 212

Fortune's mahonia, 67

Fort Worth Botanical Garden, 71

found roses, 439–49

fountain grass, 215

four o'clock, 342–44

Fragilee, 501–10

fragrant olive, 368–70

French hydrangea, 282–85

French influence, 17–21

French Roman hyacinth, 279–81

fringe tree, 206–8

frost grape, 481

fruiting plants: blackberry lily, 162–63; butcher's broom, 455–57; citrus, *13,* 61, 209–14; fig, 240–46; grapes, 7, *10,* 59, 478–84; kumquat, 66, *107, 209,* 211, 212–13; mayhaw, 220–22; maypop, 377–78; nandina, 348–50; overview, 106–14; pawpaw, 159–61; persimmon, 234–37; pomegranate, 399–402; prickly pear, 364; quince, 195–202; Turk's cap, 336–39

fulvous daylily, 259–66

furniture, garden, 146–47

Gainey, Ryan, 300, 395

Gallica rose class, 438–39

Galveston, Texas, 361–63

gardenia, 247–49

Gardenia jasminoides, 247–49

Gardenia jasminoides 'Martha Turnbull,' *248,* 249

Gardenia jasminoides radicans, 249

Gardenia thunbergia, 249

garden lilies, 96, *104,* 316–20, *505*

Gaura lindheimeri, 42, 45

Gelsemium nitidum, 250–51

Gelsemium sempervirens, 78, 250–52

Gelsemium sempervirens 'Pride of Augusta,' 251

"Georgetown Tea" found rose, 443

geranium, *88*

German influence, 39–50

German iris, 50

German myrtle, 347

Gladiolus byzantinus, 253–55, *514*

Gladiolus dalenii, 253–54, *255*

Gladiolus natalensis, 253–54, *255*

Gladiolus psittacinus, 253–54, *255*

globe amaranth, 256–58

Godshall, Nancy, 446

gold dust plant, 67

gomphrena, 256–58

Gomphrena globosa, 256–58

gourds, 5

grancy graybeard, 206–8

grapefruit, 213

grape holly, 67

grapes, 7, *10,* 59, 478–84

Graptopetalum paraguayense, 15

grasses, *69, 91, 139,* 215–19, 490

Gray, Asa, 44

Greek laurel, 310–12

greenbrier tubers, 8

"The Green Rose" (China rose), 427

Griffin, Bill and Florence, 199

Guatemalan sugar maple, 156–57

Guernsey lily, 326–30

Gulf Coast muhly, 217, *219*

Gulf fritillary butterflies, 378

gumbo, 28

Habranthus robustus, 101, 103, *491–92,* 493

Hall's honeysuckle, 322

Hamamelis spp., 8

hardiness zones for Texas, **153**

heavenly bamboo, 348–50

heirloom plants: catalogue introduction, 151–52; at Emanis House, 511–25; at Fragilee, 501–10; noninvasive, 77–78; propagation of, 86–94; rustling (collecting) of, 78–81

Helianthus tuberosus, 8

Hemerocallis × 'Apricot,' 263

Hemerocallis asphodelus, 260

Hemerocallis × 'Florham,' 263

Hemerocallis fulva, 259–66

Hemerocallis fulva 'Europa,' 262

Hemerocallis fulva 'Flore Pleno,' 263

Hemerocallis fulva 'Green Kwanso,' 263

Hemerocallis fulva 'Kwanso,' 260, *260,* 265

Hemerocallis × 'Hyperion,' 264–65

Hemerocallis 'Kindly Lights,' *262*

hemp tree, 475–77

Herbert, William, 225–27

Hibiscus coccineus, 267, 269

Hibiscus × 'Lord Baltimore,' *268*

Hibiscus moscheutos 'Peppermint Flare,' *267*

Hibiscus mutabilis, 267–69

Hibiscus syriacus, 62, 270–73

hickory nuts, 8

Hill, Madelene, 454

Hippeastrum × *johnsonii,* 274–78

Historic Iris Preservation Society (HIPS), 292

Hogg, Ima, 175

holly, 286–88

honeysuckle, 321–25

hoop petticoats, *352*

hortensia, 282–85

Howard, Thad, 225, 229

hummingbirds, 180

Hunt, William Lanier, 491

Hurricane Katrina, 445

hurricane lily, 329

Hutson, Lucinda, *12, 134*

hyacinth, French Roman, 279–81

Hyacinthus orientalis albulus, 279–81

hybrid perpetual roses, 434–36

hydrangea, 282–85

Hydrangea macrophylla, 282–85

Hydrangea quercifolia, 80, 283, 284, *285*

Hymenocallis spp., 327

Hymenocallis occidentalis eulae, 218

Ikebana philosophy in Japan, 69–70

Ilex spp., 286–88

Ilex cassine, 287

Ilex decidua, 120, 287, *288*

Ilex opaca, 286

Ilex vomitoria, 18, *287,* 288

Ilex vomitoria 'Nana,' *287,* 288

Indian azaleas, 408–10

Indian bean, 188–91

Indian fig, 364–67

Indian grass, 217, 219

Indian pink, 8

Indian spice, 475–77

informal vs. formal balance, 128

inland sea oats, *216,* 217–18

invasive exotics, avoiding, 76–77

Ipomoea pandurata, 519

iris, 289–92

Iris spp., 289–92

Iris × *albicans,* 289, 290

Iris × *germanica,* 50, 290

Iris pseudacorus, 290–91

Iris versicolor, 8

Italian cypress, 58

Italian influence, 51–61, 210–11

Italian stone pine, 58

Japanese boxwood, 166

Japanese honeysuckle, 63, 322

Japanese maiden grass, 215, 216, *217*

Japanese maple, *155, 156,* 158

Japanese rose, 299–300

Japanese wisteria, 488

japonica, 195–202

jasmine, 293–95

Jasminum spp., 293–95

Jasminum floridanum, 295

Jasminum mesnyi, 295

Jasminum nudiflorum, 294

Jasminum polyanthum, 293, 295

Jasminum sambac, 294

Jekyll, Gertrude, 36–38, 134

Jerusalem artichokes, 8

jessamine, 293–95

Jew's myrtle, 455–57

Johnny-jump-up, 474

Johnson's amaryllis, 274–78

jonquil, *87,* 96, *97, 353, 354,* 355, *359*

jujube, 49, 55, 114, 497–98

junipers, 17

Juniperus spp., 17

Juniperus virginiana, 8, 296–98

kerria, 299–300

Kerria japonica 'Mr. Airlie,' *300*

Kerria japonica 'Pleniflora,' 299–300

King, Aubrey, 447

Knopf, Ruth, 387

kumquat, 66, *107, 209,* 211, 212–13

Kurume azaleas, *409,* 410

lacecap, *282,* 283

Lady Banks rose, 300, *508*

Lagenaria siceraria, 5, 29

Lagerstroemia × 'Basham's Party Pink,' *304*

Lagerstroemia fauriei, 303

Lagerstroemia fauriei 'Fantasy,' 303–4

Lagerstroemia indica, 301–9

Lagerstroemia indica 'Catawba,' *303*

Lagerstroemia indica 'Dynamite,' *303*

Lagerstroemia indica 'Siren,' *304*

Lagerstroemia limii, 305

Lagerstroemia speciosa, 305–6

Lagerstroemia subcostata, 304

landscape design: art elements, 133–41; Asian, 70–71; collector's garden, 141–42; cottage garden at Fragilee, 502–10; Emanis House, 512–25; English naturalistic, 21, 31–38; French influence on, 17–21; Italian/Roman, 53–54, 59–61; New Orleans, 14; overview, 123–25; parterre, *20,* 21, *60,* 164–66; principles of, 127–33; Spanish influence, 9, 11

Langford, Herb and Betty, 456

Lathyrus × 'Painted Lady,' *145*

Laura Plantation, *27*

laurel, 54

Laurel Hill, Natchez, Texas, 421

Laurus nobilis, 54, 310–12

Lawrence, Elizabeth, 178

layering method for propagation, 92

Le Duc, Alice, 342

Lehmiller, David, 225

lemon, 214

lemon daylily, 260, 264–65

lemon grass, 216

"Lemon Tea" found rose, 449

Lent lily, 96, 354

LeRoy, Tom, 320

Leucojum aestivum, 35, 96, *100–101,* 313–15

Leucojum aestivum 'Gravetye Giant,' 314, *315*

Leucojum × 'Gravetye Giant,' 35

Leucojum vernum, 315

Liatris aspera, 218

Ligustrum japonicum, 17

Ligustrum sinense, 17–18, 63

lilac of the South, 301–9

lilies: blackberry, 162–63; canna, 184–87; Chinese sacred, 95, *100, 354, 357;* crinum, 29–30, 93, 223–31; garden, 96, *104,* 316–20, *505;* Guernsey, 326–30; milk and wine, 223–31, *515;* oxblood, 44, 50, 99, 100, *102,* 278; planting advice, 99–100; rain, 101, 103–4, *105,* 489–93; spider, 96, 100–101, 218, 326–30; St. Joseph's, 274–78

Lilium spp., 96, *104,* 316–20, *505*

Lilium candidum, 61, *316*

Lilium formosanum, 316, *317, 318,* 319–20, *505*

Lilium formosanum var. *philippense,* 96, 104

Lilium × *lancifolium,* 316, *317,* 318

Lilium × *lancifolium* 'Flore Pleno,' 318

Lilium longiflorum, 316, 318–19, *320*

Lilium regale, 320

lime, 214

Lindheimer, Ferdinand Jakob, 44–45

Lindheimer's gaura, 45

line element in landscape design, 136–38

Linnaeus, Carolus, 259

Liriodendron tulipifera, 7

little bluestem, 217, 219

little-leaf boxwood, 166

live oak, *28,* 403–4

loblolly pine, 513

Lonicera spp., 321–25

Lonicera × *americana* 'Pam's Pink,' *321, 323,* 325

Lonicera fragrantissima, 322–23, *324*

Lonicera × *heckrottii* 'Gold Flame,' *323,* 325

Lonicera japonica, 63, 322

Lonicera japonica 'Halliana,' 322

Lonicera japonica 'Purpurea,' 322

Lonicera prolifera, 325

Lonicera sempervirens, 321–22, *324, 508*

Lonicera sempervirens 'Sulphurea,' 322

loquat, 107

Louisiana, 12, 14–15

Louisiana iris, 291–92

Louisiana phlox, 388

Lowrey, Lynn, 197, 213

Lucullus, Lucius, 52–53

Lupinus subcarnosus, 391

Lutyens, Sir Edwin, 38

Lycoris spp., 96

Lycoris africana, 329

Lycoris × *albiflora,* 100, 329

Lycoris aurea, 100, 329

Lycoris × *haywardii, 327*

Lycoris × *incarnata, 328*

Lycoris × *jacksonian,* 329

Lycoris radiata, 96, 100–101, *104,* 326–30

Lycoris squamigera, 96, 101, 329

MacNeil, Grace, 456

Madonna lily, 61, *316*

magenta, *386*

"Maggie" found Bourbon rose, 433–34, 439

Magnol, Pierre, 332

magnolia, 331–35

Magnolia acuminata, 334

Magnolia Gardens, Charleston, South Carolina, 174

Magnolia grandiflora, 331–35

Magnolia heptapeta, 334

Magnolia macrophylla, 334

Magnolia quinquapeta, 334, 335

Magnolia × *soulangiana, 333,* 334

Magnolia tripetala, 334

Magnolia virginiana, 333

Mahonia bealei, 67

Mahonia fortunei, 67

maize (corn), *4,* 5

Malpighia glabra, 90

Malus augustifolia, 110

Malvaviscus arboreus drummondii, 336–39

Malvaviscus × 'Big Momma,' *337,* 338

Malvaviscus × 'Pam Puryear,' 338, *339*

maple, 154–58

marigolds, *508*

"Martha Gonzales" found rose, *423, 507*

Martin, Peggy, 444, 445–46, 448

marvel of Peru, 342–44

mayhaw, 220–22

maypop, 7, 377–78

"McClinton Tea" found rose, 443

McDonald, Bob, 299–300

mealy sage, *458*

medicinal plants, 8, 290, 312, 399–400, 450, 471

Meiwa kumquat, 212

Meusebach, John O. (Baron Otfried Hans Freiherr), 47–49

Mexican bush sage, *460,* 461

Mexican sugar maple, 156–57

Michelia figo, 67, 340–41

Michelia maudiae, 340

Middleton Place, Charleston, South Carolina, 174

milk and wine lily, 223–31, *515*

mimosa, 517

Mirabilis jalapa, 342–44

Mirabilis longiflora, 343

Miscanthus spp., 215

Miscanthus sinensis 'Gracillimus,' *217*

Miscanthus sinensis 'Variegatus,' 216, *217*

Miscanthus sinensis 'Zebrinus,' *218*

missions, Spanish, 16

Mobile, Alabama, 15

mock orange, 382–84, 392–95

modern hybrid vs. open pollinated seeds, 92–93

Monarda fistulosa, 8

mondo (monkey) grass, *69, 91,* 490

Montezuma cypress, 470

morning glory, *519*

moss pink, 387–88

Mueller, Cynthia, 103, 347

Muhlenbergia capillaris, 139, 217, 219

muhlygrass, *139*

Munson, T. V., 481–84

Murraya paniculata, 295

muscadine, 481

muscadine grape, 108–9, 478–84

mustang grape, 480

myrtle, 54, 345–47, *507*

Myrtus communis, 54, 345–47, *507*

Myrtus communis compacta, 345–46

Nagami kumquat, 212
naked ladies, 326–30
nandina, 62, *63*, 348–50
Nandina domestica, 62, *63*, 348–50
Nandina domestica 'Nana Purpurea,' 350
narcissus (daffodil), 8, 95–101, 351–59
Narcissus spp., 351–59
Narcissus bulbocodium bulbicodium, 352
Narcissus 'Grand Primo Citroniere,' *355–56*
Narcissus × *incomparabilis*, 358–59
Narcissus × *intermedius, 357*, 358
Narcissus × *intermedius* 'Golden Dawn,' 96, *352–53*
Narcissus italicus, 95, 96, *101*
Narcissus jonquilla, 96, *97*, 353, 355, *359*
Narcissus × *medioluteus*, 358
Narcissus × *odorus*, 96, *97*, 354, 359
Narcissus pseudonarcissus, 96, 354
Narcissus pseudonarcissus telemonius plenus, 354
Narcissus tazetta, 354, 355–58
Narcissus tazetta 'Grand Primo,' 95–96, *99*, 351, 358, *518*
Narcissus tazetta italicus, 357–58
Narcissus tazetta orientalis, 95, *100, 354*, 357
Narcissus tazetta papyraceus, 356–57
Nassau lily, 230
"Natchitoches Noisette" found rose, *424*, 442
native American grasses, 217–18
Native American influence, 3–8
native plants overview, 75–81
naturalistic landscape design, English, 21, 31–38
Nehrling, Henry, 230, 274–76, 328–29, 331
Nelson, Robert, 406
Nerine sarniensis, 327–29
Nerium oleander, 360–63
New Orleans, Louisiana, 14
New Orleans Old Garden Rose Society (NOOGRS), 444
Nicotiana spp., 8

night-blooming jasmine, 295
Noisette roses, 430–31
northern catalpa, 190–91
nurseries, 49, 85
nuts gathered by Native Americans, 8

oakleaf hydrangea, *80, 283, 284, 285*
oaks, 8, *28*, 403–4
Oberwetter, Peter Heinrich, 50
Ogden, Scott, 226–27, 230, 329–30, 358
okra, 28
old European roses, 431–32
old-maids, 494–96
Olea europa, 59
oleander, 360–63
olive trees, ancient, 59
Olmsted, Frederick Law, 35–36, 42
Onderdonk, Gilbert, 202
open pollinated vs. modern hybrid seeds, 92–93
Ophiopogon clarkei, 91
Ophiopogon japonicus, 69, 490
Opuntia spp., 9, 11, 364–67
orange jasmine, 295
orangeries, 148
Oriental arborvitae, 389–91
Osmanthus fragrans, 368–70
oxblood lily, 44, 50, 99, 100, *102*, 278

Paca Garden, Annapolis, Maryland, 31, 33, *34*
Paeonia spp., 371–76
Paeonia albiflora 'Festiva Maxima,' 372–73
Paeonia × *hybrida, 371–72*, 375
Paeonia lactiflora, 373, 374
Paeonia officinalis, 373–74
Paeonia officinalis rubra, 373
Paeonia suffruticosa, 374
pampas grass, 215–19
Panax quinquefolius, 8
Panicum virgatum, 218
Panicum virgatum 'Northwind,' 218
paperwhite, 356–57
Parker, Frances, 242
parrot gladiolus, 253–54

Parsons, Jerry, 214, 381
parterre garden design, *20*, 21, *60*, 164–66
Passiflora incarnata, 7, 377–78
passionflower, 377–78
passionvine, 377–78
pattern element in landscape design, 140–41
pawpaw, 114, 159–61
pear, 110, 112
pearlbush, 67, 238–39
peas, 27–28, *116*
pecans, 6, 8
"Peggy Martin" found rose, *429, 432, 435*, 444, 445–48, *503, 512*
Pelargonium hortortum, 88
Pennisetum spp., 215
peony, 371–76
perennials: bouncing Bet, 462–63; cherry sage, 458–61; Confederate rose, 267–69; four o'clock, 342–44; grasses, 69, *91, 139*, 215–19, 490; marigolds, *508;* peony, 371–76; phlox, 385–88; salvia, 458–61; Turk's cap, 336–39; violet, 471–74. *See also* bulbs/corms/rhizomes
persimmon, 7, 112, *113*, 114, 234–37
petunia, 379–81
Petunia axillaris, 380
Petunia × *hybrida*, 379–81
Petunia integrifolia, 381
Petunia violacea, 380, 381
Petunia violacea 'Laura Bush,' 381
Phaseolus spp., 5
Phaseolus coccineus, 5
Phaseolus lunatus, 5
Phaseolus vulgaris, 5
Philadelphus spp., 382–84
Philadelphus coronarius, 382–84
Philadelphus inodorus, 383
Philippine lily, 96, *104*, 316, *317, 318*, 319–20, *505*
phlox, 218, 385–88
Phlox spp., 385–88
Phlox divaricata, 388
Phlox drummondii, 385
Phlox paniculata, 385–86, *387*

Phlox paniculata 'John Fanick,' 385–86, *388*

Phlox pilosa, 218, 386–87, *388*

Phlox pilosa 'Forest Frost,' *386*, 387

Phlox subulata, 387–88

Phytolacca americana, 8

Pickens, Mary Anne, 347

pineapple guava, 114

pineapple sage, 461

pink rain lily, 490

Pinus pinea, *58*

Pinus taeda, 513

plane tree, 60

Platanus orientalis, 60

Platycladus orientalis, 389–91

plumbago, 314

Plumbago auriculata, 314

"pocket prairie," 218–19

pokeberry, 8

polyantha roses, 436

polyanthus narcissus, 356

pomegranate, *52*, 112, 399–402

Poncirus trifoliata, 66, *209*, 211

Poncirus trifoliata var. *monstruosa*, 211

pond cypress, 470

Ponder, Jayme and Harley, 501

popcorn spirea, 67, *465*

possumhaw holly, *120*, 287, *288*

post oak grape, 481

Powell, Jason and Shelley, 85, *447*

prairie phlox, 218, 386–87, *388*

prairies, restoration of, 217–19

prickly pear, 9, 11, 364–67

primrose jasmine, 295

primrose-leaf violet, 473

primrose peerless, 358

propagation of heirloom plants, 86–94

proportion (scale) principle in landscape design, 131, *132*, 143

prostrate rosemary, *451*

Prunus caroliniana, 392–95

Prunus glandulosa, 90, 396–98

Pseudocydonia sinensis, 197, 198–99, 200–201

Punica granatum, *52*, 399–402

purple coneflower, *3*

purpletop, 219

Puryear, Pam, 78, 337

"Queenie" found rose, 449

queen's crapemyrtle, 305–6

Quercus spp., 8

Quercus fusiformis, 404

Quercus virginiana, *28*, 403–4

quince, 195–202

rabbiteye blueberry, 108

rain lily, 101, 103–4, *105*, 489–93

Rain lily × 'Labuffarosa,' *489*

Raulston, J. C., 251

ravenna grass, 216

Rawlings, Earl, 163

red cedar, 296–98

red maple, 157

"Red Survivor" camillia, *169*

Reeve's spirea, 464, 466, *467*

regal lily, 320

repetition principle in landscape design, 130–31

reproductions of antique garden art, 145

rhizomes. *See* bulbs/corms/rhizomes

Rhododendron spp., 405–12

Rhododendron indicum, 408–10

Rhododendron obtusum 'Kurume,' *409*

Rhodophiala bifida, 44, 50, 99, 100, *102*, 278

Ricinus communis, 26, 29

River Oaks Garden Club, 177–78, 411

Robinson, William, 35

Roman hyacinth, 279–81

Roman influence, 51–61

roof gardens, 14, 55–56

Rosa spp.: Bourbon roses, 432–34; China roses, 422–28; Chinese influence, 67; class overview, 418–19; found roses, 439–49; from German pioneers, 50; hybrid perpetuals, 434–36; introduction, 413–15; landscaping with, 415–18; Native American use of, 7; Noisettes, 430–31; old European roses, 431–32; polyantha roses, 436; ramblers, 437–39; spe-cies and related hybrids, 419–22; tea roses, 428–30

Rosa banksiae × 'Alba Plena,' 67, *508*, *510*

Rosa 'Blush Noisette,' 430

Rosa 'Buff Beauty,' *442*

Rosa 'Champneys' Pink Cluster,' 430

Rosa chinensis, 422–28

Rosa chinensis 'Cl. Cramoisi Superieur,' *413–14*, 419, 425–27

Rosa chinensis 'Cl. Old Bush,' 424–25

Rosa chinensis 'Old Bush,' 423–24, *447*

Rosa 'Cl. American Beauty,' *417*, 434, *442*

Rosa 'Cl. Cécile Brünner,' 436

Rosa 'Duchesse de Brabant,' *416*, 443

Rosa × 'Fortuniana,' 67

Rosa gigantea, 428

Rosa laevigata, *420*, 421

Rosa 'Louis Philippe,' 427

Rosa 'Marie Daly,' 449

Rosa 'Nacogdoches' (Grandma's Yellow), 449

Rosa 'New Dawn,' 437–38

Rosa palustris scandens 'Swamp Rose,' 439–40

Rosa 'Paul Neyron,' 434

Rosa pennsylvanica, 440

Rosa 'Rêve d'Or,' *438*

Rosa 'Russell's Cottage Rose,' 440

Rosa 'Silver Moon,' 437, *438*

Rosa 'Veilchenblau,' 45

Rosa wichuraiana, 437

Rosa 'Zéphirine Drouhin,' *441*

rose bay, 360–63

Rosedown Plantation, St. Francisville, Louisiana, 165, 201, 330, 394

rose hips, 7

rose laurel, 360–63

rosemary, 450–54

rose of Sharon, 270–73

Rosmarinus corsicus, 454

Rosmarinus officinalis, 450–54

Rosmarinus officinalis 'Albus,' 454

Rosmarinus officinalis 'Collingwood Ingram,' 453

Rosmarinus officinalis 'Lockwood de Forest,' 453

Rosmarinus officinalis 'Prostratus,' *451,* 453–54

Rosmarinus officinalis 'Tuscan Blue,' 453

Rubus spp., 7

Rubus coronarius, 438

ruscus, 455–57

Ruscus spp., 455–57

Ruscus aculeatus, 455–56

Ruscus hypoglossum, 456

Rushing, Felder, 152

"rustling" of heirloom plants, 78–81

Saccharum giganteum, 217, *219*

sage tree, 475–77

salvia, 458–61

Salvia × 'Anthony Parker,' *460,* 461

Salvia elegans, 461

Salvia farinacea, 459–60

Salvia farinacea 'Henry Duelberg,' *458,* 459–60

Salvia greggii, 458–59, 461

Salvia greggii 'Hot Lips,' 459

Salvia guaranitica, 461

Salvia × 'Indigo Spires,' *460,* 461

Salvia leucantha, *460,* 461

Salvia madrensis, 461

Salvia officinalis, 461

Sambucus spp., 7

San Antonio, Texas, 16

sand dropseed, 219

sand lovegrass, 219

Saponaria officinalis, 462–63

Saponaria officinalis 'Flore Plena,' 462

sasanqua, 169–79

satsuma 'Brown Select' orange, 211

satsuma mandarin, 214

saucer magnolia, *333,* 334

scale (proportion) principle in landscape design, 131, *132,* 143

Schizachyrium scoparium, 217, 219

schoolhouse (oxblood) lily, 44, 50, 99, 100, *102,* 278

scuppernong, 108–9, 478, *479*

seeds, saving, 92–94

seeds/pits, propagation from, 90–92

"sense of place," 58–61, 125, 511–25

Shantung maple, 158

Sharpe, Margaret, 78

Sheesley, Heidi, 447

Shoup, Jean, 85

Shoup, Mike, 85, 446

shrubs: althea, 270–73; arborvitae, 389–91; azalea, 405–12; banana shrub, 340–41; boxwood, 164–66; bridal wreath, 464–67; butcher's broom, 455–57; camellia, 169–79; Carolina cherry laurel, 392–95; chaste tree, 475–77; cherry sage, 458–61; crapemyrtle, 301–9; deutzia, 232–33; flowering almond, 396–98; gardenia, 247–49; Greek laurel, 310–12; holly, 286–88; honeysuckle, 321–25; hydrangea, 282–85; jasmine, 293–95; kerria, 299–300; mock orange, 382–84; myrtle, 345–47; nandina, 348–50; oleander, 360–63; pearlbush, 238–39; pomegranate, *52,* 112, 399–402; prickly pear, 9, 11, 364–67; quince, 195–202; rosemary, 450–54; *Spiraea* spp., 464–67; sweet olive, 368–70; sweet shrub, 167–68; winter honeysuckle, 322–23, *324. See also Rosa* spp.

sideoats grama, 219

Sims, Catherine, 168

site planning, Native American, 6–7. *See also* landscape design

slips (cuttings or tops), 86–90

slow box, 164, *165*

Smilax spp., 8

Smith, Robert, 314

snow drops, 313–15

snowflake, 96, *100–101,* 313–15

soapwort, 462–63

Sorghastrum nutans, 217, 219

sour winter grape, 481

southern catalpa, 188–91

southern pea, 27

southern sugar maples, 154–56

southern swamp lily, 225

Spanish-dagger, 11

Spanish influence, 9–16

Spanish moss, 468

species roses, 419–22

"Speedy Gonzales" found rose, 449

spider lily, 96, 100–101, 218, 326–30

Spigelia marilandica, 8

spineless prickly pear, 366

Spiraea spp., 464–67

Spiraea cantoniensis, 464, 466, *467*

Spiraea prunifolia, 465

Spiraea prunifolia 'Plena,' 67, 464, *465,* 466

Spiraea reevesiana, 464

Spiraea thunbergii, 464, *465,* 466–67

Spiraea × *vanhouttei,* 464, 466

spirea, 464–67

splitbeard bluestem, 219

Sporobolus cryptandrus, 219

Sprekelia formosissima, 278

spring snowflake, 315

squash, 5

standing phlox, 385

star jasmine, 68, *294,* 295

starts, 79–81, 86–90

St. Augustine, Florida, 9–11

Stein, Larry, 214

Sterne, Adolphus, 42–43

Sterne home, Nacogdoches, Texas, *41*

St. Joseph's lily, 274–78

Stout, A. B., 264

strawberry, *111*

strawberry shrub, 167–68

structural ornamentation, 143–49

Studebaker, Russell, 8

succulents, prickly pear, 364–67

sugarcane plume grass, 217, *219*

summer phlox, 385, 386, *387*

summer snowflake, 313–15

surprise lily, 96, 329

swamp magnolia, 333

sweet bay, 310–12, 331–35

"sweetheart" rose, 436

sweet myrtle, 345–47

sweet olive, 368–70

sweet orange, 210, 214

sweet pea, *145*

sweet shrub, 167–68

sweet winter grape, 481

swept yard, 22–24
switch cane, 393
switch grass, 218
Symmes, Jane, 325
symmetrical vs. asymmetrical balance, 128

Tabernaemontana divaricata, 295
Tagetes lemmonii, 508
tangerine 'Changsha,' *210, 212*, 213
tawny daylily, 259–66
Taxodium ascendens, 470
Taxodium distichum, 49, 468–70
Taxodium mucronatum, 470
Taxus baccata, 17
tea, 169–79
tea olive, 368–70
tea roses, 428–30
tetraploids, 265
Texas mission gardens, 16
Texas Rose Rustlers, 78, 85
Texas star hibiscus, 269
texture element in landscape design, 138–40
Thomas, Nancy, 446
tiger lily, 316, *317*, 318
Tillandsia usneoides, 468
tobacco, 8
toothache tree, 8
topiary, 17–18, 60–61
Trachelospermum jasminoides, 11, 15, 68, 294, 295
Trachycarpus fortunei, 67
tree box, 164
tree fruits, 109–10
tree peony, 374
trees: baldcypress, 468–70; cedar, 296–98; cherry laurel, 392–95; citrus, 209–14; crapemyrtle, 301–9; desert willow, 203–5; fig, 240–46; fringe tree, 206–8; jujube, 49, 55, 114, 497–98; live oak, *28*, 403–4; magnolia, 331–35; maple, 154–58; mayhaw, 220–22; pawpaw, 159–61; persimmon, 234–37; quince, 197–200; southern catalpa, 188–91; vitex, *93*, 475–77. *See also* shrubs

Tridens flavus, 219
trifoliate orange, *209*, 211
trilobed maple, 158
Tripsacum dactyloides, 219
trumpet creeper, 180–83
trumpet flower, 180–83
trumpet honeysuckle, 321–22, *324*
trumpet vine, 180–83
Tucker, Art, 263
tulip tree, 7, 334
Turk's cap, 336–39
Turnbull, Martha, 165, 201, 330, 394
twin sisters, 358

umbrella magnolia, 334
unity element in garden design, 141–42

Vaccinium spp., 7, 108
vegetables, *4*, 5, 115–16, *117*
Vestal, Frank, 283–84
Viburnum spp., 7
Viburnum plicatum, 67
Vigna unguiculata, 27
vines: American wisteria, 485–88; Carolina jessamine, *78*, 250–52; grape, 7, *10*, 59, 478–84; honeysuckle, 321–25; jasmine, 293–95; passionvine, 377–78; trumpet creeper, 180–83; *Wisteria* spp., *65*, 485–88. *See also* climbing roses
viola, 474
Viola affinis, 473
Viola odorata, 471–74
Viola pedata, 473
Viola primulifolia, 473
Viola tricolor, 474
Viola walteri, 473
violet, 471–74
violet petunia, 380
Virginia snake root, 8
Virginia wildrye, 219
Vitex agnus-castus, 475–77
Vitex agnus-castus 'LeCompte,' *475–76*, 477
Vitex agnus-castus 'Montrose Purple,' 477
Vitex spp., *93*, 475–77

Vitis spp., 7, 478–84
Vitis 'Black Spanish,' 484
Vitis candicans, 480
Vitis 'Champanel,' *479, 482*, 483
Vitis cinerea, 481
Vitis cordifolia, 481
Vitis 'Herbemont,' 484
Vitis labrusca, 481
Vitis 'Lenoir,' 484
Vitis lincecumii, 481
Vitis rotundifolia, 478, 481
Vitis vinifera, 481

Walker, Zada, 438
wall flower, 61
Walter's violet, 473
water features, Italian/Roman, 59
watermelon, 28–29
water resources, landscaping considerations, 125
wax leaf ligustrum, 17
western catalpa, 190–91
Wheaton, Steve, 457
Whitcomb, Carl, 309
white false indigo, 218–19
white garden, 135
white magnolia, 333
white petunia, 380
white rain lily, 490
white spider lily, 218
Wiesinger, Chris, 136
wild bud hyacinth, *46*
wild Easter lily, 490, 492
wildflowers, Texas, *46*, 98
wild honeysuckle, 405–12
wild jonquil, *353*, 355, *359*
wild onion, 8
wild plants, Native American use of, 7–8
Wilson, Lindie, 178, 280–81
windmill palm, 67
winter honeysuckle, 322–23, *324*
winter jasmine, 295
winter squash, 5
Wisteria floribunda, 488
Wisteria frutescens, 485–88
Wisteria frutescens 'Delta Blues,' *486*
Wisteria sinensis, 65, 485, *487*

witchhazel, 8
woodbine, 321–25
worm tree, 188–91

yard art, African American influence on, *24*, *25*
yaupon holly, 18, *287*, 288
yellow flag, 290–91
yellow jasmine, 250–52
yellow spider lily, 329
yew, 17
Yucca aloifolia, 11
yulan magnolia, 334, 335

Zanthoxyllum clava-herculi, 8
Zea mays, *4*, 5
zebra grass, *218*
zebra swallowtail butterfly, 120–21, *122*, 161
Zephyranthes atamasco, 490, 492
Zephyranthes candida, 101, 489–93
Zephyranthes drummondii, 492
Zephyranthes grandiflora, 101, 490, 492
Zephyranthes × 'Grandjax,' 101, 103, *105*, 493
Zephyranthes treatae, 490
zephyr lily, 489–93

zero lot lines, 11
zinnia, 494–96
Zinnia augustifolia, 495–96
Zinnia elegans, 494–96
Zinnia haageana, 496
Zinnia linearis, 495–96
Zizyphus jujuba, 49, 55, 114, 497–98
Zone IX Horticulture Restoration Fund, 446